Against Continuity

Gilles Deleuze's Speculative Realism

Arjen Kleinherenbrink

EDINBURGH
University Press

Edinburgh University Press is one of the leading university presses in the UK. We publish academic books and journals in our selected subject areas across the humanities and social sciences, combining cutting-edge scholarship with high editorial and production values to produce academic works of lasting importance. For more information visit our website: edinburghuniversitypress.com

Edinburgh University Press Ltd
The Tun – Holyrood Road
12(2f) Jackson's Entry
Edinburgh EH8 8PJ

Typeset in 11/13 Adobe Sabon by
Servis Filmsetting Ltd, Stockport, Cheshire,
and printed and bound by CPI Group (UK) Ltd, Croydon, CR0 4YY

A CIP record for this book is available from the British Library

ISBN 978 1 4744 4777 5 (hardback)
ISBN 978 1 4744 4780 5 (webready PDF)
ISBN 978 1 4744 4778 2 (paperback)
ISBN 978 1 4744 4779 9 (epub)

Contents

Series Editor's Preface

In this book, Arjen Kleinherenbrink gives us a provocative interpretation of the philosophy of Gilles Deleuze, one that questions whether the great French thinker has been rightly assessed by either his allies or his opponents. It has generally been agreed on all sides that Deleuze, like his forerunner Henri Bergson, is a thinker of continuous processes and unbroken lines of flight rather than of discrete individual entities. To give just one example, Deleuzeans have often faulted Object-Oriented Ontology (OOO) on precisely this score, citing the works of their comrade-in-arms Gilbert Simondon to insist that fully formed individuals are less important than processes of individuation beginning from some sort of metastable pre-individual field. For the most part it has been assumed that this picture gets Deleuze right, and the remaining debate has been over whether Deleuze is philosophically correct to adopt such a position. But in the pages that follow, Kleinherenbrink adds a startling twist to the discussion by arguing that Deleuze is in fact a full-blown thinker of individual entities. Therefore, against all expectation, Deleuze is presented as a natural ally of OOO.

Although Kleinherenbrink has already published several philosophical works in Dutch, his native language, he was unknown to me until he pitched this book to Edinburgh University Press a year ago. From the ruthless clarity of his style, his fondness for exploring counter-intuitive lines of thought, and his refreshing sense of humour, it was easy to recognise signs of a previously hidden philosophical talent. More recently, I have been able to learn a bit about his life, which has been both unconventional and fascinating.[1] Kleinherenbrink was born on 15 September 1984 in Apeldoorn, The Netherlands. Being in poor health as a child, he

---

[1] Personal communication, 14 May 2018.

avoided sports and became an avid reader, primarily of fantasy and science fiction. In his late teens he aspired to become a rapper, going so far as to study rhyming dictionaries after the example of Supernatural, the New York-based MC. Philosophy was still years away when he became a student of business administration at Radboud University in Nijmegen. Although a business school might sound like alien terrain to most continentally trained philosophers, Kleinherenbrink would eventually encounter critical management studies, a subfield in which philosophy features heavily. Additionally, he was fascinated by the simulations he was asked to run, and found himself energised by the need to consider the interaction among the countless different entities (office space, equipment, budgets, environmental regulations) confronted by any organisation. This set of issues leads some organisational theorists naturally to Bruno Latour and actor-network theory (ANT). But under the influence of a respected professor, Kleinherenbrink was directed instead to the Deleuze and Guattari classic *A Thousand Plateaus*, and encouraged more generally to focus his studies on philosophy. He did just that, even while briefly pursuing a career in waste management consulting. Following a doctoral thesis *cum laude* and a period of postdoctoral work at Erasmus University in Rotterdam, he is now back at Radboud University as Assistant Professor in the Faculty of Philosophy, Theology, and Religious Studies. With the present book, we are able to introduce him to a wide Anglophone audience for the first time.

We now return to the surprising claims about Deleuze made in *Against Continuity*. In order to bolster his case for Deleuze as a thinker of discrete individual entities rather than amorphous trajectories and becomings, Kleinherenbrink adopts a well-defined stance towards the development of Deleuze's career. It is common, if by no means universal, to find that Deleuzean philosophers reserve their greatest admiration for *Difference and Repetition* and *The Logic of Sense*, the two difficult treatises of the late 1960s in which Deleuze says –somewhat unfairly to his earlier self – that he stopped writing commentaries and began to philosophise in his own voice. Such admirers often declare themselves somewhat embarrassed by Deleuze's later collaborations with the psychoanalyst Félix Guattari, stuffed as they are with swear words and intellectual gestures even more irreverent than those of the early Deleuze. Kleinherenbrink's interpretation is completely different. Perhaps unsurprisingly for someone who began his philosophical life with *A Thousand Plateaus*, Kleinherenbrink takes the Deleuze of the collaboration with Guattari to be the philosophically mature Deleuze. *Difference and Repetition*, far from being the crowning systematic masterwork of its author's career, marks the dead end of a younger Deleuze who *was* a thinker of continuities and trajectories, but who then abandoned this position in favour of a more object-oriented standpoint in the co-authored *Anti-Oedipus* and *A Thousand Plateaus*. Among other things, this entails that Kleinherenbrink's reading of Deleuze unabashedly reduces the importance of 'the virtual realm', often treated as Deleuze's most important concept. While it might be assumed that I as an object-oriented philosopher am unreservedly happy with such an interpretation, the effect for me has actually been somewhat unsettling, since until now I have largely been convinced by the standard view of Deleuze as a thinker of pre-individual continua, and have had to reconsider this view while reading Kleinherenbrink's pages.

In closing, allow me to point to another signal merit of this book. Kleinherenbrink's reading of Deleuze does not just unfold in a vacuum, since it also provides a powerful tool for examining the strengths and weaknesses of various authors in contemporary continental thought. Seven of his nine chapters include substantial section-length 'intermezzos' on related thinkers that give evidence of Kleinherenbrink's serious engagement with his contemporaries. His critical treatment of my own philosophy comes at the end of Chapter 7. The other intermezzos, in order of appearance, touch on the works of Levi Bryant, Maurizio Ferraris, Markus Gabriel, Manuel DeLanda, Tristan Garcia, and Bruno Latour. I would point out that, aside from Latour, all of these authors have either already been published in this series or (in the case of Ferraris) soon will be.

New philosophical movements tend to spring up amid small circles of friends and professional acquaintances, as we have seen in the case of such recent groupings as Speculative Realism, Object-Oriented Ontology, and New Realism. This sometimes leads to the misunderstanding that these movements are produced by powerful 'old boys' networks', though in fact most such movements begin from positions of remarkable isolation and weakness: outsiders are rarely excluded, but more often simply uninterested. Who really wanted to join the quartet of obscure professional outliers who met up at Goldsmiths in 2007 to launch Speculative Realism? Only retroactively, following surprising successes, does membership in such groups appear to be some sort of coveted honour or prize. Far from excluding newcomers, they tend to crave fresh members – being tired of hearing their own voices – but the newcomers tend to be slow in coming. The point of these remarks is that Kleinherenbrink's arrival in this series marks the first time that a complete philosophical outsider, someone whose very existence was unknown to me as late as last year, has come in from nowhere and made an important and surprising contribution to the literature of Speculative Realism. Nothing could be more welcome than this. As new generations emerge who have had a chance to digest the new continental philosophies of the past decade, I suspect we will see many more such cases.

Graham Harman
Dubuque, Iowa
May 2018

Acknowledgements

The analysis of Deleuze's ontology presented here was prepared in my dissertation at the Faculty of Philosophy, Theology and Religious Studies at Radboud University in Nijmegen, the Netherlands. I would like to thank my friends and colleagues there for their guidance and support. I am especially grateful to my professors Philippe van Haute and René ten Bos.

The process of reworking and expanding that initial manuscript into a book that also addresses Deleuze's relation to object-oriented ontology has benefited tremendously from many lively conversations with Mike Ardoline. The book also owes much to discussions with Rockwell Clancy, Jasmin Dücker, Simon Gusman, Annelies Kleinherenbrink, Sarah Mann-O'Donnell, Tim Miechels, Maaike de Pooter, Stefan Schevelier, Piotrek Świątkowski, and Sjoerd van Tuinen.

Finally, I would like to thank the two anonymous reviewers of the text for their valuable feedback, and I want to extend my gratitude to Carol Macdonald and Graham Harman for their efforts during the book's publication process.

Preface

This book argues that the beating heart of Gilles Deleuze's philosophy is an ontology of individual and irreducible entities, and of discontinuity between such entities. It is perhaps the first of its kind, as supporters and critics alike take Deleuze to dissolve entities into more fluid fields, forces, or events. This ruling consensus holds that Deleuze regards entities such as rocks, volcanoes, planets, people, horses, festivals, and thoughts as mere aspects of processes that exceed them. Deleuze's concepts are therefore almost invariably seen as tools to help us grasp this reduction of discrete entities into a far more continuous kind of flux.

Yet Deleuze is in fact a thinker of irreducibility and withdrawal. His crucial insight is that entities are never a mere part, representation, effect, moment, or sign of anything else. No entity can ever be reduced to another substance, subject, world, structure, movement, description, perception, content, context, future, past, or any combination of those. Nothing can stand in for anything else, and even the famous 'virtual realm' cherished by many Deleuzians fails to account for all existing things – which is exactly why Deleuze, as we will see, abandons the notion of such a realm quite early in his career. Starting from the thesis that nothing can be reduced to anything else, Deleuze designs and refines an ontology to account for the absolute singularity of entities. This one thesis motivates his resistance to representation in *Difference and Repetition*, to what he calls 'false' depth and height in *The Logic of Sense*, to transcendence in *Anti-Oedipus*, to so-called 'arborescent' thinking in *A Thousand Plateaus*, and to communication in *What is Philosophy?*.

This book aims to show how Deleuze's major concepts are all part of a coherent system that charts the nature and interactions of entities. Instead of positing a separate movement or process to account for change, it demonstrates that entities themselves are always already excessive over their relations, constituting a surplus that suffices to ground change and novelty. All of Deleuze's famous neologisms will thus be shown to *strengthen* rather than *weaken* the irreducibility of entities.

This is not an attempt to be contrarian for the sake of being contrarian. It is the necessary outcome of reconstructing Deleuze's philosophy from its central insights. In no particular order, these include that 1) everything is a machine, rhizome, or assemblage; 2) Being is univocal; 3) relations are external to terms; 4) a body is first a body without organs; 5) a body is not defined by its predicates, but by its powers; 6) nothing is a representation of anything else; 7) difference is first and foremost internal difference; and 8) machines never touch directly, but only encounter others as translated into partial objects and flows. These theses are part of a systematic ontology in which a tune hummed by a philosopher on his way home is just as real as the Waal river, an electron, Frank Herbert's *Dune*, the city of Nijmegen, a meteor, the Wu-Tang Clan, or a bicycle.

In addition to offering a fresh new reading of Deleuze, there is a second purpose to this book. It aligns his ontology with some notable thinkers associated with speculative realism and – to a lesser degree – new materialism. Deleuze is already a frequently cited source in both genres, but he is again consistently misinterpreted as reducing entities to something decidedly non-ontic. As this book already critiques such readings as they are found in Deleuze exegesis, it would be superfluous to repeat that analysis for his reception in the aforementioned genres. Instead, this book opts for a more constructive approach and compares key elements of Deleuze's ontology to salient points in so-called 'object-oriented' philosophies in these genres, which, too, hold that individual entities are the basic constituents of reality. The aim of these comparisons is twofold. The first is to show that Deleuze is a fellow traveller and a source of valuable insights for philosophers who theorise reality in terms of a radical *discontinuity* between *irreducible* entities, even if current orthodoxy suggests the exact opposite. Second, the comparisons will highlight several problems in contemporary object-oriented philosophies and indicate how these might be remedied.

Abbreviations

AO *Anti-Oedipus*
ATP *A Thousand Plateaus*
BSP *Balance Sheet Program for Desiring Machines*
B *Bergsonism*
C1 *Cinema 1 – The Movement Image*
C2 *Cinema 2 – The Time Image*
D *Dialogues*
DI *Desert Islands and Other Texts 1953–1974*
DR *Difference and Repetition*
ECC *Essays – Critical and Clinical*
EPS *Expressionism in Philosophy: Spinoza*
ES *Empiricism and Subjectivity*
F *Foucault*
FB *Francis Bacon – The Logic of Sensation*
FLB *The Fold – Leibniz and the Baroque*
K *Kafka – Toward a Minor Literature*
KCP *Kant's Critical Philosophy*
LAT *Lettres et autres textes*
LS *The Logic of Sense*
N *Negotiations*
NP *Nietzsche and Philosophy*
PS *Proust and Signs*
SC *Seminars on Cinema*
SCS *Seminars on Capitalism and Schizophrenia*
SK *Seminars on Kant*
SL *Seminars on Leibniz*
SPP *Spinoza – Practical Philosophy*
SS *Seminars on Spinoza*
SU *Superpositions*
TRM *Two Regimes of Madness*

WG   *What is Grounding?*
WP   *What is Philosophy?*

Speculative Realism

Series Editor: Graham Harman

Editorial Advisory Board

Jane Bennett, Levi Bryant, Patricia Clough, Iain Hamilton Grant, Myra Hird, Adrian Johnston, Eileen A. Joy.

Books available
Onto-Cartography: An Ontology of Machines and Media, Levi R. Bryant
Form and Object: A Treatise on Things, Tristan Garcia, translated by Mark Allan Ohm and Jon Cogburn
Adventures in Transcendental Materialism: Dialogues with Contemporary Thinkers, Adrian Johnston
The End of Phenomenology: Metaphysics and the New Realism, Tom Sparrow
Fields of Sense: A New Realist Ontology, Markus Gabriel
Quentin Meillassoux: Philosophy in the Making Second Edition, Graham Harman
Assemblage Theory, Manuel DeLanda
Romantic Realities: Speculative Realism and British Romanticism, Evan Gottlieb
Garcian Meditations: The Dialectics of Persistence in Form and Object, Jon Cogburn
Speculative Realism and Science Fiction, Brian Willems
Speculative Empiricism: Revisiting Whitehead, Didier Debaise, translated by Tomas Weber
Letting Be Volume I: The Life Intense: A Modern Obsession, Tristan Garcia, translated by Abigail RayAlexander, Christopher RayAlexander, and Jon Cogburn
Against Continuity: Gilles Deleuze's Speculative Realism, Arjen Kleinherenbrink

Forthcoming books
Letting Be Volume II: We, Tristan Garcia, translated by Abigail RayAlexander, Christopher RayAlexander, and Jon Cogburn
Letting Be Volume III: Let Be and Make Powerful, Tristan Garcia, translated by Abigail RayAlexander, Christopher RayAlexander, and Jon Cogburn
After Quietism: Analytic Philosophies of Immanence and the New Metaphysics, Jon Cogburn
Infrastructure, Graham Harman
Speculative Grammatology: Deconstruction and the New Materialism, Deborah Goldgaber

Visit the Speculative Realism website at: edinburghuniversitypress.com/series/specr

Introduction: The Machine Thesis

1 All Entities are Machines

Consider the following list. A song, novel, bird's nest, fictional character, hallucination, rock, orchid, wound, brain, battle, chemical, painting, love, sickness, toy, movie, person, crowd, house, play, and river. What do philosophers usually do with such diversity? We organise it. More specifically, we tend to theorise that the chaotic multitudes of discrete entities comprising reality do not truly exist in and of themselves, because they are just reflections or expressions of a mere handful of entities or forces said to 'really' make the world what it is. We then proclaim that some entities, laws, agents, perspectives, structures, rules, or domains are more real or fundamental than others. We turn those things into the backbone, source, truth, or rule for all others. A list of famous candidates for these coveted positions would include primordial matter, eternal forms, God, substance, Spirit, subject, vital impetus, consciousness, power relations, discourses, ideology, evolution, culture, human nature, Nature, 'nature and nurture', neurons, and subatomic particles. Whatever the selection, the inevitable result is a dualism that effectively divides reality into two sides. One side will contain one or some of the contestants just listed, and only it or they will truly cause and determine what happens and exists. The other side will consequently contain only appearances, effects, moments, representations, points, or derivatives of that first side. This reductionist tendency is among our most deeply ingrained habits.

The greatness of Gilles Deleuze is his rejection of this habit. He renounces all forms of dualism by systematically endowing all entities with equal reality. Any two entities – for example an orchid and a nation-state – may of course differ tremendously if one considers their components, their history, the conditions for their survival, their actions, and their relations to other beings. According to Deleuze, however, no amount of such *existential differences* can change the fact that the orchid and the nation-state are *ontological equals*. Neither can be reduced to anything else. Neither can ever be said to be nothing but the expression or representation of something else. Both are first and foremost things in themselves, which is to say forces that create their own difference in the world. This is the case for every entity listed at the beginning of this section, plus for every other being of whatever type that we may want to consider.

Deleuze emphasises this ontological equality of all mental, physical, chemical, fictive, organic, and digital entities by calling each and every one of them a 'machine': 'everything is a machine' (AO 12). It will take this entire book to explain the full meaning of that deceptively simple statement, but at this point it simply means that nothing can be reduced to anything else. Every entity is a machine in that it has its own operations in reality. No love can be reduced to biological drives or hormonal activity, no disease can be reduced to the will of some divinity, no word can be reduced to a language, and no hurricane can be reduced to an expression of an overarching Nature. Instead, every love, sickness, utterance, and storm is itself a force unleashed in the world. The idea that everything is such a machine is not just a manner of speaking. For Deleuze, it should be taken completely literally: 'everywhere it is machines – real ones, not figurative ones: machines driving other machines, machines being driven by other machines, with all the necessary couplings and connections' (AO 11). We will call this Deleuze's 'machine thesis'. The thesis implies what Deleuze calls a 'hyper-realism' (K 70), because it places volcanoes on the same ontological footing as fleeting thoughts, Genghis Kahn, neutrons, and office chairs. In contrast to almost all major philosophers since Kant, Deleuze holds 1) that an astonishing variety of discrete and irreducible entities comprise the fundamental texture of reality, and 2) that thought is capable of adequately discerning the ontological structure with which each such entity is endowed. He has perhaps created the first univocal ontology of individual entities without any recourse to some 'machine of all machines', however conceived. The core of his philosophy is a systematic defence and elaboration of this hyper-realism or 'universal machinism' (ATP 256). In order to better grasp the full scope of his machine thesis, let us first exclude some possible misinterpretations.

First and again, 'we are not using a metaphor [. . .] when we speak of machines' (BSP 118; cf. AO 12, 50, 56; ATP 69; BSP 131; DR 190; K 22). Deleuze does not claim that everything is like lawnmowers or chainsaws. Machines 'have nothing to do with gadgets, or little homemade inventions' (BSP 117). They are 'neither imaginary projections in the form of phantasies, nor real projections in the form of tools' (BSP 119). Instead of the weak thesis that everything is *like* machines, Deleuze advocates the strong thesis that everything *is* machines. No serious understanding can be attained by watering down the machine thesis in advance and pretending that we are merely speaking 'as if'.

Second, machine being is not a state. Someone could think that entities are sometimes machines and sometimes something else. After all, does Deleuze himself not also write that everything is a rhizome, an assemblage, and a multiplicity? Yet an entity is never a machine today and a rhizome tomorrow. These concepts are synonyms, not modalities. Deleuze writes that '"rhizome" is the best term to designate multiplicities' (TRM 362), that all multiplicities are assemblages and that assemblages are machines (D 69, 71, 132), that a rhizome 'is a multiplicity and an assemblage' (K 37), and that a machine is a multiplicity and an assemblage (ATP 34). When writing that the assemblage is 'the minimum real unit' (D 51), or that 'multiplicities are reality itself' (TRM 310; cf. 305), Deleuze therefore simply repeats the machine thesis. The variation in terminology serves to emphasise various aspects of machines which will be explained later. The same holds for concepts such as 'social machine', 'technical machine', and 'desiring-machine'. These are but different aspects of how all machines function: *they are the same machines, but it is not the same regime'* (BSP 130).

Third, 'everything is a machine' does not designate a privileged group of beings. Socrates may deny that eternal forms exist for 'worthless things' like mud, hair, and dirt (Plato 1997: 364/130d). Deleuze, however, affirms that 'hair *is* a thing in its own right' and that even the sunbeams hallucinated by the schizophrenic Judge Schreber are machines (AO 211, 12). Consider also the variety of what are called machines, assemblages, rhizomes, and multiplicities in *Anti-Oedipus* and *A Thousand Plateaus*. It includes ships, knife rests, hotels, circuses, books, castles, courts, music, hallucinations, writers, plants, animals, orchids, wasps, rocks, rivers, societies, Glenn Gould's music, packs of rats, couch grass, bureaucracies, brains, clocks, ants, Amsterdam, potatoes, children, and toys. It also includes clerks and office equipment (labour machine), mounted archers (man-horse-bow machine), phalanxes (hoplites-lances-shields machine), and dancing (dance-floor-dancer machine) (BSP 118). Deleuze even grants 'a day', 'a spring', and 'a five o'clock' the irreducibility of machines (SCS 150277). Note that these are entities from many domains, including biology, chemistry, fantasy, geology, politics, language, astronomy, and myth. Deleuze is not constructing a bizarre Borgesian taxonomy for obscure poetic reasons. He is simply asserting time and again that everything is a machine, whether 'real, contrived, or imaginary' (TRM 17). He insists that machines are neither the set of objects emerging from the hands of a maker (BSP 118), nor the set of objects used as extensions by organisms (AO 324). Multiplicities do not merely concern the unconscious, or nature, or our bodies (TRM 310). The machinic is neither a mechanical domain opposed to a non-mechanical one, nor an organic domain opposed to a non-organic one (D 104). Where machines are concerned, 'Nature = Industry, Nature = History' (ATP 37), which refuses all distinctions between the artificial and the natural or a primitive past and an evolved present (ATP 69). The machine thesis is univocal, and hence 'there is no biosphere or noosphere, but everywhere the same Mechanosphere' (ATP 69).

The machine thesis obviously raises two series of questions. First, what does it mean to define entities as machines? What are their features? How do they work? Second, why would it be necessary to define entities as machines? To which problem does the machine thesis respond? The nine chapters following this introduction answer both questions in detail, but we briefly foreshadow those answers here. We start with the second question, because it allows us to introduce the one principle from which Deleuze's entire ontology is progressively deduced.

The principle is that relations are external to terms (ES 66). This 'externality thesis' is absolutely central to Deleuze's thought. Much like the *cogito* for Descartes, the externality thesis is 'a thunderclap in philosophy' for Deleuze.[1] No element of his philosophy is so important yet simultaneously so frequently disregarded. The externality thesis launches Deleuze into the creation of one of the great systematic philosophies of the twentieth century. The entire second chapter of this book is dedicated to this thesis, but its main features can be previewed here. A term can be anything: a tornado, a truck, a game of tennis, a pang of fear, or a tomato. It does not need to be human or even alive. Relations include but are not limited to touching, seeing, colliding, pulling, having, knowing, crushing, seducing, rubbing, placing, containing, destroying, and creating. Externality means that an entity in itself is never present in its relations. It posits a difference in kind between an entity itself and its manifestations, which makes direct contact between entities impossible (as an entity can only ever encounter other manifestations, not other entities as such). It implies that each entity has properties constituting an excess over and above its current, past, future, and even possible relations. This is the case even if it exists for a mere second, during which it is at the complete mercy of other forces. Even in the most smooth-running machine imaginable, all parts will thus remain ontologically irreducible to that machine as well as to each other (K 37). There are such machines all the way to infinity: 'each segment is a machine or a piece of the machine, but the machine cannot be dismantled without each of its contiguous pieces forming a machine in turn, taking up more and more place' (K 56; cf. FLB 8). In short, externality means that nothing is reducible to anything else, even if 'anything else' is everything else.[2] It follows that relations, lying at the surface of things, are not reducible to their machines either (LS 19, 132). Nevertheless, entities are not self-caused or uncreated. As we will see, externality also does not lead to an old-fashioned dualism that divides reality into 'relational stuff' and 'term stuff'. Externality merely states that entities are not exhausted by their relations, whether they be atoms in a molecule or notes in a symphony. Every entity is always itself a force to be reckoned with. This view of entities as forces is what Deleuze means by his notion of 'non-organic' or 'anorganic' life (ATP 503):

> From this point of view natural substances and artificial creations, candelabras and trees, turbine and sun are no longer any different. A wall which is alive is dreadful; but utensils, furniture, houses and their roofs also lean, crowd around, lie in wait, or pounce. (C1 51)

What can we say about a reality in which externality holds? Most importantly, it cannot have an ultimate ground or even privileged points. Everything must happen between entities themselves. After all, a universal ground by definition concerns direct relations with the interior of entities. Yet nothing will be reducible or essentially related to a specific God, Spirit, substance, material, part, whole, or pattern. Not a single emotion is reducible to a brain or to a combination of a brain, a genome, and a culture. Not a single rock is reducible to its atoms and the events that shape it. All internalism, no matter how subtle, will be forbidden by externality:

> [R]*elations are external to terms*. Such a thesis can be understood only in opposition to the tireless efforts by rationalist philosophers to resolve the paradox of relations: either a means is found to make the relation internal to the term, or a more profound and inclusive term is discovered to which the relation is already internal. (DI 163)

Externality is the main problem animating Deleuze's thought: how can reality be what it is if direct contact between entities is impossible? The pursuit of this question culminates in an ontology 'where terms exist like veritable atoms, and relations like veritable external bridges, [. . .] a Harlequin world of colored patterns and non-totalizable fragments, where one communicates via external relations' (DI 163; cf. D 55).

As for the first question, Deleuze will argue that, ontologically, each entity is a fourfold. Or as he puts it, every machine or assemblage is 'tetravalent' (ATP 89). As we will see in the chapters to follow, the externality thesis allows Deleuze to progressively deduce that each entity must necessarily possess four basic features which comprise its ontological structure. As early as *Difference and Repetition*, he is already quite explicit about this fourfold nature of beings, writing that 'everything has two odd, dissymmetrical and dissimilar "halves", [. . .] each dividing itself in two' (DR 279–80). It is easy to see why every entity would have at least two different aspects. If externality holds, then each being is split between what it is in itself and how it manifests to other entities, and those two aspects must differ in kind. Understanding why each of these aspects must then be a further twofold requires more effort to explain, so this will have to wait until later chapters. Note, however, that if reality is comprised of discrete and irreducible beings, Deleuze must do more than simply describe the nature of such entities. In the absence of an overarching order or principle to determine which entities actually exist and what happens between them, he also needs to explain how entities among themselves produce, alter, and destroy each other. This is why in addition to the fourfold structure of machines, Deleuze's ontology also outlines three types of synthesis between entities, which account for their genesis, endurance, alteration, and termination.

As said, an adequate explanation of the full meaning and scope of the machine thesis requires the entire length of this book. These introductory citations and remarks, however, should provide an initial grasp of why Deleuze opts for the term 'machine' to describe any entity whatsoever. First, if reality would be animated by a single entity, principle, or structure (or a limited set thereof), then it (or they) would be the 'motor', 'factory', or 'machine' that produces everything that exists, drives all that transpires, and accounts for every detail of reality. In denying the existence of such an overarching 'Machine', Deleuze will instead argue that every entity is *itself* a machine, in the sense of being a causally effective agent that makes its own difference in the world. Second, Deleuze means to signal that each entity has complex inner workings, which our elaboration of the fourfold structure of machines will uncover over the course of this book.

2 A Speculative Philosophy

This book reconstructs Deleuze's ontology of fourfold entities and the three syntheses that characterise their interactions. Quite surprisingly, it is the first work to do so. Despite Deleuze's explicit insistence on the externality thesis, the machine thesis, and the fourfold nature of entities (the passages cited in the previous section are but a few among many more that we will encounter later), Deleuze's readers interpret him as anything but a thinker of irreducible entities. For example, the recently published *Deleuze and Metaphysics* contains neither a single reference to how Deleuze accords all entities equal ontological dignity by virtue of being machines, nor a single trace of the fourfold nature of such machines.[3]

In fact, many interpretations of Deleuze's philosophy can broadly be grouped into three categories, each of which is incommensurable with the machine ontology to which he adheres (as we will see). First, there are those who claim that Deleuze is a philosopher without a system. They read Deleuze as proposing that philosophers can never do better than design individual concepts which are neither part of nor derived from a rigorous and coherent theory of what comprises reality. Such concepts are then but isolated tools whose meaning one can tailor to whatever political or aesthetic project is at hand. Second, there are interpretations of Deleuze as a metaphysician who reduces entities to something decidedly non-ontic: a chaotic and pulsating flux of quasi pre-Socratic processes or an ephemeral multitude of events. Third and finally, there are those who read Deleuze's philosophy as a sustained assault on metaphysics. These treat Deleuze as deconstructing the very possibility of ontology, and as agreeing that phenomenology and hermeneutics are all that remains after the death of metaphysics.

Much of this is explained by the context in which Deleuze's works were written and subsequently read. The major currents of twentieth-century continental philosophy are arguably phenomenology, Marxism, critical theory, and their various hybrids. In each of these, to consider an entity as an autonomous force in reality, as a thing in itself that affects other things *qua this thing*, amounts to an astonishing display of naivety. 'True' philosophy should always consist in showing that what we initially think of as real beings are in fact the signs of something entirely different: ideologies, economic structures, power relations, language, cultural context, or the structure of human consciousness and perception. The assumption is that thinking about the being of beings themselves can never amount to anything but a deluded scientism, according to which we know the exact properties of entities without any distortion caused by the finitude and particularity of their observers. Quentin Meillassoux has neatly summarised this axiom of continental philosophy as 'correlationism': the belief that we can only ever think about the correlation between thinking and whatever we think about, and never just about *those things* (2011: 5). If correlationism is true, then of course, 'everything is a machine' cannot possibly be a thesis about the actual being of entities themselves. It can then merely be a thesis about *human* interaction with the world as we experience it.

Yet the fact that the interpretations of Deleuze just mentioned are understandable given their historical context does not make them correct. The first chapter of this book shows that no interpretation of Deleuze as anything but a thinker of irreducible entities comprising the very texture of reality can stand up to scrutiny. Spending an entire chapter on this may seem slightly excessive, but the notion that Deleuze is anything but a thinker of irreducible entities is sufficiently widespread to warrant such attention.

That being said, we now move on to note that our presentation of Deleuze's ontology will show that he is both a forerunner and a high point of what is called *speculative realism*, and more specifically of its 'object-oriented' branch.

It is reasonable to assume that readers of this book are somewhat familiar with the basic tenets of speculative realism, so that a brief overview will suffice here.[4] Speculative realists seek to do away with or move beyond correlationism. In different ways and for varying reasons, they aim to theorise reality independently of however human beings may experience it. 'Realism' therefore signifies (at the very least) a commitment to the existence of a reality beyond the world of human experience. The adjective 'speculative' signals that thought *qua thought* can conceive of this reality.[5] A speculative realist can of course hold (as some do) that the natural sciences or mathematics give us access to reality as it is in itself, but the idea that this is the case is not based on a scientific or mathematical datum: it is rooted in thought itself.

Speculative realism takes its name from an eponymous 2007 conference hosted at the University of London's Goldsmiths College. It brought together the work of Graham Harman, Ray Brassier, Iain Hamilton Grant, and Quentin Meillassoux. Each of these four seeks to break with the correlationist dogma that holds (continental) philosophy in thrall, but their positions differ significantly. This is not the place to provide a detailed description of how they arrive at those positions, but recalling some of their basic features is nonetheless useful to get a better sense of some of the ways in which speculative realists characterise reality as it exists independently from human experience.

For Meillassoux, reality as such is (characterised by) a hyper-contingency or 'hyper-Chaos' (2011: 64). When we peer beyond our relatively stable and predictable world of experience, what there ultimately is turns out to be 'a rather menacing power' by which anything can change into anything else at any moment, without needing any real reason to do so. Rather than a somewhat sensible and logical order that neatly dictates what transpires, the Real is the absence of any form of universal order whatsoever. This absence makes for hyper-contingency: anything can become anything at any moment. As Meillassoux writes, by this power anything can be instantly destroyed, monstrous absurdities can emerge, every dream and every nightmare can be realised, or the entire universe could just freeze into a motionless lump of inactivity three seconds from now.[6] He also holds that mathematics is able to adequately deal with this infinite mutability of reality, so that despite our inability to rely on anything solid and durable 'out there', humanity still has at least one tool with which to orient itself.

Based on the writings of Schelling, Grant argues that underlying the vast scores of entities that we may discern is a universe that we should understand as being pure productive power. Before anything particular that may exist, there is always the inexhaustible productivity of nature as such.[7] This productivity should not be thought of as yet another 'thing' underlying all other existing things, but rather as a pure dynamism that cannot be captured in ontic or substantial terms. We are certainly able to think its existence, but it is impossible to then take the further step of accurately representing it in thought.

Brassier's position offers a somewhat bleak view of reality. Taking his cue from nihilism, eliminativist philosophy, physics, and neurology, he argues that reality beyond human experience is a cold, indifferent, and above all *dying* domain. The combined efforts of human reason and scientific investigation force us to acknowledge that reality, once we successfully purge it from our human (all too human) projections, simply mocks our hopes and dreams. It is not just the case that there exists a reality beyond human experience; it also turns out that this reality is largely antithetical to our aspirations, and in particular to our (vain) efforts to ascribe meaning to the world. The world is not attuned to our needs, and the only thing humanity has to look forward to is the death of our sun and the ultimate extinction of the universe. Philosophy's task is therefore to replace all anthropocentric views of reality with the disenchanted, traumatic realisation that extinction is the ultimate horizon of existence. As Brassier writes at the end of *Nihil Unbound*, the subject of philosophy must simply realise that he or she is already dead.[8]

Finally, Harman has an ontology according to which objects harbour a withdrawn reality warded off from all human access (and also from access by other non-human objects, it should be added).[9] Atoms, chairs, centaurs, poodles, wars, and circus tents all have a private, interior aspect that constitutes their fundamental reality, as opposed to how they manifest or function in their being experienced by others. This leads to a view of reality as a vast carpentry of different types of entities that engage in constant negotiations and translations of each other's features, all the while withdrawing their interior being from their engagements with others.

These positions are quite divergent, and then there are some additional factors that make it difficult to determine who (and what) does (or does not) belong to speculative realism. Ray Brassier, for example, has been trying to disassociate himself from the label. Quentin Meillassoux actually refers to his position as 'speculative materialism', and is also counted among a second group of thinkers seeking to break the correlationist circle. In addition to Meillassoux, these *new materialists* also include thinkers such as Manuel DeLanda and Karen Barad. Moreover, during the past decade or so, a variety of other thinkers have also come to be associated with either or both labels (for varying reasons, at various times, in some cases perhaps against their wishes, et cetera), including but not limited to Levi Bryant, Tristan Garcia, Bruno Latour, Markus Gabriel, Maurizio Ferraris, Jane Bennett, and Elizabeth Grosz.

The fact that none of these thinkers fully agrees with any of the others is somewhat confusing, but let's be pragmatic and simply state that each of them is a speculative realist in the *minimal* sense of holding that thought can arrive at meaningful statements about reality as it is beyond direct experience. Each of them is in some way involved in drawing new attention to reality itself and in the construction of some new form of metaphysics after the long night of correlationism. After the previous section, it should be clear that Deleuze ought to rank among these speculative realists (and the remainder of the book will demonstrate this in detail). His machine ontology is clearly realist in the sense that entities are machines *qua themselves*, and not 'for us'. And it is speculative in the sense that the ontological structure of these machines is progressively deduced from the externality thesis, instead of being empirically observed.

The question, however, is *where* among speculative realists Deleuze's machine ontology should be ranked. An interesting way of categorising speculative realists is to ask whether their philosophy is 'object-oriented'. This is the case if it holds that individual entities are the most fundamental constituents of reality. For example, Grant's philosophy is emphatically not object-oriented, as he considers individual entities to be the expressions of a more fundamental productive and dynamic power. Conversely,

Harman's ontology is a textbook case of object-oriented ontology, as he holds that there is nothing to be found beyond objects. Rather, the 'deeper' reality lying beyond how entities are encountered by others is simply a feature of objects themselves.

In addition to Harman, six other thinkers among those just mentioned classify as object-oriented thinkers, as they hold that microbes, shoes, pieces of slate, unicorns, human societies, sequoias and countless other entities *are* reality. These six are Bruno Latour, Maurizio Ferraris, Tristan Garcia, Markus Gabriel, Manuel DeLanda, and Levi Bryant. The others would argue that such beings are distorted representations, fragments, derivatives, or expressions of something more fundamental and decidedly non-ontic, for example a hyper-contingency, chaos, intensities, materiality, processes, interactivity, and so on. This book will argue that object-oriented thinkers are the speculative realists to whom Deleuze is closest. As the previous section has indicated, his ontology accords equal reality to entities from any domain whatsoever, and holds that rocks, rivers, cities, songs, and brains are basic constituents of reality, without requiring any support from some more fundamental force, process, or substance. The interesting part, however, is not just that Deleuze should be counted as an object-oriented thinker *avant la lettre*. His position is also *unique* among object-oriented philosophers. And as we will see throughout the book, his ontology of fourfold machines and the three syntheses arguably avoids some of the weaker points and inconsistencies that haunt the ontologies of other object-oriented thinkers.

Yet even though we will identify some of the more interesting similarities and differences between Deleuze's machine ontology and the object-oriented thinkers, this book is nonetheless primarily an investigation and reconstruction of Deleuze's machine ontology *as such*. Since it claims to offer an entirely new account of Deleuze's hitherto overlooked machine ontology, it would not do to muddle the analysis with a constant back and forth between Deleuze and other philosophers. That would merely distract the reader from the deductive rigour of Deleuze's argument. Even worse, it could engender the suspicion that Deleuze's machine ontology is not truly there in the source material, but rather a projection from object-oriented ontology on to his works. Our exegesis will therefore be interspersed with seven brief intermezzos, each offering a comparison between Deleuze and another object-oriented thinker. These seven intermezzos will not present the positions of those thinkers in full detail. Rather, they will focus on key points of (positive and negative) resonance that will hopefully lay some of the groundwork for more extensive future comparisons.

At this point, however, anyone vaguely familiar with speculative realism might already wonder about Deleuze's relation to both Harman and Bryant. After all, Harman, too, claims that entities are irreducible fourfolds, and Bryant's *Onto-Cartography* (2014) also defends an ontology in which all entities are defined as machines. If both fourfolds and machines are already well-established notions in speculative realism, one can wonder what Deleuze's machine ontology can possibly have to add. As we will see, however, there are significant differences between Deleuze's machine ontology and Harman's or Bryant's ontology. Harman and Deleuze both hold that entities are fourfolds, but they have a radically different account of how entities change. As we will see, Harman holds that objects can only ever change on a very limited number of occasions, whereas Deleuze thinks that change is far more continuous and incremental than Harman would ever accept. As for Bryant, even though he also calls entities 'machines' and draws heavily on Deleuze's work, Bryant's machines are twofolds and not fourfolds. This might seem like an insignificant difference, but we will see that it is actually crucial. Whereas Deleuze's fourfolds lead to a pluralist ontology in which each entity is irreducible because of absolute *discontinuity* existing between entities, Bryant's own machine ontology leads to a monism in which reality is characterised by *continuity*, and machines are merely local points in a single dynamic field.

All in all, there are two aspirations to this book: first and foremost, to present the first rigorous reconstruction of Deleuze's ontology of irreducible machines, presenting readers with an entirely fresh and unexpected perspective on Deleuze's philosophy; second, to align Deleuze with contemporary speculative realism by comparing his ontology to some of the more salient features of other object-oriented thinkers.

3 Method and Structure

Except for the seven intermezzos, this is a book on Deleuze *qua* Deleuze. It does not compare his concepts and arguments to their roots in other philosophies, scientific theories, or works of art, except when necessary to understand a specific aspect of machine ontology. Someone may object that Deleuze writes that 'philosophy cannot be undertaken independently of science or art' (DR xvi). This, however, refers to the construction of a philosophy. Once finished, it can be reconstructed without paying too much attention to the scaffolding used in its assembly. Given our focus on ontology, this book also offers little in terms of the political, aesthetic, and other more practical aspects of Deleuze's thought.

Second, given the sheer scale of Deleuze's work, we must avoid straying from the core of his thought. We therefore focus on *Difference and Repetition*, *The Logic of Sense*, and *Anti-Oedipus*, which contain the most explicit elaborations of the fourfold and the syntheses.[10] These works use wildly different vocabularies, so in the interest of clarity we give a slight preference to the terminology of *Anti-Oedipus*. The other two books use jargon weighed down by decades or centuries of accrued meaning, but the machinic terminology is barely burdened by such distractions.[11] Moreover, as Deleuze explicitly chose this terminology to minimise undue associations with other philosophies (DI 220), it is only reasonable to follow suit. Focusing on three core works also solves the problem of 'who is talking here?' that haunts Deleuze's books about others. For example, it is difficult to determine if *Bergsonism* is an account of Bergson's philosophy, Deleuze's, or a Bergson–Deleuze hybrid. We circumvent this issue by referring to such works only where they prefigure or repeat theses and arguments from the core works just mentioned. Despite these measures, many neologisms and obscure formulations still remain to be dealt with. Quotations in earlier chapters will therefore sometimes contain terms which cannot be explained until much later ('desire' is one of those). The book may also contain more citations than readers are used to, but the excess of reference will emphasise the parsimony and constant recurrence of the model that consistently underlies Deleuze's writings. Also, we do not presume that the reader is already familiar with Deleuze's jargon. The many citations and their corresponding explanations will serve to slowly give readers a good grasp of Deleuze's conceptual apparatus, so that in later chapters of the book, sentences in High Deleuzian will actually be intelligible.

Third, not all of *Difference and Repetition* is useful in elaborating Deleuze's machine ontology. In that first work where Deleuze tried to 'do philosophy' rather than write historical commentaries (DR xv), he still largely adheres to a somewhat pre-Socratic metaphysics according to which entities are merely the expressions of more fundamental 'intensities'. Fortunately, Deleuze explicitly repudiated this early infatuation, so that we are now able to retain whatever is useful to machine ontology in *Difference and Repetition*, and discard the rest (TRM 65). Section 2 in Chapter 1 addresses this issue in more detail.

Fourth, reconstructing Deleuze's ontology necessitates that we carefully separate the wheat from the chaff. As his readers know, Deleuze rarely writes about one thing at a time. To extract his ontology, many other things about which he writes must go, including his reflections on politics, aesthetics, subjectivity, and language. This will help focus on the very ontology in which his resistance to reductionism in all those domains is grounded. We are questing for nothing less than his 'cry': 'When a philosopher is great, although he writes very abstract pages, these are abstract only because you did not know how to locate the moment in which he cries. There is a cry underneath, a cry that is horrible' (SL 060580). Finding this cry necessitates our eliminative method. As Deleuze says of a philosopher's central problem: 'sometimes the philosopher states it explicitly, sometimes he does not state it' (SL 060580), and he himself falls squarely in the latter category. He even calls *Difference and Repetition* a book 'like a soup' where everything good was located at the bottom, making it the hardest to discern.[12] Uncovering a central problem and organising a philosophy's concepts around it is also exactly what Deleuze proposes as a method to read philosophers:

> [I]t's not a matter of asking oneself what a concept represents. It's necessary to ask oneself what its place is in a set of other concepts. In the majority of great philosophers, the concepts they create are inseparable, and are taken in veritable sequences. And if you don't understand the sequence of which a concept is part, you cannot understand the concept. (SS 251180)

Fifth, there is Félix Guattari. This book refers to their collaborative works as 'Deleuze', not 'Deleuze and Guattari'. As Deleuze writes, their collaborations can be read as containing Deleuze's philosophy and as containing Guattari's, as long one does not designate them as 'exclusively Deleuze' or 'exclusively Guattari'.[13] We will refer to them by 'Deleuze', because Deleuze's ontology is not necessarily Guattari's. As Deleuze says in *L'Abécédaire*, they did not interpret their collaborative work in the same way. For example, their correspondence shows that Guattari coins the notion 'machine', but Deleuze determines what this concept will mean and how it will be positioned in a system (LAT 40–1). According to Deleuze, a more Guattarian reading of machines would not rely on irreducibility, but on 'structure, signifiers, the phallus, and so on' (N 14). It is therefore unsurprising that Guattari did not recognise himself in the system elaborated in *Anti-Oedipus*:

> I still have no control over this other world of systematic academic work [. . .] Keep my penmanship, my style. But I don't really recognize myself in the A.O.. I need to stop running behind the image of Gilles and the polishedness, the perfection that he brought to the most unlikely book. (Guattari 2006: 404)

We must therefore emphasise that we investigate *Deleuze's* ontology, postponing the analysis of possible differences with Guattari's views and how these differences manifest in their collaborations on future projects.

Sixth and finally, references will be to English translations of Deleuze's work whenever possible. Translations are sometimes modified to correct errors and inconsistencies. One example of a (grave) error is that the English edition of *Kafka* consistently mistranslates *transcendante* as 'transcendental' instead of 'transcendent'. References to untranslated works are accompanied by notes with the original French text. Within the notes themselves, references to non-English sources will remain untranslated. With these provisos in mind, we can now discuss the structure of the book.

Chapter 1 is largely dedicated to a comparison between machine ontology and other, more orthodox interpretations of Deleuze that are incommensurable with this ontology. Readers uninterested in a skirmish with existing Deleuze interpretations can skip the first two sections of this chapter. After showing why these interpretations are not consistent with the source material, we also take a first look at Deleuze's fourfold structure of individual beings and the three syntheses that connect them.

Chapter 2 starts the analysis proper by describing the centrality, necessity, and initial scope of the externality thesis. Its first section demonstrates how externality is a key notion in both Deleuze's own systematic works and in his exegetic work on others. Two other sections reconstruct Deleuze's arguments for externality. Three of these arguments are drawn from everyday experience, whereas another three rely on more purely conceptual concerns. Externality forces us to consider into how many aspects an entity's being is partitioned. By comparing Bryant's machine ontology to Deleuze's, we show why *two* such aspects are not sufficient for a coherent result, so that four aspects are required.

Chapter 3 shows how the externality thesis (and *only* the externality thesis) motivates Deleuze's well-known rejection of several other modes of thinking. In each of those cases full comparisons would require a separate monograph, but we have sufficient space to show how Deleuze takes his opponents to violate externality. This always revolves around demonstrating that a certain mode of thinking cannot accommodate the internal difference in kind between an entity's relational presence and its private interior which the externality thesis demands. The chapter also includes a section on why Deleuze takes these other philosophies all to belong to the same 'image of thought'. This image of thought is characterised by 'common sense' or the idea that an entity can be identified with one or several of its relational manifestations, as well as by 'good sense' or the idea that an entity can be reduced to and fully explained from a previous state or point of origin.

Chapter 4 then starts the deduction of the features that entities must possess if externality holds. It starts by explicating the first aspect of fourfold machines: its 'body' or 'body without organs' in its withdrawal from all possible relations. The body of a machine is its unity outside of all its engagements. The second section of the chapter explains how such non-relational bodies lead Deleuze to define reality as being fundamentally 'schizophrenic' or 'problematic'. Here, the central idea is that if each entity has a non-relational body, then no entity can ever be fully integrated in any of its engagements. Hence contingent work and effort are always required to make things function, to keep them where they are, or to remove them from their current situations. The problematic nature of machinic bodies will also allow us to draw some comparisons between Deleuze's position and Maurizio Ferraris's 'new realism', as the 'unamendability' of objects is central to the latter's position.

Chapter 5 deals with the question of what machines relate to if not the non-relational bodies of others. Its three sections explain how there are two actual, relational aspects of machines: extension and qualities. We will see how the first, connective synthesis accounts for this contact between a withdrawn entity and the actual, relational manifestation of another machine. A good part of this chapter concerns Deleuze's theory of what he calls 'sense' or 'sense-events', as these are precisely machines as encountered by others (rather than as they are in themselves). We will also contrast Deleuze's theory of sense to Markus Gabriel's ontology of 'fields of sense'.

Chapter 6 elaborates how machines manage such asymmetrical connections between virtual bodies on the one hand and actual manifestations on the other. Such relations cannot be accounted for by the actual aspect of machines, as these twofolds are precisely what must be grounded. Moreover, the body without organs in and of itself can also not account for the diversity of relations, let alone for their content. The body is the bare fact of non-relational unity for a machine, and as all machines are strictly equal in this regard, the differences between them cannot be explained through bodies alone. Hence Deleuze must posit a second aspect to the virtual side of machines. This is what he calls its 'powers', 'desire', 'Idea', '*puissance*', 'code', or 'singularities'. As such desire is that which characterises a machine while simultaneously being non-relational and unextended, Deleuze also refers to this as a machine's 'intensive matter'. We will see that the two virtual aspects of body and singularities constitute the essence of a machine, though one without permanence or simplicity. A machine's desire constitutes what it can do. A machine only ever encounters other entities in terms of its own desire. Hence desire is the ground for its relations. The chapter also contains a comparison between Deleuze's position and Manuel DeLanda's, as the latter holds that 'assemblages' can exist and function *without* having any essence whatsoever.

Chapter 7 then brings us to the notion of disjunctive synthesis. Each connection is forged based on a disjunction, which is to say grounded in a machine's desire, the latter differing in kind from its actual manifestations. The upshot of this is that a machine's desire is always already excessive over its relations, making disjunctions inclusive rather than exclusive. Simultaneously, desire is that which a machine's relations 'inscribe', 'register', or 'record' in a machine's virtuality. This is what Deleuze calls 'becoming'. Hence each relation is forged based on the traces left by other relations, the result not resembling its production due to the difference in kind between virtuality and actuality. Such becoming is neither constant nor always even significant, as it depends purely on the contingent content and intensity of encounters that characterise a machine's existence. As this chapter contains Deleuze's account of how machines can change, we here compare Deleuze's machine ontology to Harman's object-oriented ontology. This is because whereas Deleuze argues that real alterations of the being of entities are somewhat continuous and incremental, Harman holds that they are highly exceptional.

Chapter 8 details the third, conjunctive synthesis to account for how new machines can be made, and how machines themselves function as the medium through which two or more other machines can interact. As Deleuze argues, each newly forged relation is itself immediately an irreducible machine, which incidentally allows him to avoid relapsing into a dualism between relations and machines. To refer to this immediate irreducibility of machines from the moment of their inception, Deleuze uses the term 'celibate machines'. The third and final synthesis completes our reconstruction of Deleuze's ontology. This chapter also contrasts Deleuze's machine ontology with Tristan Garcia's position, as 'celibate machines' allow for close comparison with Garcia's formal ontology of things.

Chapter 9 explores some of machine ontology's implications, first by defining several standard philosophical notions (such as self, time, space, and world) from the perspective of machine ontology. This is followed by a section on what Deleuze in a Kantian vein calls the 'paralogisms' of thought. These errors of thinking explain why we do not 'naturally' think according to machine ontology, but instead tend towards internalist thinking. The last section of the chapter provides an account of what Deleuze calls 'transcendental empiricism', which can be regarded as a general method for philosophy based on machine ontology's central insights. The chapter also contains the seventh and final intermezzo, in which we discuss some of the similarities and differences between Deleuze's position and that of Bruno Latour.

Notes

1. 'cette proposition est absolument pour moi comme un coup de tonnerre dans la philosophie! [. . .] Les relations sont extérieures à leurs termes' (SC 141282).

2. Note that Deleuze calls himself an empiricist and a pluralist, and defines both as studying multiplicities in their irreducibility (D vii; TRM 304).

3. Beaulieu et al. (2014).

4. Bryant et al. (2011) and Shaviro (2014) are good introductions.

5. As we will find, 'conceive of' does not necessarily mean something like 'lay bare for all to see'. Also note that 'speculative' can also be taken simply to mean something like 'adventurous' or 'daring'.

6. Meillassoux (2011: 64).

7. Grant (2006: 137).

8. Brassier (2007: 239).

9. Harman (2011a).

10. As for continuity between these works, note that the concept of the machine is already present in works pre-dating *Anti-Oedipus* (DR 78; LS 72), that the theory of sense from *The Logic of Sense* is found in *Difference and Repetition* in condensed form (DR 153–67), and that Being is already called delirious and schizophrenic before the publication of *Anti-Oedipus* (DR 58, 227; LS 84). Also there is Deleuze's statement that '*Difference and Repetition* was the first book in which I tried to "do philosophy". All that I have done since is connected to this book, including what I wrote with Guattari' (DR xv), and that it 'serves to introduce subsequent books up to and including the research undertaken with Guattari' (DR xvii; cf. TRM 308).

11. Deleuze partly borrows it from Michel Carrouges (1976). Incidentally, Deleuze explicitly expressed his hope that *Anti-Oedipus* would be rediscovered after its many misreadings (*L'Abécédaire*, 'desire').

12. 'Ah ma thèse, c'est une soupe où tout nage (le meilleur doit être dans le fond, mais c'est ce qui se voit moins)' (LAT 28).

13. Cf. '[V]ous faites abstraction de Félix. Votre point de vue reste juste, et l'on peut parler de moi sans Félix. Reste que *L'Anti-Oedipe* et *Mille plateaux* sont entièrement de lui comme entièrement de moi, suivant deux points de vue possible. D'où la nécessité, si vous voulez bien, de marquer que si vous vous en tenez à moi, c'est en vertu de votre enterprise même, et non pas du tout d'un caractère secondaire ou "occasionnel" de Félix' (LAT 82).

Deleuze and Ontology

Faced with the notion that the combination of the externality thesis and the machine thesis leads Deleuze into a systematic ontology of irreducible entities, many of Deleuze's commentators would dig in their heels. They would raise at least one of the following objections to the suggestion that Deleuze is an object-oriented philosopher:

1) Deleuze's philosophy is just a loose assortment of concepts whose meaning ought to be (re-)defined in light of whatever project they are used in.
2) Deleuze's philosophy is more cohesive than adherents of 1) suggest, but it amounts to something radically different from or even hostile to ontology.
3) Deleuze's philosophy is an ontology, but one in which the notion of discrete entities perishes in favour of something decidedly non-ontic.

Regarding the first point, some think Deleuzism is unsuitable for systematic reconstruction, which would suit neither the spirit of the works nor the intentions of their author. This is sometimes asserted with reference to Deleuze's remark that a theory is 'exactly like a tool box [. . .] A theory has to be used, it has to work' (DI 208). A popular approach to Deleuze's work has thus become to treat concepts as individual aphorisms rather than as pieces of a larger puzzle. Fredric Jameson even writes that it is 'misguided to search for a system or a central idea in Deleuze: in fact, there are many of those' (1997: 393). Elizabeth Grosz insists that she does not want to be 'in any way "faithful" to the Deleuzian oeuvre but [. . .] keeping with its spirit, to use it, to make it work, to develop and experiment with it' (1994: 166). Likewise, Isabelle

Stengers writes that 'I used [Deleuze's] concepts only when they had become tools for my own hand, when I would not explain them but be able to take them on. I felt that this was what those books asked' (Stengers n.d.). Or take Michel Foucault, writing in his preface to *Anti-Oedipus* that 'one must not look for "philosophy" amid the extraordinary profusion of new notions and surprise concepts [. . .]. I think that *Anti-Oedipus* can best be read as an "art"' (2013: xii).[1]

Here we can simply express disagreement. Any philosophy worth its salt merits systematic study on its own terms. Not that taking creative licence with a philosophy is somehow wrong, but there is always *more* to a philosophy than its deployment in new contexts. The two other objections, however, will be discussed at some length in the next two sections. As getting bogged down in endless comparisons with the countless books and articles about Deleuze is undesirable, we only discuss exemplary cases of the remaining objections. Section 3 then returns to Deleuze's fourfold, expanding on its brief introduction in section 1 of the introduction.

1 Much Ado about Ontology

The existence of Deleuze's ontology is frequently ignored or denied. Take the example of *Anti-Oedipus*. Even though its first two chapters contain a programmatic write-up of Deleuze's machine ontology and the intricacies of machinic being, commentaries on *Anti-Oedipus* barely retain a hint of this metaphysics. It is either read as a sociopolitical critique of family life, capitalism, and psychoanalysis (Sibertin-Blanc 2010: 6, 27), or as a method to revolutionise psychiatry and realise individual and social liberation (Gandillac 2005: 147). According to its English translator, *Anti-Oedipus* is meant to 'break the holds of power and institute [. . .] a revolutionary healing of mankind' (AO 7). For Ian Buchanan, its principal thesis 'is that revolution is not primarily or even necessarily a matter of taking power', and he suggests that Deleuzian machines are only ever human organisations and practices (2008: 21).[2] Eugene Holland takes *Anti-Oedipus* to combine Marx and Freud via Nietzsche, thus integrating Marxism and psychoanalysis (2001: 7–8).[3] Although these authors skilfully reconstruct important social and political aspects of Deleuze's philosophy, they ignore the ontology in which those aspects are grounded. This is a most peculiar approach to a book which opens by asserting that 'everything is a machine', by identifying a motley crew of hal-lucinations, knife rests, stones, and societies as examples of such machines, and by disputing all taxonomical distinctions between natural, cultural, mental, and physical entities. Still, one can of course simply not be particularly interested in Deleuze's metaphysics. Things, however, are more complicated when we encounter *explicit* claims that Deleuze's philosophy contains no ontology.

First, there are interpretations of Deleuzism as phenomenology. Joe Hughes declares it impossible that Deleuze's work contains an ontology (let alone a realist one), because this would shackle Deleuze to 'the false alternative – mind or matter – that French philosophy had just overcome' (2011: 184). Unperturbed by Deleuze's insistence that machinic being precisely overcomes such false oppositions, Hughes insists that Deleuze is instead a phenomenologist who reinterprets Husserl and Merleau-Ponty (Hughes 2008).[4] Despite everything previously cited on the non-modal, non-metaphorical, non-local scope of machinic being, Hughes claims that machines exist only *for us*: 'In *Anti-Oedipus* we find the central problem to be that of the production of rep-resentation and of a Husserlian subject – a subject, that is, which is nothing more than its constant genesis' (2008: 52). Similarly, he holds that Deleuze's account of syntheses does not describe encounters between any two machines, but only between machines and humans: 'synthesis makes no sense if it takes place outside a passive and transcendental ego' (2011: 183).

Even though large parts of Deleuze's work do concern repre-sentation and subjectivity, it remains impossible to reduce his phi-losophy to phenomenology. First, there are Deleuze's dismissals of phenomenology as mere opinion (WP 149), mere common sense (DR 137), as mistakenly focusing on effects instead of causes (DR 52), and as 'psychoanalytic' (AO 37). Second, it demands the dis-missal of numerous passages in which entities among themselves are at stake (recall the first section of the introduction) as poetic hyperbole. Third and more seriously, one would have to deny that Deleuze theorises relations between entities themselves. One would have to read 'multiplicities for themselves' (TRM 309) as 'multiplicities for themselves for consciousness'. Externality would then be overruled by a single defining exception, as everything would happen for and within the genesis of subjectivity and rep-resentation. This is simply not the case. Deleuze explicitly denies that machinic being 'points' to a subject: 'It may be said that the machine [. . .] points to the unity of a machine operator. But this is wrong: the machine operator is present in the machine [. . .]' (D 104). Machines operate in relation to one another and not to-one-another-for-us. Deleuze insists on this 'great principle: things do not have to wait for me in order to have their signification. [. . .] There is this large round sun, this uphill street, this tiredness in the small of the back. As for myself, I had nothing to do with it' (2002: 17; cf. LS 48).[5] The point of machinic being is that the sun warms the uphill street regardless of my existence. Likewise, the roots of a tree relate to the soil even if no subject potentially relates to their relation. Machines of all kinds flow and crash into each other, as affirmed in a 1972 round-table discussion:

> *Maurice Nadeau*: Indeed, in your first chapter [of *Anti-Oedipus*], there is this notion of a 'desiring-machine', which is obscure to the layman and needs to be defined. Especially since it answers everything, suffices for everything. . .
> *Gilles Deleuze*: Yes, we've given the notion of machine its maximum extension: in relation to flows. We define the machine as any system that interrupts flows [. . .] Again, it is any system that interrupts flows, and it goes beyond both the mechanism of technology and the organization of the living being, whether in nature, society, or human beings. (DI 219)

Deleuze insists that his philosophy concerns 'electrons in person' and 'veritable black holes' (ATP 69). The autonomy of entities is taken to such extremes that one could sooner call Deleuze a panpsychist than a phenomenologist: 'even when they are nonliving, or rather inorganic, things have a lived experience because they are perceptions and affections' (WP 154; cf. C1 50–1). His machine philosophy theorises the 'spider–fly relation' as well as the 'leaf–water relation' (ATP 314). We even find Deleuze writing that 'every body, every thing, thinks and is a thought to the extent that [. . .] it expresses an idea the actualization of which it determines' (DR 254). And when asked if this 'drama' of machines among machines is essentially oriented towards us, Deleuze replies:

> And you would like to know what is the scope of this dramatization. Is it exclusively psychological or anthropological? I don't see it as privileging mankind in any way [. . .] All kinds of repetitions and resonances intervene among physical, biological, and psychic systems. (DI 114)

The very reason Deleuze uses 'machine' and not 'object' is that the latter suggest entities as experienced in space and time by an observer, and hence as images experienced by something else (B 41).[6] He denies that entities are mere objects for subjects, even for potential subjects whose genesis is still incomplete. He rejects this 'sleight-of-hand' (LS 97) in which 'to every object "that truly is" there intrinsically corresponds [. . .] the idea of a possible consciousness in which the object itself can be grasped in a primordial and also perfectly adequate way' (LS 343 n.3). But note that Deleuze would not just reject the idea of a *perfect* grasp of objects. Even an imperfectly grasped object is still defined as *grasped* by a subject, not as external to it. The predicate 'imperfect' changes nothing, just as an unemployed philosopher is still a philosopher. Contra Hughes, machines first and foremost concern 'the non-human' (BSP 123), should not be conceived 'in relation to a human biological organism' (BSP 131), and constitute 'the Real in itself' in its irreducibility to structure or persons (AO 69). Machines are not in our heads or our imagination and we are neither 'the cerebral fathers nor the disciplined sons of the machine' (BSP 129).

Second, some interpret Deleuze's philosophy as a hermeneutics. They take him to declare the impossibility of attaining metaphysical truths and to turn philosophy into a meditation on this impossibility. Philosophy then becomes a means to cope with a certain unavoidable tension. For example, John Caputo claims that 'Deleuze's more radical intentions [. . .] fall under the influence of what I call here a radical hermeneutics' (1987: 301 n.24):

> Radical hermeneutics is a lesson in humility [. . .] It takes the constructs of metaphysics to be temporary cloud formations which, from a distance, create the appearance of shape and substance but which pass through our fingers upon contact. *Eidos, ousia, esse, res cogitans* and the rest are so many meteorological illusions, inducing our belief in their permanence and brilliant form yet given to constant dissipation and reformation [. . .] Now it is not the function of radical hermeneutics to put an end to these games [. . .] Its function is to keep the games in play, to awaken us to the play, to keep us on the alert that we draw forms in the sand, we read clouds in the sky, but we do not capture deep essences or find the *arché*. (Caputo 1987: 258)

Jean-Luc Nancy advocates a similar reading and thinks that Deleuze participates in 'what Heidegger calls the end of philosophy'.[7]

Nancy then forces Deleuze down fairly standard hermeneutical paths. First, he insists that Deleuze's philosophy is not a theory about reality, but a philosophy seeking a 'philosophical real', or a philosophy about the (im)possibility of philosophy.[8] Second, philosophy in general and Deleuze's thought in particular are defined as 'another poetry'.[9] Third, this poetry primarily communes with the various other poetries of faith, religion, and ideology (Nancy 1998: 123).

Some take this interpretation to its logical conclusion and realise that it renders the very idea of 'explaining a philosophy' absurd. After all, to explain a poem is always to diminish it. François Zourabichvili therefore writes that 'nobody knows nor claims to say what "the" philosophy of Deleuze is; we feel affected by Deleuze, we who are its explorers, inasmuch as we try to do philosophy today' (2012: 41). Zourabichvili thereby puts himself in the unenviable situation of having to end his book with an apology for writing it. He concludes with his 'only fear being that I might have slightly diminished or ossified, or rendered confused by a will to clarify, a work nevertheless so "distinct-obscure"' (2012: 135).

Yet Deleuze's philosophy is no hermeneutics. Where hermeneutics insists on attentiveness to language and meaning in approaching the world, Deleuze rejects philosophies that foreground matters of epistemology or linguistics (WP 10). The gesture of twisting philosophy into itself is treated with equal scorn:

> To say that the greatness of philosophy lies precisely in its not having any use is a frivolous answer that not even young people find amusing any more. In any case, the death of metaphysics or the overcoming of philosophy has never been a problem for us: it is just tiresome, idle chatter. Today it is said that systems are bankrupt, but it is only the concept of system that has changed. (WP 9; cf. WG 115)

Elsewhere, Deleuze again insists that 'questions that address "the death of philosophy" or "going beyond philosophy" have never inspired me. I consider myself a classic philosopher' (TRM 361; cf. 214; N 88). He calls the very idea of the death of philosophy imbecilic and idiotic.[10] He dismisses hermeneutics for obsessing over 'original sense, forgotten sense, erased sense, veiled sense, reemployed sense, etc. All the old mirages are just rebaptized under the category of sense; Essence is being revived, with all its sacred and religious values' (DI 137).[11] Any philosophy premised on *our* incomplete grasp of things, inability to grasp essences, or aware-ness of a certain residue, outside, Other, or undecidability is still centred on *our* relation to the world.[12] This is why Deleuze refuses to align himself with Heidegger: he thinks the latter still subordi-nates that which exists (*l'étant*) to its relation to us (DR 66). As with the phenomenological reading, the hermeneutical interpreta-tion violates the externality thesis by migrating everything into a single relation between human beings and their world. Conversely, Deleuze's philosophy accounts for how irreducible entities arise from among themselves, without any need for a world understood as background for a human observer. This, as we will see, is what Deleuze means by thinking '*transcendence within the immanent*' (ATP 47).

Third and finally, there are claims that Deleuzism is a tool to obliterate ontology. It is again Zourabichvili who provides a strong formulation of such a position:

> [T]here is no 'ontology of Deleuze'. Neither in the vulgar sense of a metaphysical discourse which could inform us, in the last instance, what there is of reality [. . .] nor in the deeper sense of a primacy of being over knowledge [. . .] If there is an orientation of the philosophy of Deleuze, this is it: *the extinction of the term 'being' and therefore of ontology*. (2012: 36)

Wherever Deleuze discusses concrete entities, Zourabichvili thinks that something else is in fact at stake. He holds that for Deleuze an 'object' is not an object at all, but 'a sign through which the force of a way of living and thinking affirms itself' (2012: 9). All entities are thus reduced to representations of our own possibilities. On this point, the timid and apologetic explorer Zourabichvili cannot resist resorting to mockery:

> The introduction of *A Thousand Plateaus* ends with these words: 'establish a logic of the AND, overthrow ontology.' Contemporary philosophy – Foucault, Derrida, to say nothing of the Anglo-Saxons – has abandoned or overcome ontology; what fun, naïve or perfidious, to want by all means to rediscover one in Deleuze! (2012: 37)

Yet he ignores the second half of that phrase from *A Thousand Plateaus*: 'establish a logic of the AND, overthrow ontology, do away with foundations, nullify endings and beginnings' (ATP

25). This, as we will see later, makes all the difference. Deleuze merely opposes a certain *kind* of ontology: one that claims to discern something *fixed* from which all of reality derives. But since Zourabichvili is far from alone in thinking that Deleuze is ontology's assassin, we must first ask why one would proclaim Deleuze a herald of ontology's doom. It cannot be the fear that Deleuze would otherwise be taken for a naive realist who takes science to uncover metaphysical truth. Deleuze mocks the 'morons' who think that science has evolved to the point where it can replace metaphysics.[13] Instead, it comes from assuming 1) that any ontology is either an ontotheology, or a metaphysics of presence, or both; 2) that such philosophies are inherently flawed; and 3) that all philosophers worthy of the name know this and abide by it. For pragmatic reasons, we here define ontotheology as any philosophy claiming to know that there is something (however conceived) on which everything else relies. We define a metaphysics of presence as any philosophy claiming direct access to things (regardless of the comprehension or extension of 'things' that one prefers).

Now, Deleuze does abolish the distinction between essence and appearance and between truth and falsity (DI 74). The abolition of essence can be read as rejecting all ontotheology, whereas the abolition of truths can be read as a rejection of presence. Such a reading seems warranted, as Deleuze's work brims with rejections of God, substance, stable essences, eternal forms, knowing subjects, and so on. But at the same time, Deleuze writes that 'we have the means to penetrate the sub-representational' (DI 115), that we can 'place thought in an immediate relation with the outside' and grapple 'with exterior forces instead of being gathered up in an interior form' (ATP 377, 378). And when asked 'are you a non-metaphysical philosopher?' Deleuze replies: 'No, I feel I am a pure metaphysician' (2007: 42; cf. LAT 78). He is not being inconsistent here. Instead, as Henry Somers-Hall notes, Deleuze 'does not reject Heidegger's analysis of onto-theology, but rather Heidegger's equation of metaphysics with onto-theology' (2012: 344).[14]

Deleuze proposes an ontology of entities *among each other*, without any recourse to foundations, endings, beginnings, second worlds, or eternal substances, and without direct access to anything. This is almost unique in twentieth-century continental philosophy: an ontology that is neither an ontotheology nor a metaphysics of presence. Deleuze aims to show that the externality thesis necessarily holds, and that the aspects of any entity whatsoever can be deduced from it. Yet such an ontology will neither tell us what exists, nor what any specific existing thing is or means. Hence Deleuze explicitly jettisons the question 'what is "X"?' from his philosophy.

> The question *what is this?* biases the results of the inquiry, it presupposes the answer as the simplicity of an essence, even if the essence is properly multiple [. . .] This is just abstract movement, and we will never be able to reconnect with real movement, that which traverses a multiplicity as such. (DI 113; cf. 94; AO 132, 209; DR 94)

Deleuze's ontology respects 'a frontier between the thing such as it is [. . .] and the expressed, which does not exist outside of the proposition' (LS 132). Instead of determining what something is or what must exist, Deleuze outlines *how* entities exist, relate, endure, and emerge. It is what A. W. Moore calls a 'non-propositional metaphysics' (2012: 583). Such an ontology never makes objects fully present to subjects, never posits a constitutive subject, and never pretends that language is a transparent medium that can access internal realities. Deleuze's thus avoids 'the three figures of [. . .] objectality of contemplation, subject of reflection, and intersubjectivity of communication' (WP 92). His ontology is not one of infinite understanding or absolute knowledge. Instead, it rigorously respects human finitude (DI 16; WG 167–73). This is why Deleuze insists that proposing a systematic ontology does not amount to proclaiming oneself a philosopher-king with privileged knowledge of Being and the authority to justify everything (AO 257; WG 130, 167).

Let us avoid further confusion by distinguishing between metaphysics and ontology.[15] A metaphysics will be any philosophy that claims knowledge of a final instance or direct access to things. Such is the 'old metaphysics' of Essences and divine Being (LS 105). It is any philosophy that internalises terms to relations:

> It is correct to define metaphysics by reference to Platonism [. . .] The primary distinction Plato rigorously establishes is the one between the model and the copy. The copy [. . .] stands in an internal [. . .] relation with the Idea or model [. . .] Moreover, because the resemblance is internal, the copy must itself have an internal relation to being and the true which is analogous to that of the model. (DR 264)

On the other hand, we will define ontology as any philosophy that accounts for the being of entities while respecting the externality thesis. In Deleuze's case such an ontology retains the notion of essences for entities, but we will see how these are unknowable and malleable.[16] Hence also the 'powerlessness at the heart of thought' (C2 166). Ontology cannot say what specific things are, what generates them in this or that case, what affects them here and there, or what destroys them sooner or later.[17] Its outline of entities and relations remains completely formal.

The machine and externality theses imply a philosophy that is systematic, ontological, and centred on individual entities. The many moments where Deleuze affirms this cannot be dismissed as mere 'ambiguous formulations'.[18] One must affirm Deleuze's non-metaphysical ontology, in which the existence and genesis of entities comes only from machines themselves:

> I believe in philosophy as system. The notion of system which I find unpleasant is one whose coordinates are the Identical, the Similar, and the Analogous. Leibniz was the first, I think, to identify system and philosophy. In the sense he gives the term, I am all in favor of it [. . .] For me, the system must not only be in perpetual heterogeneity, it must also be a *heterogenesis*, which as far as I can tell, has never been tried. (TRM 361)[19]

This system aims 'to return to the things themselves, to account for them without reducing them to something other than what they are, to grasp them in their being' (DI 32). Such an ontology is 'a logic of multiplicities' (N 147) in which 'all we know are assemblages' (ATP 22–3). It is a 'philosophical theory of systems' (DI 107) seeking 'the categories of every system in general' (DI 98), with anything counting as a system or machine.[20] Instead of an empiricist philosophy which equates beings with being experienced, Deleuze proposes a 'transcendental' or 'superior' empiricism premised on 'the superior type *of everything that is*' (LS 107), this type being its ontological status as machine. It also follows that the syntheses between machines are the 'general laws of reality' (DR 108). As Deleuze writes of Henri Bergson, such a philosophy takes *the leap into ontology* and arrives at 'the variable essence of things, providing the theme of a complex ontology' (B 57, 34).

2 To the Things Themselves

This brings us to interpretations according to which there *is* an ontology central to Deleuze's thought. These have contributed much to the mainstream image of Deleuze as a philosopher who sees reality as a swirling ocean of flows, events, intensities, and processes.[21] According to such interpretations, the notion of discontinuity between irreducible entities exclusively pertains to the realm of experience. Humans and non-humans alike may *encounter* the outside world in terms of individual and mutually external entities, but such discreteness has no ontological bearing. Specific things such as governments, books, rocks, and orchids would exist in the minimal sense that we (and others) truly experience them as being thus and so, but it would be a naïve mistake to think that these ultimately *are*. What *is*, rather, is an intensive (meaning unextended and therefore unavailable to direct, unmediated experience) 'virtual' swirl of flows and processes, which differs in kind from the 'actual' realm of concrete experience.

To be fair, much in Deleuze's writings seems to warrant such an interpretation. This starts in *Difference and Repetition*, which is at times treated as Deleuze's 'magnum opus' (Smith 2012: 21). Deleuze there posits a single, continuous dimension of intensive processes that would underlie our everyday world. He refers to this as 'the realm of the in itself', 'the transcendental realm', 'the realm of the Idea', and 'the chaotic realm of individuation' (DR 88, 166, 171, 258). Our senses may trick us into thinking that there is discontinuity between, say, a skyscraper, a horse, and the number six, but they would in fact be expressions of this single realm to which 'continuousness truly belongs' (DR 171; cf. 179, 182). Skyscrapers, horses, and numbers may therefore *seem* to be equivocal, meaning that they seem to be different individuals with different natures, but they *are* univocal, meaning that they are all equal in being expressions of the same realm. Hence Deleuze writes that univocity 'signifies equality of being', that it refers to a 'prior field of individuation', and that it means that 'the identity of things dissolves' (DR 37, 38, 67).

Despite shifts in vocabulary, this idea seems (and we will see why 'seems' is really the proper verb here) to retain a presence in Deleuze's later works. He will write, for example, that philosophy 'proceeds by presupposing or instituting the plane of immanence' (WP 42), that there exists 'unformed matter on the plane of consistency' (ATP 56), and that such a plane is 'a plane of continuous variation' (ATP 511). Deleuze also frequently refers to a 'chaosmos' or 'smooth space', again suggesting the existence of a continuous, albeit chaotic, realm of processes that underlies the quasi-existence of discrete machines and assemblages. It would be superfluous to present a full litany of such passages here, because the simple point is that they all seem to suggest that the notion of a virtual realm always and everywhere remains at the heart of Deleuze's philosophy. This has given rise to many closely related interpretations of Deleuze's ontology in terms of 1) processes and intrinsic relations that would underlie and ultimately dissolve all discontinuity and separation between things, 2) the existence of a virtual realm that would be the real (and only) causal agent 'behind' or 'under' the merely apparent existence and causal efficacy of discrete machines and assemblages, and 3) a single intensive and self-differentiating force that would account for (and, strictly speaking, *be*) all of reality.[22] In all three cases, discrete entities or machines are dissolved into something decidedly non-ontic that they ultimately *are*.

We can briefly look at some representative examples. Bergen holds that, for Deleuze, individual differences (the 'thisness' of entities) are ultimately exclusively constituted by intrinsic relations with other individual entities. Each thing is then nothing but a processual knot of relations with others (2001: 11, 675).[23] This abolishes all separation between thinking and the world, and presumably between non-thinking elements in that world as well (2006: 15). This resonates with James Williams writing that, for Deleuze, 'to be is not to be a thing with recognizable limits – on the contrary, it is to be a pure movement or variation in relation to well-defined things' (2003: 64). Another way to dissolve entities into processes is to invoke their relation with what they have not yet become as an essential tendency. Patton writes that Deleuze 'presents a world of interconnected machinic assemblages, the innermost tendency of which is towards the "deterritorialization" of existing assemblages and their "reterritorialization" in new forms' (2007: 42). In all these cases, entities are mere intersections in a wider ocean of events. Their apparent discreteness is no different from sharp twists and folds in a tablecloth: there seem to be discrete 'things' here and there, but it is actually tablecloth all the way down.

The process interpretation tends to slide into positing an entire realm behind our experiences of concrete entities. This is Manuel DeLanda's well-known interpretation. DeLanda insists that Deleuze is not a realist about essences, 'so in his philosophy something else is needed to explain what gives objects their identity and what preserves this identity through time. Briefly, this something else is *dynamical processes*' (2002: 3). These processes turn out to be a single dimension resembling an agitated version of a pre-Socratic substance:

> Unlike essences [. . .] multiplicities are *concrete universals*. [And] unlike essences, which as abstract general entities coexist side by side sharply distinguished from one another, concrete universals must be thought as *meshed together into a continuum*. This further blurs the identity of multiplicities, creating zones of indiscernibility where they blend into each other, forming a continuous immanent space [. . .] (2002: 22)

To account for how continuous space comprises individual entities, DeLanda insists it is 'continuous yet heterogeneous', an oxymoron further left unexplained (2002: 29). We are simply asked to accept that individuals simultaneously do and do not exist. Yet when push comes to shove, individuals are really nothing but positions in a meshwork that dissolves them into a wider field or process. Position, after all, is relational. Hence James Williams suggests that, for Deleuze, discrete entities *are* mere intersections in a seamless web, in a 'virtual realm' populated by 'Ideas' (2003: 197, 198):[24]

> [All] things are individuals or incomplete parts of individuals defined as reciprocal relations between Ideas, intensities, sensations and actual identities. Any individual is an expression of all Ideas, though more or less clearly and obscurely [. . .] Through the Ideas it expresses and the intensities that envelop it, an individual's actual side is connected to all other things. (2003: 191)

Also adhering to the process or realm interpretation, Alain Badiou claims that Deleuze is 'a pre-Socratic' who thinks 'on the basis of an ontological precomprehension of Being as One' (2000: 101, 19). Since this One, process, or realm must account for emergence and change, it must also be an active force. Peter Hallward, too, concludes that, for Deleuze, 'all existing individuals actualise varying degrees of a single virtual force or differing, a single abstract animal or machine' (2006: 19).[25] This force is not mere shorthand for activities of entities among themselves, but truly a separate dimension: 'At the limit, we'll see that *purely* creative processes can only take place in a wholly virtual dimension and must operate at a literally infinite speed' (2006: 3). This virtual dimension is seen as a primordial totality unaffected by its own division into concrete things (2006: 16).

Interpretations such as these are quite understandable in light of the externality thesis. If there is discontinuity between entities or machines such as grass, horses, skyscrapers, and hurricanes, then it makes sense to think that *something else* accounts for interactions between them, changes within them, and the emergence of new entities among them. For example, Hallward is well aware of the externality thesis and affirms that in Deleuze, 'just like Leibnizian monads, each essence [here to be understood as an actual expression of the virtual realm] subsists in its radical isolation, in its self-sufficiency' (Hallward 2006: 123–4). If every actual thing is isolated, accounting for causation and change becomes difficult. The solution is to posit a self-differentiating realm beneath or across things, and then call entities isolated yet simultaneously intermeshed. Individual entities then immediately lose all relevance, as they have no weight of their own to throw around. No matter how unique or original, every individual only ever *is* a manifestation of a single creative force (Hallward 2006: 5). Such interpretations must agree with Slavoj Žižek that, for Deleuze, there is only '*pure becoming without being* [. . .] This pure becoming is not a particular becoming *of* some corporeal entity [. . .] but a becoming-it-itself, thoroughly extracted from its corporeal base' (2004: 9).

Entities are then reduced to our incomplete, flawed representations of something that is not an entity at all. An example from Williams clarifies how ephemeral machines then become. Using 'field of sense' as a synonym for 'virtual realm', he asserts that when barricades are raised during a protest,

the urgency for authorities to make sure that the first barricade is rapidly overcome [. . .] does not lie in the actual crushing, but in the danger the first raising presents through its effect on sense and through the way that sense can be expressed anew in a second, third and any subsequent uprising [. . .] [T]here is an effect linking two barricades beyond their spatio-temporal location. They may become materially isolated, but from the point of view of sense, they communicate. (2008: 35–6)

Williams calls this 'ethereal communication' with 'a distant and disembodied destiny that different events intermittently connect to, feed off and alter for all other events' (2008: 36). This clearly introduces an inconsistency between the machine thesis on the one hand and the 'virtual realm' interpretation on the other hand. We see that what Deleuze insists is irreducible becomes reduced, and that what he posits as being radically isolated becomes a set of relations within a field. Barricades, banners, crowds, and police charges become but moments, appearances, regions, or derivatives of perturbations in a universal Whole (however excessive, non-totalisable, creative, and active this Whole may be). Badiou identifies the move at the heart of this reading: to externalise relations between terms but simultaneously internalise all their relations into this Whole:

> If one had to define the whole, it would be defined by Relation. Relation is not a property, it is always external to terms. Hence, it is inseparable from the open, and displays a spiritual or mental existence. Relations do not belong to objects, but to the whole, on condition that this is not confused with a closed set of objects. (2000: 122)

These interpretations may be understandable, but that does not necessarily make them true. In fact, there are exegetic as well as philosophical reasons to consider them flawed. To start with the first, after *Difference and Repetition* Deleuze explicitly abandons the notion of a virtual realm that serves as a metaphysical depth from which all of reality would be produced:

> *Difference and Repetition* still aspired [. . .] toward a sort of classical height and even toward an archaic depth. The theory of intensity which I was drafting was marked by depth, false or true; intensity was presented as stemming from the depths [. . .] In *Logic of Sense*, the novelty for me lay in the act of learning something about surfaces. The concepts remained the same: 'multiplicities', 'singularities', 'intensities', 'events', [. . .] but reorganized according to this dimension. (TRM 65)

Recall that the defining feature of the virtual realm is that *its* denizens (events, processes, intensities) exist in mutual continuity (up to the point of collectively comprising one 'force'), whereas their expressions in actual experience (skyscrapers, horses, mimosas) do not. As we will see later, the introduction of 'surfaces' in *The Logic of Sense* signifies that, there and in later works, Deleuze replaces the notion of a virtual *realm* with an ontology according to which entities themselves have a private virtual *aspect*.[26] This virtual aspect constitutes an excess over and above all of an entity's relations, and we will show that this allows Deleuze to account for change and interaction, thus rendering the existence of a virtual realm to do such work superfluous.

The philosophical reason for this change is that neither the machine thesis nor the externality thesis can be reconciled with the notion of a virtual realm (however conceived). Everything is not a machine if the virtual realm exists, because then every machine is a mere representation or expression of something decidedly non-machinic (continuous instead of discontinuous, intensive instead of extensive, and so on). Yet after *Difference and Repetition,* Deleuze will be adamant that 'the machine stands apart from *all* representation' (BSP 121, emphasis added). Second, if the virtual realm exists, relations are external to terms only in a very limited sense. Things would ultimately just be loci of connections, parts of processes, or folds of larger spaces that would be continuous with (i.e. internal to) each other. Most importantly, the very notion of the virtual realm is itself incoherent, because there is no way in which something (a process, an event, an intensity) can simultaneously be continuous with its neighbours *and* ever hope to change.

At this point of our analysis, however, these assertions – especially that last one – are unlikely to convince anyone (certainly not someone accustomed to decades of Deleuzian orthodoxy). The rest of this book will be needed to supply the arguments behind them by reconstructing Deleuze's 'second' ontology in which machines are 'the minimum real unit' (D 51). This analysis will everywhere respect Deleuze's mentioned abandonment of an 'archaic depth' of intensities, which is to say that we will refer to *Difference and Repetition* only in so far as it helps clarify the machine ontology to which Deleuze ultimately adheres (because, naturally, there are many points of overlap between the two positions, for example in the notion that beings should be understood as fourfolds, which we introduce in the next section). This second ontology, as said, is no longer premised on a single, universal difference in kind that divides reality into a virtual and an actual *realm*, but on an internal difference in kind between a virtual and actual *aspect* that constitutes the ontological structure of any entity whatsoever:

> If philosophy has a positive and direct relation to things, it is only insofar as philosophy claims to grasp the thing in itself, according to what it is, in its difference from everything it is not, in other words, in its *internal difference* [. . .] – in a word, difference is not exterior or superior to the thing. (DI 32–3)[27]

After all is said and done, the conclusion will then return to the popular interpretation of Deleuze as a proponent of a virtual realm. It will show that notions such as 'plane of immanence' and 'plane of consistency' have simply been read in the wrong key by commentators who have overlooked the change in Deleuze's thinking after *Difference and Repetition*.

3 A Fourfold and Three Syntheses

Machine ontology, then. Machines neither exist just for us, nor can they be reduced to another realm or process. They are not blank slates, derivatives, representations, moments, regions, elements, points, or effects. They cannot reduce anything to discourse, power relations, ideology, subjectivity, language, consciousness, neurons, elemental particles, or biological drives. Machines are as real as it gets, and each machine is a fourfold. Deleuze's concepts do not weaken entities, but strengthen them by carefully calling attention to their four ontological features. In *Difference and Repetition*, Deleuze already states that every object has two halves, each of which is again split in two. Each half can always undergo change, though in different ways. Hence one is described in terms of 'dif-feren*t*iation' and the other in terms of 'differen*c*iation':

> Every object is double without it being the case that the two halves resemble one another, one being a virtual image and the other an actual image. They are unequal odd halves. Differentiation itself already has two aspects of its own [. . .] However, differenciation in turn has two aspects [. . .] (DR 209–10)

Or later:

> [I]t is as though everything has two odd, dissymmetrical and dissimilar 'halves' [. . .] each dividing itself in two: an ideal half submerged in the virtual and constituted on the one hand by differential relations and on the other by corresponding singularities; an actual half constituted on the one hand by the qualities actualizing those relations and on the other by the parts actualizing those singularities. (DR 279–80)

And elsewhere:

> [E]ach thing has two 'halves' – uneven, dissimilar, and unsymmetrical – each of which is itself divided into two: an *ideal half*, which reaches into the virtual and is constituted both by differential relations and by concomitant singularities; and an *actual half*, constituted both by the qualities that incarnate those relations and by the parts that incarnate those singularities. (DI 100)

That last quote is from 'The Method of Dramatization', a 1967 lecture for the *Société Française de Philosophie*. After Deleuze's presentation, Jean Wahl thanked him for outlining 'a world understood perhaps as fourfold' (DI 103), a striking remark that subsequent scholarship has completely ignored. Yet Wahl was right. Deleuze holds that each entity has a twofold virtual depth and a twofold actual surface. This distinction is 'in every respect, primary in relation to the distinctions nature-convention, nature-custom, or nature-artifice' (LS 187). This fourfold carries many names.[28] Sometimes the actual is a 'physical' or 'corporeal' surface, and the virtual 'a second screen' (LS 207). In *The Logic of Sense*, the virtual aspect of entities is split into 'body' and 'singularities', and the actual into 'sense' and experienced qualities from which sense is 'inferred indirectly' (LS 20). In *Anti-Oedipus*, every machine has a 'body without organs' full of 'desire', and manifests in relations with other machines as a 'partial object' on to which 'flow' is grafted. All this will be explained, but the point is that a fourfold template is everywhere the form of all things or 'the unique cast for all throws' (LS 180). Even though the aspects of the fourfold carry different names in different works, this 'tetravalence of the assemblage' is constant (ATP 89). This universal structure is what Deleuze means by the univocity of Being. *The Fold* even includes a picture of this fourfold entity (FLB 146; figure 1).

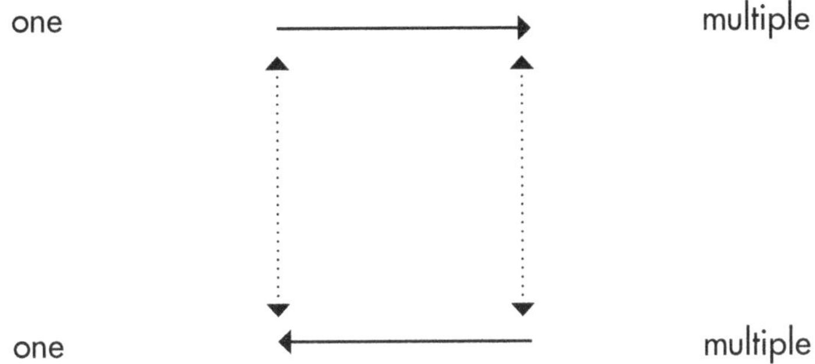

Figure 1 The fourfold

As Deleuze writes, there is

> always a unity *of* the multiple, in the objective sense; the one must also
> have a multiplicity 'of' one and a unity 'of' the multiple, but now in
> a subjective sense. Whence the existence of a cycle, 'Omnis in unum',
> such that the relations of one-to-multiple and multiple-to-one are com-
> pleted by a one-to-one and a multiple-to-multiple [. . .] (FLB 145)

In other words, the objective, virtual, irreducible aspect of each
entity must be one and multiple at the same time. One to be
this, but multiple to distinguish *this* from *that*, as Deleuze learns
from Leibniz.[29] The same is needed on the subjective, relational,
actual side. One to be *this* encounter, event, or experience which
is related to, but multiple in the sense of having qualities distinguishing *this* from *that*. As we will see, Deleuze takes this from
Husserl. The fourfold will account for stable being as well as
for becoming, resulting in an ontology of production as well as
products, as *Anti-Oedipus* would put it. And unlike essences in
classical systems, Deleuzian essences are entirely (though never
randomly or without effort) malleable, so that each machine is
meta-stable at best (DI 86).

It is important to note that the 'heterogeneous elements' constituting machines are simply more machines (BSP 118). The resulting
reality in which production and alteration can only be grounded
in individual entities is what Deleuze confusingly calls 'process':

> There is no such thing as either man or nature now, only a process that
> [. . .] couples the machines together. Producing-machines or desiring-
> machines everywhere, the schizophrenic machines, all of generic life:

self and non-self, exterior and interior no longer have any meaning whatsoever. (AO 12, translation modified)

Process has three senses. First, that there 'is no such thing as relatively independent spheres or circuits', so that no transcendent factor causes or connects machines behind the scenes (AO 14). Secondly, that there is 'no distinction between man and nature' (AO 15), so that nothing is posited 'for us'. In these two senses, 'process' simply means that machinic being happens everywhere. Yet thirdly and most importantly, process 'must not be viewed as a goal or an end in itself, nor must it be confused with an infinite perpetuation of itself' (AO 15). It is not some continuous, universal, or underlying event existing in addition to machines. Instead, externality necessitates that reality is riddled with breaks and cuts (AO 26), and this breaking and cutting among machines is what Deleuze calls 'process'. There is only a schizophrenic pandemonium of interlocking yet irreducible machines, each ignoring, transforming, recruiting, excluding, absorbing, consuming, producing, recording, targeting, fleeing, trapping, or displacing others. It is what Deleuze calls 'the metaphysical production of the demoniacal within nature' (AO 64).

Nevertheless, Deleuze must account for production, generation, change, permanence, emergence, and so on. Without a universal medium or background, *entities* will have to produce, mediate, uphold, transport, and annihilate each other. Enter Deleuze's notion of passive syntheses. These feature prominently in *Difference and Repetition*, *The Logic of Sense*, and *Anti-Oedipus*, and capture the indirect nature of relations between machines. *Difference and Repetition* calls them 'passive syntheses of time'. In *The Logic of Sense* they are simply called connective, disjunctive, and conjunctive syntheses (LS 174). In *Anti-Oedipus* they are syntheses of 'production, registration, and consumption', or three 'syntheses of the unconscious' (AO 86).[30] Yet these are the same syntheses in each case. They describe how one entity relates to another (connection), how it manages to do so while remaining irreducible (disjunction), and how new entities are created (conjunction).[31] They are 'temporal' because they account for how things happen; 'passive' because they are independent of memory, understanding, will, recognition, and consciousness; 'productive' because they account for the forging of relations; 'registrative' because they account for the alteration of individual essences; and

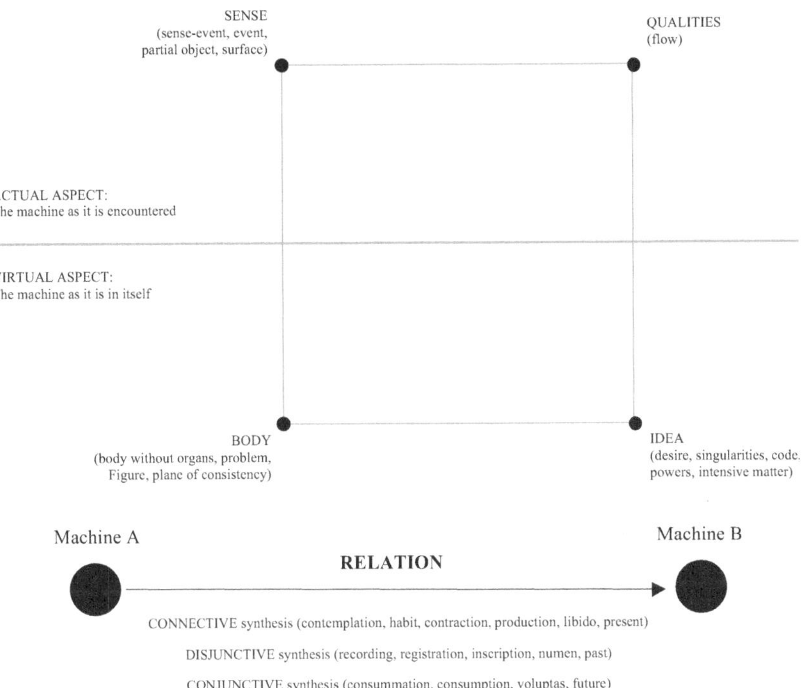

Figure 2 The fourfold and the syntheses

'consumptive' because they account for the birth and death of entities. These syntheses are not successive, but always 'overlap' (AO 24). They are 'beneath' instead of 'after' each other (cf. DI 24, 29), and they are as universal as the fourfold. A human spotting a friend is a case of the three syntheses, but so is a meteor striking the moon, or my finger striking my keyboard.

Figure 2 is a basic diagram of the structure of entities and relations according to Deleuze's ontology. As said, any machine whatsoever has a fourfold ontological structure. Two of its aspects are 'actual' and concern how a machine is encountered by others. Two further aspects are 'virtual' and concern the non-relational being of a machine *qua* machine. Any relation whatsoever between machines comprises three syntheses. The diagram lists the most important terms (and some of their main synonyms) that Deleuze uses to designate specific aspects of machines and their relations.

Subsequent chapters will explain these aspects in detail, show why each of them is necessarily thus and so, and elaborate on the often complex interplay between them. As we progress through our reconstruction of machine ontology, readers may find it convenient to use the diagram as a reference sheet to keep track of 'where' we are in our analysis.

First Intermezzo – Levi Bryant and Twofold Machines

The previous section showcased Deleuze's assertion that all entities are fourfolds. This can only leave us to wonder *why* this would be the case. Subsequent chapters will explain this via careful reconstruction of Deleuze's specific arguments for machinic being. In anticipation of these analyses, however, we should first gain a somewhat more general understanding of why fourfold entities are the only game in town *if* one accepts the externality thesis stating that all entities have an extra-relational aspect.

To arrive at such an understanding, it is useful to compare Deleuze's *fourfold* machines with Bryant's version of machine ontology, according to which machines are *twofolds*. This is not because both choose to call entities 'machines'. The mere use of identical terms need not make for identical theories, or even for theories that are interesting to contrast. The real reason is that whereas significant portions of Bryant's writings are *also* premised on the externality thesis, his resulting ontology of twofold machines would suggest that externality does not necessitate fourfolds. If that is the case, then everything we have claimed about Deleuze being able to deduce fourfold being from externality between relations and terms would obviously be mistaken. In addition, Bryant's machine ontology is also instructive in that a twofold theory of entities is arguably the first thing that comes to mind when confronted with the externality thesis. Entities would have their manifestations in relations to others, plus their non-relational interior constitution, full stop. Despite Deleuze's assertions in the previous section, it initially feels superfluous to then split these two aspects into two further twofolds. Finally, as Bryant's philosophy always draws heavily on Deleuze's writings, our brief comparison here also helps to familiarise ourselves with some of the concepts and arguments that later chapters will feature more extensively.

One might think that a comparison between these two machinic ontologies should wait until later in the book, so that the subtler aspects of their respective ontologies could also be meaningfully compared. This, however, is one case in which the devil is not in the details. The difference between Bryant and Deleuze concerns the fundamental outline of their philosophies, not the fine print. Interesting as they may be, any further similarities and differences between their systems would merely distract us from their incommensurability at a very basic level. That being said, Bryant's exegetic work on Deleuze and his writings on the many facets and implications of (his version of) machinic philosophy are some of the most inspiring and thought-provoking texts that someone interested in Deleuze and/or speculative realism could encounter, making it somewhat of a shame that there is no space to dwell on them more extensively. Instead and as said, we limit our reflections to those parts of his ontology which help us gain an initial, general grasp of why a fourfold ontology is necessary *if* the externality thesis is accepted in the sense of an ontological thesis stating that entities themselves have a dimension that withdraws from their presence in relations.

Difference and Givenness (2008) is the first of Bryant's three published monographs. It is a study of the philosophical method that Deleuze calls 'transcendental empiricism' (we discuss this method in Chapter 9). Bryant's reading emphasises Deleuze's critique of *presence*, the belief that the experience of an entity is identical to its being. Bryant shows how Deleuze systematically attacks all 'presentist' philosophies according to which reality can be reduced to our thoughts about it:

> Whether it be a world absolutely immanent to the subject in the form of a pure immanence to consciousness producing being through its perception or differentiating itself through contradiction, or an absolute materialism where all is matter and configurations of atoms, or a naïve realism where the subject somehow immediately knows the world, or a transcendental idealism where the subject imposes form on the world, all of these positions assume the primacy of some form of presence. (Bryant 2008: 264)

This attentiveness to a fundamental difference between the relational appearances of entities to others, as opposed to their private being, later becomes a central feature of Bryant's initial object-oriented ontology, the 'onticology' which he outlined three years later in *The Democracy of Objects* (2011). Bryant's onticology is a speculative realist theory premised on his own take on what we have here called the machine thesis and the externality thesis. As for the first, he argues that all objects equally exist and that no final or initial entity (or anything else, for that matter) serves as the universal ground for (any of) the others (Bryant 2011: 19). As for the second, he insists that 'we must avoid, at all costs, the thesis that objects *are* what our access to objects *gives* us', following Harman's thesis that objects have interior dimensions that withdraw from their relations (2011: 18). Note that 'our' and 'us' also refers to non-humans. Bryant holds that *no* entity ever directly encounters the interior of another being.

This acceptance of externality leads Bryant to discern two dimensions that characterise the being of objects. First, their manifestations in relations with others. Think of a couch that is experienced as heavy, black, leathery, and comfortable. Second, their extra-relational and interior 'irreducible structure' (Bryant 2011: 215), which may be among the causes that generate these manifestations, but is nevertheless different in kind from them. Bryant calls this interior aspect the 'powers' of an entity (much like Deleuze, as we will see in Chapter 6). Note that at this point in our analysis, it is still somewhat irrelevant how one precisely characterises the interior being of entities. Indeed, various alternatives are available. For example, Harman refers to it as 'real qualities', and Deleuze will also use 'singularities' and even 'Idea' in addition to 'powers'. Nonetheless, Bryant's use of 'powers' has one notable advantage in clearly emphasising the difference between an object's being and its manifestations. For example, my speaking English in a conversation with colleagues is a relational manifestation of my private capacity or power that characterises my interior being. What manifests in the conversation is not the capacity itself, but rather a translation or expression of it engendered by circumstances. Whomever I am speaking with naturally does not have the sensuous experience of a *power* floating in thin air before them. Powers ought to be understood as always being excessive over and outside of however they manifest in actuality or extension.

The same difference between powers and manifestations animates Bryant's most recent book, *Onto-Cartography* (2014). This is where Bryant changes his term for any entity whatsoever from 'object' to 'machine'. Large parts of *Onto-Cartography* concern interesting series of practical (i.e. social, political, and epistemological) implications of object-oriented thought and the heuristics that might be nurtured in light of it. Yet as said, we are here concerned with Bryant's basic ontological commitments. The key section in that regard is 'Machines are Split Between their Powers and Products' (Bryant 2014: 40–6). It again defines objects, now machines, as twofolds split between the powers (which Bryant also calls 'virtual proper being' or 'operations') that they are in themselves, and their manifestations to others. And again, these manifestations are said to be expressions or products of powers, with the latter nonetheless remaining different in kind from such relational appearances.

The question in which we are interested here is whether differentiating entities into twofolds is sufficient in light of the externality thesis. Starting with manifestations, we must therefore ask whether there can be such a thing as a machine made manifest, without having to make further distinctions concerning manifestation. This does not seem to be the case, because the qualities characterising the experience of an entity are different from the qualified thing that is experienced. When I experience the black, heavy, and leathery couch, 'couch' does not designate a fourth quality in addition to the first three. It is the thing of which the qualities are qualities. These qualities can change while 'their' object remains that same thing. Exposure to harsh light will eventually make the black fade to a dark grey, but that does not mean that the light is manufacturing a new couch. To recall Deleuze's terminology from the previous section, the multiple qualities characterising the experience of a thing must be the qualities of a unity that is itself not a quality. This unity cannot be the thing in itself (its interior being), because externality demands that the thing in itself never enters into relational givenness. Could this unity then pertain to who- or whatever experiences the couch? If that were the case, 'couch' would be a unity that I add on to a perception of otherwise free-floating qualities (a Humean position). Yet this is also precluded by externality. If the thing-in-manifestation would be reducible to me, then the entire relation (the experience of the couch and its qualities) would be internal to its term (the perceiver). The only viable option for externalist philosophy is therefore that this unity is proper only to the relation itself, that is, irreducible to either term.

Full support for this argument and its many implications is given in Chapters 5 and 8. For now, the important thing is that the manifestations of an entity to others is not a single, homogeneous phenomenon. Manifestations are split into two aspects: the qualities characterising an experience on the one hand, and on the other hand the unified thing – immanent to the relation – of which they are qualities. Even though he does not dwell on it too much, Bryant tacitly seems to acknowledge this point in his machine ontology. He distinguishes between the bare fact of a machine's manifestation on the one hand, and on the other hand the effect of a manifestation on who- or whatever experiences it (Bryant 2014: 42–3). Manifestation as such can then refer to the simple fact of a machine expressing itself outside of its interior being, and in addition relations would concern what Bryant calls a 'qualitative', 'agentive' or 'material' dimension, the latter referring to what we call the 'content' of an experience. A generous reading of *Onto-cartography* might therefore already characterise Bryant's machine ontology as a threefold rather than a twofold.

The real difference between Bryant's and Deleuze's machine ontology concerns the non-relational, private interior of entities. Note again that, for Bryant, the interior being of a machine is its powers, full stop. The externality thesis then immediately raises the question as to what separates the powers of *this* thing from those of *that* thing. This separation cannot be accounted for by the difference between powers and manifestations, for the simple reason that manifestations are relational. Externality is an ontological thesis that states that there must be discontinuity between entities-as-such, not a phenomenological thesis that states that entities-in-experience appear *as if* they are mutually incommensurable. If externality holds, then any two entities must remain radically separate even when nobody is looking (better yet: even when *they* are not 'looking'). Or again in Deleuze's terms, the interior being of a machine must have a unity in addition to its multiple powers, a unity that acts like a firewall or blast shield that prevents the powers of *this* machine from being continuous with the powers of *that* one.

Without such a unifying aspect, all powers of all entities would ontologically be continuous with each other. This would violate externality, because powers would then be directly present to other powers. The result would be an internalism according to which the fractured and diverse world of experience would 'really' be a single, continuous, and ultimately homogeneous mass. To summarise, *if* externality holds, then it is not just the case that each entity is some X over and above how it is experienced by others. It must also be the case that each entity is some X that has no direct access to or contact with the X of any other entity. So, if entities are powers, then they also need additionally to be something else (some Y) that prevents all powers from dissolving into one great universal mush.

Bryant is well aware of this exigency, because he has simply opted to do away with externality altogether. In a 2016 article, he announced a shift in his ontological thinking.[32] Bryant now explicitly renounces the object-oriented externality thesis that entities are withdrawn from one another and irreducible to their relations. What seem to be discrete entities in experience, he argues, are nothing but 'folds' or 'pleats' in a wider field. Contra the externality thesis, these folds are continuous with one another. To use his example, a tree in Albuquerque is not a separate entity with respect to the soil, insects, rain, and other beings that generate it. Instead, the tree 'pleats all of these things into it'. To recall a metaphor we used earlier, this reality seems to be somewhat like a giant tablecloth that has been twisted and knotted in myriad ways. The knots and folds seem to be discrete entities, but in fact they are nothing but local points in a single continuum. To avoid the charge that this reduces all that exists to a single blob, Bryant adds that such folds also involve a 'becoming something other'. The aforementioned tree is not literally tiny pieces of soil, rain, and animal life, but rather a folding-transformation of these things into bark, leaves, roots, and so on.

Yet from the perspective of the externality thesis, this is not enough. Strictly speaking, externality does not depend on whether or not alterity exists. Instead, it depends on whether entities (be they different from each other or not) exist in discontinuous isolation, or are part of a single integrated continuum. By opting for the latter, Bryant is therefore completely right in noting that his new ontology must renounce the externality thesis (the 'withdrawal' of entities). Should he choose to expand his article (which is just an opening salvo, not a full-blown system) into a more detailed ontology, it would therefore have to be a monism in which entities are but points in a single dynamic field, rather than the machinic pluralism proposed by Deleuze. As we have already indicated in section 2 of Chapter 1 and will further elaborate in Chapters 2 and 3, any such monism will be haunted by a series of problems whose overcoming will prove quite a challenge. Such problems, of course, are for Bryant to overcome. The point of this intermezzo was merely to increase our initial understanding of why the externality thesis leads to the notion of fourfold beings. *If* externality holds, then entities are split between relational manifestations and their private being (their 'powers'). We saw that relational manifestations are actually a twofold of qualities and qualified thing. More importantly, if externality holds as an ontological thesis, then there must also be a strict separation and discontinuity between the interior being of *this* entity and the interior being of *that* entity. Hence, whatever X is said to comprise, this interior must be supplemented by some further Y that prevents all existing cases of X from dissolving into a single great mass, because in the latter case only a single entity could truly be said to exist (Big X). Having said this, Chapter 2 will go on to discuss why Deleuze thinks that externality necessarily holds. After that, Chapter 3 will use a series of examples drawn from Deleuze's own writings to reinforce the point that not even a shred of internalism is compatible with the notion of entities that *really* exist as the very base of reality.

Notes

1. Foucault is closer to the truth when calling *Difference and Repetition* an ontology, and *The Logic of Sense* a metaphysical treatise (1970: 91, 79).
2. Moreover, Buchanan holds that whereas relations are machines (e.g. the relation between a breast and a mouth), the terms of such machines *are not* (2008: 57). This reinstalls precisely the kind of dualism that Deleuze aims to overcome.
3. Contra Deleuze's insistence that 'we prefer not to participate in any effort consistent with a Freudo-Marxist perspective' (DI 276).
4. Also see Bryant's *Difference and Givenness*, which defines Deleuze's thought as a 'phenomenology of the encounter' (2008: 13).
5. Cf. 'Les objets sont hors de nous, ne nous doivent rien, sont leur propres significations' (LAT 293).
6. This is also his reason for avoiding 'thing': 'thingness is the property of the sensible, perceived, formed things, for example the plate or the sun or the wheel' (SCS 270279).
7. 'Dans ma tradition, Heidegger nomme cela "fin de la philosophie"' (Nancy 1998: 117).
8. '[Deleuze] effectue un réel philosophique. L'activité philosophique est cette effectuation' (Nancy 1998: 118).
9. 'Elle se comporte tout naturellement comme une autre poésie' (Nancy 1998: 120).
10. *L'Abécédaire*, 'histoire' and 'résistance'.
11. Cf. LS 71–2.
12. Cf. Deleuze's rejection of 'a subjective emptiness which is then attributed to Being' (DR 196).
13. 'Aujourd'hui il y a une série de crétins qui ont pensé, parce que la science avait évolué, elle pouvait se passer de métaphysique' (SL 100387; cf. ATP 22; WG 115).
14. As also acknowledged by Véronique Bergen (2006: 7, 15–16), François Lyotard (1997: 12), Antonio Negri (1995: 97), Paul Patton (DR xi), and Nathan Widder (2012: 10), among others.
15. As per Deleuze's recommendation (DR 293).
16. As Arnaud Villani writes: '[Deleuze] gives philosophy the definition

of a *concrete metaphysics, free from the universal and all vestiges of transcendence*' (2006: 229).

17. At one point, Deleuze rejects realism for sticking to 'the requirements of simple representation' (DR 104), but this is merely a rejection of any realism positing something as 'ultimate or original' (DR 104).

18. '[M]algré quelques rares formulations ambiguës, cette philosophie [. . .] soit irréductible à une ontologie' (David-Ménard 2005: 115).

19. Cf. 'It's become a commonplace these days to talk about the breakdown of systems [. . .] Systems have in fact lost absolutely none of their power' (N 31).

20. 'mechanical, physical, biological, psychic, social, aesthetic, or philosophical, etc. [Even though] each type of system undoubtedly has its own particular conditions' (DR 117–18; cf. 184, 187, 190).

21. A near exception is Bryant (2011), as we will see.

22. Peter Hallward, for example, calls the virtual a process, but also an energy, a force, a plane, a field, a movement, a space, and a dimension (2006: 16).

23. Bergen stages this as a Hegelian dialectic voided of negativity, seeing 'secret affinities between Hegel and Deleuze' (2002: 664). Deleuze is also read as a closet Hegelian by Jameson (1998: 385) and Žižek (2004: 69).

24. Or as Žižek puts it: 'the infinite potential field of virtualities out of which reality is actualized' (2004: 4).

25. Hallward refers to the single abstract animal or machine mentioned in *A Thousand Plateaus* (ATP 45), a passage which, however, does not refer to a unified *force*. Deleuze merely mentions 'a specific unity of composition' for entities, which refers to the fourfold, not to some cosmic *élan vital*.

26. Deleuze will from then on rail *against* the existence of a (quasi) pre-Socratic realm that underlies reality and in which 'each individual system comes undone' (LS 79; cf. 107, 132; ATP 70).

27. Cf. how 'the sublime principle of the *differend*' must be regarded as coming 'from the heart of *things*' (DR 230, second emphasis added).

28. Badiou is right to note that 'Deleuze arrives at conceptual productions that I would unhesitatingly qualify as *monotonous*, [using] a virtuosic variation of names, under which what is thought remains essentially identical' (2000: 14). DeLanda (2002: 157–80) and Hughes (2008: 156) also point this out.

29. 'Je dirais que la matière à plusieurs caractéristiques internes [. . .] Toute chose à plusieurs caractéristiques internes, il n'y a pas de chose qui n'ait qu'un seul réquisit' (SL 170387).

30. We later see that 'unconscious' is synonymous with 'virtual'.
31. The name 'syntheses of time' is confusing, not in the least because Deleuze has a very counter-intuitive theory of time, which we address in Chapter 9.
32. Bryant (2016) is a French translation of his original English text. The latter is available at Bryant's blog: https://larvalsubjects.files. wordpress.com/2016/11/ethicalbodies.docx (last accessed 22 August 2017). We cite from the English version, hence the lack of reference to specific pages.

2

The Externality Thesis

Until now, we have merely repeated Deleuze's *assertions* that, ontologically, every being is a fourfold entity that he designates with the term 'machine'. Yet an assertion is little more than an opinion if it is not grounded in something that makes it count as an actual argument. The machine thesis is rooted in the more fundamental thesis proclaiming the externality of entities. This externality is the point of departure from which the fourfold is deduced as the necessary structure of all machines. This chapter first establishes the simple fact that the externality of entities is a central motivating force in Deleuze's philosophy. We then show why Deleuze thinks that the externality thesis holds. We will first see how experience itself already puts us on the scent of externality, and then proceed to more speculative arguments.

1 Relations are External to Terms

The realisation that relations are external to terms is the 'thunderclap in philosophy' for Deleuze (SC 141282). A term can be anything: a person, riot, festival, planet, storm, thought, or subatomic particle. Relations, for their part, include touching, pointing, consuming, recruiting, forcing, destroying, and so on. Every feature of an entity that can be registered, experienced, or measured by anything else is relational. If relations are external to terms, entities must therefore have a private, internal reality. It follows that an entity, the entities which are in it, and the entities in which it is, never fully touch. A beaver dam cannot exhaust its wooden parts, but neither could the trees whence those came. Externality is thus the condition of the possibility of encountering, removing, transforming, or destroying something. If the being of wood would be its residing in trees, then beaver dams could never become. Hence relations never signify an essential belonging or final destination. Instead, they are alliances, gifts, hijackings, shelters, tools, and constructs. As Deleuze writes, all machines function 'amid hiatuses and ruptures, breakdowns and failures, stalling and short circuits, within a sum that never succeeds in bringing its various parts together so as to form a whole' (AO 56). A passage from *Dialogues* further surveys this externalist world:

> *Relations are external to their terms* [. . .] relation is neither internal to one of the terms which would consequently be the subject, nor to two together. Moreover, a relation may change without the terms changing [. . .] If one takes this exteriority of relations as a conducting wire or as a line, one sees a very strange world unfold, fragment by fragment: a Harlequin's jacket or patchwork, made up of solid parts and voids, blocs and ruptures, attractions and divisions, nuances and bluntnesses, conjunctions and separations, alternations and interweavings, additions which never reach a total and subtractions whose remainder is never fixed. (D 55)

Externality and irreducibility are the heart of Deleuze's philosophy. Hence his 'hatred of interiority' (N 6). 'Interiority' marks any philosophy that denies entities a private reality. Interiority reduces entities to representations of something else, thereby internalising their being to their relation with something beyond themselves. 'No surplus' is the mantra of internalism.

Externalist philosophies support the exact opposite view. Deleuze first encounters the externalist intuition in David Hume's empiricism (ES 108). For Hume, the content of direct experience is not an object such as a glass or a table. Direct experience merely contains simple impressions ('hot', 'painful', 'red') which are *then* objectified ('fire') via habituation, which is a principle of human nature. Deleuze calls this externality of objects to direct experience the 'point common to all empiricisms' (ES 99; cf. LAT 124, 130, 140). More importantly, he radicalises this externalist intuition. It comes to define a 'superior' empiricism in which entities are withdrawn from *all* relations, not just from our perceptions (DR 143). Conversely, 'non-empiricist' is any theory 'according to which, *in one way or another*, relations are derived from the nature of things' (ES 109). It is any theory according to which at least one relation is internal to the being of beings ('tornadoes are the will of God', 'love is hormonal activity', 'all things are subatomic particles'). In short, externality is an ontological axiom: 'the truly fundamental proposition is that relations are external to terms' (ES 98; cf. x, 66, 98, 99, 101, 105, 107, 123; DI 163, 166; SC 211282, 010383; TRM 365).

It is often remarked that Deleuze's work on other philosophers does not faithfully repeat their theories, but rather transforms them according to his own needs (Smith 2012: xii). Yet perhaps it has not been noticed that the externality thesis is always the key to this transformation. For example, in reading Bergson, Deleuze consistently tries to downplay Bergson's idea that there exists a single creative and all-pervading force (the *élan vital* or universal duration). He instead presents Bergson as proposing a pluralism of parts which remain external to each other (B 104). Likewise, after dismissing Leibniz as an internalist thinker in *Difference and Repetition*, Deleuze later recasts him as a thinker of externality. In this later reading, individual monads express the entirety of the world, but they themselves remain external to all such expressions (LS 110).[1] Leibniz is taken to realise that monads are substances with essential attributes, but that these attributes are irreducible to relations.[2] In a third example, it is externality that forces Deleuze to break with his philosophical hero Spinoza. For Spinoza, relations are internal to one term, as individual modes are reducible to substance. Spinoza consequently cannot account for the full individuality of things, which is precisely what Deleuze aims to accomplish.[3]

Yet as indicated, the externality thesis is not merely a principle by which to read others. The very project of *Difference and Repetition* is already to develop an '*internal difference* [referring] only to an *external relation* with extensity' (DR 231). If relations are external to entities, entities contain an internal difference between their inner selves and their manifestations in relations. The reference to extensity emphasises spatial externality, asserting that entities are irreducible to one another even if they are conjoined. *The Logic of Sense* also asserts externality temporally in stating that 'the paradoxical situation of the beginning [. . .] is that it is itself a result, and that it remains external to that which it causes to begin' (LS 218). Furthermore, *Anti-Oedipus* asserts externality mereologically:

> We believe only in totalities that are peripheral. And if we discover
> such a totality alongside various separate parts, it is a whole *of* these

particular parts but does not totalize them; it is a unity *of* all these particular parts but does not unify them; rather; it is added to them as a new part fabricated separately. (AO 57)

Moreover, the very opening page of *A Thousand Plateaus* warns readers not to overlook the fact that matters and the relations between them are exterior to each other (ATP 3). The book later again asserts the 'essential irreducibility of assemblages' (ATP 256). Deleuze writes that an assemblage 'has only itself, in connection with other assemblages and in relation to other bodies without organs' (ATP 4). A book, for example, has many connections to other entities (its author, cover, ink, words, index, readers, publisher, language . . .), but none of those are its being. Despite its relations, it *has only itself* as demanded by externality.

This theme of solitude returns in Deleuze's books on cinema, and even structures them.[4] Again Deleuze affirms that 'relation is not a property of objects, it is always external to its terms' (C1 10).[5] The first book then explores the 'movement-image', which is Deleuze's name for images of the movements common to several 'vehicles or moving bodies' (C1 23). Movement-images are thoroughly relational and include actions, perceptions, and affections (C1 ix). They can hint at externality, but never embrace it fully. The first book ends with a consideration of Hitchcock, who according to Deleuze realises that relations are external to terms, but 'constantly refuses' the full implication of that thesis (C1 x, 215). Hence the second volume on 'time-images', which move beyond movement-images as paradoxical perspectives on 'an outside more distant than any exterior, and that of an inside deeper than any interior' (C2 261).

Deleuze's reflections on literature are animated by similar concerns. He famously proclaims the 'superiority' of Anglo-American literature in *Dialogues*, and again externality is the reason behind it.[6] Deleuze detects 'a principle dear to English philosophers, to which the Americans would give a new meaning [. . .]: *relations are external to their terms*' (ECC 58). He takes most literature to obsess over internality (where do I belong?, where is my home?, how to fall in love?, what have we lost?, what is my place in my family?), but American writers do the exact opposite by focusing on the solitude and non-inclusion of non-humans as well as humans. Deleuze writes that T. E. Lawrence's genius is to reject a world of images, as images are always images *of* something, and therefore relational. Lawrence instead 'moves from images to *entities*' (ECC 120). Deleuze takes Lawrence not to write about shame and glory as images or effects (the shame after battle, the glory of the army), but as entities in their own right.

Finally, even Deleuze's appreciation of the baroque in *The Fold* revolves around externality. Deleuze interprets the baroque as an attempt to aesthetically separate all entities from their relations with others, as exemplified in baroque architecture:

> This is baroque layout *par excellence*. A chamber with neither a door nor a window! Such a chamber literally realizes the formula: 'an interior', at the limit an interior without exterior. What is the correlate of this interior without a door or a window? The correlate of this interior is an exterior which includes doors and windows, but, and this here is precisely the baroque paradox, that no longer corresponds to an interior. What is that? It is the façade! The façade is pierced by doors and windows, only the façade no longer expresses the interior. The façade becomes independent while simultaneously the interior has conquered its autonomy. (SL 2001 87; cf. FLB 31–2)[7]

Again, we see the thesis that an entity has a private reality on the one hand, and a completely different manifestation in relations on the other. It is should now be clear that 1) Deleuze encounters externality in Hume's empiricism, and aims to radicalise it into a 'superior empiricism', 2) externality is a central notion in *Difference and Repetition*, *The Logic of Sense*, *Anti-Oedipus*, and *A Thousand Plateaus*, and 3) Deleuze's readings of other philosophers and of the arts are also centred on externality. Having determined that externality is central, we must now know *why* this is the case, and then outline some immediate implications. Deleuze often defends externality *a contrario* by highlighting shortcomings in internalist philosophies. Yet he also presents at least six more general arguments, which fall into two groups. The first contains three arguments drawn from lived experience, the second three more speculative, ontological arguments.

2 The Experience of Externality

In the first group, the first argument concerns our interactions with objects. For example: I see a cube, but I cannot see more than three of its sides at any given moment. I cannot integrate it fully into a relation with myself. Nonetheless, I can extract the cube from where I find it (say, in a stack of cubes) and proceed to manipulate it. From this Deleuze concludes that entities are 'totally objective', by which he means irreducible to their relations with us or with other things.[8] By removing an entity from its previous engagements, we detach it 'from a ground constituted by an ensemble of other objects'.[9] This ground is its existential ground. It is the situation in which it was involved a mere moment ago. Since objects can traverse wide varieties of such grounds, Deleuze reasons that the cube must have a private, internal ground in and of itself. There must be something by virtue of which it remains *this* cube throughout different settings.[10] Its being can neither be in the relations it had before entering the stack of cubes, nor in its recent relations within the stack, nor in its current relations with me. And since there is no reason to assume that human relations with a random object are different from relations with non-human entities, Deleuze concludes that entities must have a private ground or internal reality that has nothing to do with us.[11]

The formula 'everything is a machine' expresses this idea in the original French *tout fait machine*. 'Tout fait' refers to Duchamp's readymade artworks, such as the famous urinal and the bottle-drying rack. Given the references to Dadaist art in *Anti-Oedipus*, Deleuze is certainly aware of this.[12] Does not each readymade confront us with the fact that entities can be detached from their relations? They are always objects migrated from one context to the next. More importantly, they force us to see that what we usually call the essence of the object is a mere relational function. The urinal turned artwork is no longer a sanitation fixture, but before Duchamp's intervention the urinal was not yet an aesthetic sensation. Both 'essences' are mere functions depending on contextual relations. It is nonetheless the same urinal in both situations, so there must be something external to relations which constitutes the urinal's 'thisness', to borrow a term from Duns Scotus. This readymade lesson must be generalised. Everything is a readymade, and is irreducible to our perceiving, labelling, or using it. Anything is equally irreducible to its surroundings. The urinal belongs neither to a dump, nor to a museum, nor to a toilet. Duchamp's readymades also suggest that entities cannot even be reduced to their parts. *Fountain* does not need its 'R. Mutt' signature in order to exist, nor does *L.H.O.O.Q.* need the moustache added to Mona Lisa. The parts of an entity are always somewhat redundant, a complex notion to which we will return later. For now, observe how readymades reveal that objects have no natural place, function, or meaning. There is nothing external constituting their essence. Each is simply a force unleashed in the world.

All this is a necessary consequence of the irreducibility of entities. If an entity would be reducible to X, then X would after all be its natural origin, place, movement, function, destination, or meaning. Duchamp's readymades mock this idea. As Michael North notes, Duchamp adopted 'tout fait' from Bergson, the latter using it pejoratively to designate everything mechanical and rigid (North 2009: 97–9). Bergson's 'tout fait' is what humour exposes and ridicules, as when we laugh at seeing someone stumble. In stumbling we suddenly encounter our legs as foreign, reluctant objects. Bergson thinks such moments are unnatural exceptions to an 'inner suppleness of life' (1914: 44, *passim*). Duchamp inverts this model and shows that harmony is not naturally given, but rather an exception, an artificial construction, a temporary situation that requires effort to be maintained. A readymade is indifferent to where it is and to how it is experienced. It teaches us that entities are obstinate and withdrawn from their relations. Smooth totalities only exist if sufficient forces cooperate to *make* entities act in harmony. An entity is an irreducible machine that only functions smoothly with others if effort is spent in putting it to work. Moreover, such efforts necessarily involve shattering some relations that the entity used to entertain. As Deleuze writes: 'the artist is the master of objects; he puts before us shattered, burned, broken-down objects, converting them to the regime of desiring-machines, breaking down is part of the very functioning of desiring-machines' (AO 45). No entity is automatically reducible to or aligned with anything else, and resistance and rigidity are primordial facts instead of unnatural exceptions. A readymade does not tell us that entities *await* a practical or aesthetic function, it tells us that they *resist* it.

Yet irreducibility is not autarchy. As we will see, there is no entity without connections to other entities serving as its parts, allies, enemies, and ecology. This is precisely why Deleuze uses 'assemblage' as a synonym for 'machine', the former being a system emerging from relations between heterogeneous parts. Note that if entities were autarchic, they would not be irreducible, but self-identical and thus reducible to themselves. As indicated earlier, collectivity and solitude go hand in hand (K 18), as Deleuze's main thesis paradoxically implies that any entity whatsoever is irreducible to all relations, but that it always needs other entities to pull that off.

The second observation from lived experience concerns learning. Deleuze characterises learning as familiarising oneself with something that remains hidden. When we learn to swim or to speak a language, the object (water, Japanese) never fully reveals itself. We merely experience 'signs' of the object (DR 22). 'Sign' should be broadly understood. The water perceived is a sign, but so is swimming in it. A Japanese textbook is a sign of Japanese, but so is a Japanese conversation. Signs signify 'two orders of size or disparate realities between which the sign flashes', and envelops 'another "object"' (DR 22). On the one hand, the sign is the object in its manifestation in a relation. On the other hand, the object in itself remains enveloped in its signs and withdrawn from direct contact. Learning suggests this because one can, in principle, always learn new things about the same entity. Moreover, to learn is to vary the relations that an entity entertains in order to familiarise ourselves with it. (Is this not also the central notion of scientific experiment?) If a shift in relations were to correspond to an equal shift in entities, the notion of learning about *this* entity would be nonsensical. It is precisely because we only ever encounter translated signs of objects, and not objects themselves, that we can increase our familiarity with swimming, the Japanese language, a lover, an institution, or a memory.

The third argument from experience concerns novelty. Our first great love, the First World War, the French Revolution, the invention of the internet, the first jazz recordings, all these things derive part of their significance from having truly been new. Yet this cannot really be the case if things have an internal relation to some ground (however conceived). If all things are mere representations or derivatives of something permanent and stable that does not change, then novelty is merely an illusion. Even the end of the world will then be reducible to the same old ground (whether God, history, substance, matter, or natural law) of which telephones, yesterday evening, tennis shoes, and burlesque theatre were also mere effects. As Deleuze writes: 'if the ground lets that which grounds subsist, we can wonder what purpose it serves. Conversely, if grounding changes something, then we see the point. Does not every ground lead to an unexpected surprise? Does the ground not lead to something we did not expect?' (WG 41). Experience suggests that reality holds genuine surprise, which implies that there is no universal ground, but rather a change in what gets to ground what as soon as something new has been grounded.

3 Speculative Arguments for Externality

This first group of arguments for externality is not yet decisive. One could object that Deleuze merely makes externality plausible in a phenomenological or epistemological sense. Yet the first three arguments do pave the way for the second group, whose arguments rely on speculative, conceptual considerations. Deleuze first insists that if relations were internal to terms, the current state of affairs could not pass. In *Bergsonism* he asks: 'how would a new present come about if the old present did not pass at the same time that it *is* present? How would any present whatsoever pass, if it were not past *at the same time* as present?' (B 58). This resurfaces in *Difference and Repetition*:

> If a new present were required for the past to be constituted as past, then the former present would never pass and the new one would never arrive. No present would ever pass were it not past 'at the same time' as it is present; no past would ever be constituted unless it were constituted 'at the same time' as it was present. (DR 82)

Crucially, Deleuze is *not* referring to our usual notion of time here. As he writes, 'the past and the future do not designate instants distinct from a supposed present instant, but rather the dimensions of the present itself in so far as it is a contraction of instants' (DR 71). 'Present' refers to entities in their relations, and 'past' refers to the dimension of entities which remains external to all previous, current, and future relations. It is a 'past which never *was* present, since it was not formed "after"' (DR 82). It is 'posed as already-there' and 'in itself, conserving itself in itself' (DR 82). If the being of entities were purely present and relational, each entity would be exhausted in its current affairs. No entity would have the non-relational surplus required to ditch old relations and forge new ones. Each entity must have an internal reality during each moment of its existence, an 'always already past' with which relations are forged.

Second and similarly, if internalism were true and entities would be their relations, the universe would have reached a 'final state'

(NP 47). Suppose that the non-relational aspect of entities is merely what they will become at a later point in time: it then becomes very hard to understand why change or becoming has then not yet ceased. If being is fully relational, one would expect reality to be at a standstill in full equilibrium, because everything would already be exhaustively deployed. As Deleuze writes:

> But why would equilibrium, the terminal state, have to have been attained if it were possible? By virtue of what Nietzsche calls the infinity of past time. The infinity of past time means that becoming cannot have started to become, that it is not something that has become. But, not being something that has become it cannot be a becoming something. Not having become, it would already be what it is becoming – if it were becoming something. That is to say, past time being infinite, becoming would have attained its final state if it had one. And, indeed, saying that becoming would have attained its final state if it had one is the same as saying that it would not have left its initial state if it had one. (NP 47)

Changing into something implies having been something. Therefore, if everything is to become reducible to something, then everything must have equally been something. At the very least, it must have formally been that which becomes reduced to something at the end. Yet if that were the case, it becomes inexplicable why everything is not reducible to that something between the beginning and the end. The externality of entities to terms concerns absolute irreducibility and cannot be a mere moment within a larger process of interiorisation (DI 163). If that were true, we would end up with a frozen reality in which everything is utterly stuck in its relational present, and not even illusory change would be possible. This is why Deleuze remarks that even if there is a God who creates our world, 'his calculations never work out exactly, and this inexactitude or injustice in the result, this irreducible inequality, forms the condition of the world. [If] the calculation were exact, there would be no world' (DR 222).

Third, 'Nature would never repeat [. . .] would it be reducible to the superficiality of matter' (DR 290). This again concerns the necessity of externality. If all entities plus their relations and alterations are reducible to a single material stratum, then this stratum entertains an internal relation with all entities and relations. After all, to be something would mean to be a representation or permutation of this layer. Several things would then be unintelligible: for one thing, why this single material layer broke up into fragments in the first place and why its human section experiences the illusion of diversity. Next, why there is *this* in this case and *that* in that case. If everything is reducible to the same natural substance, law, or principle, the existence of different actual entities becomes a mystery. Finally, what the reality of this material stratum would be. If materialism is true, then to be something is to be reducible to a final matter. Being would ultimately mean 'to consist of substance'. Yet a final material layer cannot contain itself, because in order to be final it cannot be constituted by anything, not even itself. This is the contradiction in materialism of an 'infinitely repeated element' which Deleuze denounces (DR 271). As he writes, any 'bare and material model is, properly speaking, unthinkable' (DR 286). Within materialism, we would once again expect everything to be wholly actual and homogeneous, so that no future events would be possible. This is why Deleuze writes that nothing would 'repeat'. Note that this is not just a problem for materialism, but also for idealism (C1 56; AO 35). For example, as the post-Kantians had already seen, similar problems arise when Kantian transcendental subjectivity has to account for the phenomena of experience. First, how to account for diversity if the same conditions are to fully account for every minute detail of experience. Second, how to account for the same conditions producing *this* here yet *that* there. Third, how to account for the genesis of the transcendental subject and the various faculties, how to account for that which accounts for everything.[13] Deleuze denounces not just materialism, but any philosophy that internalises entities and their relations to a substance, agent, principle, movement, or an exceptional and overarching relation (such as the one between human and world).[14]

But why be so strict? Why Deleuze's insistence that there is always *full* externality of relations to terms?[15] Why must each entity have an interiority that is *absolutely* separate from others by an 'external envelope' (DR 24)? Why must there be relations *and* terms at all? This is because ontology is a zero sum game. First, reality cannot solely consist of relations.[16] A fully relational reality cannot account for change. Hence each relation must be accompanied by something else: the private reality of its entity, which constitutes a surplus to account for change. Moreover, if only relations existed, what relations relate to would be unintelligible.

There would be 'infinite representation' (DR 56), so that a house would be nothing but the infinity of possible and current relations of others to it. Yet a relation to something is never a relation with another relation to something. My view on the house is neither an experience of your view of the house, nor my experience of all possible views of the house.[17] I experience the *house*, though accounting for this will not be as simple as it sounds. Or take another example. Colour and position are relational qualities: colour requires a source of light and position is always relative. Now, an entity's colour is not the colour of its spatial coordinates or even its extension. 'Two metres of green' simply does not exist. Relational qualities can converge, but only ever on the same non-relational *entity*.

It is equally impossible that relations are merely somewhat, sometimes, or possibly internal to terms. Someone may posit that relations are merely somewhat external to terms, if only to introduce some modesty into the bold division that Deleuze proposes. However, one then merely posits a 'big' extra-relational aspect for entities and donates part of it to their relations. A 'small' extra-relational aspect still remains, and it will still be the private reality of entities. Likewise, relations cannot sometimes be external and sometimes not. Someone might propose this as an easy explanation of how everything seems to hang together. We would have an accidental play of external relations safely residing on the solid backbone of a few privileged internal relations. However, even if entities had just one internal relation with something else, all the problems previously mentioned return. We would once again be left with entities lacking a surplus beyond their present actuality. Their being would be fully exhausted in a single current relation. Nor can the being of something reside in a possible relation, because possibility always requires other entities. Suppose that, for example, a festival were its possible appreciation by a reviewer after it has taken place. This leads to the absurdity that if the reviewer dies prematurely, thereby eliminating the possibility, the festival will not have been! Nothing is solved by saying that festivals are *all* their possible relations. After all, even if the universe ends immediately after the festival, it will still be the case that it took place. Evasive strategies such as these are 'common to metaphysics and transcendental philosophy', because of 'this alternative which they both impose on us: *either* an undifferentiated ground, a groundlessness, formless nonbeing, or an abyss without differences and without properties, *or a supremely individuated Being and an intensely personalized Form. Without this Being or this Form, you will have only chaos*' (LS 105–6; cf. 103; WP 51). Internalist philosophies assume that reality would be absolute chaos if it were not curtailed by a substance, God, or a cosmos (metaphysics); by a Kantian subject (transcendental philosophy); or by a relation between humans and world.

Whatever the strategy, there are two general ways to oppose externality: 'either a means is found to make the relation internal to the terms, or a more profound and inclusive term is discovered to which the relation is already internal' (DI 163). In both cases, we replace entities and their real interactions with 'an abstract relation which is supposed to express them all' (NP 74). The result is always a dualism. If relations are internal to terms, something must be posited beyond entities and their interactions to account for change. If relations and terms are all internal to a more profound relation, there is dualism between that in which everything stands and everything that stands within it. In both cases, the multiple is embraced by a One. Deleuze instead defends a pluralism which is at the same time a type of monism. Pluralism, because each entity has a private and irreducible reality making it a force of its own. Monism, because each entity will, in a formal sense, have this same interior:

> There is only one form of thought, it's the same thing: one can only think in a monistic or pluralistic manner. The only enemy is two. Monism and pluralism: it's the same thing [. . .] This is because the source of dualism is precisely the opposition between something that can be affirmed as one, and something that can be affirmed as multiple [. . .] (SCS 260373; cf. DR 56)

It will not be easy to 'see things from the middle, rather than looking down on them from above or up at them from below' (ATP 23). We can 'no longer expect salvation from the depths of the earth or from autochthony, any more than expect it from heaven or from the Idea' (LS 129), because *there is no longer depth and height* so understood (LS 130). Instead, we need to consider entities in and of themselves, and systematically doing so is what Deleuze modestly calls his 'own little contribution' to philosophy.[18]

Before we move on, let us note some implications of the

externality thesis. First, as already said, every single entity will be absolutely irreducible, whether pores, scars, breasts, bees, soccer players, Tuaregs, wolves, or jackals. Moreover, it does not matter if they are physical, hallucinated, or poetic: real is real (ATP 30; cf. FLB 10). A world of externality is one in which 'no two grains of dust are absolutely identical, no two hands have the same distinctive points, no two typewriters have the same strike, no two revolvers score their bullets in the same manner' (DR 26). Second, the absolute refusal of internality means that 'the principal frontier is displaced. It no longer passes, in terms of height, between the universal and the particular; nor, in terms of depth, does it pass between substance and accident' (LS 132).[19] Instead, we must install a difference in kind between the 'metaphysical surface' and the 'physical surface' of each entity (LS 125), so that entities are spatially, temporally, and mereologically irreducible. Both aspects must have an element of permanence as well as change. Otherwise either identity or alteration is referred to one side of their being; this side will consequently be indistinguishable from that same aspect in other entities, which would fuse all those sides into one, thus re-establishing dualism. Third, all primary and secondary qualities, parts, wholes, functions, and predicates belong to the relational aspect of entities. To describe or even define an entity in terms of its colour, weight, size, mathematical structure, components, memberships, age, origin, smell, public, users, location, or the time between its birth and death is always relational. It always involves other entities as well. Deleuze will have to account for the private reality of entities without referring to any of these relational aspects. Fourth, this account cannot be an epistemological realism. Deleuze has barred himself from answering the 'what is . . .?' question for any specific entity, precisely because answering it would imply that the being of an entity can become present in a relation with a human being. Hence the following:

> It is not certain that the question *what is this?* is a good question for discovering the essence or the Idea. It may be that questions such as *who? how much? how? where? when?* are better – as much for discovering the essence as for determining something more important about the Idea (TRM 94)

If things 'endure in their own way', withdrawn from direct access, then still 'ontology should, of necessity, be possible' (B 49). Yet it must be purely formal. An ontology can outline the general structure of any entity whatsoever, but it cannot tell us exactly what the private reality, essence, or Idea of any specific entity is. Such discoveries are made in other human activities, but even there, externality demands that 'what is. . .?' can never receive a definitive answer. To learn about a machine or assemblage is to grow acquainted with its manifestations in various relations, with its descriptions, with its parts, with its uses, and so on, but never to know it in itself.

Notes

1. See also 'Ce que j'exprime clairement c'est, dans le monde, ce qui a rapport à mon corps [. . .] Mais ce qui arrive dans mon corps, mon corps lui-même, je ne l'exprime pas clairement du tout' (SL 120587). In this reading, monads will express events (also called predicates), but never their private attributes. See 'la relation c'est le prédicat [. . .] un prédicat c'est un verbe [et] le verbe, c'est l'indice d'événement' (SL 200187); 'ce qu'il appelle prédicat, c'est la relation' (SL 100387); 'un prédicat c'est toujours un rapport' (SL 120587).

2. '[Leibniz] est le premier à savoir que les mathématiques et la logique sont des systèmes de relations irréductibles à des attributs'; 'Une substance est inséparable de son attribut essentiel et inversement la substance est définie par l'attribut essentiel' (SL 200187).

3. For Spinoza, 'il faut bien que la relation soit finalement intérieure à quelque chose. Il ne veut pas penser à des relations qui seraient de pures extériorités' (SS 170381).

4. I agree with Jacques Rancière that Deleuze's cinema books include – among other things – a theory about the world written in cinematographic vocabulary (Rancière 2006: 109).

5. Cf. SC 141282, 211282. The cinema books call what remains external in entities the 'out-of-field' (*hors-champ*) (C1 16).

6. Cf. Clancy (2015) on the 'metaphysical commitments' that Deleuze discerns in American literature.

7. '[C]'est l'aménagement baroque par excellence. Une pièce sans porte ni fenêtre! [. . .] C'est la pièce qui réalise à la lettre, littéralement, la formule: 'un intérieur', à la limite un intérieur sans extérieur [. . .] Quel est le corrélat de cet intérieur sans porte ni fenêtre? Le corrélat de cet intérieur, c'est un extérieur qui lui comporte des portes et des fenêtres, mais, justement et c'est cela le paradoxe baroque, il ne correspond plus à un intérieur. Qu'est-ce que c'est? C'est la façade!

La façade est percée de portes et de fenêtres; seulement la façade n'exprime plus l'intérieur [. . .] la façade prend de l'indépendance en même temps que l'intérieur a conquis son autonomie.'

8. 'Or ce n'est nullement le signe d'une dépendance de l'objet, au contraire c'est la manifestation de son objectivité totale' (LAT 293).

9. 'Il est bien connu l'objet contemplé se détache sur un fond, constitué par l'ensemble des autres objets' (LAT 293)

10. 'Mais précisément l'objet ne pourrait pas entrenir avec les autres un rapport quelconque, si ce rapport lui restait extérieur: pour que tel objet se détache comme forme sur le fond des autres objets, il faut qu'il soit déjà à lui-même son propre fond' (LAT 293).

11. 'Ce phénomène renvoie à l'objet lui-même, et pas du tout à celui qui le perçoit' (LAT 293).

12. Cf. Zepke (2008).

13. Kant, of course, conveniently defers to God (Maimon 2010: appendix II, 234, *Letter from Kant to Herz*).

14. Deleuze would also reject objections that the issue of internalism versus externalism is a 'pseudo-problem', which someone could raise based on the intentionality thesis. The latter says that all consciousness is consciousness of something that is not itself this consciousness. Hence we seemingly obtain externality (something irreducible to consciousness) and internality (something in consciousness) at the same time and without contradictions. Yet the irreducible part of the object in consciousness cannot be produced by or accounted for by consciousness itself. If that were the case, both aspects of the object (its presence and its otherness) would be reducible to consciousness, and the problems arising for all internalism return. So the object's withdrawn otherness must belong to *it*. The same goes for relations between entities. If consciousness were to fully account for them, the result would be a pre-Socratism in which a unified *physis* is shaken and fragmented by *nous*, so that we are again confronted with the same problems that hamper materialism.

15. '[L]a relation, c'est forcément en trois puisqu'elle est extérieure à ces termes, dont on a au moins deux termes et la relation n'est réductible à aucun de deux ni à la totalité de deux. Donc la relation est toujours un tiers' (SC 010383).

16. '[P]eut être qu'à la limite, il n'y a pas de terme, il n'y a que des parquets de relations, ce que vous appelez un terme, c'est un paquet de relations, voilà' (SC 141282); '[J]e crois que qu'on peut pas penser les relations indépendamment d'un devenir au moins virtuel, quelle qu'elle soit la relation, et que ça à mon avis, les théoriciens de la rela-

tion, pourtant si forts qu'ils soient, ils l'ont pas vu, mais je voudrais insister beaucoup plus sur ce point' (SC 141282).

17. Foucault is right that *The Logic of Sense* (and, by extension, Deleuze's entire philosophy) is 'the most alien book imaginable from *The Phenomenology of Perception*' (1970: 79). This is because Merleau-Ponty precisely defends the claim that 'the house itself is not the house seen from nowhere, but the house seen from everywhere. The completed object is translucent, being shot through from all sides by an infinite number of present scrutinies which intersect in its depths *leaving nothing hidden*' (2005: 79, emphasis added).

18. 'mon seul petit apport' (SC 141282).

19. As we will see, relational aspects of entities are not 'accidental' because they can alter an entity's essence.

3

Critiques of Internalism

Having established the centrality of the externality thesis to Deleuze's thought, we can now show how this very thesis motivates his various critiques of other philosophers and philosophies. This serves a dual purpose. First, it demonstrates that Deleuze's critiques are not a loose aggregate of individual problems that he discerns in 'competing' systems of thought. Every single one of them is instead rooted in his adherence to externality and the resulting irreducibility of entities. Second, it provides further support for our conviction that Deleuze's philosophy and ontology cannot be properly understood unless one proceeds from the externality thesis. This is to say that ignoring, at any point in the analysis, the externality of relations and terms amounts to nothing less than aligning Deleuze with those very philosophies he seeks to do away with.

1 Difference and Repetition

Each machine or multiplicity (a single thought, a dashing party, a massive mountain) has a difference between its internal reality and its interactions with others. It has a difference in itself (DR 55). It is an ontological difference between two aspects of a machine rather than a difference between it and something else. In turn, repetition must be 'the production of the "absolutely different"; making it so that repetition is, for itself, difference in itself' (DR 95). Repetition is the eternal return of this difference in kind between all actual relations and all interior realities of all entities. This internal repetition repeats the same ontological difference in all existential cases.[1] As every entity is irreducible to anything else, it is also a repetition of a different difference, this time existentially. Existentially, the repeated difference between a mountain in its externality and in its relations is not the same as the difference between those two aspects of a flower. And since a mountain enters into different types of relations, it is not even the same repeated difference for the mountain itself![2] We can now understand Deleuze's critique of difference and repetition in their 'maledictory state' (DR 29). These are concepts of difference and repetition that suggest that the being of machines is something exterior to them, something shared with others, something below, above, or beyond them. This can be an entity, process, force, consciousness, history, and so on. In each case we see a 'primacy of identity' rather than an internal difference, demoting difference to a representation of something else rather than a difference within something itself (DR xix).

Repetition in its usual sense refers to cases of *different* entities, events, or forces that are nonetheless in a certain sense *identical* (DR xv). Take the cruel example of several beatings. They are only 'repeated beatings' if there is at least someone who repeatedly beats, or someone repeatedly being beaten, a single location where beatings occur, or a single individual who reads about them. The same is true for repetitions of festivals, seasons, birthdays, sounds, lessons, weather patterns, stylistic elements, explanations, and mistakes. Such repetition is not understood as an internal repetition of a difference. It is an external repetition of an identity: one thing repeats in different cases. This becomes problematic once we think that external repetition does not just associate entities existentially, but also explains them ontologically. An entity is then the common element discerned in it and others. Deleuze presents several ways in which we can come to think this.

First, there are laws, which determine 'the resemblance of the subjects ruled by it, along with their equivalence to terms which it designates' (DR 2). Someone may think that everything is fully accounted for by transcendent natural, religious, or cosmic laws. All terms are then internal to their relation with those laws. Being would mean being a representation of laws, and nothing besides. Every storm, rock, or thought would be a determination by general, self-identical laws, without internal reality in and of itself. Second, there is scientific experiment which defines things 'in terms of a small number of chosen factors' (DR 3). Someone could think that some measurable properties of entities must be essential. It would follow that the being of an entity can become present in a relation under the right conditions. By repeatedly and reliably showing an entity to display such a property, one could grow convinced that this property is its real being ('the dog is a barker', 'water is H_2O'). Third, someone may think that an entity can be fully grasped via its concept. Since a concept's comprehension (its specificity) and its extension (the objects to which it applies) are inversely proportional, a concept for a single entity would require infinite comprehension. Yet this does not work. The comprehension of a concept can only be increased by adding predicates: we specify 'dog' by adding 'grey', 'aggressive', 'thirty-pound', and so on. But as already established, predicates are always relational. Rather than grasping an entity in itself, infinite comprehension merely 'allows the greatest space possible for the apprehension of resemblances' and remains 'applicable by right to an infinity of things' (DR 12). Infinite comprehension merely lists all relations that an entity (possibly) entertains. It lists the memberships of a thing, but it disregards its external being. This makes for an extreme case of external repetition, because a being is equated with an infinity of other possible beings to which the same predicates apply.[3]

Such ontologies premised on external repetition and internal relations display what Deleuze refers to as 'generality' (DR 1), 'mechanism' (AO 59), or 'functionalism' (AO 210). It 'expresses a point of view according to which one term may be exchanged or substituted for another' (DR 1). It equates entities with how something makes them manifest and function in a certain relation. Both the change and the permanence of rivers, beliefs, societies, and monuments are then mere illustrations of demands issued from something beyond them (DR 2). For instance, a functionalist theory would hold that organic tissue and silicon surrogates are strict equals if they perform the same function for their host. The price to pay is that, at the limit, the very notions 'organic tissue' and 'silicon surrogates' become senseless. The words suggest a difference where their functions reveal no such thing. Functionalism and mechanism cannot account for *this* entity which at some point *started* to function. They are hampered by a 'fundamental inability to account for [a machine's] formations' (AO 323).[4] By focusing only on the surface performance of things, they overlook the inner regions of the things themselves.[5]

Repetition in its 'maledictory state' ignores that external repetition is logically preceded by an internal repetition which 'affirms itself against the law, which works underneath laws, perhaps superior to laws' (DR 2). They forget the 'condition or constitutive element' of external repetition, which is 'the interiority of repetition *par excellence*' (DR xvi). If everything is merely its function or manifestation, everything is internal to terms. The present would not pass, the universe would be finished, nothing would be able to happen. We require a 'positive principle' of internal repetition (DR 19), which is the absolute difference between how a machine functions and what resides within it. We need to account for the internal repetition beneath the bare, external repetitions that obscure it (DR 25).

Deleuze similarly rejects philosophies in which the most fundamental difference is a difference between an entity and something else. Such a 'difference which falls back into exteriority', however conceived, presupposes an identity (DR 24). As with repetition, the point is not that difference between entities does not exist, but that this tends to obscure a more fundamental internal difference. This leads Deleuze to reject all philosophies premised on identity, resemblance, opposition, and analogy (DR xv). He calls these 'the four shackles' which 'betray the nature of Being', and a cross on which 'difference is crucified' (DR 29, 269, 138). If the very being of an entity is to be identical to something, to resemble something, to stand opposed to something, or to be analogous to something, then this being is relational. To be would be to represent one's relation with this other or to dissolve into a movement beyond oneself. This turns each difference into a moment of a more profound identity. If two horses are different, they must first both be horses (identity). If a mental asylum is like a prison, their differences become secondary to their shared features (resemblance). Hot differs from cold, but both concern temperature (opposition). If I am to this text what a badger is to its burrow, we are both first and foremost builders (analogy). Whenever such differences are taken to be fundamental, 'we do not think difference in itself' (DR xv).

These considerations lead Deleuze to reject key elements in the philosophies of Aristotle, Hegel, and Leibniz in *Difference and Repetition*.[6] Starting with the first, Aristotelianism is an exemplary case of what Deleuze calls 'organic representation' (DR xv, 35).[7] The term denotes any philosophy that defines entities in terms of some 'bigger thing' to which they belong. A non-philosophical example would be taking the (incidentally false) statement 'opposable thumbs are only found in primates' to mean that there is something essentially 'primatish' about opposable thumbs. Now, for Aristotle the greatest possible difference is contrariety, as for example in rational versus non-rational animals. This is because 'opposites alone cannot be present together' (Aristotle 1991a: 1055b33–4). Contrariety indicates a specific difference that relies on a higher identity, here the genus 'animal'. Hence 'two terms differ when they are other, not in themselves, but in something else; thus when they also agree in something else' (DR 30; cf. 31–2). This violates externality in four ways. First, individual things have a defining, internal relation to their genus, as genera concern that which is common to the essence of their species. Second, primary substances ('an individual man') as defined in the *Categories* are numerically one and self-identical, meaning they lack the internal difference necessitated by the externality thesis (Aristotle 1991a: 4a 10). Third, genera 'remain the same in themselves while becoming other in the differences which divide them' (DR 31). Only through specific difference does 'animal' become something else in humans than in horses (DR 12), but the genus itself has no internal difference. Fourth, the categories or highest genera must be defined analogically, as Being cannot be the highest genus (DR 33–4). This is because specific differences cannot contain their genera. If they did, a human being would be a 'rational animal animal', which is absurd. If being were a genus, its division into categories would thus require a specific difference without being, which is impossible because a specific difference which *is not* (i.e. does not exist) cannot be operative. The result is definition by analogy, which is utterly relational.

Next, Deleuze presents Leibniz and Hegel as examples of 'orgiastic representation' (DR xv, 42). This stands for philosophies that, instead of subordinating discrete entities to discrete 'bigger things', assimilate all things into a whole of which they are expressions or on to which they converge (DR 42). They absorb entities into a 'womb in which finite determination never ceases to be born and to disappear, to be enveloped and deployed within orgiastic representation. [Representation] no longer refers to the limitation of a form, but to the *convergence* towards a ground' (DR 43). There are two methods for doing this. First, by absorbing everything into the 'infinitely large', as exemplified by Hegel (DR 45). An entity or finite thing is not subordinated to a finite thing, but incorporated into infinity itself. Consider:

> We have before us the *alternating determination of the finite and
> the infinite*; the finite is finite only with reference to the ought or the

infinite, and the infinite is only infinite with reference to the finite. The two are inseparable and at the same time absolutely other with respect to each other; each has in it the other of itself; each is thus the unity of itself and its other, and, in its determinateness – *not to be* what itself and what its other is – it is existence. (Hegel 2010: 112–13, 21.129)

According to Hegel it is senseless to consider that which is finite in and of itself. The finite is inseparable from what it is not: the infinite. He regards every finite thing as a mere temporary limitation of the infinite, a mere moment in a larger and circular movement of the finite into the infinite and back again, so that each limit is something to be sublated or transcended. The most fundamental notion of difference is, then, that between the finite and the infinite, and such difference concerns a perpetual process of vanishing or negation. In this 'infinite movement of evanescence as such', 'the thing differs from itself because it differs first from everything it is not' (DR 43, 42). Yet externality forces Deleuze to posit that 'the thing differs from itself *first, immediately*' (DI 42). Deleuze rejects Hegelianism because it does not allow entities their private reality outside of their relations. For Hegel, 'behind the curtain, there is nothing to see' (SL 200580), whereas for Deleuze, reality is riddled with curtains, and all of them are hiding something.

The second method, discerned in Leibniz, takes the opposite route and 'introduces the infinite into the finite [. . .] in the form of the infinitely small' (DR 45). For Leibniz, the basic elements of the world are monads or simple substances. They have no extension, no shape, and cannot be divided (Leibniz 1989: §3). They are utterly impervious to change and have 'no windows', so that 'neither substance nor accident can come into a monad from outside' (Leibniz 1989: §7). This seems promising for an externalist reader, until Leibniz accounts for interactions and relations between monads. To explain diversity and change despite their absolute isolation, Leibniz posits that monads always already have 'relational properties that express all the others, so that each monad is a perpetual living mirror of the universe' (Leibniz 1989: §56). Absolute isolation is combined with total relationism, so that each monad's being comprises expressing the totality of the world, with the difference between monads being that each expresses only part of this world clearly (DR 47). As each individual expresses everything that exists and happens, and most clearly expresses that which is nearest to it, crossing the Rubicon thus essentially pertains to Caesar (to his concept, strictly speaking), as does every other thing that ever happened to Caesar. This is infinitely small representation, in which 'the essence contains the inessential in essence' (DR 47). Even though the notion of monads clearly inspires Deleuze, the fact that each monad entertains an internal relation with the entirety of the world leads him to reject Leibniz. The difference between monads is only a difference in perspective on the same world, an external difference premised on an identity: 'the world, as that which is expressed in common by all monads, pre-exists its expressions' (DR 47).

Despite its difference from finite representation, infinite representation still defines entities relationally. Where finite representation links entities to something discrete, infinite representation links them to a totality (DR 49, 263). Infinite, orgiastic representation defines each entity in its coextension with a larger whole, one that 'maintains a unique center which gathers and represents all the others, like the unity of a series which governs or organizes its terms and relations once and for all' (DR 56). Like finite representation, infinite representation disregards the internal difference and non-relational surplus that externality demands from each entity. In Deleuze's words, 'what is missing is the original, intensive depth which is the [. . .] first affirmation of difference' (DR 50). Philosophies of representation merely give us entities in terms of something else, not in and of themselves. In those cases, 'the net is so loose that the largest fish pass through' (DR 86). It always misses the machines themselves, for the simple reason that a thing is never equal to its representation. Instead, any given machine and every picture, drawing, description, or theorisation is an irreducible entity with a private reality. In terminology to which we return later, being a machine is to be uncoupled and deterritorialised, both simply meaning 'extra-relational':

> [T]he machine is not a represented object any more than the drawing of it is a representation [. . .] The induced machine is always other than the one that appears to be represented. It will be seen that the machine proceeds by means of an 'uncoupling' of this nature, and ensures the deterritorialization that is characteristic of machines [. . .] (BSP 121)

2 Depth and Height

After *Difference and Repetition* Deleuze never repeats his extensive critiques of 'maledictory' uses of the concepts in the book's title. Yet the externality thesis keeps motivating new criticisms. These can be organised around the notions of 'false height' and 'false depth' as introduced in *The Logic of Sense* (LS 127–34). The critique runs parallel to that of *Difference and Repetition*, but reconstructing it here helps emphasise that Deleuze is criticising fundamental ontological presuppositions and not just individual concepts.

The paradigmatic philosophers of depth are the pre-Socratics who try to discover the 'secret of water and fire' (LS 128; cf. 10, 72, 129). They posit fundamental elements or the more abstract *Apeiron* as the ultimate reality from which entities derive. In their deepest, final depth, everything is one. Diversity is at best an illusion of the senses or a temporary state of injustice. The manifold of existing things is ultimately one in 'the infernal below, unfathomable for us, of an Ocean of dissemblance' (DR 262, translation modified). We may think that discrete tables, cats, jet fighters, and moons exist, but in truth these are mere compressions and relaxations of one or several primal elements. Yet if everything is one, objections with which we are now familiar resurface. Why and how would such elements fragment into discrete parts? Why *this* fragment here yet *that* fragment there? How to explain emergent properties? How to account for alteration if everything is solidly one? Again the problem is that all things are thought to entertain an internal relation to a single 'deep' term, so that the present should not be able to pass and the universe should be frozen. As Deleuze puts it this time, such an original world would simultaneously be a 'radical beginning and absolute end' (C1 124). Such problems never disappear by simply multiplying the number of 'deep things', which Deleuze clarifies by referring to Empedocles:

> Indifference has two aspects: the undifferenciated abyss, the black nothingness, the indeterminate animal in which everything is dissolved – but also the white nothingness, the once more calm surface upon which float unconnected determinations like scattered members: a head without a neck, an arm without a shoulder, eyes without brows. (DR 28)

The black nothingness refers to run-of-the-mill pre-Socratism, the white nothingness to Empedocles. Part of the latter's thought is that multiple *archai* exist, namely the four elements plus love and hate (Empedocles 2001: 64/57). He also holds that parts of bodies used to be separate from one another because of the malign influence of hate. The problem is that Empedocles' separated objects are always already *heads* and *necks*. Their being is already defined relationally in terms of future functions within a body. They start out 'unconnected' and 'scattered', but always as unconnected *determinations* and scattered *members*. As Aristotle already saw, the separate basic elements and discrete things in Empedocles already presuppose a unity (1991b: 301a19). This presupposition turns change into an illusion, because the generation of things is a mere process of extracting from a body what was in it all along (Aristotle 1991: 305b1–5). So as with the rest of the pre-Socratics, Empedocles internalises relations and terms. As Deleuze politely puts it, 'all the parts converge in an immense rubbish-dump or swamp, and all the impulses in a great death-impulse' (C1 124).

Why is it important to repeat Deleuze's wholesale rejection of such universal depths and original elements? First, because it lends support to our earlier rejection of the popular image of Deleuze as a thinker of a heterogeneous yet continuous 'virtual realm' from which discrete objects derive. Deleuze insists that 'contrary to what the pre-Socratics thought, there is no immanent measure [. . .] capable of fixing the order and the progression of a mixture in the depths of Nature (*Physis*)' (LS 131). A single final material layer cannot explain the generation and existence of compounded things. Therefore, such is *not* the point of Deleuze's famous insistence on immanence. If it were, he would not have dedicated *The Logic of Sense* to the Stoics, but to the pre-Socratic Anaxagoras. For Anaxagoras, everything exists in a single mass in indistinguishable yet differentiable ways. All things have in a sense always existed as infinitesimally small units of themselves, mixed together in endless numbers and spread throughout reality. Hence each entity is 'homoiomerous', meaning that everything already contains all the wholes of which it can become a part and everything into which it can change. This is hardly different from reducing entities to a virtual realm in which excessive intensities swarm and produce the myriad things of experience. A second reason is that, contra Badiou's reading mentioned earlier, it is important to see that Deleuze is not a Bergsonian. Bergson is a vitalist who holds that each living thing stands in a universal, organic continuity of Life itself, which Deleuze must reject for being another reductionist case of false depth. Third and perhaps most importantly, ontologies of false depth are surprisingly popular in our time. Deleuzism is thus not just an alternative to ancient philosophical positions, but also to various reductionisms centred on elementary subatomic particles, waves, forces, fields, or even neurons, which are contemporary versions of the same flawed pre-Socratism.

The prime example of a philosophy of heights is of course Platonism (LS 127). Philosophies of depth evoke the image of everything resting on or emerging from a single common base 'beneath' or 'within'. Conversely, philosophies of height bring to mind the image of being tied to a cosmic puppeteer. They always try to penetrate the puppeteer's heaven and discern the truths and principles of all things (LS 127); in Platonism, eternal forms or Ideas which determine what entities are essentially. As Deleuze reminds us, 'the Idea responds only to the call of certain questions. Platonism has determined the Idea's form of question as *what is X?* This noble question is supposed to concern the essence and is opposed to vulgar questions which point merely to the example or the accident' (DI 95). The eternal forms ground entities while remaining entirely exterior to them, as nothing that happens to an entity can alter an Idea. This gives thought a 'geography before having a history' (LS 127). Since the essence of everything that happens (history) is derived from that which determines it from up high (geography), thought merely has to survey the heights to acquire insight into things. 'What is X?' can be answered by taking recourse to 'voice from on high' which yields a truthful, essential relation into a thing (AO 238). Hence entities themselves come only in second place, after that which determines their essence (DR 62).

Deleuze calls philosophies of height 'philosophical diseases' (LS 127), as everything is again premised on internality. The being of entities depends on an internal relation with Ideas that are beyond them. They lack a private reality which externality demands be secluded from all else that is, because their essence is completely determined by the eternal forms. And this is not just the case in Platonism. Deleuze also identifies metaphysics premised on God (LS 71–2), the natural laws of naïve scientism (LS 127), and idealism and dialectics (LS 128) as philosophies of height. Moreover, Kant also ranks as a thinker of heights (DR 58; LS 71, 105–6).

Kantian phenomena are utterly conditioned by transcendental subjectivity. Even the laws of nature derive from pure understanding which, through the categories, unifies and structures all that appears (Kant 1996: A 128). Hence for Kant, 'relations depend on the nature of things in the sense that, as phenomena, things presuppose a synthesis whose source is the same as the source of relations' (ES 111). One could object that Kantian things in themselves remain withdrawn from experience, but that is not the point. Kantianism is an internalism because all entities and relations in human experience can be reduced to their universal relation with the transcendental subject and its categories.[8]

To qualify as a philosophy of heights, it does not matter if the height is constituted by Ideas, God, or a subject. What matters is that everything 'under' this height entertains an internal relation with it and is held to be understandable and possible only through it. In this sense, the heights of Kantian idealism are no different from medieval occasionalism. Hence another type of thought is also denounced in *Anti-Oedipus*. It is what Deleuze calls 'culturalism' or 'symbolism', defined as any philosophy that defines things in terms of an overlying structure (AO 202–3). In *Anti-Oedipus*, Deleuze's critique is aimed at any psychoanalyst who holds that our lives and experiences are fully determined by the Oedipus complex. Yet we can think of other examples. Anyone who holds that entities, events, and our experiences are (over)determined by language, history, ideology, or similar edifices is a philosopher of the heights. It merely requires holding that structures are not just operative on things, but also 'present in things' (AO 201). And in fact, one does not even have to hold that *entities* are linguistic or historical through and through. As with Kant, the problem already starts when the *relation* between two entities is taken to be fully determined by language or ideology. Such a relation would then be a mere representation of another overarching thing. It would render its two terms utterly inoperative, reducing them to something like 'ideal poles' of the overarching entity which would be the real cause or agent.

Finally, false height and false depth can be combined within a single theory. This is done by not only positing that an ultimate ground or puppeteer exists, but also that it is fully intelligible. It is 'the scientific image according to which the philosopher's heaven is an intelligible one' (LS 127). This is the idea behind Deleuze's pun that 'God is a Lobster, or a double pincer, a double bind', because it nullifies entities twice over (ATP 40). Naïve scientific realism is an excellent example. On the one hand, it holds that all entities can be reduced to a final layer of ultimate elements (false depth). On the other hand, it simultaneously holds that these elements conform precisely to our models of them (false height). In a strange combination of pre-Socratism and Kantianism, entities are reduced to smaller elements, but these elements and our experiences or descriptions of them harmoniously coincide. We see this, for example, in Wilfrid Sellars's famous idea that in addition to a manifest (quotidian) image of objects, we can also attain a scientific image that reveals them as they are in themselves (Sellars 1962: *passim*). Like a Protagoras in a lab coat, Sellars concludes that 'science is the measure of all things, of what is that it is, and of what is not that it is not' (1991: 173). Deleuze sums it up as follows:

> It in effect operates with two 'universals', the Whole as the final ground of being or all-encompassing horizon, and the Subject as the principle that converts being into being-for-us [. . .] Between the two, all of the varieties of the real and the true find their place in a striated mental space, from the double point of view of Being and the Subject, under the direction of a 'universal method'. (ATP 279)

In a more vulgar example, think of a cynic who insists that love can be reduced to more basic biological determinants, yet also believes that corporations and advertisements can accurately manipulate these (AO 333). The thing itself, love, is thereby reduced to a representation of a biological base clashing with a cultural operation, to a mute result of hormones and Valentine's Day commercials.

Deleuze's repeated critique of false difference, repetition, height, and depth is that such notions violate the externality thesis. Externality demands we do away with them, such that *there is no longer depth or height* (LS 130). Yet this *only* refers to the abolition of universal depths and heights, not to local ones. After all, externality demands a difference between the 'deep' reality of individual bodies or machines and the 'high' surfaces of their relations. As Deleuze writes, 'if bodies [. . .] assume all the characteristics of substance and cause, conversely, the characteristics of the Idea are relegated to the other side [. . .] on the surface of things: *the ideational or the incorporeal can no longer be anything other than an "effect"'* (LS 132). Under externality, each entity will have a private body or *corpus* which differs in kind from its consequently incorporeal manifestations in relations.

3 The Image of Thought

Finally, Deleuze detects a common root to all internalist, reductionist, and relational thought. As the private reality of machines is never given in a relation, we tend to overlook it and identify machines with one of their relational manifestations, signs, images, or representations. As Deleuze writes, 'to refer a sign to the object that emits it, to attribute to the object the benefit of the sign, is first of all the natural direction of perception or of representation' (PS 29). An entity is thereby equated with one or several of its appearances, making its 'internal character depend upon the simple external criterion' (DR 179). Deleuze calls this 'objectivism', because we then think 'that the "object" itself has the secrets of the signs it emits' (PS 28). Yet uncritically equating the manifestations and relations of things to their being creates trouble: not all relational aspects or signs of things can be assigned to a single entity (PS 100–1). In 'Peter is taller than Paul', 'being taller than' can never refer to only one of the two subjects. Moreover, our world is filled with frivolous, unreliable signs (PS 23). The same entities have contrary qualities at different moments, or even simultaneously for different observers.

Now, we easily accept that some qualities are inessential. Cobblestones do not need to be part of a picturesque street in a quaint little village, nor does every sponge cake have to trigger a memory. We nonetheless often think that signs (entities as related to by other entities) come in two varieties: obvious yet trivial ones and essential ones which are slightly harder to detect. Deleuze calls this response to the disappointments of naïve objectivism 'subjective compensation' or the attempt 'to become personally sensitive to less profound signs that are yet more appropriate' (PS 35). It turns us into rigorous phenomenologists in search of the *eidos* or most intimate self-being hiding beneath the immediate features of individuals (cf. Husserl 1982: 7). Yet for Deleuze, 'nothing can prevent the disappointment' (PS 35). 'The moment in compensation remains in itself inadequate and does not provide a definitive revelation' (PS 35, 36). This is because equating an entity to an image, representation, or quality is always reductionist, internalist and relational.

Subjective compensation characterises what Deleuze calls the 'image of thought', a natural yet misguided way of thinking about our thoughts. This image is grounded in three ideas (NP 103). First, that thought naturally thinks the truth and accurately grasps the in itself of things. This also implies that the in itself of things is stable and simple, that it corresponds neatly to its manifestations in relations, and that it merely differs in degree from being experienced. Second, that we can be 'diverted' from truth by passions and accidents. This is the idea just mentioned that representations come in two kinds: fickle ones and reliable ones. Third, that there exists a method to discern which is which. This implies that all human practices can be ranked on a scale of truthfulness. In *Difference and Repetition*, Deleuze describes this image of thought by highlighting its two main features: common sense and good sense.

Common sense signifies the identification of something via features of our experience of it. It is a principle of recognition. I can recognise a friend in different places, moods, and outfits because something about her remains identical and common throughout the variations. Likewise, I can recognise something as a house, a cat, or a mystery because of shared features with houses, cats, and mysteries I have already experienced. Existentially, there is nothing wrong with commonsensical acts: 'it is apparent that acts of recognition exist and occupy a large part of our daily life: this is a table, this is an apple, this is the piece of wax, Good morning Theaetetus. But who can believe that the destiny of thought is at stake in these acts, and that when we recognize, we are thinking?' (DR 135). Things become problematic when common sense is thought to give us the truth of things. This is where subjective compensation starts. Common sense becomes the idea that among the relations something entertains, one concerns its heart, being, and truth. Moreover, it will be a relation between an object and its observer. The observer selects one of its many possible and actual representations, and proclaims it identical to 1) the thing itself, and 2) a true thought of the thing itself. The thing becomes its image and since the image is *thought*, thing and thought become perfectly aligned. An ontological use of common sense thus selects at least one representation as the exception to 'relations are external to terms'. This selected image is 'common' in two senses. First, as it comprises the being of an entity, it will be common to all its manifestations. Second, as this being is being thought, anyone can recognise it in principle. This is because common sense assumes that 1) everybody can really think, and 2) that really thinking is to think the thought that comprises the being of entities.[9] Common sense has then become 'the most general form of representation' (DR 131), because it legitimises the equation of a thing to how it is experienced and reduces the being of entities to their being *for us*. Note that the precise nature of that which is common is irrelevant, because the real problem is simply that one relational property is elevated above all others. Hence it matters little whether common sense recognises the will of God, mathematical structures, power relations, or signifiers as the common aspect of things. Even formal definitions of objects as being at least potentially perceivable by subjects are commonsensical (cf. DR 131, 134). In all cases everything becomes organised around a single relation which 'brings diversity in general to bear upon the form of the Same' (LS 78). And 'whatever the complexity of this process, whatever differences between the procedures of this or that author – the fact remains that all this is still too simple' (DR 129), because it violates externality by letting thought access the heart of things. Externality demands that entities have absolutely *no* ontological community whatsoever. Whatever pertains to recognition and identification can be physical, epistemological, existential, pragmatic, contingent, subjective, or produced; but it cannot be ontological. Even formally, things have nothing to do with us.

As Descartes famously writes, good sense signifies the 'power of judging well and of distinguishing the true from the false', a power 'naturally equal in all men' (1994: 111). Deleuze does not object to good sense in its quotidian use (LS 76), but to its ontological deployment. Good sense then becomes the thesis that all products retain what produced them. It reduces an entity to its relations with a source: effects to causes, wholes to parts, and presents to previous states. Good sense therefore imparts everything (mereologically, spatially, and above all temporally) with a single direction 'which goes from the most differenciated to the least differenciated' (LS 75; cf. 1). Most features of entities will be mere decoration, and good sense will be the faculty allowing us to discern that *of which* a whole is a construct, an effect is a result, and a present is an outcome. Hence its internalism and reductionism. Good sense is a principle of prediction (DR 226), because it holds that the future is reducible to the present. Put differently, it considers everything to 'belong' somewhere, which is why Deleuze playfully suggests that agricultural pastures, middle-class values, private property, and class divisions count among its consequences (LS 76).

The combined illegitimate uses of good and common sense suggest that 1) thought can backtrack to the source, principle, being, and truth of things; and that 2) this truth or being can be recognised and predicted, meaning that thought and being entertain an internal relation. The image of thought is therefore no less than the reduction of things to things in thought, to things related to us. It is the idea that there is one exception to externality, to difference in itself, and to repetition for itself, and this exception will be thought itself. It is the idea that Being is thoroughly relational, and that attaining truth is in each case merely an exercise in avoiding error (DR 167). Hence good and common sense, like false depth and height and maledictory difference and repetition, ignore the fact that the image of thought 'presupposes another distribution' (LS 76).

It is worth noting that this general image of thought, *and not just psychoanalysis*, is the 'Oedipus' assaulted in *Anti-Oedipus*. Deleuze is not just attacking the 'familial Oedipus', but also the 'philosophical Oedipus' (SCS 260373). The latter is defined as follows:

> It is the image or the representation slipped into the machine [. . .] It is the compromise, but the compromise distorts both parties alike, namely, the nature of the reactionary repressor and the nature of revolutionary desire. In the compromise, the two parties have gone over to the same side, as opposed to desire, which remains on the other side, beyond compromise. (BSP 122)

To think Oedipally is to think according to the image of thought. It is thinking that entities and their relations can be reduced to their relations with us . . . or at least to their relations with something that has a relation to us. In both cases, everything is reduced to a mere representation (AO 70). Why does this 'compromise' distort both parties? As will be explained in more detail later, the 'reactionary repressor' is simply anything relating to an entity. This is because externality demands that the in itself of a machine is repressed in all possible relations. The second party, 'revolutionary desire', is Deleuze's name for an entity's malleable, produced, yet entirely private and irreducible reality. Oedipal thinking distorts both sides, because it holds that only *some* instead of *all* relations are repressors, and also that the truth or 'desire' of entities is found within *one* instead of *no* relation. Hence an entity's manifestations and essence are both turned relational, such that their private reality is entirely ignored. Instead of agreeing to such a misleading compromise, we must insist on our irreducible machines. After all, 'we still have not accomplished anything so long as we have not reached elements that are not associable, or so long as we have not grasped the elements in a form in which they are no longer associable' (AO 125).

Externalism demands an ontology in which we find everything 'mineral, vegetable, animal, juvenile, social each time shattering the ridiculous figures of Oedipus' (AO 123). Quoting Serge Leclaire, Deleuze envisions this project as 'the conception of a system whose elements are bound together precisely by the absence of any [. . .] natural, logical, or significant tie' (AO 125; cf. Leclaire 1996: 148). Leclaire may refer to psychoanalysis, but Deleuze refers to philosophy itself. We need a system in which all relations are contingent and therefore actually *matter*. This requires reaching the 'nomadic distribution' and 'crowned anarchy' that 'precedes all good sense and all commons sense' (DR 224; LS 79). It implies more than merely affirming the existence of a plurality of things (ATP 6). It requires that thought operates by what Deleuze frequently calls 'n-1' (ATP 377, 22, 24, 177; DR 1, 8, 68, 140, 141, 155). It is to allow every machine a reality for itself, detaching it from each '1' which would reduce its being to a representation, image, or moment. Only this gives philosophy a 'true beginning' (DR 132). Each machine or multiplicity must be seen as being 'more' than it is in any given present, not in the sense of having other possible relations, but as having a surplus over all actual as well as possible relations. With the externality thesis now firmly established, we can now begin to chart this 'unrecognized and unrecognizable *terra incognita*' (DR 136).

Notes

1. In what follows, we regularly distinguish the 'ontological' from the 'existential'. By 'ontological' we mean entities in so far as they are all equal in being irreducible fourfolds involved in threefold syntheses. By 'existential' we mean entities in their concrete existence, which is to say in their uniqueness. Existentially, there are extreme differences

between a volcano, a book, a thought, and an electron. Ontologically, they are equal.

2. Chapter 7 will show that the internal reality of a machine alters during its existence. Ontological difference is a difference in itself between a differing internal reality (differen*tia*tion) and a differing relational reality (differen*cia*tion).

3. Deleuze also refers to Kant's argument that if the only created thing were a human hand, its concept would not be able to determine whether it was a right or a left hand. Such determination must include the thumb being 'left' or 'right' and the palm being 'inside' or 'outside', predicates that refer to more than just the hand. The point would be that a concept cannot avoid reference and therefore relation to something beyond its object (cf. DR 13; SL 200580). For the original argument, see 'On the First Ground of the Distinctions of Regions in Space' (Kant 1991).

4. Cf. 'jamais la fonction ou jamais l'usage de quelque chose n'explique la production de cette chose' (SCS 18071).

5. Hence 'molar functionalism' does not reach deep enough (AO 210) and mechanism cannot capture machinic being (FLB 8).

6. Whether Deleuze's reading of these authors is *correct* is another matter.

7. Exemplary because all four shackles are present: categories are defined by analogy, specific difference within a genus as identity in a concept, opposition in predicates, and resemblance in perception for the *infima species*.

8. Even if one reads Kant's critical project 'backwards', starting with the third *Critique*, nothing changes. It allows one to posit a 'free accord' or 'free harmony' between the faculties that would precede their more rigidly defined relations as found in the two earlier *Critiques* (KCP 50, 55). Nevertheless, each accord is still reached only between the faculties.

9. Hence common sense as defined by Deleuze overlaps with both the Aristotelian *koinè aisthesis* (a common faculty for the reliable unification of various sensations) and the Kantian *gemeinschaftlichen Sinnes* (a common faculty of judgment, allowing human beings to move beyond their own private conditions) (KCP 21; Kant 2007: 69, §21).

4

The Machinic Body

We have established that the externality thesis is central to Deleuze's philosophy, and that externality is the reason why Deleuze considers his ontology to be incommensurable with a range of other philosophies. Based on the externality thesis, we can now commence the progressive deduction of the four features of machines, and their associated syntheses. We start with the aspect of machines that is neither presentable to nor derived from other entities, which is to say with the precise aspect that externality demands. Deleuze calls this first aspect of the virtual twofold of assemblages the 'body' or 'body without organs'. We first explicate what this non-relational and external body is. Next, we take a closer look at why and how machinic bodies render all entities *problematic* to the extent that they can never be fully and harmoniously integrated into whatever other entities treat a machine as a component or as part of their environment.

1 No Being without a Body

In Deleuze's philosophy, the term 'actual' indicates assemblages as experienced by other machines. Conversely, 'virtual' denotes the extra-relational reality of machines. Recall from the introductory chapter that the virtual and actual side of machines are both twofolds. Entities need to be one as well as multiple in both their aspects: one in order to be something rather than nothing or everything, and multiple in order to be this rather than that. One, because neither relational nor internal properties can ever be properties of properties (the absurdity of 'an inch of red'). Properties only ever belong to machines. Multiple and qualified, because otherwise multiplicities would not differ. Of these four, we are first interested in the non-relational unity of a machine, which Deleuze calls 'the body'.

86

The body is that which remains external to relations between machines. As everything is a machine, so everything is a body.[1] A body can be an animal, a sound, a mind, an idea, a language, a society, a group of people, and so on (SPP 127; cf. AO 372). Being an aspect of machines, bodies are not restricted to either nature or artifice (DI 103): 'bodies may be physical, biological, psychic, social, verbal: they are always bodies or corpora' (D 52). Significant parts of Deleuze's books focus on the bodies of human beings, human societies, and economic systems, but they also mention the bodies of tables, fictional characters, deserts, knights, weapons, tools, factories, metals, armies, parties, rain, wind, hail, and pestilential air (cf. ATP 261; N 26; TRM 310). Everything is a machine with its own body, which is why a 'climate, wind, season, [and] hour are not of another nature than the things, animals, or people that populate them' (ATP 263).

Given the externality thesis, a Deleuzian body has nothing to do with bodies understood as certain volumes of materials. Physical, biological, psychic, social, and verbal machines have bodies, but those bodies themselves cannot be qualified as such. Externality demands that all entities are formally identical in having a body. The body is a transcendental unity, irreducible to relational dimensions such as history, possibilities, composition, empirical qualities, users, and functions.[2] For any given machine, the body is 'what remains when you take everything away', which is why Deleuze calls it 'the body without organs' (ATP 151). When he states that 'there is not a single body without organs, there are as many as you like' (SCS 260373), it does not mean that bodies without organs are human ascriptions. It means that even those ascriptions are machines with bodies without organs. This 'glorious' or 'schizophrenic body', this 'organism without parts' (LS 90, 88) is that which guarantees that no machine can ever become fully integrated in any relation. It is why, as Deleuze writes, 'each organ is a possible protest' (AO 243–4). Even if gills are only found in fish, there is still nothing essentially 'fishy' about the being of gills, so that many machines will have to be at work in order to keep gills functioning for fish. Irreconcilable differences notwithstanding, the body without organs thus clearly has a distant cousin in the Platonic and Aristotelian ineffable individual. It is the unifying aspect of the virtual, non-relational twofold of the machinic fourfold, as Deleuze's various accounts of it will consistently confirm.

To start, 'a body is not defined by the form that determines it nor as a determinate substance or subject nor by the organs it possesses or the functions it fulfills' (ATP 260). It is neither spatially extended in something nor temporally present to something (C2 189).[3] In a mereological, temporal, and spatial sense, the body without organs is therefore neither that which a machine is in nor that which is in a machine. It is that aspect of each machine which enters into nothing and into which nothing enters. It is one half of a machine's internal difference between privacy and actuality. Deleuze's appreciation for Antonin Artaud's concept of the body further emphasises this withdrawn nature of the body. As the former cites the latter: 'the body is the body / it is all by itself / and has no need of organs / the body is never an organism / organisms are the enemy of the body' (AO 20; cf. FB 44). The body is 'deprived of organs: eyes shut, nostrils plugged, anus blocked, stomach rotten, throat ripped out' (TRM 19). Ontologically and *qua* body, it is neither in the being of a machine to have *this* as parts or organs, nor to be a part or organ of *that*. Though I depend on my organs existentially, I cannot be reduced to them ontologically. This is the point of Deleuze's mantra 'No mouth. No tongue. No teeth. No larynx. No esophagus. No anus' (AO 19). We are always quick to functionally define entities in terms of internal components or relations with an environment. Yet the body without organs remains outside all such relations and thereby contests our commonsensical perspectives on organisations and organisms (ATP 30).

If everything is a machine and each machine has a body, then Deleuze is not just critiquing our organic perspective on organisms, but organic perspectives on *anything*. Rocks, pieces of cheese, a tune stuck in your head, a car, a battle, a piece of art, a slice of bread: every entity has a body without organs. This simply means that nothing can handle anything without exercising force. As the body is never integrated into another machine, it can only be handled and never be had. Ontological externality implies the existential necessity of forcing, pressing, dragging, seducing, moving, avoiding, transforming, and aligning things. Hence Deleuze's appreciation for Nietzsche's Untimely, as the body has no determinate 'when' (DR 130); for Samuel Butler's Erewhon, because it has no determinate 'where' (DR 285); and for Herman Melville's Bartleby or the 'man without references', as the body has no determinate function or activity (ECC 71–4). Machines are always engaged with other machines in certain times, places, and relations, but they are simultaneously never reducible to such things. And only because *each* entity has a body without organs does it make sense to claim that after subtracting everything, *everything* will nonetheless be left.[4] Each machine has a body that comes into view only after abstracting from all relationality: power, language, experiences, histories, structures, components, texts, dialogues, materials and so on. Only then do we find 'the simple thing' or simply 'the entity' (ATP 151).

Deleuze makes the same argument in his book on Francis Bacon, in which the body without organs is synonymous with 'the Figure' (FB 15, 20, 45). The Figure is never a 'spatializing material structure' (FB 20). Attaining it requires solemn acts of isolation, and Deleuze interprets Bacon as carefully disassociating his subjects from their environments, gestures, and biological components (FB 1, 63, 83). The point of such subtractions is to avoid the identification of the body without organs with anything 'figurative, illustrative, and narrative' (FB 14). As Rancière notes, isolating the Figure prevents it from becoming an element in a story, the resemblance of something else, or even part of a network with other Figures (1998: 528). In short, it prevents internalising a machine into a relation with something of which it would be a representation.

To insist on the bodily withdrawal of computer programs, zebras, apples, conversations, keys, emotions, and meteors, Deleuze calls the body 'indivisible' and 'nondecomposable' (AO 106). He associates it with 'anti-production' and calls it 'the unproductive, the sterile, the unengendered, the unconsumable' (AO 19; cf. 26). Deleuze uses such terminology to distinguish this transcendental body without organs from our usual associations with the term 'body'. Consider also the following:

> The body without organs is not the proof of an original nothingness, nor is it what remains of a lost totality. Above all, it is not a projection; it has nothing whatsoever to do with the body itself, or with an image of the body. It is the body without an image. This imageless, organless body, the non-productive, exists right there where it is produced. (AO 19)

The body is not a relational image or projection, but a part of a machine's internal reality. Recalling Sellars, the body is thus neither the manifest nor the scientific image of things. That it does not refer to a totality stresses that bodies belong to individual entities. The denial of an emergence from nothingness asserts that a body without organs is not *causa sui* or autarchic. That machines have a reality beyond relations does not imply that they need no relations to exist. On the contrary, a body is no remnant of a totality, so it must be constructed from other discrete assemblages. It may be 'unengendered', but it cannot be unproduced, as that would make it testify to an original nothingness. It would then not be 'unproductive', as it would have produced itself. The correct interpretation of 'unengendered' is precisely 'not belonging to a species or genus', which simply again points to the irreducibility of multiplicities.

Deleuze indeed confirms that the body without organs 'is a thing to produce or fabricate. A body without organs does not preexist' (SCS 260373). Whenever and wherever an entity comes into existence, it immediately has its body without organs as the guarantee of its irreducibility. Whenever machines combine their forces to produce a water molecule, a marriage, a perception, a house, or a red panda, a body without organs emerges. Each of those machines is irreducible to its origins, components, and context, even if they depend on them existentially. This is precisely why the *full* destiny of entities comes from the relations, transformations, becomings, desires, vectors, events, and encounters which they inherit, create, resist, accept, or modify during their existence. What many of his commentators fail to realise is that Deleuze only emphasises the events, operations, processes, and encounters between entities because *no* relations are presupposed for anything. *All* specific events matter existentially because *none* of them are prescribed ontologically:

> Desiring-machines make us an organism; but at the very heart of this production, within the very production of this production, the body suffers from being organized in this way, from not having some other sort of organization, or no organization at all. An incomprehensible, absolute rigid stasis in the very midst of process, as a third stage [. . .] The automata stop dead and set free the unorganized mass they once served to articulate. (AO 19; cf. 18, 90)

As soon as something new is articulated, there is a new machine with its own body. Without the irreducibility of its body, no machine would ever be able to leave the site of its inception. This body is the 'third stage' which interrupts two types of relations: those concerning that which generates a machine and those concerning that which a machine generates. And of course, its generators and generations will in turn be nothing but machines, each with their own interruptive body. Deleuze had already theorised this 'third' in the 1950s: 'is it third because it arrives third? Certainly not. It is even the first [. . .] It is primary. What there is at the beginning, well that would be the third' (WG 23; cf. 43). Yet it is not until *Anti-Oedipus* that 'the third' or 'the body' takes centre stage:

> Every coupling of machines, every production of a machine, every sound of a machine running, becomes unbearable to the body without organs [. . .] Merely so many nails piercing the flesh, so many forms of torture. In order to resist organ-machines, the body without organs presents its smooth, slippery, opaque, taut surface as a barrier. (AO 20)

The body without organs is why everything takes effort. It is why nothing is permanently stuck in its relations. It is why you cannot get a tune out of your head by willing it to disappear. It is why the revolution can turn sour. It is why people survive an organ transplant. It is why hydrogen and oxygen can become water instead of a small pile of oxygen and hydrogen. It is why you can fall in love. It is why your love is irreducible to hormones and trends. It is why everything drifts apart unless it is kept together. It is why we can create what has not yet been forged. It is why all relations, organs, and functions strictly speaking have mere *'temporary and provisional presence'* (FB 48). It does *not* mean that relations are epiphenomenal. To say that bread is irreducible to its baker or that electricity is irreducible to its generator is not to say that such generators are not existentially necessary. And note that we already accept this way of thinking in many cases. We all understand that students, citizens, and words can respectively enter and leave universities, societies, and languages without any of the latter becoming entirely new entities whenever one of their relations changes. Understanding the first aspect of the fourfold is only a matter of also extending the same courtesy to all other entities.

Deleuze also describes machinic irreducibility in terms of a 'primal repression, as exerted by the body without organs at the moment of repulsion' (AO 386). This repression is not brought about from the outside, but progresses from the very nature of the body without organs. Each machine 'does' primal repression all by itself (AO 144; cf. LS 244). As per usual, Deleuze is careful to clarify that he is not theorising a mere mental operation: 'we are of the opinion that what is ordinarily referred to as "primary repression" [. . .] is not a "counter-cathexis", but rather this *repulsion* of desiring-machines by the body without organs' (AO 20). In counter-cathexis, the psyche blocks something by covering it up with another image. Yet primary repression has a much wider scope for Deleuze. It concerns the fact that no body without organs ever manifests directly in relations. It is always enveloped, covered up, or 'repressed' by its own actual manifestations, from which it differs in kind.

Yet does Deleuze not at times deviate from this course? For example, the sixth chapter of *A Thousand Plateaus* is called 'How do you make yourself a body without organs?'. And does that same chapter not call the body without organs a *practice*? Does it not state that masochism, drug addiction, and hypochondria may bring about your body without organs? And does Deleuze not write elsewhere that 'life provides many ambiguous approaches to the body without organs (alcohol, drugs, schizophrenia, masochism, and so on)' (FB 47)? That all suggests that the body without organs can be experienced 'when organization breaks down or is revealed to be arbitrary or culturally determined' (Sutton and Martin-Jones 2008: 142).

Nevertheless, Deleuze is not contradicting his own principles. The opening paragraph of the sixth *Plateau* explicitly states that 'you can never reach the body without organs, you can't reach it, you are forever attaining it, it is a limit' (ATP 150). It cannot be given as such, it can only be inferred indirectly (cf. BSP 132). Precisely because of this, we are forced to resort to indirect and exceptional experiences to illustrate its nature. This is not unlike how black holes are registered, which cannot be perceived directly so that their existence must be inferred by their effects on nearby matter. In Deleuze's case, the hypochondriac body asserts that its organs are being destroyed. The paranoid body cannot trust its organs or its environment. The schizophrenic body is locked in a struggle with its own organs. The drugged body experiences radical shifts in how organs function. Finally, the masochist body seals off 'normal' organic functions (ATP 150). In each case, a body *distances* itself or finds itself distanced from its organs. Its relations with internal components and external factors are interrupted, yet the body continues to exist, if only for a while. In none of these cases does the body without organs become tangible or otherwise directly given. Deleuze uses them as examples of lived experiences that testify to the irreducibility of bodies. When he writes that a schizophrenic 'puts us in contact with the "demoniacal" element in nature' (AO 49), Deleuze means that schizophrenia and other cases can inform us about the real structure of what exists, a structure that is not at all self-evident and often eludes us. This method is comparable to Freud's crystal principle as described in his *New Introductory Lectures on Psychoanalysis*. Freud holds that our pathologies and perversions are not opposed to a psychic and sexual normality. Instead, they are exaggerated versions of characteristics that define all psyches and sexualities. He compares this with how crystal never breaks randomly, but always according to fault lines that characterised its inner structure when it was not yet broken.[5] Deleuze similarly thinks that wherever bodies are radically distanced from relations normally deemed essential to them, we can learn something about the inner structure of all things. Such learning opportunities can be as simple as observing a child:

> It has been noted that for children an organ has 'a thousand vicissitudes', that it is 'difficult to localize, difficult to identify, it is in turn a bone, an engine, excrement, the baby, a hand, daddy's heart . . .' This is [. . .] because the organ is exactly what its elements make it according to their relation of movement and rest, and the way in which this relation combines with or splits off from that of neighboring elements. (ATP 256)

All experience is organic, which is to say relational and thereby comprised of what several machines have in common.[6] There is no way to make a body without organs as such present in experience, which is why approaches to it are 'ambiguous' (FB 47). This is again clear from Deleuze's book on Bacon, subtitled *The Logic of Sensation*. What Deleuze admires in Bacon is that his paintings allow us to realise the existence of something that can never be present. The whole point of Deleuze's analyses of Bacon's paintings is the conclusion that sensation is ultimately rooted in the unproductive, unattainable, indivisible, sterile body without organs, which is precisely *not* qualitative or qualified (FB 45). And we must be strict: even the most vague, ambiguous, unconscious, material, tentative, or bodily awareness of something is a qualified relation. The logic of sensation does not posit some kind of primordial link with the body without organs. This also clarifies what Deleuze means by his frequent references to 'direct', 'immediate', or 'intensive' sensations of the Figure. He is not claiming that Bacon pulls off the stupendous feat of creating an onto-logical rupture by painting a handful of objects that would magi-cally grant their observers unmediated access to bodies without organs. Even Bacon is not that good. It means instead that each relation always already concerns something non-qualified, non-represented, non-extensive, and non-relational. As Deleuze writes, 'when sensation is linked to the body in this way, it ceases to be representative and becomes real' (FB 45). So to paint directly or immediately is to paint in the awareness of the reality of bodies without organs. Hence Deleuze's appreciation for Bacon's paint-ings, in which bodies always find their environments and organs twisting and slipping away from them. The heart of the matter is always the withdrawal of bodies from direct contact (LS 191, 192, 236), and this withdrawal is precisely why 'clarity endlessly plunges into obscurity' (FLB 36).

Think of machinic entities, then, as having a virtual, private, and internal body enveloped by a lifetime of manifest relations. Some relations will be necessary for a machine's survival. Others will be fleeting and irrelevant. Some will change what the machine can do completely, whereas others will merely strengthen or weaken its existing capacities. A football, for example, has relations with its leather components, with air on its inside and outside, with hands and feet, and with crowds of spectators, but its body without organs never coincides with these relations. Another way to under-stand this is Deleuze's notion of 'the baroque house', conceived as an entity consisting of one 'common room' and one 'closed private room' (FLB 4). Like Leibniz's monad, the private room is com-pared to a dark chamber without windows, resonating with what happens in the common room yet remaining 'closed, as a pure inside without an outside, a weightless, closed interiority' (FLB 32). Each entity, whether a word spoken or a bullet fired, has two such rooms or floors: 'the need for a second floor is everywhere affirmed to be strictly metaphysical' (FLB 14). As Deleuze writes in his book on Proust, each entity is therefore a sealed or closed vessel (PS 117, 125, 127, 162, 174). These closed vessels com-prise a 'galactic structure' (PS 117) that forces us to see reality as 'crumbs and chaos' (PS 111). This does not mean that vast, cumbersome, and intimidating entities such as bureaucracies, galaxies, world wars, tectonic plates, family reunions, and Jupiter have to cede their reality to subatomic particles, genes, and amoebas. It only means that no entity can ever be integrated into its relations. Yet this is also to say that in a very basic sense, reality is deeply problematic.

2 All Bodies are Problematic

All problems aside, we have already learned quite a lot at this point. Relations are external to terms, a term is any entity whatsoever, every entity is a machine, each machine is a fourfold assemblage, each fourfold comprises two twofolds, one twofold is actual and relational, one twofold is virtual and withdrawn, the first aspect of the virtual twofold is the body without organs, this body is the virtual unity of a multiplicity, and this virtual unity resists all assimilation, reduction, or integration into relations. With only one of the four machinic aspects laid out before us, we are already confronted with a terrifying picture of reality. If everything is irreducible to relations, then nothing is naturally located anywhere or doing anything. Everything we love and rely on can be undone, as random forces or devious agents can pervert all we hold sacred. Likewise, everything we detest can be destroyed, and unexpected events or stubborn persistence may lead to improved circumstances. Yet in all cases, everything requires work and effort.

Even a painting by Vermeer 'is not valid as a Whole because of the patch of yellow wall planted there as a fragment of still another world' (PS 114). The patch of yellow can simply be removed from the Vermeer and put to different use. All entities, even the elements of great symphonies, are 'violently stuck together despite their unmatching edges' (PS 123). The body without organs, the closed vessel or the Figure, guarantees that 'everything is compartmentalized [. . .] There is communication, but it is always between non-communicating vases. There are openings but they always take place between closed boxes' (TRM 39; cf. PS 117). There is no contradiction in writing that 'one body penetrates another and coexists with it in all of its parts, like a drop of wine in the ocean, or fire in iron. One body withdraws from another, like liquid from a vase' (LS 5–6). The point is precisely that even the drop withdraws from the ocean like liquid from the vase. Even in his last book, Deleuze theorises bodies as 'separated, unconnected systems' (WP 123). The notion of a universe of closed vessels returns in the section on mereology in *Anti-Oedipus* ('The whole and its parts'):

> [W]e are struck by the fact that all the parts are produced as asymmetrical sections, paths that suddenly come to an end, hermetically sealed boxes, noncommunicating vessels, watertight compartments, in which there are gaps even between things that are contiguous, gaps that are affirmations [. . .] (AO 57)

It follows that everything is irrevocably problematic. If nothing is ontologically integrated into anything else, no machine ever does anything by itself. Other machines will always be required to make it do anything. This is not because a machine by itself is inert matter. After all, since all machines must be produced by other machines, activity and force are omnipresent. In a machine ontology, rest is a minimum of movement instead of its absence, and peace is a minimum of tension. Instead, irreducibility itself is again the reason. In this sense 'the problematic is [. . .] a perfectly objective kind of being' (LS 54). Deleuze writes that 'problematic structure is part of objects themselves', that Being 'is the being of the problematic' (DR 64; cf. 168). This is because 'the instance-problem and the instance-solution differ in nature' (LS 54). In our current context, a solution to a problem is simply the creation of a relation. It is to put a machine somewhere and make it do something. Putting a painting in a museum is a solution to its problem, but so are divorcing a spouse, a rock plunging into a river, a predator taking its place as leader of the pack, and a hammer smashing a blasphemous statue. Solving a problem is therefore never permanent, in the sense that no relation can ever become the being of a machine. A solution is merely a spatio-temporal actualisation. This is why 'it is an error to see *problems* as indicative of a provisional and subjective state [. . .] The "problematic" is a state of the world, a dimension of the system, and even its horizon or its home: it designates precisely the [. . .] reality of the virtual' (DR 280).

As a problem, each entity has three aspects: 'its difference in kind from solutions; its transcendence in relation to the solutions that it engenders on the basis of its own determinant conditions; and its immanence in the solutions which cover it' (DR 179). This is to say that a virtual body is never given in actual relations, that it cannot be integrated into its manifestations in relations, and that it is always enveloped by its relations. This last feature stresses that even though bodies are irreducible to relational manifestations, these are nevertheless *their* manifestations. Despite being a closed vessel, the virtual twofold is not immune to the events of the world, a point to which we will return. For now, note that the body without organs is why we never accurately know *what* something is, and why 'the things and beings which are distinguished in the different suffer a [. . .] radical destruction of their *identity*' (DR 66). It is because 'the problematic element, with its extra-propositional character, does not fall within representation' (DR 178). If the body is truly extra-relational, then all ways of relating to another machine are at best perfectly reliable descriptions of it or tried and tested ways of handling it. Yet none of that makes the body present. It is in this sense that the problematic body can only be presented in problematic form (DR 169). As a machine *qua* machine 'is an object which can be neither given nor known, but must be represented without being able to be directly determined' (DR 169), we have also found the likely reason for Deleuze's many shifts in terminology throughout his writings. If no privileged symbols or significations exist to describe machines, then it makes sense to tailor one's vocabulary to the linguistic, interpersonal, or economic machines one is describing. This is 'the problem of writing: in order to designate something exactly, anexact [*sic*] expressions are utterly unavoidable' (ATP 20; cf. AO 357; DR 11). What Deleuze writes of Pierre Klossowski is therefore equally true for his own philosophy:

> With respect to that which can only be seen and heard, which is never confirmed by another organ and is the object of Forgetting in memory, of an Unimaginable in imagination, and of an Unthinkable in thought – what else can one do, other than speak of it? (LS 284)

Klossowski reciprocates by noting that what Deleuze brings to philosophy is precisely 'the introduction of the unteachable into teaching'.[7] The externality of entities and the irreducible, non-relational body without organs opposes itself to all forms of what Klossowski calls 'laboratory conformism' (*un conformisme laborantin*). It is the idea that scientists, psychiatrists, philosophers, or artists could set up conditions under which a machine *qua* machine becomes present. Conversely, externality forces us to hold that even a perfect mathematical description of an object is not different in kind from a casual glance at it. The mathematical formula will be infinitely more reliable, accurate, useful, parsimonious, objective, rigorous, communicable, and valuable, but it never ceases to be just as relational as the glance. Both concern relations with the object, and neither of them can ever stand in for the machine related to.

The problematic status of the body without organs explains Deleuze's aversion to the question 'what is . . .?' and to the verb 'being'. To be is to be something, but in all cases except tautologies this quickly leads us to identify an entity with its qualities, parts, functions, or class. We use 'being' to designate relations, not machines themselves. As the virtual aspect of machines must nonetheless be accorded full reality, and we must find ways to talk about their being without necessarily referring to their being *in*:

> Being is also non-being, *but non-being is not the being of the negative*; rather it is the being of the problematic, the being of problem and question. Difference is not the negative; on the contrary, non-being is Difference: *heteron*, not *enantion*. For this reason non-being should rather be written (non)-being or, better still, ?-being. (DR 64; cf. 63, 202; LS 123)

The awkward formulas of '(non)-being' and '?-being' correspond to the problematic yet real aspect of entities (DI 25). They do not oppose a thing to what it is not, but rather oppose its non-relational side to its relational side. Another lexical trick that Deleuze uses to stress this point is a frequent use of the indefinite article: 'the [body without organs] is never yours or mine. It is always *a* body' (ATP 164; cf. 256; LS 103, 141; TRM 351). Like the terms '(non)-being' and '?-being', his use of 'a' and 'it' aim to steer clear of how our usual descriptions and names for machines designate their entanglements rather than their beings.

The problematic body without organs guarantees that all parts of all machines remain really distinct even if they operate in combination (BSP 125, 127). This withdrawn aspect of machines is the condition for the possibility of all emancipation. If multiplicities were fully relational, politics could only be the stewardship of old relations (conservatism), the management of current relations (*Realpolitik*), or the extension of the present into future relations (historical determinism). Consider any mode of existence that contests the 'average adult-white-heterosexual-male' societal standard (ATP 105, 176). If assemblages were their relations and nothing else, then the very being of non-standard modes of existence would include their relation to this standard. After all, a contestation is a relation. No matter how fiercely one rejected or deconstructed the standard, all roads would keep leading to Rome, because rejections and deconstructions are relations as well. This is precisely what Deleuze denounces as 'familialism' in *Anti-Oedipus* and 'arborescent thought' in *A Thousand Plateaus*. If being is relational, then any mode of existence *essentially is* a child of a parent, a branch of a trunk, and the deviation from a norm. It would be fundamentally impossible to ever get away from anything. Conversely, externality and the body without organs guarantee that a multiplicity can never be reduced to the circumstances in which it arises or to the standards it opposes.

Deleuze's famous concepts of 'lines of flight' and 'deterritorialization' also express this. To start with the latter, Deleuze remarks that the English equivalent to the French *deterritorialization* is 'the outlandish'.[8] To belong somewhere, to be found somewhere, to do something, to have a home, to be oppressed by this or liberated by that are existential situations but never ontological givens. Instead, 'multiplicities are defined by the outside: the line of flight or deterritorialization according to which they change in nature and connect with other multiplicities' (ATP 9). No relation is metaphysically implied, which is precisely why existential relations constantly define and redefine the nature of a multiplicity. There is, for example, no flower implied in a seed. A specific machine only develops into a flower if specific interactions with sunlight, insects, and nutrients in the soil are realised. Nothing 'goes wrong' if the seed is simply eaten and digested. Likewise, there is no heterosexual identity implied in human nature, no beaver dam implied in a piece of wood, and so on. It is because all multiplicities are ontologically 'asignifying and asubjective' that their actual engagements fundamentally matter (ATP 9). As a body is always a feature of each machine, such engagements never cease to be vital. A flower can wither, a sexuality can change, and a dam can break. The irreducible nature of the machine's body without organs remains primary in all cases: 'in fact, what is primary is an absolute deterritorialization, an absolute line of flight, however complex or multiple – that of the plane of consistency or body without organs' (ATP 56; cf. 270). 'Plane of consistency' here means that the many relations by which a machine undergoes the events of its existence always concern *it*, that *it* will be the depository of the traces they leave.[9] 'Line of flight' indicates that the body is a sufficient reason for the possibility of breaking with current relations. Even if it would kill me, my heart can nevertheless be removed from my chest. Even if a machine D is produced if and only if machines A and B are made to interact in a specific way caused by machine C, then subsequent machines will nevertheless have to deal with machine D, and not necessarily with A, B, or C. Deleuze gives the example of a mechanic working in the boiler room of ship, writing that 'the mechanic is a part of the machine, not only as a mechanic but also when he ceases to be one' (K 81). The mechanic has been thoroughly shaped by decades of work in the boiler room. The milieu of the boiler room has altered how he walks, talks, and thinks. It has strengthened his arms, wrecked his back, and ruined his lungs. Even when the mechanic goes on shore leave, he carries these traces with him. Nevertheless, the mechanic remains outlandish, remains unintegrated into the boiler room, simply because he can leave. Once again, 'irreducible' is not a synonym for 'immune'.

'Problematic' and 'outlandish' are alarming terms. They remind us of jealous lovers, volatile chemicals, unruly children, unforeseen consequences, hostile climates, the betrayals of solemn oaths, and hairstyles from the eighties. Yet there is another way of picturing machinic being, which is to call each machine a nomad. This refers to 'a *nomos* very different from the "law"' (ATP 361; cf. 408). 'Nomad' has a double etymology referring to dividing, distributing, and allotting lands, but also to roaming, roving, and wandering. As a nomad, each machine is constantly engaged in both types of activities. On the one hand, there are its relations, but on the other hand, there always remains this unintegrated aspect to it. A machine's nomadism lies not in its movements, but precisely in its fundamental excess over all relations, movements, and locations.[10] The nomad is *he who does not move* [. . .] one who does not depart, does not want to depart' (ATP 381; cf. D 37–8). To be a nomad is to never truly settle in any relation. Each machine or nomad is a '*local absolute*, an absolute that is manifested locally' (ATP 382; cf. 494). *Ab solus* means not being relative to anything else. It means being irreducible and external. To borrow two examples from Bergson, a town is absolute in the sense that not even all possible photographs of it can stand in for it, and a poem is absolute in the sense that none of its translations and descriptions can replace it. The absolute expresses that the object is never its representations (Bergson 1999: 22). This absolute, nomadic, problematic character of bodies without organs of machines also motivates the distinction Deleuze likes to draw between chess and go (ATP 352–3). In chess, each piece is irrevocably defined by its functions. Yet in go, pieces 'have only an anonymous, collective, or third-person function: "it" makes a move. "It" could be a man, a woman, a louse, an element. Go pieces are elements of a [. . .] machine assemblage with no intrinsic properties, only situational ones' (ATP 353). In chess, pieces are defined according to a 'milieu of interiority' or internal relations, whereas 'a go piece only has a milieu of exteriority, or extrinsic relations' (ATP 353).

Deleuze's best-known term for such a nomadic reality is 'schizophrenia'. If externality holds, then reality is 'a schizoid universe of closed vessels' (PS 175). Schizophrenia is a universal condition, such that 'there is no *specifically* schizophrenic phenomenon or entity; schizophrenia is the universe of productive and reproductive desiring-machines' (AO 25; cf. 13, 162; C2 172). To think schizophrenically has absolutely nothing to do with glorifying a pathology. At best, it is to see that certain schizophrenic experiences accord with how all of reality works (AO 13). It is to see in reality only 'the continual whirr of machines' (AO 12). It is to posit no false depths and heights. It is to posit a body or 'a soul for rocks, metals, water, and plants' (AO 12). It is *not* to posit that the constants, patterns, laws, and ratios discovered by the sciences do not exist. The schizo position is merely that machines have a private reality over and above their many relations, making them 'alone even in the company of others' (ATP 34):

We cannot [. . .] say that the schizophrenic machine is comprised of the parts and elements of various pre-existing machines. Essentially, the schizophrenic is a functional machine making use of left-over elements that no longer function in any context, and that will enter into relation with each other *precisely by having no relation* [. . .] (TRM 18)

The peculiar character of schizophrenic machines derives from their putting elements in play that are totally disparate and foreign to one another. Schizophrenic machines are aggregates. And yet they work. (TRM 18)

These two fragments state the same point. Every machine is generated by other machines, regardless of its scale. In this respect the utterance of a word is not different from the birth of a solar system. No machine coincides with its generators or components, which makes it disparate and foreign to other machines. This is perfectly expressed in the description of a table that Deleuze borrows from the Belgian artist Henri Michaux, which deserves to be quoted at length:

> Once noticed, it continued to occupy one's mind. It even persisted, as it were, in going about its own business. . . . The striking thing was that it was neither simple nor really complex, initially or intentionally complex, or constructed according to a complicated plan. Instead, it had been desimplified [*sic*] in the course of its carpentering. . . . As it stood, it was a table of additions, much like certain schizophrenics' drawings, described as 'overstuffed', and if finished it was only in so far as there was no way of adding anything more to it, the table having become more and more an accumulation, less and less a table. . . . It was not intended for any specific purpose, for anything one expects of a table. Heavy, cumbersome, it was virtually immovable. One didn't know how to handle it (mentally or physically). Its top surface, the useful part of the table, having been gradually reduced, was disappearing, with so little relation to the clumsy framework that the thing did not strike one as a table, but as some freak piece of furniture, an unfamiliar instrument . . . for which there was no purpose. A dehumanized table, nothing cozy about it, nothing 'middle-class', nothing rustic, nothing countrified, not a kitchen table or a work table. A table which lent itself to no function, self-protective, denying itself to service and communication alike. There was something stunned about it, something petrified. Perhaps it suggested a stalled engine. (AO 17; cf. LS 366–7 n.21; cited from Michaux 1974: 125–7)

The table is irreducible to its creator's intentions or to its functions. Its components and relations are additions, not its being. Other entities experiencing the table do not experience its private reality, but something else ('less and less a table'). The table *qua* table is immovable and cannot be handled physically or mentally: it remains external to relations. Yet we only realise this by moving beyond its surface, which is to say our normal ways of encountering it. We will then be left with the body without organs, a freakish and unfamiliar instrument that resists all assimilation.

Second Intermezzo – Maurizio Ferraris and Unamendable Objects

The body makes a machine problematic. Because its body can never feature in a machine's relations, no machine can fully coincide with how it features among the parts or in the environment of another entity. Any relation is but a temporary 'solution' to this persisting problem. We already noted briefly that this stubborn resistance is also a ground for political emancipation, and here someone might initially disagree. How could reality's *resistance* to our dealings be liberating? Here, a comparison between Deleuze and some key features of the 'new realism' proposed by Maurizio Ferraris is enlightening.[11] It will demonstrate that the externality of entities has immediate political implications. It will also show that – despite what some may think – Deleuze cannot be regarded as a postmodern philosopher. Finally, it will reveal the importance of the *speculative* aspect of machine ontology – in the sense of including arguments that move thought *beyond* the field of direct experience.

Ferraris initially oriented his philosophy towards post-structuralism, deconstruction, and hermeneutics. Yet in the mid-1990s he started to articulate a 'new realism' opposed to these genres of thought. Specifically, Ferraris sought to break with their tendency to jointly blend into the postmodern thesis that reality is nothing but human interpretations. Two concerns animated this turn in his philosophy. First, politically, he realised that postmodernism is not the emancipatory force it claims to be. Second, ontologically, he came to disagree with the idea that reality is just a series of interpretations (a correlationist thesis if ever there was one).

Ferraris defines postmodernism, which he also calls 'social constructivism' or 'realitism', as a combination of de-objectification, ironisation, and desublimation (2014a: 4, 15). De-objectification is the thesis that there exist no things in themselves, just human interpretations. The world is not comprised of real entities: it is nothing but a mirror of our desires, linguistic activities, and power struggles. This engenders ironisation, or the belief that taking theories seriously (as *facts* about *things*) is dogmatic. Instead, we ought to make liberal use of quotation marks (written or gestured) to always signal that we are not *really* speaking about real things when we seem to speak about real things. The final element is desublimation, defined as the belief that only desire can be revolutionary, progressive, or emancipatory. If claims to 'knowledge' mislead us into thinking that there exists a real world out there, then reason and intellect, as generators of knowledge, cannot be trusted. Desire (i.e. emotion, affect, irrationality) is at least 'honest' in not resorting to metaphysical or scientific shenanigans in an attempt to present itself as 'objective'.

Postmodernism initially feels like a liberation. If nothing but human interpretation exists, then humans can change everything by simply reinterpreting it. There would be nothing non-human in reality to oppose or resist us, as the real would just be an ephemeral dream produced by ourselves (Ferraris 2014a: 16). Unfortunately, such exuberance quickly turns into disappointment. Initially, postmodernism seemed an excellent tool for the emancipation of marginalised groups. If the status quo oppressing them was just a set of narratives and power strategies built by humans, then other humans could obviously change this status quo: first, by exposing it *as* a social construct rather than a set of facts; second, by designing more progressive stories and politics. Yet the problem is that *everyone* then gets to play the interpretation game, including the powers that be. Ferraris realised that the logical outcome of postmodernism is therefore not progressive left-wing politics, but *populism* on both sides of the political spectrum (2014a: 3). As soon as you enter the political arena armed with postmodern arguments, your opponents can respond in exactly two ways. First, they can say 'According to your own axioms, you have nothing to offer but stories. Point granted – *you* have stories. *We*, on the other hand, have stories *rooted in facts*.' This turns you into the populist, in the sense of a peddler of utopian fantasies lacking any and all recourse to facts. Second and perhaps worse, they can say 'We totally agree, everything is a story. Nothing is real, there is just interpretation. Bring it on!' The result is full-blown populism, in the sense of a world in which might makes right. Science and history are out of the window, and politics transforms into a Machiavellian, solipsistic shouting match. We should not need to add that those already in power have the best odds of prevailing under such conditions.

This political disappointment provided Ferraris with a motive to develop a 'new realism', but it is not yet an argument against postmodernism. Reality can still be X even if X has terrible consequences (otherwise, carcinogenic substances would have been erased from existence once we noticed that they were indeed carcinogenic). The actual argument lies in Ferraris's identification of three fallacies respectively underlying de-objectification, ironisation, and desublimation. In addition to critiquing postmodernism, we will also see that the identification of each fallacy leads to a positive feature of Ferraris's realism.

The first fallacy is the 'fallacy of being-knowledge' (Ferraris 2014a: 23).[12] The postmodernist confuses epistemology and ontology by reasoning 'if I think X, then X is obviously something thought, therefore the existence of X depends on conceptual schemes'. Instead, she should reason 'if I think X, then my thought of X is obviously something thought, therefore my thought of X depends on conceptual schemes'. As Ferraris puts it, *our knowing* that there are mountains on the moon that are over 4,000 kilometres tall depends on our having conceptual schemes by which we can attain such knowledge, but *there being* such mountains does not depend on the existence of thinking human beings (2014a: 23). Or to make the absurdity in postmodernism even more clear: if being was not different from thinking, then we would need a concept 'even to slip on a patch of ice' (2014a: 24).[13]

Ferraris's point is that reality is brimming with entities that do not require human concepts in order to exist. They (the entities) are irreducible to them (the concepts). He drives the point home with what he calls 'the slipper experiment' (2014a: 28). Take a carpet with a slipper on it. One person can ask another person to pass them the slipper (and the other person can comply) even if their worldviews, thoughts, and opinions are radically different. It is not their concepts that make for intersubjectivity, it is the *slipper* (that makes for inter*objectivity*, we should add). This becomes clearer when we imagine a dog bringing someone the slipper. Here, too, it is the slipper constituting a shared world between dog and human. Third, Ferraris asks us to imagine a worm crawling over the slipper. Even though the worm has no conceptual apparatus worthy of the name, it still encounters and has to navigate the slipper. Fourth, the same would still be the case if ivy was growing over the slipper. Fifth and finally, even another slipper thrown on to the slipper would of course encounter the slipper!

The conclusion Ferraris urges us to draw from his experiment is that objects are *unamendable* (2014a: 35). Unamendability does not mean that an object cannot be changed. It means that an object cannot be reduced to that by which another object relates to it. The slipper is just as irreducible to my conceptual schemes as it is to however worms, ivy, and other slippers register their encounter with it. This is even true for social objects such as promises, bets, or marriages (2014a: 52–6; cf. Ferraris 2014b; De Sanctis 2015: 221–4). These certainly need human minds to construct and maintain them, but it does not follow that their being is identical to such generators. They, too, are unamendable. Otherwise, we could simply erase a tune stuck in our head by wishing it away. The fallacy of being-knowledge lies in the disregard for unamendability, and this same unamendability of objects constitutes the first positive feature of Ferraris's ontology: 'the fact that what we face cannot be corrected or changed by the mere use of conceptual schemes' (2014a: 34).

Second is the 'fallacy of ascertainment-acceptance' (Ferraris 2014a: 45). The ironic postmodernist thinks that ascertaining the real existence of something equates to the dogmatic acceptance that it must be kept in the exact same state as that in which we first encounter it. For the postmodernist, change is only possible if objects are fully reducible to our own constantly changing experiences of the world. Yet unamendability implies the precise opposite. If any object is irreducible to how others currently relate to it, then it is possible to change both the object and our relations to it. As Ferraris writes, doctors want to ascertain what diseases are, precisely in order to treat or eliminate them (2014a: 46). Exposing this fallacy immediately flips into a second positive feature of Ferraris's ontology: change and emancipation are always possible because objects are not restricted to their current givenness.

The third fallacy is the 'fallacy of knowledge-power' (2014a: 67). According to the postmodernist, any claim to knowledge is a thinly veiled power strategy. Within the game of competing interpretations, whoever claims real and objective knowledge is merely trying to pull off an Orwellian 'some interpretations are more equal than others' manoeuvre. The problem is that this leaves the postmodernist unable to counter absurdities such as Holocaust denials (2014a: 69), because he denies himself access to the argument that we *know* for a *fact* that the Holocaust happened. By his own admission, anything the postmodernist says is simply one power move pitted against others. Here, too, unamendability exposes the fallacy and provides the solution. If the world is nothing but the mirror of our interpretations, then 'Holocaust' is merely an empty signifier whose 'existence' and 'truth' is constantly (re-)established in human struggles. But if it is a real and unamendable *object* (i.e. really *something*), then it cannot be reduced like that. Here it is important to note that – even though Ferraris does not dwell on it – 'unamendable' does not mean 'undetermined'. The whole point of unamendability is that an object is not some empty void that passively accepts human projections. Unamendability means *resistance* to interpretation, which means that objects must have their own *character*. This again leads to a positive feature for Ferraris's realism: the prospect of certainty (2014a: 76).

The fact that objects resist random interpretation and treatment is the condition for the possibility of some interpretations being more accurate than others, and for *knowing* it (via repeated scientific experiment, for example). Unamendability therefore allows for *progress* in our understanding of the world.

The similarities between Ferraris's notion of unamendability and Deleuze's machinic bodies are obvious. Deleuze's bodies withdraw from becoming present in relations, so that an entity is always irreducible to how we interpret it. As he writes, no machine, not even the tools that we make for ourselves, can ever be reduced to human projections (BSP 118–19). Deleuze is clearly far from a postmodernist who holds that books, tigers, diseases, atrocious events, and slippers are reducible to however we choose to think about them. Externality warrants that a machine *qua* body can never be dissolved into whatever schemes by which it is encountered – be they conceptual or otherwise. Just as for Ferraris, this very irreducibility of entities must be regarded as providing the condition for the possibility of change, emancipation, certainty, and progress. Or in Deleuze's terms: the irreducibility of machines to our projections on to them is the condition for the possibility of 'new connections' (BSP 121). We can only ever change things in the world because these things are more than their current deployment, and we can only ever acquire knowledge about which interpretations are the more accurate ones as long as entities have some being of their own that precludes them from surrendering themselves equally to just any interpretation. The notion of a specific *character* for entities implied in the latter will be explained in detail in Chapter 6.

Nevertheless, one crucial difference between Deleuze and Ferraris must be pointed out. Section 2 of Chapter 2 showed that, like Ferraris, Deleuze identifies a series of experiences that point to the externality of entities to their relations, that is, to their irreducibility or unamendability. Yet unlike Ferraris, Deleuze supplements these observations with speculative arguments in support of the externality thesis. He supplies arguments as to why reality could not be otherwise than be comprised of irreducible entities, even if human experience would not suggest it to us. This is not the case for Ferraris. In fact, Ferraris is, strictly speaking, not making a distinction between entities as related to and entities as they exist in themselves, but between entities *as conceptualised* and entities *as perceived*:

> For me, the first step to overcome the transcendental fallacy and resolve the confusion between ontology and epistemology has lied [*sic*] in

understanding that perception is autonomous from thought [. . .] (De Sanctis 2015: 227)

Ferraris does not just present his philosophy as a new realism; he also refers to it as an attempt to revalorise aesthetics as a philosophy of perception (Ferraris 2014a: 18). By this he seems to mean that *perception* is irreducible to *concepts*, which in turn means that unamendability would refer to the irreducibility of perceived objects to conceptualised objects. This raises the question of whether Ferraris really manages to establish the unamendability of objects *qua objects*, or merely the irreducibility of perception to thought. An ungenerous critic might accuse Ferraris of merely proving that our relation to objects contains something that cannot be reduced to concepts. This certainly seems to be Ferraris's point when he critiques Kant for burdening us with the fallacy of being-knowledge:

> [We have] to agree that knowing a thing is not the same as encountering it, for instance, banging into a chair in the dark. And, however our experience might become, we must admit that most of it has this opaque and incorrigible undertow, where the conceptual schemes that organize our knowledge count for very little. (Ferraris 2013: 46)

Indeed, a major part of Ferraris's critique of Kant is that we *can* have meaningful intuitions without concepts, which the latter famously denied (Ferraris 2013: 52–61). But from the perspective of Deleuze's externality thesis, this is insufficient to establish a realism of objects. It merely establishes that our experience of objects is a twofold of non-conceptual content supplemented by conceptual interpretation. Ferraris, then, still requires an argument to expand unamendability-as-perceived into an irreducibility of objects even when no other entity is relating to it. After all, a slipper perceived as unamendable always remains a slipper *perceived*. Ferraris seems to confirm this suspicion: 'in general, the "external world" is external to conceptual schemes, and, from this point of view, its paradigm lies in the unamendability of perception' (2014a: 37). If we take this seriously, the unamendable slipper would not be an object existing independently from human relations to it (note the ironic quotation marks around 'external world'). The unamendability of the slipper just seems to be a feature of human experience, albeit a non-conceptual perceptive aspect of experience that exaggerated attention to the conceptual side of experience tends to overshadow. Whereas realism is certainly the spirit of Ferraris's philosophy, this may not be entirely warranted by its letter. This point of critique helps us realise why Deleuze also uses speculative arguments in addition to experiential ones in order to establish the externality thesis and the irreducibility of machinic bodies.

Notes

1. Deleuze may write that '*the* body without organs reproduces itself, puts forth shoots, and branches out to the farthest corners of the universe' (AO 22, emphasis added), but there he is describing the infectious behaviour of a specific body without organs: capitalism. There is never just a single body without organs, except in the sense that one can be the protagonist of a case.

2. Some English readers of Deleuze may think that the transcendental aspect of his philosophy disappears in the Guattari collaborations. One reason may be that the English edition of *Kafka* mistranslates *transcendante* (transcendent) as 'transcendental'. This suggests that Deleuze criticises something 'transcendental' in favour of something 'immanent' (K 73), whereas the actual target of the critique is transcendence. Also recall that *Anti-Oedipus* refers to the 'unconscious' of machines as their transcendental aspect, and that schizoanalysis is also called 'transcendental analysis'.

3. 'le corps, ce n'est pas de l'étendue' (SL 120 587).

4. 'Vous commencez par soustraire, retrancher' (SU 103); 'Mais qu'est-ce qui reste? Il reste tout, mais sous une nouvelle lumière' (SU 104).

5. 'Wenn wir einen Kristall zu Boden werfen, zerbricht er, aber nicht willkürlich, er zerfällt dabei nach seinen Spaltrichtungen in Stücke, deren Abgrenzung, obwohl unsichtbar, doch durch die Struktur des Kristalls vorher bestimmt war. Solche rissige und gesprungene Strukturen sind auch die Geisteskranken' (Freud 1961: 64).

6. Cf. 'We know that things and people are always forced to conceal themselves, have to conceal themselves when they begin. What else could they do? They come into being within a set which no longer includes them and, in order not to be rejected, have to project the characteristics which they retain in common with the set' (C1 3).

7. '*introduire dans l'enseignement l'inenseignable*' (Klossowski 2005: 43).

8. '"Outlandish", c'est exactement le deterritorialisé, mot à mot' (*L'Abécédaire*, 'animal').

9. Hence the plane of consistency also being called the 'immanent field

of desire' (SCS 140573). Being a body without organs, a plane of consistency, too, must always be produced: 'Jamais un plan de composition ou de consistance ne préexiste' (SCS 150277).

10. 'The *nomos* [designates] first of all an occupied space, but one without precise limits [. . .] – whence, too, the theme of the "nomad"' (DR 309 n.6; cf. LS 60).

11. This is based on available English translations of Ferraris's work. Also, Ferraris's *Manifesto of New Realism* (2014a) and *Introduction to New Realism* (2015) are nearly identical in content, so that we can cover both by simply citing from the former. We apologise for any exegetical errors and omissions resulting from not taking into account his Italian work.

12. Ferraris also calls this the 'transcendental fallacy', and traces its origins to Kant's *Critique of Pure Reason*, blaming the latter for a 'reduction of objects to the subjects that know them' (Ferraris 2013: 45).

13. One cannot solve this by saying that our thoughts *and bodies* shape the world, because it is still absurd to think that the existence of patches of ice would depend on human bodies being around to slip on them.

5

Relations between Machines

Despite the splendid isolation in which the bodily aspect of machines resides, relations must nevertheless exist. First, because we determined that machines are produced by other machines. Second, because an internal difference in kind between a non-relational virtuality and actual manifestations implies that actuality is always relational. Yet the externality thesis forbids a direct encounter between machines *qua* bodies. The question therefore becomes how on earth machines ever manage to relate at all. This will bring us to the first of three syntheses which account for contact, assembly, alteration, and disintegration among entities, and to Deleuze's concept of 'sense'. We will learn that no relation is ever a relation with a simple unit. What machines encounter in relations is an actual twofold of what Deleuze calls 'flow' or 'qualities' on the one hand, and 'partial object' or 'extension' on the other. By the end of the chapter we will have grown acquainted with the first synthesis and three of the four aspects of machines: their non-relational body plus the two aspects pertaining to how they are experienced by other assemblages.

1 The Connective Synthesis

Given that *everything* is a machine, we must account for all types of relations. This includes someone spotting a friend, a mouth meeting a flow of milk, a meteor striking the moon, rain landing in a puddle, a bullet piercing a skull, a hand receiving a signal from a nervous system, a crumb being part of a cake, a virus infiltrating software, and a wasp landing on an orchid. Deleuze needs to account for all forms of having, pushing, landing, spotting, touching, suspecting, destroying, recruiting, generating, qualifying, quantifying, and so on. This implies the necessity of syntheses, a synthesis being an operation by which two distinct entities are drawn together:

> It is true that one might [. . .] wonder how these conditions of dispersion, of real distinction, and of the absence of a link permit any machinic *régime* to exist [. . .] The answer lies in the passive nature of the syntheses, or – what amounts to the same thing – in the indirect nature of the interactions under consideration. (AO 370)

In an externalist reality, synthesis is presupposed wherever entities meet (ES 100). Synthesis must provide a form of *indirect interaction*, because externality forbids two bodies from ever relating directly. Deleuze posits three such syntheses. The first accounts for the basic fact of relating. The second concerns that on which relations are based, and the third concerns that which makes relations hold.

Difference and Repetition calls these 'syntheses of time': a connective synthesis of the present, a disjunctive synthesis of the past, and a conjunctive synthesis of the future. Yet they have little to do with temporality as usually understood. This is why *The Logic of Sense* simply calls them the connective, disjunctive, and conjunctive synthesis (LS 43–7), and why *Anti-Oedipus* calls them the synthesis of production, registration, and consummation. And already in *Difference and Repetition*, Deleuze is careful to describe what exactly he means by 'synthesis of time':

> The past and the future do not designate instants distinct from a supposed present instant, but rather the dimensions of the present itself in so far as it is a contraction of instants. The present does not have to go outside itself in order to pass from past to future [. . .] In any case, this synthesis must be given a name: passive synthesis. (DR 71)

The syntheses concern three dimensions of each relation. They are temporal only in the sense of being the formal structure of whatever happens. The connective 'present' refers to the relation as such, the disjunctive 'past' refers to that which grounds the relation and must therefore exist *during* the relation, and the conjunctive 'future' refers to how each disjunctive connection immediately creates a new machine. That last point seems counter-intuitive, but it is in fact absolutely necessary that each relation between machines implies the generation of a new machine. Understanding why this is the case, however, requires familiarity with all major aspects of Deleuze's ontology. We will therefore postpone the analysis of the generation of new entities until Chapter 8. For now, simply note that if relations are external to terms, then there must always be something that prevents two machines from becoming permanently absorbed in a single relation. A connection between two multiplicities must therefore immediately generate something that exceeds them. Despite its obviousness, another thing to note is that the syntheses neither concern our perceptions of objects nor human experience more generally. Even though Deleuze frequently uses perception as an example, 'perceptual syntheses refer back to organic syntheses which are like the sensibility of the senses; they refer back to a primary sensibility that we *are*' (DR 73). And we, of course, are but particular cases of fourfolds, so that the same syntheses also concern rocks, wood, nitrogen, sulphates, and other assemblages (DR 75). This is why the syntheses are 'passive'. Synthesis is not something someone decides to do. Synthesis is what everything does in all cases, and it is the condition for 'active' synthetic activity such as remembering and understanding (DR 71).

To start with the first synthesis of connection and the bare fact of relation, we must first ask ourselves what relates to a machine. Recall a remark cited earlier, that 'the third' or the body is primary (WG 23). It is where relation starts. What relates is the body itself, the third thing standing between the components generating a machine and the machines it alters or generates itself. *I* walk through the museum. Granted, I need legs, feet, lungs, and arteries to do it. Also required are the museum itself, the street in front of it, the floors inside it, and so on. Agency is quite obviously distributed, as I could not walk in a vacuum. Nevertheless, *I* walk through the museum, not my shoelaces or my left kidney. Likewise, *I* perceive a river. I do so thanks to many other assemblages or rhizomes coupled to me, but those cannot stand in for me. This is identical to how the EU has its citizens, even though it needs countless politicians, laws, office buildings, and other entities to have them. It is the body that relates, not one of its components. Also note that the actual aspect of a machine cannot be what relates to other multiplicities. The actual is what is manifest in relations. It is that which is experienced, and an experience cannot directly experience experiences for the same reason that a quality is never directly a quality of a quality. It would be absurd to hold that when we look at each other, that which perceives you is your perception of me.

On one side of every relation we find a body without organs. As Deleuze writes, 'from Leibniz, we have already learned that there are no points of view on things, but that things, beings, are themselves points of view' (LS 173; cf. DR 69; FLB 20–1; PS 161). To be a body without organs, a Figure, or a problem is being a point of view on other machines.[1] In the context of machine ontology, this is neither a phenomenological nor an epistemological thesis. It is a necessary corollary of the externality thesis. If nothing is reducible to anything else, then there are no general perspectives to which things would be internal. Everything has its own perspective on the world, but 'perspective' refers to relations of whatever kind, not just visual ones. When Deleuze writes that 'each composing representation must be distorted, diverted and torn from its center. Each point of view must itself be the object, or the object must belong to the point of view' (DR 56), we must be careful not to confuse epistemology and ontology. Deleuze's machines are highly similar to Leibnizian monads in this regard: 'at the basis of *each individual notion*, it will indeed be necessary for there to be a point of view that defines the individual notion. If you prefer, the subject is second in relation to the point of view' (SL 150480; cf. SL 161286).

None of this violates externality. Externality would be violated if a virtual component of a machine, at this point its body, would manifest *as such*. Yet to relate to something is not at all the same thing as being related to. To look at someone does not imply being looked at. Even if the other person reciprocates, she or he would not experience a body without organs, but an actual, manifest entity. This is why passive synthesis 'is essentially asymmetrical: it goes from the past to the future in the present' (DR 71; cf. 81); why 'everything goes from high to low, and by that movement affirms the lowest: asymmetrical synthesis' (DR 234); and why 'everything ties together in an asymmetrical block of becoming, an instantaneous zigzag' (ATP 278). The carpentry of beings is forged one unilateral relation at a time, and each relation exclusively runs from a virtual body (the 'past' or private 'depth' underneath the present relation) to the actual and manifest aspect of one or several other machines (their local 'height' in a present relation).[2] This constitutes what is the case and therefore that upon which machines will act (bringing about a future). Unilaterality and asymmetry are necessitated by the fact that direct body–body relations between machines are impossible, as there is always an ontological 'indifference toward the act of producing and toward the product' (AO 18) by which the body remains withdrawn from any machine experiencing it. Being experienced therefore implies a 'rupture' between a machine's virtual body and its actual manifestation:

> Doubtless each organ-machine interprets the entire world from the perspective of its own flow [. . .] the eye interprets everything – speaking, understanding, shitting, fucking – in terms of seeing. But a connection with another machine is always established, along a transverse path, so that one machine interrupts the current of the other or 'sees' its own current interrupted. (AO 16, translation modified)

The body is a point of view. Each machine can only have relations according to its own capacities. A machine's relations are therefore contractions of other machines into actualisations according to what that first machine can do, even if its relations are forced upon it. Each entity is a 'contracting machine' (DR 73), each relation is fundamentally a contraction (LS 225). Having a relation with another machine is to contract 'a multitude of divergent series in the successive appearance of a single one' (LS 175). An eye sees everything in terms of seeing, and by that simple act unites a multitude of mutually irreducible machines into a single experience. Since this is true for all entities, the first synthesis reveals the glue of reality: entities are combined in the experience of other entities. They are brought into a single present: 'the passive synthesis of habit [constitutes] time as a *contraction* of instants with respect to a present' (DR 81; cf. 70–1). The connective synthesis is a synthesis of 'habit' for two reasons. First, all entities are in the habit of contracting others. It is simply what happens whenever a relation is forged or entertained. Second, for sentient beings it is the condition for the possibility of recognition and anticipation. To act from habit, after all, is to meet the future based on something retained from the past, the latter having come to 'style' one's point of view. Yet despite this terminology, contraction is not just a visual phenomenon. It refers to how experience is never experience of a machine *qua* machine, but instead a case of bringing machines into actuality based on a specific point of view. As other machines are brought into that same point of view, their disparate realities become unified to the extent that the relation can manage to hold:

> A contractile power: like a sensitive plate, it retains one case when the other appears. It contracts cases, elements, agitations or homogeneous instants and grounds these in an internal qualitative impression endowed with a certain weight. (DR 70)

Relation is contraction. Even a relation with a single machine expresses its untimely and unextended virtual body in a qualified actual relation. Ontologically, all relations are contemplations or contractions, even in existential cases of relaxation (DR 75). It is irrelevant if a specific relation is strong or weak, enduring or momentary, physical or social. To synthesise, to contemplate, and to contract is to pull other entities into an experience. All relations are indirect contact with a contracted expression of a machine rather than with its body. From that point on, nothing stands in the way of machines shaping other machines: everything, even that which a machine can contract, results from what a machine contracts:

> We are made of contracted water, earth, light and air – not merely prior to the recognition or representation of these, but prior to their being sensed. Every organism, in its receptive and perceptual elements, but also in its viscera, is a sum of contractions, of retentions and expectations. (DR 73)

> Habit is creative. The plant contemplates water, earth, nitrogen, carbon, chlorides, and sulphates, and it contracts them in order to acquire its own concept and fill itself (enjoyment) [. . .] We are all contemplations, and therefore habits. (WP 105)

These quotations stress the ontological importance of the synthesis of contraction. It is impossible to properly grasp Deleuze's philosophy without understanding that the 'machining' that each assemblage does is first and foremost the contraction of otherwise withdrawn machines into actual manifestations that thereby come to shape what something becomes. Consider the following passage from *Difference and Repetition*:

> What we call wheat is a contraction of the earth and humidity, and this contraction is both a contemplation and the auto-satisfaction of that contemplation [. . .] What organism is not made of elements and cases of repetition, of contemplated and contracted water, nitrogen,

carbon, chlorides and sulphates, thereby intertwining all the habits of which it is composed? [. . .] Perhaps it is irony to say that everything is contemplation, even rocks and woods, animals and men, even Actaeon and the stag, Narcissus and the flower, even our actions and our needs. But irony in turn is still a contemplation, nothing but a contemplation. (DR 75; cf. SL 170387)

Our introduction asserted that Deleuze is closer to being a panpsychist than a phenomenologist. We now see that a more accurate name would be 'polypsychist', as he endows each entity with a private stance on reality.[3] That each entity has a body from which it encounters other beings in the form of contractions according to its own characteristic style of being is what Deleuze seeks to express when writing that each machine has a 'soul' or 'larval self':

> A soul must be attributed to the heart, to the muscles, nerves and cells, but a contemplative soul whose entire function is to contract a habit. This is no mystical or barbarous hypothesis. On the contrary, habit here manifests its full generality: it concerns not only the sensory-motor habits that we have (psychologically), but also, before these, the primary habits that we are; the thousands of passive syntheses of which we are organically composed. (DR 74)

Such musings are anything but poetic.[4] To be a multiplicity is to assemble other entities via contractions, but each of those is also a contracting entity in turn. Even 'matter is, in effect, populated or covered by such souls, which provide it with a depth without which it would present no bare repetition on the surface' (DR 286). Even lifeless machines have a soul, a private depth, a body without organs underlying the actualisations by means of which they encounter one another. Contra the Socratic gesture of barring unworthy things from ontological speculations, 'contemplative souls must be assigned even to the rat in the labyrinth and to each muscle of the rat' (DR 75). The first synthesis or the bare fact of relation implies that contraction or contemplation defines 'all our rhythms, our reserves, our reaction times, [and] the thousand intertwinings, the presents and fatigues of which we are composed' (DR 74). The first synthesis is a synthesis of production, and what it produces is an actualisation of whatever it contracts, engendering a togetherness to envelop the solitude of bodies.

Connections can be of whatever type. As Deleuze writes, 'to enter or leave the machine, to walk around it, to approach it – these are still components of the machine itself' (K 7). Synthetically, there is no difference between the relations you have with your lungs or those you have with your clothes, your language, or this text. You synthesise relations with a plethora of such things and, in whatever way, contract them into really encountered manifestations. There is no ontological difference between insides and outsides, only an existential one. Your relations with your car keys and your lover are ontologically equal to those with your arteries and your eyeballs. Only a virtual body is the true interior of Mars, Oxford University, a grain of sand, or an awkward moment during a blind date. 'Being part of' is no longer the privilege of things that are physically located in other assemblages. 'Being part of' must come to mean 'being contracted by'. Each machine is part of whatever encounters it, and the impact of such encounters can range from pitiful irrelevance to brutal domination. My biological components help forge the perspective that I am, but so do the city of Nijmegen and the surrealist collages in my living room. In terminology to which we will return later, those machines are all equal in contributing to the becoming of my powers. Machine ontology implies an exotic mereology in which machinic parts are both more numerous and less internal than we would normally think.

Machine ontology replaces the inside–outside distinction with a more fundamental distinction between contiguity and rupture, or in other words between production and anti-production: 'a characteristic of the connective or productive synthesis is the fact that it couples production with anti-production, with an element of anti-production' (AO 19). Contiguity and rupture are not opposites. Rather, 'the break or interruption conditions this continuity: it presupposes or defines what it cuts into as an ideal continuity' (AO 50; cf. 51). As we saw, that which remains external to terms is the virtual aspect of machines. Machines are barred from body–body contact. Each relation is a synthesis by which the virtual aspect of a body indirectly relates to an actual manifestation of other machines, the latter differing in kind from their respective virtuality. This difference in kind is the break or interruption Deleuze mentions. Direct contact between virtual entities is impossible, but the actual aspects of those same entities can meet as encountered by yet another machine. And remember that this is not just a point made about perception, but about *all* relation. My perception of a small globe and a wooden owl displayed on my fireplace contracts a number of irreducible entities into one manifestation, but so does a tornado that gathers up innumerable multiplicities in its passing. Contraction is the glue of the world. The Real is animated only because *another* machine can treat *these* machines as a contiguous series or a single thing. Such contiguity and rupture are even at work in relations with but a single object. This is because entering into a relation implies becoming extended, and any object is always contiguous with its spatio-temporal context. No matter how hard I focus on my telephone, the world never consists of my telephone, then the void surrounding it, and only then the table on which it lies. Instead, experience is always a plenum, for humans as well as for non-humans. It is an ontological fact that relation pulls entities from their virtual bodies into manifestations: 'desiring-machines work only when they break down, and by continually breaking down' (AO 19; cf. 45):

> For the machine possesses two characteristics or powers: the power of the continuum, the machinic phylum in which a given component connects with another [. . .] but also the rupture in direction, the mutation such that each machine is an absolute break in relation to the one it replaces [. . .] Two powers which are really only one, since the machine in itself is the break-flow process, the break being always adjacent to the continuity of a flow which it separates from the others by assigning it a code, by causing it to convey particular elements. (BSP 121)

A machine defines what it cuts into as an 'ideal continuity' in the sense that no machine can experience other machines fundamentally on *their* terms, that is, as bodies. Being only able to encounter entities on *its* terms, a machine's relations introduce a common notion into that which is encountered, so that an ideal continuity or contiguity is a genuine feature of all relation.[5] Since each machine is a machine of further machines, this play of rupture and contiguity is a defining feature of reality. Each machine is a 'system that interrupts flows' (DI 219) in the sense that each machine's contiguous world is cut off and reinterpreted by yet other machines, each working on their own terms. Grass contracts water and nutrients in the soil, a cow contracts the grass, a painter contracts the cow and the meadow into a painting, a curator contracts various paintings into an exhibition, and so forth. This is what Deleuze refers to as a 'logic of the AND' (AO 50). Each machine gathers up multitudes of others in its experiences (this

AND that AND that . . .), and each of those others is doing the same. Machinic contact is magnetic or binary. A virtual body never touches another virtual body, but only the other, actual side of machines which constitutes the flow of actuality:

> Desiring machines are binary machines, obeying a binary law or set of rules governing associations: one machine is always coupled with another. The productive synthesis, the production of production, is inherently connective in nature: 'and. . .' 'and then. . .' This is because there is always a flow-producing machine, and another machine connected to it that interrupts or draws off part of this flow [. . .] And because the first machine is in turn connected to another whose flow it interrupts or partially drains off, the binary series is linear in every direction. (AO 16)

In no way does this abolish the body without organs. 'Desiring-production forms a binary-linear system. The full body is introduced as a third term in the series, without destroying, however, the essential binary-linear nature of this series' (AO 26). One body encounters a second entity, not as body but as actuality. A third body encounters the first body, also not as body but as actuality. This is what Deleuze calls 'bare repetition': 'in every way, material or bare repetition, so-called repetition of the same, is like a skin which unravels, the external husk of a kernel of difference and more complicated internal repetitions' (DR 76). The contiguity of actuality is bare repetition. For every machine, everything is 'the same' in the precise sense that it registers everything on its terms, even if those terms change. This repetition is the manifest skin that envelops the bodies of all machines. Internal repetition and difference between a machine's own virtual and actual aspects remains hidden from direct experience. The very structure of contact between entities 'causes [internal repetition] to disappear as it appears, leaving it unthinkable' (DR 71).

Yet we must explain what we have merely posited until now. Machinic virtuality is withdrawn and irreducible, machinic actuality is present and contiguous. What is this initial result of contraction or contemplation? What is this actual aspect of entities? Quite obviously, it cannot simply coincide with a perceiving body. First, because it is an aspect of that which is encountered. Second, if entities were fully drawn into that which encounters them, we would regress into internality. As we have seen, 'bodies caught in the particularity of their limited presents do not meet directly in line with the order of their causality' (LS 131). Actuality must be a form of indirect contact. As Deleuze writes about machines, 'one of the halves is always lacking from the other, since it exceeds by virtue of its own deficiency [. . .] The question is less that of attaining the immediate than of determining the site where the immediate is "immediately" as not-to-be-attained' (LS 136). The virtual must in other words be fully absent from the actual if their difference in kind is to be upheld. In contracting another machine, the result of the connection must make 'the absolute appear in a particular place', but never *as such* (ATP 382). This brings us to *The Logic of Sense*, in which Deleuze theorises this radical distinction between 'corporeal things and incorporeal events' (LS 23; cf. 4). Sense or the event is this actual, relational, and manifest unity of machines.

2 Sense at the Surface

Every relation is a connection to another machine. A connection is a contraction of other entities into an actual manifestation. This result of the interaction between corporal machines is what Deleuze calls 'sense': 'sense is never a principle or an origin', 'sense is produced by bodies' (LS 71, 124). This already establishes that Deleuze does not use 'sense' exactly as we do in everyday conversations. For example, when we say 'it finally made sense to me', we mean that there was a moment at which we attained a true apprehension of what something or someone *is*. As we will see, however, Deleuze does not use 'sense' to refer to what a machine *is*, but to what a machine *does* when engaging with others. For him, a machine makes 'sense' as soon as it does *anything* to another machine. Hence being confused or disoriented by a book is a case of that book making sense in the exact same way that fully understanding a book is. Because it is not the *being* of a machine, sense is not reducible to the machine's generating a relation, it is rather their 'common result' (LS 8). Sense is something that must be made to *happen*, which is why Deleuze uses 'event' as its synonym. He writes that 'the event is sense itself' (LS 211) and that sense and event are the same entity (LS 182). *The Logic of Sense* frequently repeats this strict equivalence by referring to 'the flat world of the sense-event', 'the sterility of the sense-event', and 'the organization of the sense-event' (LS 22, 32, 245, 167).[6]

It is important to emphasise this identity of sense and event. The first third of *The Logic of Sense* uses linguistic entities (sentences, phonemes, proper names, predicates) as a case study to illustrate more general ontological points. The last third of that same book performs a reinterpretation of Kleinian psychoanalysis to the same effect. This could mislead readers into thinking that 'sense' applies exclusively to language, and 'event' only to human experience.[7] Yet 'sense and event are the same thing – except that [. . .] sense is related to propositions' (LS 167). Does this then mean that *all* of the book is about language? Far from it. Deleuze's machine ontology uses 'proposition' as a synonym for 'relation', which is why 'there are many forms of possibility for propositions: logical, geometrical, algebraic, physical, syntactic' (LS 18). Sense and event are synonyms for the actuality that manifests when machines enter into relations. The two concepts do not imply different theories about two natural kinds of relation. They concern the same theory of relations between machines.

Formally, each relation has a body without organs on one side and a sense-event on the other. Machine ontology therefore implies 'a dualism of bodies or states of affairs and effects or incorporeal events' (LS 6). This duality among entities is the price to pay when one abolishes all traditional dualisms between the One and the Many.[8] The sense-event 'articulates what is separate' and 'brings about the convergence of divergent series, but it neither abolishes nor corrects their divergence' (LS 183). It stands between the bodies of machines and warrants internal difference: each machine is virtual in itself, yet it equally is an actual sense-event for others. This is the only way to assure that difference 'is never between two products or between two things, but *in one and the same thing*' (DI 26). It is the difference between the virtual and the actual, between 'surface zones and stages of depth' (LS 245). Sense-events are the hallmarks of the contiguity of actual experience, and 'being incorporeal effects, differ in nature from the corporeal causes from which they result' (LS 144). This is important to grasp: sense-events are *always only effects* which radically differ from things (LS 144; cf. 8).

With these general remarks in place, we can now detail the concept of sense or the 'incorporeal, complex, and irreducible entity, at the surface of things' (LS 19; cf. 94). That which a machine encounters cannot be reduced to the machines encountered. Throughout *The Logic of Sense*, Deleuze insists that sense is not reducible to denotation, manifestation, or signification. It is neither a machine related to, nor the perspective of, the relating machine, nor the meaning or context of the relation. Sense is 'irreducible to individual states of affairs, particular images, personal beliefs, and universal or general concepts' (LS 19). A sense-event 'skirts' bodies, but never equals them (LS 10). Whereas the body without organs is the *virtual* and non-relational unity of a machine, a sense-event is its *actual* and relational unity. It is the bare fact that *this* rather than *that* is encountered, and that *this* or *that* can never be a body. Deleuze here claims to revive a Stoic insight:

> The Stoics distinguished radically two planes of being, something that no one had done before them: on the one hand, real and profound being, force; on the other, the plane of facts, which frolic on the surface of being, and constitute an endless multiplicity of incorporeal beings. (LS 5)

Sense is the impassable envelope or surface around machines (LS 133; cf. 123, 124, 182). It is the impenetrable and non-consumable frontier between things (LS 25). Its function is to organise the terms of relations 'as two series which it separates' (LS 182). I look at a mug on my table. Neither I nor the table encounters the virtual, internal reality of the mug, which remains external to relations. Instead, we encounter a sense-event, an expression of the mug into relation.[9] Recall for the following that 'proposition' is a synonym for 'relation':

> [Sense] turns one side toward things and one side toward propositions. But it does not merge with the proposition which expresses it any more than with the state of affairs or the quality which the proposition denotes. It is exactly the boundary between propositions and things. (LS 22)

As propositions include physical and many other types of relations, we can say that sense is the brute and empty givenness of something to an assemblage. The sense-event further strengthens Deleuze's 'disavowal of false depth' (LS 9). Instead of a universal depth from which all things emerge, the superficial nature of sense emphasises the private depth of each entity's (non-)being. We can also point to Deleuze's frequently cited statement that 'Paul Valéry had a profound idea: what is most deep is the skin'

(LS 10; cf. 103). This does not mean that there is nothing beyond sense-events, as that would make everything Deleuze writes about bodies without organs, machines, and externality unintelligible. Rather, in the context of machinic being it means that all ways of relating to something, including the most accurate descriptions, are but skin deep. They concern the actual, sense-event side of machines and not their virtual aspect. The old universal depth is traded in for local ontic depths, and as such finds itself 'reduced to the opposite side of the surface' (LS 9). It is thus false to think that it is the 'same object which I see, smell, taste, or touch' (LS 78). Instead, it is the same *sense-event* that I see, smell, taste, and touch in a given relation, a sense-event which is not the object *qua* object, but a translation or actualisation of it.

With the French *sens* carrying a connotation of 'direction', we can say that sense amounts to a machine being directed into a relation. Another way to put this is to say that having a sense means being comprehended by something else. Water comprehends hydrogen, wars comprehend soldiers and bullets, my country comprehends me, and so on. To have a sense is to have something connect to you. Conversely, to experience a sense-event is to connect to something. Comprehension is contiguous, as it means entertaining a relation to a plurality of machines that do not entertain this same relation to each other (nor does the comprehending machine entertain this relation with itself). I am a citizen of my country, but my fellow citizens are not citizens of me, nor is my country a citizen of itself. Hydrogen is a component of water, but oxygen is not a component of hydrogen, nor is water a component of itself. You are reading this book, which means you comprehend its pages and words into a sense-event which we can call 'your reading'. Fortunately, you are not the only machine comprehending it. Many others comprehend it in many other ways, so that it does not fall apart once you toss it into a corner and forget all about it:

> There is no event, no phenomenon, word or thought which does not have a multiple sense. A thing is sometimes this, sometimes that, sometimes something more complicated – depending on the forces [. . .] which take possession of it. (NP 4)

Machines are kept together, shattered, transformed, removed, captured, hidden, and recovered by the contingent and universal play of comprehending and being comprehended, that is, of constituting sense-events for one another. There is a sense-event whenever a machine is comprehended by another machine. The production of sense is therefore the production of that which is the case in a given situation (DR 154). Another way of putting this would be to say that a sense-event amounts to extension, to a manifestation in a certain time and in a certain place.

Deleuze expresses this sense of sense by constantly emphasising that sense is 'expressed' (LS 110), an insight first developed in his studies on Spinoza. The 'expressor' of this expressed is the virtual aspect of that which is related to. Hence sense 'brings that which expresses it into existence' (LS 166), with 'into existence' meaning 'into relation' rather than 'into reality'. Sense is a result of the transition from (non)-being into being-for. Being that which is expressed, sense cannot be reduced to a designated object or to that which experiences the expression (LS 20; DR 154). And in a surprising move for an avowed anti-phenomenological thinker, Deleuze credits Husserl with the invention of this concept of sense.

> [W]hen Husserl reflects on the 'perceptual noema', or the 'sense of perception', he at once distinguishes it from the physical object, from the psychological or 'lived', from mental representations and from logical concepts. He presents it as an impassive and incorporeal entity, without physical or mental existence, neither acting nor being acted upon – a pure result or pure 'appearance' [. . .] When therefore Husserl says that the noema is the perceived such as it appears in a presentation, the 'perceived as such' or the appearance, we ought not understand that the noema involves a sensible given or quality, it rather involves an ideational objective unity as the intentional correlate of the act of perception. (LS 20)[10]

A crucial difference between Deleuze and Husserl is that the former's theory of sense-events also concerns relations between entities in which consciousness does not even feature potentially. Nonetheless, the last part of the cited passage highlights an important point: sense has *nothing* to do with quality or with the sensible given. The sense-event is not the redness, sweetness, and roundness of an apple, but rather the brute fact of that which is related to being the *apple*, which is a unified entity over and above its many qualities. As discussed earlier, qualities require a unit of which they are qualities, as qualities cannot adhere to qualities themselves. There is simply no way to make roundness sweet without involving something like apples. This is not just the case for humans. For example, there is no such thing as a material encountering heat *qua* heat. Heat is always a quality emanating from an entity, whether this entity is a fire, a wave, or an aggregate of microscopic particles. Quite obviously, the body without organs itself cannot be the unity that supports such actual qualities, because it remains withdrawn in its own virtuality. Only sense fulfils this function, being a machine's unity in actuality.

The body is the unity of the virtual twofold, and sense (extension, comprehension, event) is the unity of the actual twofold. Sense is a dangerous game for machines, because of the twin principle of contiguity and rupture introduced earlier. Any machine A can be treated as two different machines by machines B and C, if their respective perspectives differ sufficiently. Simultaneously, machine D can treat machine A and a completely different machine X as one single machine. Moreover, nothing prevents a further machine E from being blissfully unaware of the actual unity of machine A, and it can carry A's components *a* and *a'* off in different directions, which may herald A's demise. For example, let A be a work of art consisting of a pile of sticks, B a dog, C an art connoisseur, D a philistine fooled by A's proximity to X (X being, say, a fire extinguisher), and E the cleaner who mistakes A for a mess that the wind blew in through an open door. Yet such trials and tribulations do not just befall postmodern kitsch. If machine A were a political issue, a war, a planet, a river, or an amoeba, the scenario could easily be the same, though of course with different actors for B, C, D, and E. This play of pulling and being pulled into relations results from the fact that sense is *immanent to relations*. Contrary to the virtual body, '[sense] has an entirely different status which consists in *not* existing outside the proposition which expresses it' (LS 21). Sense is not the relation itself, but rather its correlate, and this correlate is not the virtuality but the actual manifestation of a machine. A sense-event is therefore that which 'inheres' or 'subsists' in relations (LS 19; cf. 5, 34, 94): 'we cannot say that sense exists, but rather that it inheres or subsists [. . .] What is expressed has no resemblance whatsoever to the expression' (LS 21).

Being the unity but not the quality of actuality, sense is utterly neutral. Sense always has 'this dryness [. . .] and this splendid sterility or neutrality. It is indifferent to the universal and to the singular, to the general and to the particular, to the personal and

to the collective; it is also indifferent to affirmation and negation' (LS 34–5; cf. 31).[11] Take, for example, a statue of Thomas
Aquinas on a university campus. Humans around it, birds on
top of it, the ground underneath it, and the wind and rain slowly
eroding it do not encounter the statue's internal reality, but only
its expression in relations with them. Each of them encounters
the statue as a sense-event. This sense, being the relational surface
of actuality surrounding a body, is utterly indifferent in so far as
each universal, singular, general, or particular predicate attached
to it concerns the statue's qualities, components, or its relations to
other entities. Sense is that to which such predicates are attached,
it is not such a predicate itself. It is neither personal nor collective,
because the rule of contiguity and rupture can make it the sense
of one or many experienced bodies, as well as the sense of one
or many bodies experiencing. Finally, it is indifferent to affirmation and negation, because those again concern qualities. In a
single drawn-out experience of the statue (staring at it for fifteen
minutes, for example), that which I can affirm or must deny of the
statue can change. It can be grey now, but a different colour later,
intimidating now, but pompous later, and so on. The qualities can
shift, but the sense-event remains the same.

Much like the body without organs in virtuality, a sense-event is
neutral, sterile, and impassible (LS 95; cf. 100, 148). It is entirely
different from the qualities and significations of entities (LS 167;
cf. 94). Strictly speaking, sense is not that which happens, but
rather the givenness, the presentation, the extension of that which
happens: 'the event is not what occurs (an accident), it is rather
inside what occurs, the purely expressed' (LS 149). Hence sense is
an event '*on the condition that the event is not confused with its
spatio-temporal-realization in a state of affairs*' (LS 22). This statement simply reiterates the fact that sense has nothing to do with
quality, affirmation, negation, quantity, or modality (LS 33, 70).
No mode of the proposition is able to affect sense (LS 32), precisely because sense is *always* there in *all* relations. Sense is nothing
but formal unity in actuality, and Deleuze again cites Husserl to
insist that 'its productivity, its noematic service, is exhausted in
the expressing' (LS 32; cf. Husserl 1982: §124, 296). This explains
why 'sense is never an object of possible representation' (LS 145),
because representation by definition concerns qualities. So, strictly
speaking, sense is not equal to function: 'shall we at last say that
[sense] is useful, and that it is necessary to admit it for its utility?

Not even this, since it is endowed with an inefficacious, impassive, and sterile splendor. This is why we said that *in fact* we can only infer it indirectly' (LS 20). At the limit, we could even say that there is a 'part of the event that we should call non-actualizable, precisely because it belongs to thought and can be accomplished only by thought and in thought' (LS 220). This is because the actual unity of, for example, my telephone is something I can only realise by subtracting all qualities from the telephone up to the point that only its formal unity or its empty givenness as a unit remains. This is why 'the first paradox of sense [. . .] is that of proliferation (DR 155; cf. LS 28). Sense cannot be accurately represented, as it differs in kind from all representational or relational content (DR 158). It is not a qualified experience, but the mere unity of that experience. If I see my telephone, that is a sense-event. No matter how hard I try, I cannot make that sense-event present *as such*. If I focus on the telephone *qua* sense-event, I always end up relating to the sense-event of my telephone, but that relation will once again have a sense of its own which envelops that which the relation concerns. Hence 'given a proposition which denotes a state of affairs, one may always take its sense as that which another proposition denotes' (LS 29).

Yet sense-events never cease being the sense-events *of something*. It is true that Deleuze writes how all his books are attempts to 'discover the nature of events' (N 141), but that does not mean events are all there is. As he notes, 'how could the event be grasped and willed without its being referred to the corporeal cause from which it results?' (LS 143). Likewise, he writes that the sense-event 'emanates [. . .] from the eternally decentered ex-centric center' (LS 176), with the adjectives referring to the unextended, non-localised nature of the withdrawn body. The very nature of sense is 'to point beyond itself towards the object designated' (DR 154). It always refers to non-sense (LS 81), as it refers to the virtual aspect of an encountered machine that does not manifest in relations.[12] This relation to non-sense is 'internal and original' (LS 81) because the virtual side of the body and the actual side of sense both belong to the same machine. There is a difference in kind between the expressing body and expressed sense, but that difference in kind is an internal difference within multiplicities themselves. Despite this difference, a machine has no choice but to become committed to how it is encountered in actuality. Otherwise we would end up in the absurd situation where meteors would smash into moons without those moons being smashed into by meteors. In other words, sense is immanent to the relation and not to its machine, yet it is nonetheless attributed to the latter:

> The event *results* from bodies, their mixtures, their actions, and their passions. But it differs in nature from that of which it is the result. It is, for example, attributed to bodies, to states of affairs, but not at all as a physical quality, rather, it is ascribed to them only as a very special *attribute*, dialectical or, rather, noematic and incorporeal. (LS 182)

Sense is attributed. It is not the attribute of the relation or proposition, but rather of 'the thing or state of affairs' (LS 21). Sense is thus a frontier: 'in the surface organization which we [call] secondary, physical bodies [. . .] are separated and articulated at once by an incorporeal frontier. This frontier is sense, representing, on one side, the pure "expressed" [. . .] and on the other, the logical attribute of bodies' (LS 91). Sense 'relates to the object as though it were its logical attribute, its "statable" or "expressible"' (DR 156). If the moon is struck by the meteor, it must be the case that the moon was capable of having the meteor entering into relations with it, as opposed to, for example, a subatomic particle that passes through it unnoticed. Sense is the proof that a machine could become given to another machine. Deleuze cites Émile Brehier to illustrate this point:

> When the scalpel cuts through the flesh, the first body produces upon the second not a new property but a new attribute, that of being cut. The *attribute* does not designate any real *quality*, [the attribute] is, to the contrary, always expressed by the verb, which means that it is not a being, but a way of being. This way of being finds itself somehow at the limit, at the surface of being. (LS 5)

Sense is the extension of something into a relation. To have a sense is to be comprehended, and to undergo a sense-event is to comprehend something. Sense-events envelop bodies which themselves remain withdrawn, and give them a spatio-temporal location (a where and a when). Differing in kind from the body, sense is an incorporeal surface effect (LS 70–1). Because of this difference in kind, a sense-event does not simply correspond to the body. Sense is never essence. Sense is not like a predicate or adjective defining a body, but rather a 'verb' (LS 5). Sense expresses that something is happening, for example, the tree 'greens' (LS 6). To say 'the tree is green' would suggest that the tree is essentially green. 'The tree greens' instead invokes the image of an entity that just happens to be doing something. It tells us that there is a 'tree occurrence' (LS 21) of a machine entering into a specific relation. Hence '"to green" [. . .] is not a quality in the thing, but an attribute which is said of the thing. This attribute does not exist outside of the proposition which expresses it in denoting the thing' (LS 21). Hence a wolf is a 'wolfing', a louse is a 'lousing', and so on (ATP 239). The qualities of machines concern their actual manifestations, not their virtual being. As we will see, this virtual being will still provide the sufficient reason for those manifestations of those qualities, but nevertheless a difference in kind exists.

Recall that the withdrawn, transcendental, virtual, unextended, non-relational, external status of the virtual body caused Deleuze to call it (non-)being or ?-being, in order to emphasise that the virtual aspect of machines is not given in relations, yet is far from being a nothingness or something unreal. Sense, being the actual yet local unity of a machine where the body is its virtual yet real unity, is likewise called 'a non-existing entity' (ATP xiii). Sense-events are 'pure infinitives of which it cannot even be said that they ARE, participating rather in an extra-being [. . .] Such an event, such a verb in the infinitive is also the expressed of a proposition or the attribute of a state of things' (D 63). Since a sense-event is the bearer of actual qualities and not those qualities themselves, we again need such terminology to insist on its full reality:

> As an attribute of states of affairs, sense is extra-being. It is not of being; it is an *aliquid* which is appropriate to non-being. As that which is expressed [. . .] sense does not exist, but inheres or subsists. (LS 31–2)

Sense is an 'objective entity, but one of which we cannot say that it exists in itself: it insists or subsists, possessing a quasi-being or an extra-being, that minimum of being common to real, possible, and even impossible objects' (DR 156). Or as Deleuze writes, if we call the virtual body a substance with being, then sense is 'an *extra-Being* which constitutes the incorporeal as a non-existing entity. The highest term therefore is not Being, but *Something (aliquid)*, insofar as it subsumes being and non-being, existence and inherence' (LS 7).

3 Actuality is a Twofold

We have elaborated two of the four aspects of machinic assemblages. First, there is the body without organs, the virtual, unextended, withdrawn, non-relational, never given, irreducible, transcendental unity of each machine. Second, there are sense-events that constitute the actual unity of machines manifesting in relations. Sense-events are that of which the qualities of a machine are qualities. They are the actuality, the extension, the being-comprehended and being-contracted into relations of machines. Though both are markers of machinic unity, sense and body differ in kind. Sense is relational, spatial, and temporal, whereas the body is not. Yet sense and bodies are not sufficient to account for things. Recall that they are both neutral and sterile, which is to say unqualified. Formally, *qua* bodies and sense-events there is no difference between a war, a comet, a thought, a bottle, a chemical, a poster presentation, and a bout of despair. The body is only ever *a* body, and a sense-event is merely something or *aliquid*. Yet both are absolutely necessary features of entities: the body, because relations are relations with an entity and not with other relations with that entity; sense, because qualities are qualities of an actual object and not of other qualities of that object.

Still, actuality cannot merely be sense. If that were the case, each relation would concern a pure and empty happening, which is never the case. The tree *greens*, the wolf *wolfs*, and the louse *louses*. The impact of a bullet is different from that of good news. This brings us to the second aspect of the actual twofold, which is quality itself. As we saw, sense is irreducible to qualities, representations, lived experiences, and so forth. Yet it is always 'encrusted' with qualities, if you will.[13] Formally, sense is irreducible to quality, but existentially, qualities are always grafted on to sense-events. Sense is 'the verb' in the sense that it concerns something becoming manifest in a relation. Yet in another sense, the verb expresses that which envelops sense in actuality (LS 21, 182). This brings us to Deleuze's distinction between 'partial objects' and 'flows'.

Actualisation, the becoming comprehended of a machine, or in other words a machine becoming part of something else through connective synthesis, is what Deleuze calls 'differenciation'. Differenciation does not just concern sense, but sense as well as qualities or the given as well as the specificity of the given: 'differenciation differenciates itself into these two correlative paths:

species and parts, determination of species and determination of parts. [. . .] there is a differenciation which integrates and welds together the differenciated' (DR 217). Sense-events are merely one aspect of the connective synthesis, which in truth concerns the entire actual twofold. Hence Deleuze also refers to the contractive labour of entities as 'the partial object-flow connective synthesis' (AO 15).

'Partial object' is another term for 'sense'. A partial object is a machine such as it manifests in a relation. Such a manifest entity is 'partial' in two ways. First, it is not the manifestation of an object in general, but rather the manifestation of a specific machine or specific machines. Second, each manifest object is 'styled' by the machine to which it manifests, as each machine can only experience other machines on its own terms. We must therefore take care not to interpret the term as if 10 per cent of a body without organs were to enter into relation, which would violate externality. As Deleuze puts it, they are 'not partial (*partiels*) in the sense of extensive parts, but rather partial (*partiaux*) like the intensities under which a unit of matter always fills a space in varying degrees' (AO 352). Being identical to sense, a partial object is naturally opposed to the body without organs (LS 188), as the former is relational whereas the other is not. 'Partial object' expresses the idea that sense-events, despite being formal and neutral, nevertheless have a type of character. It is a term intended to ward off interpretations of actuality as being 'something in general'. Instead, each manifestation concerns a specific 'organization' (DI 99). Connecting to a machine means making that machine into a part or an organ, which implies that it immediately starts to function in a certain way.

This is why a body without organs is the *'raw material of the partial objects'* (AO 372), the former being that which expresses and the latter being what is expressed. A partial object is 'an elective bodily zone', 'the isolation of a territory', and 'a fact of the surface' (LS 196–7), descriptions that emphasise that a partial object is identical to the sense-event, to the fact of being comprehended, or extension itself. This is why partial objectivity and extension are inseparable (DR 173). To manifest a partial object is to assign to 'agents a place and a function [. . .] They are relations of production as such, and agents of production and anti-production' (AO 62). In other words, there is a partial object wherever and for as long as the production of a relation endures.

Entities encounter partial objects in relations, which is to say the actual surfaces and not the virtual reality of others:

> Partial objects are what make up the parts of the desiring-machines; partial objects define the working machine or the working parts, but in a state of dispersion such that one part is continually referring to a part from an entirely different machine, like the red clover and the bumble bee, the wasp and the orchid [. . .] (AO 368)

The bumble bee only experiences a partial object of the red clover, just as the wasp only experiences a partial object of the orchid. As readers of *Anti-Oedipus* will experience, Deleuze consistently couples the notion of partial objects to that of 'flow'. Flow is precisely what Deleuze means by the second 'fork' of differenciation into actuality that leads to 'qualities' and 'specification' (DI 99). Flow is 'what is given' (SL 150480). If sense or a partial object is that which supports and relays quality (DR 238), flow is this quality itself.[14] The cup on my desk is a partial object in actual experience (for me as well as for the desk), but its flow is the varying set of qualities of this object: its colour, weight, and density; its evocation of some personal memories; its precise pressure on the desk; and so on. As 'every partial object emits a flow' (AO 379), the distinction between the two elements of actuality is formal.[15] In another sense it is also real: the flow of qualities can shift and slide while observing the same entity in experience. Nevertheless, despite this plasticity the one is never encountered without the other: 'differenciation is always simultaneously differenciation of species and parts, of qualities and extensities: determination of qualities or determination of species, but also partition or organization' (DR 210; cf. 228). It is thus correct to say that machines only encounter partial objects, but also to say that each machine only encounters a continuity of flow. A machine can after all only encounter that which it is capable of encountering. Everything thus perceives a world of its own:

> A machine may be defined as a *system of interruptions* or breaks [. . .] Every machine, in the first place, is related to a continual material flow (*hylè*) that it cuts into [. . .] Each associative flow must be seen as an ideal thing, an endless flow [. . .] The term *hylè* in fact designates the pure continuity that any sort of matter ideally possesses [. . .] (AO 50, translation modified)

In becoming comprehended, in occurring to other machines, machines are interrupted or broken, which refers to the difference in kind between virtuality and actuality. Yet from the perspective of any given machine, there are strictly speaking no breaks to be noticed. Recall that the connective synthesis contracts a multitude of irreducible entities into contiguous experience. Experience contains different things because, ultimately, different machines are being comprehended and, as we will see, the perspective of the machine to which they manifest is not the *only* thing styling experience. Yet because it nevertheless concerns machines according to a certain perspective, experience will be contiguous. Moreover, because partial objects are always qualified, we can say that each machine, by virtue of being a perspective, acts or 'cuts into' the material flow that it experiences. This *hylè* is simply the total world of a given machine. Because of the rule of contiguity and rupture, it is ideal and endless in principle, as no machine ever encounters a void. Once again, this contiguity and continuity of actuality (where there is none in the virtual) is the glue of the world. Each entity is generated from other entities and generates other entities in encounters that are only ever partial object-flow combinations. From the perspective of a machine itself, it is therefore undeniable that partial objects are produced 'by being drawn from (*prélevés sur*) a flow or a nonpersonal *hylè*, with which they re-establish contact by connecting themselves to other partial objects' (AO 61). This is because a machine is never in another position than that of having contiguous experiences. This is why any specific relation with a specific entity is always experienced as if a figure emerges from a background that was always already the *Welt* of the multiplicity in question. As always, the scope of these theses is fully ontological. Partial objects and flows are not fantasies or representations of human beings, but genuine productions of reality itself (cf. AO 59).[16]

The contiguity implied in connective synthesis explains how different flows can be combined into the patchwork of the Real. All it takes is a third flow. As Deleuze writes, 'two flows could never be said to be coexistent or simultaneous if they were not contained in a third one [. . .] There is therefore a fundamental triplicity of flows' (B 80). For example, how can a philosopher reading a book and a dog chewing a bone be part of the same reality? Only because they are comprehended by other machines which by that very fact constitute spaces in which they can coexist. The manifestations of two machines coexist directly only in so far as there is at least one other machine that comprehends them both according to its own perspective. And this is how a *milieu* or context can exist. 'A milieu is made up of qualities, substances, powers, and events: the street, for example, with its materials (paving stones), its noises (the cries of merchants), its animals (harnessed horses) or its dramas (a horse slips, a horse falls down, a horse is beaten)' (ECC 61). These irreducible machines are only together because there is at least the street which comprehends their partial-object flows or sense-events. This also allows us to understand Deleuze's frequent use of 'series' throughout *The Logic of Sense* and other works. Though Deleuze never provides a definition, we can now state that a series is simply any number of actual manifestations of machines organised into parts (and wholes) within the contiguous experiences of another machine.[17]

Flows are inherently variable, even if the partial object they concern remains constant. They are 'produced by partial objects and constantly cut off by other partial objects, which in turn produce other flows, interrupted by other partial objects' (AO 16). For example, the changing light of the setting sun will change the colour of the cup of my desk, but this flow can be cut off by closing a curtain, the effect of which can be altered again by turning on a lamp. This is only possible because sense or partial objectivity, despite being the sense or partial object of a specific machine or machines, is neutral and immune to affirmation or negation. This is why qualities of an assemblage can change while it remains the same experienced machine. Otherwise, each minuscule change in the colour of my cup would turn it into a different actual cup. If that were the case, nothing in reality would be able to differenciate (chemically, cognitively, or otherwise) anything from anything else. Each entity would go mad in its own private, kaleidoscopic pandemonium.

Actuality is twofold. On the one hand, there is the sense-event, extension, partial object, or the being comprehended of a machine. On the other hand, there is the quality, specificity, the flow of a machine. The latter is always grafted on to the former: 'there is no quality without an extension underlying it' (DI 96). It is important to remember that the actuality of an entity is never simply 'there'. It is never simply at large in the world or in reality as such. All actuality is immanent to specific relations. Again crediting Husserl, Deleuze therefore concludes that all relations are characterised by 'immanent transcendence'.[18] When I perceive a table, the actual table is inside my experience. This is its immanence. Yet at the same time, the table's Figure remains different in kind from my experience of it. This is its transcendence. As cited earlier: 'a problem has three aspects: its difference in kind from solutions; its transcendence in relation to the solution that it engenders on the basis of its own determinant conditions; and its immanence in the solutions which cover it' (DR 179).

At this point we can understand what Deleuze means by 'energy', a recurring term in *Difference and Repetition* and *Anti-Oedipus*. As he writes:

> When we seek to define *energy* in general [it] will not be confused with a uniform energy at rest, which would render any transformation impossible [. . .] energy in general or intensive quantity is the *spatium*, the theatre of all metamorphosis of difference in itself which envelops all its degrees in the production of each. [It] is a transcendental principle, not a scientific concept. (DR 240–1)

Energy is the theatre of all that difference in itself undergoes. It is, in other words, the synthetic activity of machines. Given that there are three syntheses, Deleuze also distinguishes three types of energy, which he respectively calls 'Libido', 'Numen', and 'Voluptas'. We are now in a position to explicate the first, Libido. Blithely ignoring the usual connotations of the term and explicitly distancing himself from both Jung and Freud in the process (AO 61–2), Deleuze writes that 'what we term Libido is the connective "labor" of desiring-production' (AO 24). Libido is the connective synthesis itself, and it is *always* happening. This is because, as we saw, bodies without organs must be produced. This means that each existing machine is always at the very least comprehending other machines that are producing it, so that each machine is always already engaged in the 'libidinal' activity of drawing something from the actualisations of virtual bodies into twofold extensions of partial objects and qualified flows. Simply put, in order for a volume of water to continue existing, hydrogen and oxygen must continue to be comprehended in a specific, qualified way that has determinate effects. The same is true for the continued existence of planets, festivals, friendships, marriages, political unions, betrayals, and all other assemblages in all possible domains.

We now have a better understanding of three of the four aspects of machines, plus one of the three aspects of the syntheses between assemblages. To repeat once more: each machine is a fourfold. Each is a virtual twofold surface of non-relational being, plus an actual twofold surface of relational being. The twofolds are necessary because both virtual and actual being must be unified and singular as well as multiple and qualified. In actuality, machines must be qualified because otherwise different encounters would not exist. They must be unified because qualities are not qualities of qualities, but qualities of something. In virtuality, machines must be unified to guarantee externality, but also because a relation to an entity is not a relation to a relation to that entity. They must be qualified because otherwise only a single virtual machine would exist, to which all relations would then be internal.[19] The virtual and non-relational unity of a machine is its body without organs or Figure. As soon as an entity is produced, it has a body that guarantees its irreducibility. Because *all* physical, historical, chemical, political, linguistic, imaginary, literary, technological, cultural, biological, geological, philosophical, galactic, and subterranean entities have such a body without organs, reality is fundamentally schizophrenic or problematic. Nothing is ever fully integrated into anything else. Equilibrium and harmony are only ever achieved and maintained, never preordained and given. All rest is but a minimum of movement. All peace is but a minimum of tension.

Externality makes it impossible that two bodies meet directly. All relations are unilateral and asymmetric. A body only ever relates to the actual surface of other machines. It does so on its own terms, meaning that a machine's body is a point of view or perspective. It also follows from the externality thesis that each machine is produced and that no relation is ever ontologically presupposed. All relations are contingent syntheses. Deleuze distinguishes three such syntheses: connection, disjunction, and conjunction. These do not exist in separation. Rather, all three are constitutive of all relations. The connective synthesis concerns the bare fact or present of a relation. Every 'libidinal' connection is a contraction in which machines that remain irreducible to each other are combined to the extent that a third machine unifies them in its experience. Connection-contraction is the glue of the universe, and rupture-contiguity the dual nature of all connective labour. Each actual twofold with which anything comes into relation consists of sense and qualities. Sense is what is expressed in a relation. It is the unity of that which is experienced. Much like the body, it is produced, neutral, and sterile. As it is always something produced, all sense is an event. Differing in kind from its own body and being encountered on another machine's terms, a sense-event is a partial object. Being relational, sense equals being comprehended, or being part of something. Yet there is no part without specificity, no extension without quality. Expressed sense does not exist outside the qualified expression (FLB 39). The rule of rupture and continuity ensures that qualified experience constitutes a flow. It assures that the content of machinic relations combines into a contiguous whole in which flows interrupt one another without any void between them.

Third Intermezzo – Markus Gabriel and Fields of Sense

We can now compare Deleuze to Gabriel on the topic of senses.[20] Such a comparison is interesting for a number of reasons. First, Gabriel's position provides support for the notion that the sense of an entity is not some private property, but rather something attributed to an entity by virtue of another entity comprehending it. Second, we will see that the sense of an entity is never general, but only ever local. Third, Gabriel's ontology of fields of sense is an actualism in which entities withhold nothing from their relations. We will see how this leads to problems that Deleuze manages to avoid by virtue of machines having bodies. Fourth, we will see how Gabriel's position is haunted by what we will call 'infinite deferral of specification', which happens to teach us why Deleuze has to introduce a fourth machinic aspect in addition to bodies, senses, and qualities.

Much like Deleuze, Gabriel distinguishes ontology from metaphysics. A metaphysics posits some universal X in which (or by which, or as which) everything exists. Ontology, however, is 'the systematic investigation into the meaning of existence' (Gabriel 2015: 5). Since there is no a priori rule dictating that the existence of things is the existence of all things *together* in or as the same thing, there is no reason to equate ontology with metaphysics from the start. In fact, Gabriel's inquiry into the meaning of existence will lead to the conclusion that existence can never be existence in some universal domain, so that metaphysics is pointless (because the object it claims to study is impossible). In addition, the inquiry into existence is not an inquiry into 'existence-for-us': 'ontology should not be a particular study of human existence, but primarily a study of existence full stop'

(2015: 37). Here we already discern the first parallel with Deleuze's machine ontology, as we are dealing with what it is for an object to be and not with what it is for objects to feature in human experience.

Gabriel's inquiry starts by asking if existence is a property of individuals in the same way that '. . . is green' or '. . .is heavy' are properties. This turns out to be impossible, because such properties are 'proper properties' (2015: 43, 53). A proper property distinguishes an object from other objects in the same domain.[21] For example, '. . .is green' distinguishes green objects from all non-green objects in the domain of entities with colours. 'Existence' is not such a property, because all objects existing in a domain obviously *exist*. It follows that '. . . exists' can never distinguish one object from others.[22] Is existence then a non-proper property that all individuals simply have? This would make existence a 'metaphysical property', a property common to all individuals in a domain (2015: 55). Yet this is also impossible. If there is a domain in which all individuals are, then this domain exists. But if existence comes down to featuring in that domain (which is different from *being* that domain), then the domain itself does not exist. This leads to the absurd notion of a non-existing domain that exists so that entities exist, so that existing entities do not exist, precisely because the domain needed to exist does not exist.

We now know that existence is neither a proper property of some individuals, nor a metaphysical property of all individuals. Gabriel concludes that existence is therefore not something pertaining to objects *as such*. Instead, it concerns a *relation* between an object and the domains in which it appears, domains being defined as 'fields of sense' (we will soon see why). As he writes: 'To exist is to appear in specific fields of sense where the fields of sense characterize what exactly it is for something to appear in them' (2015: 44; cf. 158). Hence, existence is not a property of individuals, but of those fields, 'namely their property that something appears within them' (2015: 65; cf. 144). For example, a university allows individuals to feature as academics, a war allows them to feature as combatants, and an ecosystem allows them to feature as prey. In other words, whatever exists only exists *as such* because it features in something that makes it feature *as such*.

Note that there is no such thing as bare existence. A university does not first determine that individuals exist and only then determine that they are students and academics. Determining their existence *is* determining them as students and academics: 'there is no bare existence, but only existence as this or that' (2015: 61; cf. 96,

166). Existence always has a local 'as-structure'. This is why domains are fields of sense and not fields of existence. Every entity that makes things feature is sense-bestowing in that it characterises objects in their appearance. Here, Gabriel's ontology supports Deleuze's theory of sense-events on two important points. First, that the sense of a machine is not the being of the machine in itself. Rather, sense is attributed to it by some other entity that makes it feature (actualises it) in a relation. Second, that the sense of a machine is never general or universal. Instead, sense is a local occurrence (hence 'sense-event') engendered by some other entity that makes a machine manifest as this-or-that. The difference is, of course, that actuality is not a twofold for Gabriel. For him, sense and qualification simply coincide. Yet insisting on this difference is somewhat pointless, since Gabriel could arguably concede a formal (though perhaps not a real) distinction between sense and qualities without having to change too much in his overall ontology. The more fundamental difference between Gabriel and Deleuze lies elsewhere, and we will get to that in a moment.

If existence means featuring in a field of sense, it follows that each field of sense features in some other field(s) in order to exist (2015: 140, 225). Gabriel's ontology is therefore a relationism in that it relies on a 'functional concept of objecthood' (2015: 167). To be an entity is to feature other objects or fields (to bestow a sense upon them) and to feature in other objects or fields. Each entity is both specified in a field or fields, and a field specifying objects – *and it is nothing further*:

> Existence is a relation between a domain and its objects (its denizens). As a result, objects could not exist alone; they are not absolutes, but only exist as *relata*. Objects only exist relative to their domain, as existence is the property of their domain to contain exactly them. (2015: 140)

To use terminology from the previous section, Gabriel's ontology defines entities as their comprehending others, plus their being comprehended by others, full stop. Hence, a university *is* the fact that it makes students and academics appear as such, plus the fact that it features in a certain way in further fields of sense, for example an educational system or a legal system. Or to use one of Gabriel's favoured examples, there are things featuring in Faust (characters, events), plus there is Faust featuring in things (literary studies, libraries, this sentence), and the combination of those two simply *is* Faust. It is nothing beyond those two types of relations: 'appearances are as real as it gets' (2015: 166). This also implies that indefinitely many fields exist, because each field, in order to exist, has to appear in some other field (2015: 167).

A first problem with Gabriel's relational ontology of fields of sense is that it cannot account for identity and change. To start with the former, one wonders what guarantees that *this* object remains *this* object as it traverses various fields of sense and determines the sense of various objects that appear in it *qua* field. What makes it so that the plethora of senses bestowed upon me by countless others during my lifetime are in any meaningful way truly bestowed upon *me*? In Gabriel's words, given that objects are defined as bundles of senses, we need to know what keeps the bundle together (2015: 231). His answer is that among the plurality of fields bestowing sense on an object, there is one 'governing sense' that unifies the bundle:

> [T]he identity of an object across the plurality of descriptions holding of it does not consist in the fact that the object is a substance to which we then ascribe properties, but rather in the fact that there is a governing sense unifying the various senses in which the object is presented. (2015: 237; cf. 266)

To paraphrase an example that Gabriel frequently uses, what makes Arnold Schwarzenegger Arnold Schwarzenegger is that there is a field comprehending him (i.e. giving him a sense) such that he cannot become what he is not. This governing sense accounts for the fact that a relevant number (i.e. those making it what it is) of senses concern the object. So, hypothetically, there would be some governing sense X determining Schwarzenegger as an Austrian-American actor and politician. This sense would stipulate commensurability with everything he is (a former governor, a philanthropist, and so on) and incommensurability with everything he is not (such as a female Swedish sex worker – Gabriel's example). Yet this does not give Gabriel what he needs. It merely establishes that his ontology can account for the trivial point that entities are always determined such that they cannot exist just anywhere. Fish featuring in the ocean cannot be moved to the surface of the sun and survive, my neighbour cannot become a senator in the Roman Empire, and so on.

This is insufficient to account for identity. Take the example of an arena where ten thousand fans are watching Beyoncé perform. Beyoncé then features in (at least) ten thousand fields of sense: the individual experiences of the fans, each individuating her slightly differently from the next. What accounts for the fact that they are all watching the same singer perform? It is patently absurd to hold that it is something else that comprehends Beyoncé, because comprehending X is simply not identical to comprehending how X is comprehended by something else. That would lead to the incoherent conclusion that if I experience a house, I do not in fact see a house, but someone else experiencing the house. To further clarify the point with another example, suppose that two individuals – my twin and I – have the *same* governing sense (nothing in Gabriel's ontology precludes this). Would we then be the same entity? Gabriel can try to circumvent these problems in two ways, neither of which is satisfactory. First, he can assert that different governing senses can warrant an object's identity in different situations and at different times. This does not eliminate the problem, because it does not address how *the same entity* had *this* governing sense in 2015 and *that* governing sense in 2016. Second, he can assert that for each entity there is a field of sense determining everything it was, is, and will be, somewhat like a Leibnizian concept. Yet that leads to the tautology that each entity is ultimately satisfactorily determined by itself, like a Baron Munchausen pulling himself from the swamp by his own hair.

Gabriel's ontology equally fails to account for change. According to Gabriel, every object is exhausted by its relations, by the 'sum' of how it appears in other fields and of how other fields make it appear. It follows that everything is fully actual (2015: 264). But if there is nothing beyond how things are deployed in their current present, then change is utterly impossible. If everything *is* how it is currently determined full stop, then there is no room for anything to become otherwise. To be more precise, there is nothing *preventing* an entity from moving into a different field of sense. Unless my governing sense forbids it, I can in principle walk to my kitchen and thereby start to feature in that field of sense. The problem is that even if nothing prevents it, there is also nothing that *allows* for it in Gabriel's ontology. In accounting for the possibility of both identity and change, Deleuze's bodies succeed where Gabriel runs into insurmountable difficulties. The body of a machine is always more than its current relational deployments, so that there is sufficient ground for it to break with some of those relations and engage in new ones. As for identity, it is easy to see that the ten thousand fans are all looking at the same Beyoncé if and only if all sense-events involved are truly translations or expressions of the same body into actuality. This is of course fallible. Through some clever trickery with mirrors, half the arena could actually be looking at a stand-in while the other half gets to see the real thing. But that reinforces the point rather than undermining it, because the five thousand duped fans are precisely being duped because they are looking at expressions of *that* doppelgänger into actuality!

The second problem with Gabriel's ontology is the most interesting for our purposes here, as it shows why Deleuze still needs to add a fourth machinic aspect to bodies, senses, and qualities. We can call it the *infinite deferral of specification*. Gabriel's objects are what they do, and they do two things. First, they are fields in which objects appear. This is never appearance as a bare particular, but appearance as *something*. Fields thus bestow a specific sense on entities. Second, they are objects that appear in fields. This, too, is never appearance as a bare particular, but appearance as something. For example, students and academics feature in universities, while universities feature as juridical entities in legal systems and as Marxist strongholds in right-wing fearmongering. Call the students and academics *a*, the university *A*, and the legal systems and fearmongering *B*.

The question is: how does *A* manage to determine entities as *a*? By what does it manage to give them the sense of *a* rather than *x*? Why does the university not determine entities as tapirs or bullets? Obviously, the answer cannot be found among whatever other things also feature in the university's field, because the same question also concerns them. Nor can the reason be found in the university itself, because by Gabriel's definition the university has no 'in itself'. It *is* nothing but two sets of relations: those with things appearing in it and those with things in which it appears. The only possible answer is that the university manages to do what it does by virtue of how it features in other fields. Let's be generous and assume that this other field *B* is the legal system, not the fearmongering. This initially seems plausible, because the legal system determines a university as something that can register young people as students. But upon closer inspection, things are more problematic, because the same question must be asked for the legal system. It, too, is nothing but 'making feature' and 'featuring in'. Hence 'the legal system determines that the university determines entities as students' depends on referring the legal system to yet another 'higher' field of sense that determines the legal system for what it is, and the same operation is then repeated for *that* field of sense, *ad infinitum*. The problem is that the specific *character* required for a field of sense to determine entities as *this* rather than *that* is infinitely deferred to further fields in which it features, so that Gabriel's ontology is unable to account for how anything ever attains the quiddity required to truly function as a field of sense. Nothing ever turns out to have the specific character required to endow another entity with the proper character to make entities feature in it as *a*. Gabriel *needs* to say that the university has a specific character – and indeed he does – but the very fundamentals of his ontology provide no support for this assertion.

Our interest in this problem stems from the fact that it also factors into Deleuze's ontology. The fact that machines have bodies in addition to qualified senses does not yet account for how machines have a specific character that makes them actualise other entities as *this* rather than *that*. As we have seen, a body without organs is simply the non-relational unity of a machine, from which it follows that a machine *qua* body does not have any properties that would distinguish its operations from those of any other machine. This points to the final aspect of the fourfold, which is precisely the non-relational 'essence' supplementing each body, one that makes it *ontologically* different from other machines. The next chapter begins by showing that Deleuze is well aware of this problem, and then spends two sections on his proposed solution.

Notes

1. 'nous sentons qu'avoir un corps et avoir un point de vue, ce ne sont pas des choses indifférentes l'une à l'autre [. . .] les deux choses sont liées' (SL 120587).
2. Cf. 'it is always the case that one series has the role of signifier, and the other the role of signified, even if these roles are interchanged as we change point of view' (LS 38).
3. 'Polypsychism' used in this sense is a neologism coined by Harman (cf. Harman 2011a: 121–3).
4. 'Est-ce un formule poétique? Mais non. Chaque chose est une contemplation de ce dont elle procède [. . .] Le rocher contemple le silicium, le carbone sûrement, le x, y, z etc. . . . dont il procède' (SL 170387).
5. 'Ideal' does not mean mental. We will see that 'Idea' is Deleuze's word for the virtual essence or powers of a machine.
6. Nonetheless, Deleuze sometimes uses 'event' in a different, transcendental sense. We return to this in section 3 of Chapter 7.
7. Deleuze's ontological commitments nonetheless *do* result in a spe-

cific philosophy of language (Lecercle 2002) and a theory of psycho-social development (Świątkowski 2015).

8. 'It is not at all the dualism of the intelligible and the sensible, of Idea and matter, or of Ideas and bodies. It is a more profound and secret dualism hidden in sensible and material bodies themselves' (LS 2).

9. For a detailed analysis of the ontological clues provided by our interactions with everyday objects such as mugs, see section 3.1 of Bryant (2011).

10. Cf. that Husserl 'had uncovered sense as the noema of an act' (LS 96).

11. The same litany is repeated later in *The Logic of Sense*, and there Deleuze again credits Husserl for the discovery of sense 'in conformity with the requirements of the phenomenological methods of reduction' (LS 101–2). At one point Deleuze even wonders 'could phenomenology be this rigorous science of surface effects?' (LS 21). What Deleuze appreciates in Husserl is that for the latter, experience is always a twofold between the object immanent to experience and the qualities of that object. Nevertheless, we must keep in mind that Deleuze 1) is theorising *all* relations and experiences, not just those of consciousness, and that 2) his actual twofold is merely one half of a fourfold of which the other half rests outside relations.

12. Or, if one prefers, a 'sub-sense, a-sense, *Untersinn*' (LS 90).

13. We borrow the term from Harman (2005: 209).

14. There are passages in *A Thousand Plateaus* in which 'flow' refers to the *internal* constitution of machines, which we address in the next chapter. The same happens with 'event' in *The Logic of Sense*. Such moments, however, reflect Deleuze's habit of constantly shifting his terminology, *not* a change in the underlying ontology that this terminology expresses.

15. Cf. how out of depths 'emerge at once the *extension* and the *extensum*, the *qualitas* and the *quale*' (DR 231)

16. Deleuze credits Melanie Klein with coining the concept, but explicitly extracts partial objects from their psychoanalytic context: 'Partial objects are not representations of parental figures or of the basic patterns of family relations; they are parts of desiring-machines' (AO 61).

17. 'l'étendue c'est une série, c'est une série infinie dont les parties s'organisent selon les rapports de tout-parties' (SL 120587).

18. 'Je perçois la table, c'est une appartenance de l'ego. J'ai l'habitude de percevoir la table, c'est une appartenance de l'ego. C'est intéressant puisque les intentionnalités, les consciences DE quelque chose

sont des appartenances de l'Ego. Et [. . .] Husserl va tellement loin qu'il dit que ce sont des TRANSCENDANCES IMMANENTES. Les INTENTIONNALITES sont des TRANSCENDANCES, transcendance de la conscience vers la chose, mais ce sont des transcendances immanentes puisque ces intentionnalités sont immanentes à la monade. La monade, c'est l'EGO saisi avec toutes ses appartenances or toutes les intentionnalités sont des appartenances' (SL 190587).

19. Leibniz had already noted the same for his monads (1989: §8). As Deleuze writes, bodies must have 'physical qualities' (LS 4), in the Greek sense of a *physis* composing the interior reality of something as opposed to the law or *nomos* acting as an external determinant. For Deleuze, 'physical qualities' have nothing to do with mass or density, but rather with a transcendental interior of things (LS 24).

20. We base our analysis of Gabriel on his *Fields of Sense*. Gabriel (2013) summarises that book's ontology.

21. The notion of domains may strike the reader as somewhat unfamiliar, but simply note that – for Gabriel – it is patently absurd to hold that an individual could exist by being *nowhere*. Hence everything must feature in something else: a domain.

22. One cannot counter that '. . . exists' distinguishes objects from non-existing objects. That would require a domain in which there exist both existing and non-existing objects that we can distinguish via the proper property 'exists'.

6

Inside the Machines

Our analyses so far imply that actuality is only ever an effect and that only bodies are causes (LS 4). Yet this seems unlikely. First, as the body is but the unity of a machine, it is hard to see how bodies cause *different* encounters, events, and experiences. Second, since the body is the anti-productive and sterile warrant of irreducibility, it is difficult to see how it could *cause* at all. Moreover, we still have no way of distinguishing *this* body from *that* body, as their actualities cannot factor into what distinguishes them in their being. Yet despite these objections, the absence of universal height or depth and the necessity that each machine be produced still implies that machines themselves function as distinct causes. Deleuze is aware that the initial components of his ontology raise such questions: 'we began from absolute forms taken in their nonrelation. And all of a sudden relations [. . .] spring up [. . .]. How could the relation jump out of the nonrelation?' (FLB 52); 'how can elements be bound together by the absence of any ties?' (BSP 133); 'how can we bring disparate singularities into relationship?'[1] Such questions are answered by turning to the fourth aspect of machinic being.

As there is no event without qualities, so there is no body without properties. As this chapter demonstrates, Deleuze calls these essential yet malleable properties the 'desire', 'singularities', 'Idea', 'code', or 'powers' of machines. Like the bodies on to which they are grafted, the virtual Ideas of entities are generated from yet never given in relations. Like the body, they are transcendental rather than empirical and unextended rather than comprehended. They are the non-signifying elements from which sense and qualities result (DI 175; LS 71), so that sense is always the sense of *this* or *these* things. They are the 'pure intensive matter' and 'stationary motor' of machines (TRM 21). They are the private, internal properties of things.[2] If the body without organs is an 'egg', then desire is what fills it (ATP 164). The body and its desire constitute the 'full body' which is the 'engineering agency on which the machine installs its connections and effects its ruptures' (BSP 121). It is what makes the body a 'heterogeneous dimension' from which a machine's extensions emerge (DR 229), so that 'quality is always a sign or an event that rises from the depths' (DR 97).

Once again, we must suspend our usual associations with a term. Desire is not our craving for cigarettes and coffee. For Deleuze, desire feels like water or lava (AO 85), so it cannot be a type of need. It defines psychic as well as material reality (AO 43; cf. 38), and even irrational things desire (AO 43). If the Figure is what machines *are* and actual manifestations are what they *do*, then desire is what they *have*. As desire is the second part of the virtual twofold, it is on the side of causes. Desire is the motor behind relational manifestations. Deleuze will therefore define desire in terms of power. Desire is the virtual 'latent content' at work behind the 'manifest content' of actuality (LS 263). This is why a machine is defined as a 'desiring-machine' (BSP 132).

1 The Powers that Be

To start things off, we must first address the fact that Deleuze often calls the desiring, transcendental, and virtual aspect of machines their 'unconscious'. Much like his use of 'soul' as a synonym for the body without organs, 'unconscious' could once again mislead readers into thinking that his philosophy only concerns human beings. Nothing could be further from the truth.

Anti-Oedipus aims to demonstrate that the unconscious is not a theatre, but a factory.[3] The unconscious is not a representation or image of a transcendent, imaginary, or symbolic script (AO 71). It is not internal to a relation with something else. Rather, the unconscious is assembled through contingent encounters with machines. This does not just refer to the human psyche, but to the internal reality qualifying the being of any machine whatsoever. Deleuze does not use the term 'to denote a psychological reality outside consciousness, but to denote a nonpsychological reality – being as it is in itself' (B 56). It is precisely because all machines have such an unconscious that *Anti-Oedipus* is 'about the univocity of the real' (N 144). Desire or the unconscious 'is not imaginary or symbolic, it is uniquely machinic, and as long as you have not reached the region of the machine of desire, as long as you remain in the imaginary, the structural, or the symbolic, you do not have a genuine hold of the unconscious' (SCS 161171). For Deleuze, 'unconscious' is simply the aspect of a machine that cannot become present to consciousness or through any other kind of relation. Hence this unconscious also 'belongs to the realm of physics' (AO 323). The unconscious is the virtual aspect of machines, and in this sense it is 'matter itself' (AO 323). The *Capitalism and Schizophrenia* diptych repeatedly affirms that the unconscious is a dimension of machines, multiplicities, or assemblages, and that it is therefore found everywhere in the schizophrenic Real (AO 69, 129, 130, 135, 400; ATP 27, 35, 36). So once again, we must not be misled by our usual associations with the terms used, and must realise that what Deleuze writes about the 'desire' of the 'unconscious' fully pertains to his machine ontology.

Now, desire is what a rhizome *has* (ATP 14). As Deleuze writes, 'one is only what one has: here, being is formed or the passive self *is*, by having' (DR 79). Like the body without organs, desire belongs to the virtual aspect of entities (DR 106). The desire of a machine is its real properties, which are irreducible to that which generates the machine and that which the machine generates. Deleuze means nothing less when writing that *'where one believed there was the law, there is in fact desire and desire alone'* (K 49). Recall from the first chapter that Deleuze associates law with the idea that entities are determined from a superior depth or height. A machine may, of course, find itself doomed to exist at the complete mercy of other machines and their effects, up to the point that its behaviour and development can be predicted with law-like certainty. This is never denied. Nevertheless, even the *complete* domination, the *unique* milieu, the *sole* source, and the *necessary* relations of an entity can never be its *being*. This being, being that 'fills' each body without organs, is desire. Desire is that which the contracted and encountered partial objects functioning as parts of a machine generate. Desire is what causes machinic manifestations in actuality, while always differing in kind from such manifestations.[4]

Desire is therefore transcendental. It is that which gives actuality to a machine, but it is not itself such an actuality. It is not encountered in a specific place or moment. It is not an empirically available quality. A machine's desire is a private reality that cannot be directly experienced by anything else: 'the objective being of desire is the Real in and of itself' (AO 39; cf. 354).[5] This makes 'desire' a misleading notion, as philosophically informed readers are trained to associate 'transcendental' with a universal structure providing the conditions for the possibility of human experience. Yet Deleuze is not Kant, and the former reproaches the latter for having botched the concept of the transcendental (DR 170; cf. 135, 142, 151, 173). Instead of the condition for possible experience, Deleuze's transcendental desire is the condition for real encounters, meaning that desire is the internal, intensive *matter* of machines that comes to be translated into actuality.

This notion of intensive matter is certainly counter-intuitive. It tells us that matter or space comes in two varieties: the relational kind to which we are accustomed, but then also an intensive kind wholly alien to us. Yet if externality holds, something about entities must *be* outside relations. This cannot just be their unity or simplicity (body or Figure), so there must be a second virtual aspect that provides machinic beings with their individual character. This is desire, which Deleuze indeed defines as 'submolecular, unformed Matter' (ATP 503; cf. K6) or 'raw genealogical material' (AO 96). Yet we must not start to think that desire therefore refers to minuscule things: 'the reality of matter has abandoned all extension, just as [it] has abandoned all form and quality' (AO 104). As stated, desire or internal matter is what Deleuze calls the unconscious of machines: 'in reality the unconscious belongs to the realm of physics; the body without organs and its intensities are not metaphors, but matter itself' (AO 323). Also note that desire as internal matter cannot refer to a universal and unified substrate. Externalism precludes a matter to which all machines are internal. Desire is rather the matter internal to a machine, enveloped by the blast shields of its actuality and completely separated from direct contact with the desire of others. Were this not the case, then everything Deleuze writes about connection-contraction and the dual power of rupture and contiguity would be completely superfluous.

So, as Louis Althusser writes, the materialism Deleuze defends has little to do with the philosophies usually operating under that label (Althusser 2006: 167–8, 189). Deleuzian materialism is not the theory that everything supervenes on an ultimate layer of reality whose constituents are self-identical (reductive materialism). It is not the theory that there is contradiction within the very essence of things (dialectical materialism). It is not the theory that the mode of production of material life conditions our social, political, and intellectual existence, which in turn conditions consciousness (historical materialism). It is not the theory that some or all things are animated by a single creative force (vitalist materialism). It is not the theory that neural activity exists whereas mental states do not (eliminative materialism). It is not the theory that matter is epiphenomenal to function (token materialism). And it is not materialism defined as 'the reflexive twist by means of which I myself am included in the picture constituted by me' (Žižek 2006: 17).

Desire as intensive matter explains the difference between *this* machine and *that* one. The body without organs is only the virtual unity of a machine, and all actuality differs in kind from a machine's private being. Machines could not be different machines with only these three aspects. Desire solves this problem. If Peter, Paul, Pluto, Plato, plutonium, ploughs, placentas, and plywood are different machines, it is because they have different internal properties or desire. Desire is why two machines are different machines even if they are encountered as the same single thing by everything else. Just like each Leibnizian monad has its internal qualities, so does each Deleuzian machine have its desire. It is in this sense that a body without organs is always desire (cf. ATP 165).

Desire is essential yet malleable. As Deleuze writes, 'how are we to define this matter-movement, this matter-energy, this matter-flow, this matter in variation that enters assemblages and leaves them? It is a destratified, deterritorialized matter' (ATP 407). As 'intense matter' it is 'more fluid' than the bodies to which it belongs (ATP 109): the desire of a body can change. Why is this the case? The most important reason is that machine ontology would otherwise be inconsistent. Recall that machines are produced only by machines, as there is nothing non-machinic in machine ontology to account for genesis. So suppose for a moment that only its citizens generate the EU, only its hydrogen and oxygen generate water, and only its lovers generate a love. As soon as the EU, the water, or the love exists, it is an irreducible machine with its own body without organs. Yet just as there cannot be extension without quality, there cannot be body without matter, that is, without desire. Otherwise the citizens, the chemicals, and the lovers would initially all produce the exact same thing, which is absurd. Our citizens, our chemicals, and our lovers instead generate different entities whose internal reality immediately consists of a twofold of body and desire. Thus, a machine's initial relations generate desire. If this generation of desire were only to happen at the moment of conception, then two different kinds of relations would exist: those that truly generate a machine at the beginning of its existence, and subsequent ones that leave its private being unaltered. This would force Deleuze into precisely the kind of dualism that externalism forces him to reject. This would be a dualism of two different kinds of relations.[6] So to avoid incoherence, all relations must have a 'shot' at altering a machine's desire. That which I essentially am must be malleable over the course of my existence. Acquiring a new language or falling in love must *de jure* (the *de facto* question is existential, not ontological) be able to alter my desire or internal matter in a way that does not differ in kind from the event of my conception. The next chapter will elaborate on this point, as other matters must first be dealt with.

Because why this awful term 'desire'? If Deleuze needs a word for the internal being of machines, then why choose a word saturated with psychological and relational connotations? He knows very well that 'desire' normally refers to a unity, totality, and integration through the suggestion that something will be complete once its desire is fulfilled (AO 37–8, 349). First, desire normally concerns what I lack now but aim to have in the future. Alternatively, a teleological approach to desire would hold that my being is to become what I will be, so that the 'desire' of today's seed would be the flower of tomorrow. 'Desire' would then refer to a 'dreamed-of-object behind every real object' (AO 38).[7] Third, a more psychoanalytic notion of desire would be that my mundane desires mean or conceal other desires and problematic relations that for complex reasons do not rise to the level of clear conscious awareness (D 76).

A first reason to nevertheless opt for 'desire' is simple historical precedent, as Deleuze explicitly borrows it from the sociologist Gabriel Tarde (ATP 219). Preceding Deleuze by decades, Tarde proposed that desire is not a psychological state, but a universal constituent of the very 'molecular cohesions' that give rise to our bodies and psyches (Tarde 2012: 21).[8] The second reason is polemical. If we were to take the usual meanings of 'desire' as referring to something *essential* about entities, then entities would essentially be that which they lack. Psychologically, I would define myself in terms of the future self I hope to become. Teleologically, my being would be defined by that towards which I naturally strive. Psychoanalytically, I would be defined by a desire that I would never be able to completely fulfil. What could we do if we wanted to say that there *is* indeed something defining me essentially without it ever being empirically available, even though it has nothing to do with what I presently lack? One could take a term already closely associated with such a definition, and try to redefine it. This is precisely Deleuze's intention. Desire *does* define the singularity of entities, but positively rather than negatively and in terms of excess rather than of lack. He is thus trying to change the meaning of essentialised 'desire' into its exact opposite (AO 39). Instead of denoting something that is lacking, for Deleuze desire 'is always fulfilled as perfectly as it can be by virtue of the states of desire' (AO 154–5).

So each machine has its internal desire or intensive matter. The desire or matter of a machine is neither that which generates it nor that which it generates. It is that which connections to partial objects generate in it and that which is the cause of how it manifests to others. 'Desire' or 'matter' is just as a good a term as any for this aspect of entities. Like the body without organs, Figure, or problem of a machine, desire is non-relational. Hence every name for it is inexact. Hence 'the desiring-machines [. . .] represent nothing, signify nothing, mean nothing, and are exactly what one makes of them, what is made with them, what they make in themselves' (AO 328). Remember the problem of writing according to Deleuze: 'in order to designate something exactly, anexact [*sic*] expressions are utterly unavoidable' (ATP 20). This reminds us of the aporetic dialogues in which Socrates and company always fail to arrive at accurate definitions, with this failure emphasising human finitude rather than the existence of the subject of investigation. The solution to such unavailability is to increase the number of terms used, as lavish description is necessary whenever precise definition is impossible. This is why Deleuze also uses 'powers', 'singularities', 'code', and 'Idea' to refer to the fourth aspect of machines. 'Desire' makes us think about wishes, 'power' about might, 'code' about rules, 'singularities' about anomalous events in deep space, and 'Idea' about eternal forms, but despite such distractions these terms can still inform us about virtual being.

First, desire is 'one with the power of the machine' (K 56) and 'the sign of desire [. . .] is a sign of strength (*puissance*)' (AO 134; cf. 317, 329).[9] This points to a definition that Deleuze famously draws from Spinoza: a body is defined by what it can do (ATP 257).[10] And since everything is a machine and each machine has a body, we can say that 'everything is summed up in power' (DR 8). Deleuze will also refer to this power as 'affect', writing that 'the affect is the entity, that is Power or Quality' (C1 97).

We must pay attention to why Deleuze uses the French *puissance* rather than *pouvoir*. Power is not might. My power to crush an insect is thoroughly relational, as it requires not just me, but also the insect, my foot, and a surface on to which the insect is smashed. What Deleuze means by power is not such might, but that by which I have this might. My *puissance* is that which I contribute to the event of crushing the insect. It is more primordial than what we usually think of as being power. It is 'active primitive power'.[11] We could also call this 'potential', and Deleuze indeed equates the virtual side of a machine to potentiality (ATP 100). But again this potential cannot be relational. My *puissance* is not, for example, a potential to type the next seventy words of this section. However we call it, desire, power, *puissance*, or potential is the internal reality that characterises a machine. It can be described and experienced only indirectly. It can never manifest as such, which is why Deleuze calls all lived experience 'a paltry thing in comparison with a more profound and almost unlivable Power (*Puissance*)' (FB 44):

> So, we define things, beings, and animals by their powers. One can immediately see, at the very least, to which other points of view [*paysages*] this is opposed: one no longer defines them by or as genera or species. I will not say that a table is a manufactured thing, or that a horse is an animal, I will not say that a person is of the masculine or feminine sex; instead: tell me of which affects you are capable? In other words: what are your powers of being affected?[12]

What does it mean to define a machine by all the ways of being of which it is capable?[13] Since relations are external to terms, no definition yields the in itself of a machine. We only learn about the being of machines indirectly, by placing them in various situations, by being attentive to how they respond, and by summarising our observations in images and formulas. We thereby define a body by what it can do (D 60). Take, for example, a bridge in Rotterdam on a rainy day. There is then 'this bridge [. . .] as pure quality, this metal as pure power, Rotterdam itself as affect. And neither is the rain the concept of rain nor the state of a rainy time and place' (C1 111). The capacities or potentials of the bridge, the metal, Rotterdam, or the rain are not what they are doing to each other, nor do they neatly correspond to that. Instead, all their interactions are but signs ('partial definitions', if you like) of what they can do. Being trod on by pedestrians, oxidising in the rain, being home to a bridge, and soaking pedestrians are not powers, but actualisations of powers. As for another example, my power to walk is obviously not identical to the entities (my feet, my legs, my toes, and so on) that generate this capacity. There is nothing 'walkish' about a toe muscle. And my actual walking is not identical to my capacity to walk, but rather an actual manifestation thereof. Walking is an extensive, social, relational event, whereas the *puissance* by which I walk is an intensive, private, withdrawn property. The very name 'capacity to walk' is a mere nominal definition, as it is not certain whether that capacity is a capacity for other things as well. For example, a capacity to smell is intricately related to the capacity to taste, so that perhaps it makes no sense to speak of two separate capacities at all. As Aristotle already realised, there is thus a sense in which potential is one, and another sense in which it is many.[14] For machine ontology, it is one in the sense of belonging to *this* entity and not to others, but it is many in the sense of being that which comprises the internal diversity of this entity, as well as being at the heart of the entire spectrum of its actualisations. Nominal definitions of desire are all we can have. Insight into the internal reality of machines will always be approximate and indirect, even when the insight takes the form of a completely accurate and reliable symbolic description. Defining machines by their powers is what Deleuze calls 'ethology':

> This kind of study is called ethology [. . .] [Look] for the active and passive affects of which the animal is capable in the individuated assemblage of which it is a part. For example, the tick, attracted by the light, hoists itself up to the tip of a branch; it is sensitive to the smell of mammals, and lets itself fall when one passes beneath the branch; it digs into its skin, at the least hairy place it can find. Just three affects; the rest of the time the tick sleeps, sometimes for years on end, indifferent to all that goes on in the immense forest. (AO 257)

Our hypothetical tick only acts if the sun heats it, a mammal passes it, or blood entices it. To each of these encounters corresponds a different action: climbing up, falling down, digging in. Three exercises of its powers, three actualisations of its virtuality, three manifestations of its desire. If all mammals were to suddenly vanish from the earth, this apocalyptic event would not change the *puissance* of the tick. The tick will simply no longer actualise it as before. This is why a 'power to X' is only ever a rough description of the powers that be for rocks, thoughts, ticks, perceptions, mountains, commodities, financial markets, proteins, and my miniature Eiffel Tower replica. Potential or power is not a potential 'for something'. The power of wood is not dams, boats, trees, or desks. Instead, any given piece of wood has its irreducible, transcendental, internal desire contracted from connections with its parts (remember our strange mereology in which every encounter is one with a part). Wood can be put to work in producing dams, boats, trees, or desks, but that will never make its internal reality 'boatish' or 'deskish'. If that were the case, no piece of wood could ever survive the annihilation of a ship or the destruction of a table.

A next synonym for desire or power is 'singularities'. This is confirmed when Deleuze writes that singularities 'correspond to potentials' (DI 87) and that matter is never homogeneous but instead 'essentially laden with singularities' (ATP 369; cf. 43, 49).[15] Once again this is not matter understood as a universal and extensive substrate. Instead, singularities inhabit a 'nomad space' (DI 143), with 'nomad', as we have seen, always referring to a machine. Singularities are always 'distributed in a properly problematic field' or in 'objectively distinct instances' (LS 104–5). Singularities are not in space as such, but always in '*a* space of nomad distribution in which singularities are distributed' (LS 121, emphasis added). Each machine has its desire or powers, so that 'each individual envelops a certain number of singularities' (DI 102). As with powers and desire, 'actual terms never resemble the singularities they incarnate' (DR 212):

> Singularities are turning points and points of inflection; bottlenecks, knots, foyers, and centers; points of fusion, condensation, and boiling; points of tears and joy, sickness and health, hope and anxiety, 'sensitive' points. Such singularities, however, should not be confused either with the personality of the one expressing herself in discourse, or with the individuality of a state of affairs designated by a proposition, or even with the generality or universality of a concept signified by a figure or a curve. The singularity [. . .] is essentially pre-individual, non-personal and a-conceptual. It is quite indifferent to the individual

and the collective, the personal and the impersonal, the particular and the general – and to their oppositions. (LS 52)

Singularities are not the manifestations of machines, but the internal characteristics of which actualities are manifestations. Singularities 'determine the conditions of the problem' (DR 163; cf. LS 55) to the extent that they are the real conditions for the actualisation of a body without organs into a sense-event. This is why singularities are defined as 'pre-individual being' (DI 87). Singularities are the conditions for the possibility of encountering a machine as *this* or *that* individual.[16] If I return home from an intensive language course abroad and you hear me speaking French, then this is a sign that I have gained new singularities (altered my desire, increased my powers or capacities). Singularities are thus 'turning points' in the precise sense that actualisations revolve around them. Whenever water starts to boil, a person starts to cry, or a philosopher starts to think, singularities are 'activated'. Whenever iron starts to melt, it is a sign that a singularity is being actualised (ATP 406).

It is in various passages on singularities that one can really see how Deleuze is struggling to find appropriate terms for the internal being of machines. He calls them 'certain atomic elements [. . .] which by themselves have neither form, nor signification, nor representation, nor content, nor given empirical reality, nor hypothetical functional model, nor intelligibility behind appearances' (DI 173). He also calls them 'unstable matters', 'free intensities', and 'mad or transitory particles' (ATP 40). Of course, none of these terms means that we regress into talking about minuscule things:

> They are not atoms, in other words, finite elements still endowed with form. Nor are they indefinitely divisible. They are infinitely small, ultimate parts of an actual infinity, laid out on the same plane of consistency or composition. They are not defined by their number since they always come in infinities. However [. . .] they belong to a given Individual. (ATP 254)

Like the bodies without organs to which they belong, singularities are real yet not actual. So Deleuze uses terms such as 'atomistic', 'molecular', 'microphysical', and 'machine-electrons' (AO 212; BSP 130) in a purely transcendental sense.[17] Singularities do not dwell in extensive space, but rather in a 'topological space' or a 'pure *spatium*' (DI 174). It is precisely the body without organs of a machine that serves as this intensive 'space' in which collections of singularities are distributed. This is why each *spatium* is a point of view.[18] The body is thus 'necessarily a Place, necessarily a Plane, necessarily a Collectivity' (ATP 161). Yet far more than his physicalist terminology, Deleuze's assertion that singularities are 'pre-individual' (DI 87) is the source of many misreadings. It may even be the main culprit behind the popular idea that Deleuze posits a universal virtual force, realm, process, or dimension pervading or underlying all things. Yet as already stated, this idea is wrongheaded.

The notion of pre-individuality hails from Gilbert Simondon's *L'individu et sa gènese psycho-biologique* (1966), which according to Deleuze 'presents the first thought-out theory of impersonal and pre-individual singularities' (LS 344 n.3). Deleuze's enthusiasm for this book clearly speaks from a glowing review he wrote (DI 86–9), which is, however, not at all a celebration of a discovery of a unified realm behind all things. The concept of pre-individual singularities, Deleuze tells us, allows us to overcome a certain deadlock: must the coming about of individual entities be understood as resulting from fully formed individuals, in the sense that exact models or blueprints would pre-exist each entity? Or is an entity a result of its total environment? The first option puts individuation *before* the existence of the entity. The second puts individuation *besides* the existence of the entity. We either internalise an entity into a generator pre-existing it or into generators surrounding it. Yet Simondon offers a third alternative. He sees that 'in reality, the individual can only be contemporaneous with its individuation' (DI 86). That is to say, 'loading' entities with singularities allows us to understand individuation as a 'moment' or 'movement' which causes a 'passage from the pre-individual to the individual' (DI 86) in which the *entity itself* is truly involved. If entities possess their own singularities, then they are not mere passive mirrors of other forces working upon them. They are then a force among forces, actively involved in how they manifest as concrete individual objects in determinate settings. They are then no longer passive playthings of the forces that grapple with them. They allow us to see entities as 'meta-stable systems' defined by 'at least two different dimensions, two disparate levels of reality' (DI 86), which are of course the actual and virtual twofolds. Each meta-stable system is 'defined as *pre-individual* being, [and] is perfectly well endowed with singularities' (DI 87; cf. DR 246).[19] Individuation is what comes to '*resolve the problem*' (DI 87). So individuation is *not* the emergence of deceptively thing-like entities from a primordial flux. Individuation is actualisation,[20] and the actualisation of an entity refers to its irreducible internal reality, to its body without organs and the powers, capacities, desire, or singularities filling it. So singularities, as Deleuze has it, are 'pre-individual and impersonal, but [this] does not qualify the state of an energy which would come to join a bottomless abyss' (LS 213).

A third synonym for desire is 'code' (cf. AO 27). As with desire or powers, code always has a body without organs serving as its 'support' (AO 53). It is, of course, not just a linguistic concept, as if words would have code but hamsters not. A flow of words is just as much an actualisation or realisation of code as a flow of electricity (AO 277). Deleuze affirms that 'every machine has a sort of code built into it, stored up inside it' (AO 52). As with singularities, codes are not minuscule things, so that we cannot follow Claire Colebrook in equating code to DNA and chemicals (2002: 142). It would also be a mistake to interpret code as a relational concept. 'Coding' is certainly relational, as it concerns the exercise of powers upon another entity, but 'code' is not. The two are easily confused, leading to suggestions that 'a pattern of repeated acts is a "code"' (Massumi 1992: 51). Yet Deleuze is careful to distinguish a code from the activity of coding, as he takes there to be 'codes *and* processes of coding and decoding' (ATP 54, emphasis added). Take the example of hairstyles. Hair can be 'coded according to very different codes: widow code, young girl code, married woman code, et cetera' (SCS 161171). If everything is a machine, then so is the latest fashion trend. Like all machines, the latest fashion trend will have code stored inside it. When it connects to specific entities (via young people reading fashion blogs, for example), one possible outcome is that the young woman submits to the code, that is, to the powers of a machine. Circumstances can conspire to have the code of the fashion trend code the young woman's hair, so that this code functions as a condition for the actual style of her hair. Of course, this connection-contraction may also alter the code, power, or desire of the hair itself. In fact, there is little doubt that the many rituals involving straighteners, curling irons, and cosmetic products will have their effects on what hair can do.

As with singularities and power, Deleuze insists that code in and of itself never neatly corresponds to any actual manifestation. We can conceive of the interior of each machine as containing a plethora of chains of code, so that in the heart of machines there are '"signifying chains" because they are made up of signs, but these signs are not themselves signifying. The code resembles not so much a language as a jargon, an open-ended, polyvocal formation' (AO 53; cf. 91). Due to the difference in kind between the actual and virtual aspect of machines, code cannot be exhausted by any actuality. In fact, even the demise of an entity cannot undo its irreducibility to actual manifestations. Take, for example, a great love. Its lovers have no privileged access to it, which is why love always remains an unfinished project. Even though the love certainly has its singular character (desire or code), the lovers only ever register its actualisations. And as all lovers know, a love changes over the course of its existence. Now, suppose that in addition to our lovers, many others are also determined to supply their love with adequate words, descriptions, and formulas. Poets write endless sonnets about it, scientists provide all the details concerning its biological and sociological nuances, and critics compose vitriolic tracts to denounce the love as a mere superficial fling. None of these relations to the love would yield the love in itself. Not even the best poet or the harshest critic could present us with love's code.

Instead of a correspondence theory between manifest symbols and internal content, the notion of code suggests that powers are in a sense carved into the very heart of things: 'if this constitutes a system of writing, it is a writing inscribed on the very surface of the Real [. . .] a writing that constitutes the entire domain of the "real inorganization" of the passive syntheses' (AO 53–4). Moreover, code can be put to work in two different ways. Code can be used to code, but also to 'overcode'. This happens when 'brick and blocks' of code become 'encased and embedded' so that they only have a 'controlled mobility' (AO 227). When I merely look at a river, this is coding: I perceive the river as I do because of the capacities, powers, desire, or code that I have. The river itself remains completely oblivious to my looking at it. Yet when I start to manage the river by constructing dams, quay walls, and other machines to tame it, this is overcoding. I still encounter the river in terms of my own code, but I am also mobilising the powers of myself and others to change what the river does. Note that overcoding is not a human privilege. There can be no doubt that a village that is economically dependent on wool is overcoded by its sheep. After all, without the sheep even realising it, everyone in the village will try to attune their lives and surroundings to the continued production of wool.

The fourth and final synonym for desire is 'Idea'.[21] As Deleuze writes, 'beneath representation there is always the Idea and its distinct-obscure depth, a drama beneath every logos' (DI 103).[22] As with the other synonyms, 'Idea' again concerns the internal reality or private depth of entities which functions as the ground for their actual twofolds of sense and qualities. It is therefore unsurprising that Deleuze associates Ideas with potentiality (DR 181). And if we recall that a body without organs is also called a problem, with its solutions being its manifestations into actuality, the following makes perfect sense: 'even if the problem is concealed by its solution, it subsists nonetheless in the Idea which relates to its conditions and organizes the genesis of the solutions. Without this Idea, the solutions would have no *sense*' (LS 54). Were the virtual aspect of a machine a mere body or problem, then the specificity of encounters with *this* or *that* entity would become unintelligible. Hence each problem must have its idea to constitute a full virtual 'unconscious' twofold (DR 100, 279, 192). An Idea is always already 'provided with a specific mode – namely, the "problematic"' (DR 267). Saying that a body has its desire is no different from saying that a problem has its Idea. In both cases, there is 'the identity of Ideas and problems' (DR 187; cf. 169). No entity ever encounters a bare machine or a machine in general. One never encounters a mere body. Instead, relations are always relations with specific machines, with *this* or *that* or *them*. The qualified sense-event resulting from a connection-contraction (seeing a landscape, feeling an emotion, and so on) always results from an encounter with something endowed with its own character. So though formally distinct, 'problems are Ideas themselves' (DR 244) and 'problematic Ideas are precisely the ultimate elements of nature' (DR 165). When Deleuze writes that 'only the Idea or problem is universal' (DR 162) or that 'the problematic element [. . .] is the object of the Idea as a universal' (DR 178), he does not mean that only one problem or Idea exists. He means that the problem-Idea twofold is a universal characteristic of each individual machine.[23] So unsurprisingly, Ideas 'include singularities in all its varieties' (DR 176) and 'subsume the distribution of distinctive and singular points' (DR 176), so that the 'existence and distribution of singular points belongs entirely to the Idea' (DR 189). Being identical to the distribution of singularities for a body without organs, the Idea of a machine is its pre-individual internal reality: 'it is always a question of pre-individual singularities distributed within the Idea. It is unaware of the individual' (DR 247).

The Idea is therefore never an object, or at least not to the extent that philosophers equate 'object' with 'object of experience'. It is instead an 'objectality' (DI 95).[24] Deleuze borrows 'objectality' (*objectité*) from Sartre's *Being and Nothingness*. Yet for Sartre, objectality concerns 'being-for-others' (1993: 273) and is thus 'one of the modalities of the Other's presence to me' (1993: 253). For Sartre,

> if the Other is to be a probable object and not a dream of an object, then his object-ness [*objectité*] must of necessity refer *not to an original solitude* beyond my reach, but to a fundamental connection in which the Other is manifested in some way other than through the knowledge which I have [. . .] (1993: 253, emphasis added)

So for Sartre, a friend's objectality is part of his relation to her and of her manifestation to him. Conversely, for Deleuze a friend's Idea or objectality is precisely that which is neither connected to nor manifesting for me. It is the fact that she *is* a virtual body which *has* an intensive Idea.[25]

The Idea (power, singularities, code, desire) of a machine is 'completely determined' yet simultaneously lacks 'determinations that constitute actual existence (*the thing is undifferenciated*')' (DI 100).[26] On the one hand, at any given moment a machine has precisely the powers that it has and no others: complete determination. On the other hand, these powers are never actual, never differenciated into a manifestation. From the perspective of actuality, the virtual is thus always indeterminate.[27] Powers are always that which the sense-events of a machine in actual relations express, but the expression never resembles that which is expressed. The Idea of a machine constitutes its private 'depth' which cannot be encountered directly, but only ever in terms of how it differs from itself when rising to the surface of its own actuality:

> In truth, all the forms are dissolved when they are reflected in this rising ground. It has *ceased to be the pure indeterminate which remains*

below, but the forms also cease to be the coexisting or complementary determinations. The rising ground is no longer below, it acquires autonomous existence. (DR 28)

My walking is an actualisation of my capacity to walk, not this capacity to walk itself. Hence the virtual aspect of a machine is always 'more' than its actualisations: a machine's desire can be actualised in manifold ways. Being power or singularities, any Idea is a pure virtuality that does not resemble its own actualisations (DR 279, 201, 191, 211; DI 100, 101). Revising the Cartesian notion of clear and distinct perceptions, we can say that each actualisation is clear and confused. It is what Deleuze calls a differenciation of a machine's Idea into a present relation which nevertheless does not resemble the Idea of which it is the expression. An Idea only ever becomes 'indirectly determined' (DR 169). In turn, each Idea is distinct and obscure. It is what distinguishes the being of *this* machine from that of others, which Deleuze calls differentiation. As Deleuze writes, 'the nature of the Idea is to be distinct and obscure. In other words, the Idea is precisely *the real without being actual, differentiated without being differenciated, and complete without being entire*' (DR 214; cf. DI 101). This explains why 'distinction-obscurity becomes here the true tone of philosophy' (DR 146).

Having introduced the second virtual aspect of the fourfold, we can see why each machine is also called a multiplicity. A multiplicity is 'an ensemble of singularities'.[28] The term thus emphasises the virtual aspect of machines: 'Problems-Ideas are positive multiplicities' (DR 267). Since there is no such thing as a body without an Idea, there is little harm in saying that an Idea itself is a multiplicity (DR 182). A machine is a multiplicity because it is always one and many, without this one (body) and this many (singularities) being reducible to one another. The sense in which a machine is a multiplicity is *substantive*:

Ideas are multiplicities: every idea is a multiplicity or a variety. In this Riemannian usage of the word 'multiplicity' [. . .] the utmost importance must be attached to the substantive form: multiplicity must not designate a combination of the many and the one, but rather an organization belonging to the many as such, which has no need whatsoever of unity in order to form a system [. . .] 'Multiplicity', which replaces the one no less than the multiple, is the true substantive, substance itself. The variable multiplicity is the how many, the how and each of the cases. Everything is a multiplicity in so far as it incarnates an Idea. (DR 182; cf. DI 96)

So apparently a multiplicity is not a combination of the many and the one, but instead *an* organisation belonging to the many as such. It is a system, but not a unity. Multiplicity is not the one (or the multiple), but it is substance. How can these seemingly contradictory statements be reconciled? For starters, opposing multiplicities to the one and the many means opposing them to 'the one in general' and 'the multiple in general' (B 44). The being of an entity is never to be a One for others. The EU is more than the comprehension of its citizens, a flower is more than the comprehension of its parts, and so on. Likewise, the being of an entity is never to be among the Many which are part of something. I am more than a citizen among citizens of the EU. A rose petal is more than a part among parts of the flower. Each machine has an internal reality that is singular and multiple at the same time. Singular, because each machine is this system and no others, by virtue of its body, problem, or Figure. Multiple, because it has its own desire, powers, singularities, or Idea. In what sense is a multiplicity then not a unity? In the sense that all quantity belongs to actuality (AO 327). To be 'one' is always to be 'one of . . .' To be one is to number among others (cf. B 38). To be one dog is to be among dogs, to be one phone is to be among phones, and so on. A multiplicity is one, but in a different sense. It is a single system that cannot be reduced to its members or its memberships. It cannot be reduced to actual unity, but it *is* characterised by simplicity (B 43). The body without organs is not 'one of . . .', but it is singular. Likewise, desire or power is not many as in being several things, which would be relational and actual. Nevertheless, the singularities or Idea of a machine comprise its internal diversity, its 'heterogeneity' (B 43).[29] This is why Deleuze approvingly paraphrases Samuel Butler's *Erewhon*: 'we are misled *by considering any complicated machine as a single thing*; in truth it is a city or a society' (AO 325). It is also why Deleuze associates his use of 'multiplicity' with Riemannian manifolds (ATP 32; DR 162–3; F 13). As Deleuze understands it, such manifolds are not defined or determined by external factors or coordinates. Instead, they are determined only 'in terms of their own dimensions or their independent variables' and contain 'the principle of their own metrics' (B 39). Such a manifold or multiplicity would not be reducible to anything else, and to define it we would therefore not search for external factors. Again note that if there were a single virtual dimension, force, principle, layer, process, or realm, then machines would not be multiplicities. A machine would not be an irreducible 'one-and-many-in-itself', but rather a representation acting out something else.

If relations are external to terms, each entity or machine must have an excess over and above its relations. This excess must be singular, so that each must have a body. This excess must be differentiated, because otherwise only one thing would exist. Every machine is therefore a multiplicity: singular without being a unit of something and diverse without being a diversity of things. This virtual twofold is irreducible to that which generates a machine or that which a machine generates. Or as Deleuze writes, 'every multiplicity grows from the middle' (D viii). Every entity is produced, so that all powers of all bodies result from contractions. Likewise, power is always that which is responsible for an actualisation. Yet the power to speak a language (a mere nominal definition) is not the book from which the language is learned, nor is it the speaking of the language. The power-body twofold (Idea-problem, code-Figure, singularities-body, desire-body without organs) is not what a machine *does* in manifest relations with other machines. It stands between the generators and generations of a machine.[30] A virtual twofold is a produced result as much as it is a specific point of view. It is a local source and endpoint of connections-contractions. A machine unites disparate realities of irreducible things by encountering them as behooves its powers. My desire is not the encounter with others, but the condition of the encounter. Desire is the private reality of entities, and in this sense 'the only subject is desire itself on the body without organs' (AO 90). This internal reality is a machine's matter, its substance, and its essence.

2 Essence is a Twofold

'There is only desire and the social, and nothing else', Deleuze writes (AO 42; cf. 213). There is only the private being of machines and the public, relational, contingent manifestations that machines construct among each other. Any machine is *both* 'the Real *and its artifice*' (AO 107). The private reality of a machine is as real as its tangible, quantifiable, and definable manifestations:

> The virtual is opposed not to the real but to the actual. *The virtual is fully real in so far as it is virtual.* Exactly what Proust said of states of resonance must be said of the virtual: 'Real without being actual, ideal without being abstract'; and symbolic without being fictional. The virtual must even be defined as a strict part of the real object – as if the object had one of its parts in the virtual, and plunged into it as into an objective dimension. (DR 208–9, translation modified; cf. 211; DI 178–9)

We thus cannot agree with DeLanda's assertion that Deleuze is not a realist about essences (DeLanda 2002: 3). *Anti-Oedipus* calls desire an essence at least twice (AO 342, 383), and desire is called a substance and matter itself (cf. D 78). Elsewhere Deleuze writes that 'this ideal reality, this virtuality, is essence' (PS 61; cf. 41, 89), that essence is the withdrawn, non-relational 'hidden thing' found to 'dwell in dark regions' (PS 47, 100), and that the distribution of singularities in a depth is the formation of 'individual essences' (DI 102). As for DeLanda himself, he holds that a coherent theory of how entities among themselves comprise reality can do without essences, a notion that we examine in more detail right after this section.

As we have seen in Deleuze's reference to the work of Simondon, desire as essence lies at the root of a machine's individuation into concrete objects of experience. Hence essence 'is not only individual, it *individualizes*' (PS 43). Even in his seminars, Deleuze calls the 'nomos matter' or 'vagabond materiality' or 'matter endowed with singularities' that belongs to machines their 'vague essences' (SCS 270279). This is again confirmed in his published work, when the singularities of a machine are said to constitute a 'vague corporeal essence' (ATP 408), being 'vague' precisely because actualisations differ in kind from essences. Again crediting Husserl with the finding, Deleuze holds that essence is vague because it is radically distinct from the sensible. Essence does not refer to a simple thing or object of experience, but to the internal reality of a body:

> Husserl speaks of a protogeometry that addresses *vague*, in other words, vagabond or nomadic, morphological essences. These essences are distinct from sensible things [. . .] It could be said that vague essences extract from things a determination that is more than thinghood (*choséité*), which is that of *corporeality* (*corporéité*) [. . .] (ATP 367)[31]

This corporeality 'is not to be confused with an intelligible, formal essentiality or a sensible, formed and perceived, thinghood' (ATP 407). Instead, essence is purely virtual. Deleuze's concept of essence does not return us to when 'rationalism proclaimed its possession and comprehension of essences' (DR 188). Because of the difference in kind between the virtual and actual aspects of machines, the 'singularities of the Idea do not allow any positing of an essence as "what the thing is"' (DR 191). Essence cannot be made present. As Arnaud Bouaniche writes, Deleuze's concept of essence is more akin to that of a specific yet indeterminate force that comes to express itself, [32] which is to say a *puissance*, singularities, desire or Idea.

Bruce Baugh has shown that this idea of a variable essence per entity is already found in Deleuze's work on Spinoza (Baugh 2006: 31), in which it is called 'particular essence'. These essences are neither universal, nor unchanging, self-identical, unitary, or eternal. They are not 'stable stuff' to be opposed to change and becoming. They are not fixed, transcendent, or invariant. Baugh writes: 'Deleuze's reading of Spinoza proposes, on the contrary, essences that are mobile and immanent in material things, real and material, concrete and subject to variation' (2006: 31). He notes that 'as Deleuze's essences are not ideal, invariant, or universal, they seem the opposite of what Platonism or essentialism decrees essences should be' (2006: 31). Indeed, as Deleuze writes: 'Now essences have various characteristics. They are in the first place particular essences, and so irreducible to one another: each is a real being, a *res physica*, a degree of power or intensity' (EPS 303; cf. 94, 191, 230, 231). Baugh adds that 'because of the dominance of the Platonist view of essences, Deleuze's revolutionary proposal has been ignored or misunderstood by some Deleuzians' (2006: 31–2).

Once we see that each machine is not just a body without organs, but that this body is 'full' of malleable internal properties, Deleuze's repeated insistence that the body without organs is an 'egg' becomes slightly less odd:

If we think of the organless body as a solid egg, it follows that, *beneath* the organization that it will assume, that will develop, the egg does not present itself as an undifferentiated milieu: it is traversed by axes and gradients, by poles and potentials, by thresholds and zones destined later to produce one or another organic part. For the time being, however, the egg's organization is intensive. (TRM 21; cf. AO 31)

The internality of the egg, or the second 'closed room' from Deleuze's writings on the baroque, is a 'spatium', a space without extension (AO 164; cf. ATP 153, 388, 479; DR 96–7, 230). Being different in kind from that which generates it, this internal reality has no 'veritable organizers' that predetermine it (AO 115). Instead, it only has stimuli in the form of actual encounters. It is the 'smooth space' that is 'occupied without being counted', opposed to relational 'striated space' (ATP 362).[33] Because it is counter-intuitive to think of an unextended space, this transcendental aspect of Deleuze's philosophy is probably the hardest to grasp. Yet externality leaves us no choice. As Deleuze writes:

> Though experience always shows us intensities already developed in extensions, already covered over by qualities, we must conceive, precisely as a condition of experience, of pure intensities enveloped in a depth, in an intensive *spatium* that preexists every quality and every extension. (DI 97)

The internal reality of a machine, though generated by contractive contact with other assemblages, is always exterior to its manifestations. Other machines will only perceive it on their own terms, always already rupturing it into the contiguity of their own experience. This is the 'bare repetition' that always serves as the 'external envelope' of the more profound repetition internal to things (DR 84). In other terms, each problem-Idea is always already enveloped in solutions, but never reducible to them:

> A problem does not exist, apart from its solutions. Far from disappearing in this overlay, however, it insists and persists in these solutions [. . .] The problem is at once both transcendent and immanent in relation to its solutions. (DR 163)

In *Proust and Signs*, Deleuze likewise remarks that essences are 'imprisoned' in a state of '*complication*, which envelops the many in the One and affirms the unity of the multiple' (PS 45). 'The many in the One' here indicates how other machines can never encounter the full being of a machine's essence. Walking is, after all, a mere transformed fragment or local instantiation of someone's power to walk (that intensive matter in herself that contributes to her actual walking). Recall that actual qualities are always 'more' than actual sense. The colours, sounds, and smells of an encountered object can change while the object encountered does not. Likewise, virtual qualities (singularities, desire) are always 'more' than their own actualisations: 'the content is *too big* for its form' (ATP 286). There is an 'excess in the Idea' (DR 220) and each code is always a 'surplus' (DR 53). Any actualisation is a contraction, or a transposition of powers so that 'a potential energy is actualized and falls to its lowest level' (LS 110).

Each machine has a virtual twofold of a body and desire, of (non-)being and potential, of Figure and Idea. This twofold is irreducible to any and all actuality: 'whatever the reality in which the virtual object is incorporated, it does not become integrated' (DR 101). This inability to integrate anything into anything is the condition for the possibility of all motion, change, improvement, depreciation, surprise, oppression, fear, love, construction, collapse, slowness, speed, stability, irregularity, and so on. The relations or *presents* of assemblages are always less than their internal reality. Everything is enveloped. Is this not why the twenty-second series of *The Logic of Sense* is titled 'Porcelain and volcano'? There is burning matter in the heart of each thing, always enveloped by fickle yet impenetrable surfaces of actuality. And is this not why Deleuze, throughout *Anti-Oedipus*, insists that reality is a factory rather than a theatre? In the absence of a cosmic script (ontology is not a cosmology), all machines have a shot, through connecting and contracting, at altering the essence of others, provided that they and others have the required *puissance*. Every machine has its generators and its generations. It will never be reducible to either one. As this makes final equilibrium impossible (AO 175), *tension* becomes a fundamental feature of reality:

> But what a strange, almost unbearable tension there is here . . . this embrace, this manner in which the present surrounds, invests, and encloses the other moment. The present has become a circle of crystal or of granite, formed about a soft core, a core of lava, of liquid or viscous glass. (LS 158)

It follows from the difference in kind between the virtual and actual twofold that virtual objects have the peculiar property of 'being *and* not being where they are, wherever they go' (DR 102).[34] An actuality is always precisely where and when it is. It is in this or that relation. My keyboard is beneath my hands and on my desk. A song is in a room. An organ is in an organism. Soldiers fight in wars and drones hover over weddings. It is a platitude, but machines are encountered in relations and nowhere else. Yet their essence is never in relations. It is not even *slightly* there, because it differs in kind from its manifestations. An expression is not that which is expressed. Essence is not where or when its machine is. Essence is Erewhon and Untimely. Virtual matter is after all intensive rather than extensive, and powers are unextended. A capacity (to laugh, to melt, to move) is never two hundred pounds, bright red, or six minutes. Those can be the qualities of a person who laughs, but that is a different matter altogether. It is because of this difference that there is nothing strange about the simultaneous presence of Beethoven's seventh in countless movies, records, and other media, about a single war raging in disconnected areas, about minuscule particles simultaneously manifesting in multiple locations, or about those same particles manifesting as tiny waves *and* as tiny balls. Since the internal reality of a machine does not have to be anywhere, it can be in many other machines at the same time, and each time it can be registered in radically different ways.

We have repeatedly hinted at the transcendental nature of the problem-Idea twofold. For Deleuze, 'transcendental' neither refers to a Kantian transcendental subject, nor to a Husserlian transcendental ego, nor even to a Sartrean transcendental field understood as the impersonal spontaneity of consciousness (Sartre 1960: 98). For Deleuze, 'transcendental' is the virtual aspect of a machine (cf. AO 132). The problem-Idea itself is the transcendental instance (DR 164). Readers of *A Thousand Plateaus* and *Kafka* may express some surprise here, as Deleuze there seems to argue *against* transcendental Ideas (ATP 142). *Kafka* especially seems constantly to deny that there is anything transcendental about machines (K 39, 43, 47, 52, 59, 61, 67, 72, 73, 84, 86, 87, 88). Yet the translators of these works are leading us astray. They translate *transcendante* as 'transcendental' instead of 'transcendent'. In *Kafka*, Deleuze is arguing against false transcendent depths and heights, not at all against the transcendental.[35] In fact, the transcendental status of the virtual is central to machine ontology:

> We seek to determine an impersonal and pre-individual transcendental field, which does not resemble the corresponding individual fields, and which nevertheless is not confused with an undifferentiated depth. This field cannot be determined as that of a consciousness. (LS 102; cf. 99)

The transcendental field is the virtual twofold. As we have seen, it is pre-individual in the sense that it is populated with intensive singularities, code, desire, or Idea, rather than with objects of experience: 'pre-individual nomadic singularities constitute the real transcendental field' (LS 109; cf. 102; TRM 350). And since Deleuze is by no means a philosopher who envelops the existence of entities in a human–world relation, his transcendental philosophy differs radically 'from everything that makes up the world of subject and object' (TRM 384). When Deleuze writes 'What is a transcendental field? It can be distinguished from experience, to the extent that it does not refer to any object nor belong to any subject' (TRM 384), he is saying precisely that the being of machines eludes any possible correlationist scheme.[36] The internal reality of a machine differs in kind from all actuality, from all possible objects in all possible experiences of all possible subjects.[37] The transcendental field of an entity is the 'primary order which grumbles beneath the secondary organization of sense' (LS 125). As usual, Deleuze insists that this primary order cannot be a single dimension or force underlying all things: 'the transcendental is no more individual than personal. Is this to say that it is a bottomless entity, with neither shape nor difference, a schizophrenic abyss? Everything contradicts such a conclusion, beginning with the surface organization of this field' (LS 99). Why does the surface organisation of the transcendental field preclude us from positing a single and universal virtual force or field? Because entities are enveloped in their own actuality. A body cannot interact directly with another machine's virtuality. A world of experience contains only actual manifestations according to the *puissance* of the machines in play.

By positing a transcendental field for each individual entity, Deleuze takes himself to inaugurate another Copernican Revolution, one deemed necessary because 'Kant's critical revolution changes nothing essential' (AO 38; cf. DR 40–1, 163). Kant changed nothing essential because Kant's critical project reinforces the old idea that reality is split along a single fault line between determinants and the determined, this time between a constitutive transcendental subject and constituted experience (KCP 14, 69). A true revolution would not simply turn the determinant into the determined and vice versa, but would do away with the single fissure of reality altogether. It would herald an ontological pluralism in which each entity carries such a difference in kind within itself. It would be a machine ontology in which both aspects of entities are fully real. On the one hand, a machine is real, actual, and relational. On the other hand, it is real, virtual, and non-relational. According to Deleuze, the Stoics are the only ones to have attempted this in the history of philosophy:

> The Stoics' strength lay in making a line of separation pass – no longer between the sensible and the intelligible, or between the soul and the body, but where no one had seen it before – between physical depth and metaphysical surface. Between things and events. Between states of things and compounds, causes, souls and bodies [. . .] (D 63)

As a result of this fissure in the heart of things, philosophical analysis is a 'materialist psychiatry': 'a revolution – this time materialist [will] rediscover a transcendental unconscious defined by the immanence of its criteria' (AO 93).[38] Such a revolution would be 'defined by the twofold task it sets itself: introducing desire into the mechanism, and introducing production into desire' (AO 35; cf. N 17). The introduction of desire is the acknowledgement of a private, transcendental reality for all entities. Entities are therefore more than mechanisms passively dancing to the tunes of natural laws or other things. The introduction of production into desire will be discussed later in this chapter when we analyse the notion of 'becoming'. What matters now is Deleuze's insistence that there is a transcendental or 'unconscious' aspect to entities:

> Analysis termed transcendental is precisely the determination of [. . .] criteria immanent to the field of the unconscious, insofar as they are *opposed* to the transcendent exercises of a 'What does it mean?' Schizoanalysis is at once a transcendental and a materialist analysis. (AO 132)

Schizoanalysis lines up with what we have identified earlier as ethology. It progresses from the realisation that no relation penetrates the actual manifestations of partial objects and flow. The essence of a machine can only be inferred directly, because the matter of an entity is transcendental and not extended. Consider the following:

> We can form a complex group, but we never form it *without its splitting in its turn, this time as though into a thousand sealed vessels* [. . .]

and in each vessel is a self that lives, perceives, desires, and remembers, that wakes or sleeps, that dies, commits suicide, and revives in abrupt jolts. (PS 124)

When we focus on an entity, our focus never gives us the entity in itself. No relation, whether human or non-human, ever attains the complex internal distribution of singularities or flow of a desire immanent to a machine. Instead, our focus (through perception, description, art, science, myth, or mathematics) only gives us that which generates a machine, that which a machine generates, or the actual qualities that it manifests. Even if our accounts of a machine move beyond its current present, they can only ever be accounts of that which a machine can do. They can never be presentations of that which makes a machine able to do so in the first place. Also note that an encounter with a machine always follows the rule of rupture and contiguity implied in the first synthesis. As a result, a machine's actuality is always a translation of its internal reality (its ultimate and private properties) into an actuality in which it is fully compatible with all other machines belonging to that same actuality (cf. the ideal continuity of flow). Or as Deleuze puts it: 'the ultimate quality constituting [an entity] is therefore expressed as the quality common to two different objects, kneaded in this luminous substance, plunged into this refracting medium' (PS 47). This is not to say that an account could not be true, reliable, verifiable, useful, necessary, valid, communicable, and so on. It is just to say that an actual truth about a machine is never the virtual matter of the machine.

The schizophrenia of reality is the fact that everything has its own internal reality. Everything is a machine, every machine is irreducible to its manifestations in relations. Every machine has an extra-relational non-being, which is to say a body (problem, figure, vessel) with powers (desire, singularities, Idea, code). This is its essence. Each machine can only exist due to its being generated by other machines, but being generated by others does not imply being a mere representation of others. We are perhaps not used to thinking that when a speaker speaks a single word, this word has a 'core of lava', a desire or Idea irreducible to even the combination of all other existing things. Yet this is the price to pay for externality. And come to think of it, who would really think that the speaker and her speaking can *be* the spoken word? Who really thinks that a load of bricks, some windows, and two or three doors can *be* a house? Do we not say that the whole is greater than the mere sum of its parts? So perhaps the truly counter-intuitive positions are those that hold that the amount of things can be increased without really increasing the amounts of things. This is held by those who reduce things to appearances, apparitions, effects, representations, or images. It is the thesis of all those who eliminate countless entities in favour of nature and nurture, or biology and culture, or particles and consciousness.

Yet our earlier elaboration of the first connective synthesis left us with a question. The first synthesis tells us *that* two or more mutually irreducible entities can be brought together in an encounter with yet another machine. Each machine sees, touches, reacts, interrupts, recruits, disturbs, perceives the world on its own terms, and the machines it experiences have no choice but to abide by those terms with regards to the actual surfaces that they will manifest. This accounts for a universal process of rupture and contiguity: incommensurable machines are made to manifest in actuality (twofolds of sense and qualities, or partial objects and flows), in which a 'third' machine can treat them as continuations of one another. Each 'third' machine thus has a relation to other machines which do not have this relation with each other. But knowing *that* is not knowing *how* it happens: '*how* can elements be bound together by the absence of any ties?' (BSP 133, emphasis added). Hence the first synthesis is insufficient, and there must be a second: 'the passive synthesis of habit in turn refers to [a] more profound passive synthesis of memory' (DR 79; cf. 82). With the full fourfold now available to us, we can start to analyse this second synthesis, but not before making a quick detour through DeLanda's ontology of assemblages.

Fourth Intermezzo – Manuel DeLanda and Assemblage Theory

Having discussed Deleuze's notion of individual and malleable essences, we now turn to DeLanda's assemblage theory. DeLanda's ontology also features irreducible individual entities (assemblages) existing at all scales of reality, while precisely *denying* that essences exist. As in the other notes, we will focus on DeLanda's own philosophy without worrying too much about the sources on which it is based. Nevertheless, DeLanda bolsters his claims by referring to Deleuze with such frequency that we cannot remain silent on that particular source. Our discussion of assemblage theory will therefore also briefly reflect on how DeLanda reads Deleuze.

DeLanda was famously the first to forcefully emphasise that Deleuze is a realist philosopher, and one whose theories would be in line with the state of the art in science and mathematics at that (DeLanda 2002). Shortly after, he began to outline his own ontology or 'assemblage theory', starting in *A New Philosophy of Society*. The title of that book should not mislead its readers. DeLanda explicitly states that atoms, molecules, organisms, entire ecosystems, and human institutions are all equally assemblages (2013: 3). His focus on human society is merely a case study based on an ontology that ranges over all entities. That ontology is a realism in which no entity can ever be reduced to its (relations with) other beings: 'the ontological status of any assemblage, inorganic, organic, or social, is that of a unique, singular, historically contingent individual' (2013: 40). Its primary adversaries are therefore philosophies premised on relations of interiority (what we have called internalism), in which entities are exhaustively defined by their mutual relations (2013: 9).

Due to its many similarities to Deleuze's machine ontology, we can outline the basics of DeLanda's assemblage theory relatively quickly. As with Deleuze's machines, DeLanda's assemblages are irreducible to their parts and environments, so that entities are external to their relations (2013: 4, 10). This also implies *redundancy*, as an assemblage does not necessarily require *all* components that currently contribute to its (re)production (2013: 37). Every assemblage is characterised by emergent properties that are not found in its components – think of how entities have length, area, and volume that their parts do not have. Such properties are what DeLanda counts as the actual side of assemblages (2016: 108). Assemblages are individuated and defined by the specific historical processes that account for the production and maintenance of such properties (2016: 108; cf. 2011: 185; 2013: 28, 38–9). In addition to actual properties, assemblages also have (better yet: are) what DeLanda calls 'dispositions' (2011: 185; 2013: 10, 29; 2016: 5, 108). Dispositions are the tendencies and capacities of an assemblage. These are fully real, but they need not be actualised at any given moment. Actualisation of properties depends on these dispositions (2016: 108). 'Tendencies' refer to that which allows an assemblage to change what it is already doing, for example slowly freezing as temperature drops. 'Capacities' refer to that which allows for a completely new actualisation, for example an innocent-looking plant turning out to be poisonous once you eat it. The difference between the two seems merely nominal, as both refer to the same virtual side of an assemblage. Up to this point, the similarity to Deleuze's account of powers, code, singularities, and Ideas should be obvious.

DeLanda calls the virtual capacities of an assemblage its 'possibility space' (2013: 126 n.6; 2016: 5). Its actualisations come to define the assemblage by engaging it in two types of activities (2013: 12; 2016: 22–33). First, its actualised components can take on both material and expressive roles. Think of how the same concrete façade can simultaneously be a material component of a building and trigger a bout of nausea in a spectator. Second, actualisations can stabilise or destabilise the identity of an assemblage. Here, think of how a tree transforms nutrients into itself while it can simultaneously also be losing leaves and rotting away. DeLanda adds a third type of activity called 'coding' and 'decoding' (not to be confused with how we have defined it earlier), referring to special kinds of expressions that affect the identity of an assemblage (for example, how language helps keep communities together). Yet this seems to be a subtype of stabilisation and destabilisation that requires no extra treatment here. It is also clear that assemblages are *causally active*. They affect other assemblages in their own environment (DeLanda prefers 'at their own scale'), and also retroactively affect the very assemblages that serve(d) as the components that produced them – think of how a nation-state can affect the very people that (re)produce it on a daily basis (2013: 37).

In addition to internalism, DeLanda also holds assemblage theory to be antithetical to essentialism (2013: 4; 2016: 12, 139). Specifically, DeLanda is taking aim at Aristotelian taxonomies that essentialise species and genera. This would be the idea that individuals ('Socrates') are rigidly fixed as existing as instantiations of a genus ('animal') and a species ('rational'). Genus and species are considered to be eternal, unchanging essences. In turn, all features of an individual (such as being a musician or being tall) are considered accidental, meaning not *really* making the individual what it is. We can easily see why DeLanda would be against this, because it is incommensurable with the notion that an assemblage is precisely defined by the full history of everything that has featured in its constitution. What an Aristotelian would define as a species turns out to just be another assemblage for DeLanda. A species 'is an *individual entity*, as unique and singular as the organisms that compose it, but larger in spatiotemporal scale' (2013: 27).

By analogy, think of how, for Deleuze, an individual person is a machine, and that any group constituted by multiple individuals is simply another machine, ontologically equal despite countless existential differences. As DeLanda puts it, species are not natural kinds, but 'larger scale individual entities of which organisms are component parts' (2013: 40).

Genera, however, are a different story, and this is where Deleuze's machine ontology and DeLanda's ontology start to diverge. According to the latter, assemblages among each other cannot sufficiently account for why similar assemblages keep arising (DeLanda 2011: 186). From this, it follows that replacing species with assemblages cannot be followed up by also replacing genera with more assemblages. Instead, DeLanda recasts genera as what he calls 'diagrams' (2013: 29–30).[39] A diagram is a set of 'universal singularities' shared by numerous assemblages. An example would be 'chordata', which is the phylum to which all vertebrates belong. A diagram or set of universal singularities is a structure that determines the space of possibilities associated with a specific assemblage (2013: 30). So, whereas the more quotidian encounters between vertebrates would be accounted for in terms of their private capacities or possibility space, the fact that they are *all* vertebrates is due to the real existence of a diagram determining vertebrates as thus-and-so. DeLanda also gives the example of Max Weber's typology of political authority. For Weber, there are just three sources of such authority: tradition and custom, personal charisma, and legal authority. The relevant diagram would then be a space of possibilities with three 'singularities' defining the extreme forms that political authority can take, plus (by implication) all possible hybrids of those three. The existence of this diagram would account for the high degree of similarity between authority figures. This implies that if I attempt to gain political authority by other means – say, violence – and ultimately fail, the reason is not that specific human beings (i.e. other assemblages) do not take particularly well to prolonged exposure to a regime of murder and torture, but because the diagram for political authority does not stipulate brute force as a viable option. In short, the being of assemblages is not just determined by their private capacities and their local encounters, but also by larger virtual structures ranging over entire populations of similar entities:

> As actual entities, all the differently scaled social assemblages are indi-
> vidual singularities, but the possibilities open to them at any given time are

constrained by a distribution of universal singularities, the diagram of the assemblage, which is not actual but virtual. (2013: 40, emphasis added)

Note that for DeLanda, the exteriority of relations concerns the *actual* relations between components and assemblages, and between those components themselves. Quite simply, a chair's being cannot be reduced to how it currently features in a living room. Yet since a diagram never becomes actualised (it is a virtual structure, full stop), there is then nothing by which various diagrams (i.e. sets of universal singularities determining possibilities) would be *distinct* (there is no such thing as bodies without organs in DeLanda's ontology). It would therefore follow that all diagrams are merely zones in a universal possibility space, and this is indeed precisely what DeLanda defends. He introduces a 'cosmic plane' and states that a diagram 'connects an assemblage with other diagrams, with a cosmic space in which diagrams exist free from the constraints of actuality' (2016: 6). Since DeLanda holds that no actuality also implies no real distinction, this plane must be thought of as being continuous and populated by 'gradients of intensity' instead of discrete entities (2016: 111). This cosmic plane seems to eliminate all causal efficacy of assemblages *qua* assemblages, as he adds that 'every actual assemblage or component of an assemblage is the product of a segmentation of an ideal continuous virtuality' (2016: 111). He is quite clear about this cosmic plane *not* being an epistemological construct, metaphor, or analogy for the total field of assemblages. It is literally a reality with full-blown metaphysical status (2016: 112, 126). In short, 'in addition to existing as part of concrete assemblages, diagrams are *connected to* a space of pure virtuality, a cosmic plane of consistency' (2016: 109, emphasis added).

Quite unexpectedly, what started out as a theory of assemblages mutually constituting each other now feels more like a Neoplatonic theory in which entities emanate from a cosmic height. However, instead of emanation, DeLanda speaks of 'symmetry-breaking cascades' (2016: 123). Somehow, it is then simultaneously true that 'in all cases we are dealing with assemblages of assemblages' *and* that assemblages are merely the 'lowest level' in a cascade of which the upper echelons are radically different from assemblages (2016: 126, 123). Or as he writes: 'the world begins as a *continuum of intensity* that becomes historically segmented into species' (2016: 148). All in all, it seems that DeLanda's ontology has three basic constituents (assemblages, diagrams, and the cosmic plane), even though it is not entirely clear whether the distinction between them is real, formal, or something else altogether.

Before we go further into that last point, we should briefly comment on how DeLanda reads Deleuze, as the latter is frequently cited in support of all three types of 'entities' that feature in assemblage theory. This is because previous sections argued that Deleuze, instead of positing supra-individual virtual structures, migrates essences into the interior of machines and shows why essence is malleable rather than fixed (which is his way of getting rid of 'classical' eternal essences). Whence these radical different readings of Deleuze? First, DeLanda frequently refers to the 'virtual realm' metaphysics that the early Deleuze briefly endorsed in *Difference and Repetition*. Yet we have already seen that Deleuze explicitly abandoned this early metaphysics, because it leads to a 'classical height and even toward an archaic depth' haunted by all the problems that we have extensively discussed in Chapter 3 (TRM 65). Second, DeLanda often cites *A Thousand Plateaus* in defence of diagrams and the cosmic plane. But on that point, I would argue that DeLanda confuses epistemological heuristics for ontological realities. The references to cosmic planes and diagrams are instruments to help us think a 'flat ontology' in which all entities are equally real, and to help us grasp that all beings have causally effective yet private interiors that account for a vast array of events – be they brief or smeared out over thousands of years. But they do not reintroduce the very virtual realm that Deleuze had already disposed of in the late 1960s, because that would amount to a flagrant violation of the externality thesis that is still at the heart of the *Capitalism and Schizophrenia* diptych. We will return to this last point in a moment. For now, the point is that DeLanda seems to be reading Deleuze's oeuvre from the perspective of the metaphysics proposed in *Difference and Repetition*, whereas we have argued that this is precisely the one thing that should be avoided – at least if Deleuze's own trajectory of thought is to be properly understood.

Now, though DeLanda approvingly cites Deleuze in that the virtual is strictly a part of the real object (DeLanda 2016: 109), much of what he writes about diagrams and the cosmic plane speaks against this. This raises the question of how, precisely, we should understand the world 'beginning' as a virtual continuum that then breaks into pieces. Or the 'cascading'. Or that assemblages are 'constrained' by diagrams and that diagrams are 'connected' to the cosmic plane. Are these really three distinct types of things or structures? DeLanda tends to be unclear on this point. For example, the same paragraph that states that the world is a virtual continuum of intensity that is 'then' segmented into pieces, also states that for assemblages of atoms, this intensive continuum is 'embodied' in stars (2016: 148). What does that mean? Is the intensive continuum a functional or perspectival posit, so that *if* one considers atoms, *then* the individual virtual aspect of stars is the relevant intensive continuum, in the sense of being the environment in which atoms are produced? Or is there an intensive continuum and *then*, separately, stars that somehow link atoms to a relevant zone in this continuum? *Are* the stars, virtually, the diagram and perhaps cosmic space for entities such as atoms, or not?

It seems like there are two options for DeLanda. First, individual assemblages (including their virtual capacities) could really be different from diagrams and cosmic planes. Second, individual assemblages (including their virtual capacities) could just be zones within diagrams that in turn are just zones within the cosmic plane. If we take the second option, individual assemblages would simply be perspectival illusions. Assemblages would *seem* to encounter other assemblages, but behind the scenes everything would just *be* the same continuous, unified cosmic plane. No assemblage would be an irreducible entity *qua this assemblage*, but at best simply irreducible in how it engages with other assemblages in actuality. Yet that would be wholly irrelevant, because the cosmic plane would ultimately be pulling all the strings. This would reintroduce all the problems that we have already discussed at length in previous chapters. Therefore, let's go with option one and state that assemblages are really different from diagrams and the cosmic plane.

Starting with diagrams, remember that they are introduced to account for similarity between assemblages in the absence of 'classical' species and genera which would constrain the variation in what individuals can become. As DeLanda writes: 'something else needs to be added to perform the role that genera and species play, that of explaining the regularity and stability of the characteristics of individual entities' (2016: 142). We agree, but why is this 'something else' not just assemblages? Recall that DeLanda *already* thinks that assemblages form other assemblages. They stabilise and destabilise each other, they retroactively influence their components, they constitute a material as well as an expressive world for each other, and they produce each other in specific and contingent historical processes. He even holds that the 'natural kinds' that some would posit to exist over and above species are in fact just bigger assemblages produced by the individuals in it, and retroactively influencing those individuals.

Why on earth would we then need to add diagrams to account for similarity? If I cook the same three meals every week, is that not perfectly explainable in terms of specific machines (myself, the supermarket, my kitchen, recipes I know, and so on)? If a forest full of oak trees keeps producing oak trees, is it not sufficient to explain this in terms of *oak trees*, plus rain, sun, soil, and so on? Would it not be superfluous to add a diagram that would stipulate something like oak-being as a possibility, while also precluding that oak trees would suddenly start spawning sports cars or church bells?

As for a cosmic virtual plane, we have already indicated that it reintroduces a host of problems. Why did it start breaking into segments in the first place? How is this not another version of the kind of Platonic heaven that DeLanda's assemblage theory is supposed to be against? DeLanda also claims that, for example, hunter-gatherer societies always already contained a prefigured state in their possibility space (2016: 130). But if the cosmic plane already contains all possibilities *and* if it is how the world 'first' begins, then why did everything not just come into existence from the get-go? Or why in this order and not in another? And why is it experiencing itself *as if* it is discrete entities? DeLanda is well aware of these problems:

> [W]e cannot simply postulate the existence of an ideally continuous cosmic plane [. . .] but must account for its production and maintenance. Otherwise the plane will be nothing but a Platonic heaven [. . .] (2016: 131)

Nevertheless, DeLanda states that it is *not* real assemblages that produce and maintain the cosmic plane (2016: 132). Instead, the processes by which the cosmic plane is produced and maintained are asserted to have a different temporal structure than real assemblages, one pertaining only to the cosmic plane *qua* cosmic plane (2016: 132). He mysteriously calls it 'a present without duration that is unlimitedly stretched in the past and the future directions simultaneously, so that nothing actually happens but everything just happened and is about to happen' (2016: 132). Mystical overtones aside, this clearly means that the cosmic plane is *sui generis*, as everything pertaining to its production and maintenance is wholly immanent to it, plus eternal at that. That does not protect the cosmic plane from being a Platonic heaven, it merely states that there is some form of movement or temporality within that heaven. But a dynamic Platonic heaven is, of course, still a Platonic heaven. Hence, *something* must be superfluous here. Either the cosmic plane is some 'over there' that leaves assemblages with sufficient room to be real beings that have real effects on each other, or assemblages are illusory perspectives on (and of!) an intensive virtual realm that exists wholly unified and continuous within some form of an eternal present. It seems to be the latter, and we merely note that this violates both the externality thesis and the machine thesis.

To conclude, the 'assemblage' part of assemblage theory has many obvious similarities with Deleuze's machine ontology. It posits a realism for all entities regardless of type and scale, it (initially) grants assemblages a real causal efficacy, it roots assemblages in their historical production rather than in transcendent structures, it holds that assemblages have mind-independent reality, it regards human–object relations as ontologically equal to object–object relations, and so on. Yet supplementing these assemblages with diagrams and a cosmic plane makes for some radical differences. All in all, DeLanda's reader is left wondering why diagrams and (zones of the) cosmic plane are not just theoretical constructs that ought to help us think reality, rather than structures with a real existence outside the sphere of human thought. Imagine a group of people lost in a forest. If they come to a fork in the road, should there really exist the trees, their emotions, their debate on which route to take, the splitting path, *and then also* a diagram that stipulates possibilities? Such a diagram would, of course, be a convenient tool for a scientist who might want to map the situation, but how would that diagram be anything more than simple shorthand for a situation that is in fact comprised of nothing but machines?[40]

In any case, we now return to our discussion of Deleuze's machine ontology. The following two chapters will elaborate how machines alter (Chapter 7) and create each other (Chapter 8), which accounts for both change and similarity without introducing any additional real entities or structures that would supplement machines as the basic constituents for Deleuze's ontology.

Notes

1. *L'Abécédaire*, 'zigzag'.
2. 'Les propriétés sont intérieures aux termes [. . .] mais les relations sont des extériorités' (SC 141282; cf. LS 4).
3. *L'Abécédaire*, 'desire' (cf. AO 36; DI 219, 232; TRM 17, 22).
4. 'Le désir [. . .] ne peut pas être simplement déterminé par des objets quels qu'ils soient, ne peut pas être déterminé par des sources quelles

qu'elles soient, ne peut pas être déterminé par des buts quels qu'ils soient' (SCS 180472).

5. Not even when a machine observes itself. All introspection is relational.

6. We are aware that Deleuze *seems* to use a dualism between machines and relations himself. Yet Chapter 8 will show that each relation *is in fact a machine*.

7. As Deleuze cites Clément Rosset, 'the world [then] acquires as its double some other sort of world, in accordance with the following line of argument: there is an object that desire feels the lack of; hence the world does not contain each and every object that exists; there is at least one object missing, the one that desire feels the lack of; hence there exists some other place that contains the key to desire (missing in this world)' (Rosset 1971: 39; AO 39).

8. Deleuze and Tarde also share a conviction that each entity is, in and of itself, a complex, heterogeneous, and diversified being. '*everything is a society* [. . .] Science tells us of animal societies [. . .] of cellular societies, and why not of atomic societies? I almost forgot to add societies of stars, solar and stellar systems' (Tarde 2012: 28; cf. DR 307–8 n.15).

9. So as with desire, *puissance* endows a machine with its specificity, whereas its body merely is the bare simplicity and irreducibility that it shares with all other entities: 'C'était la variation des positions et des connexions des matériaux qui constituaient les agencements dit machiniques, agencements machiniques dont le point commun était que tous réalisaient le plan de consistance suivant tel ou tel degré de puissance' (SCS 210174).

10. 'L'individu n'est pas forme, il est puissance' (SS 170281).

11. See the continual references to 'puissance active primitive' in SL 120587.

12. 'Donc, nous définissons les choses, les êtres, les animaux, par des pouvoirs. On voit tout de suite, au moins, à quels autres paysages ça s'oppose: on ne les définit plus par ou comme des genres ou des espèces. Je ne dirai pas qu'une table, c'est une chose fabriquée, qu'un cheval c'est un animal, je ne dirai qu'une personne est de sexe masculin ou féminin, mais: dites-moi de quels affects vous êtes capable? i.e. quels sont vos pouvoirs d'être affecté?' (SCS 031273).

13. 'Une chose se définit par toutes les manières d'être dont elle est capable' (SL 070487).

14. 'Obviously, then, in a sense the potentiality of acting and of being acted on is one (for a thing may be capable either because it can be

acted on or because something else can be acted on by it), but in a sense the potentialities are different' (Aristotle 1991b: 1046a 20).

15. In other words, 'unstable matters' and 'nomadic singularities' are synonymous (ATP 40).

16. Cf. *'in this sense the individual is the actualization of preindividual singularities'* (FLB 73); 'the individual thus finds itself attached to a pre-individual half which is not the impersonal within it so much as the reservoir of its singularities' (DR 247).

17. 'C'est encore en ce sens que, dans *Mille plateaux,* il est souvent dit que le moléculaire n'est pas du molaire miniaturisé' (LAT 90).

18. 'Le point de vue permet de définir, déjà, quelque chose dont on a pas du tout parlé, ce que Leibniz appelle: l'espace; à savoir en latin: le spatium' (SL 120587).

19. Cf. 'Singularities-events correspond to heterogeneous series organized into a metastable system with potential energy wherein the differences between series are distributed' (LS 103).

20. Individuation 'proceeds by a cascade of actualizations' (WP 123; cf. DI 101).

21. 'Idea' is intimately connected to the concept of differential relations. We address this in Chapter 8.

22. Deleuze would affirm Heidegger's thesis that *logos* first and foremost means 'gathering' or 'collecting', or in other words a bringing into relation (Heidegger 1976: 128).

23. In *Vibrant Matter,* Bennett makes frequent reference to Deleuze's work to argue that there exists a 'vital materiality' *before* there exist concrete things (2010). Hence, when Bennett talks about assemblages as being 'open wholes', she refers precisely to their ontological *continuity* with other entities, as they are all equally part of the intense dynamism of materiality as such. This, of course, is a far cry from Deleuze's notion of *discontinuity* between machines, by which each body *harbours* its intensive powers in splendid isolation (though generated by) those of other entities.

24. Cf. 'This new object we can call *objectile* [. . .] The new status of the object no longer refers its condition to a spatial mold – in other words, to a relation of form-matter – but to a temporal modulation that implies as much the beginnings of a continuous variation of matter as a continuous development of form' (FLB 20).

25. Deleuze also compares an Idea to a structure (DR 183). As with all synonyms for the fourth aspect of the fourfold, he insists that this structure has no sensible form, no conceptual signification, and no assignable function. Its elements are determined reciprocally so that

it is intrinsically defined. Its elements are extra-propositional and sub-representative (DR 267), and a structure can never be determined either scientifically or psychologically (DI 107).

26. 'When the Idea actualizes itself, it differenciates itself. In itself and in its virtuality, the Idea is completely *undifferenciated*. However, it is not at all indeterminate' (DI 100, translation modified).

27. Which is why Deleuze calls multiplicities 'anexact yet rigorous' (ATP 483).

28. *L'Abécédaire*, 'l'un'.

29. As we will see shortly, this diversity is *malleable*, which is another reason to deny simple unity, which suggests being self-identical, to multiplicities.

30. In his otherwise compelling *The Being of Analogy*, Noah Roderick reads Deleuzian desire as being an 'intermediary force' or 'interface' between entities (2016: 43–5). Instead of a private reality within things, Roderick takes Deleuze to posit a 'swarm of desire around the content of a thing' (2016: 46). In *this* interpretation, Roderick is right to point out that one would lack the surplus *in things* required for them to change. While being a misreading of Deleuze, Roderick's analysis points out precisely why Deleuze requires a latent content as the intensive matter of machines. Roderick's own alternative to his misreading of Deleuze, that of positing a 'surplussive identity of objects' (2016: 51), is highly similar to Deleuze's actual ontology.

31. Deleuze's reference is to paragraph 74 *Ideas I*, in which Husserl discusses concepts that are 'essentially, rather than accidentally, inexact and consequently also non-mathematical' (Husserl 1982: 166).

32. 'Le pluralisme ne consiste pas en effet à pulvériser le monde au point d'en faire un pur chaos face auquel il n'y aurait plus rien à penser. Il propose une nouvelle conception de l'essence qui dévient déterminable en fonction d'un nouvelle critère, celui de la *force* qui s'exprime' (Bouaniche 2007: 68).

33. We obviously cannot agree with Miguel de Beistegui's suggestion that oceans and the internet are smooth spaces whereas others are not (2010: 67–8).

34. In *The Logic of Sense*, Deleuze credits Lacan's analysis of Poe's *The Purloined Letter* for this insight. As Lacan notes, 'what is hidden is never but what is *missing from its place* [. . .] And even if the book be on an adjacent shelf or in the next slot, it would be hidden there, however visibly it may appear' (Lacan 1972: 55).

35. To be clear, for Deleuze 'the transcendent is not the transcendental' (TRM 385).

36. Giorgio Agamben also notes how crucial it is to detach the transcendental from human experience if Deleuze is to be understood: 'It is impossible to understand Deleuze's concept of transcendental field or its strict correlate, the concept of singularity, if one does not register the irrevocable step they take beyond the tradition of consciousness in modern philosophy' (1998: 170–1).

37. 'Aucune notion ne peut être transportée de l'empirique au transcendantal: c'est même pourquoi la notion de sujet ne peut apparaître dans le transcendantal, même purifiée, etc. tout ce qui est valable dans l'empirique cesse de l'être dans le transcendantal' (LAT 89–90).

38. The terms 'psychiatry' and 'unconscious' make it tempting to read the call for a materialist psychiatry as if it does *not* concern ontology. One can then read it as, for example, a call to introduce Marxist historical materialism into psychoanalysis. Guillaume Sibertin-Blanc explores this option (2010: 16, 20), and therefore cannot but wonder why Deleuze uses 'schizophrenia' in a metaphysical sense (2010: 56). In the Marx–Freud interpretation, schizophrenia can only indicate a dual condition of 1) schizophrenic pathology as the limit of subjective lived experience, and 2) schizophrenia as a limit of objective social codifications determining human desire (2010: 59). This confirms that once the ontological meaning of schizophrenia is disregarded, large parts of *Anti-Oedipus* become unintelligible. Moreover, *if* schizophrenia were a universal condition of a duality between subjective desire and objective social conditions, then the objects of our world would always be the mere representation or intersection of two things: material conditions and human desire. Objects would thus be reduced to two (types of) relations, forcing one to claim that *Anti-Oedipus* breaks with Deleuze's dictum that relations are external to terms.

39. Synonyms are 'phylum', 'body-plan', 'phase-space', 'possibility space', and 'topological structure' (DeLanda 2013: 29).

40. Note that in *The Rise of Realism*, a dialogue with Graham Harman published in book form, DeLanda seriously downplays the role that diagrams and the cosmic plane play in his ontology.

7

Machines and Change

As we noted at the end of the previous chapter, there must be a second synthesis to account for *how* entities manage to truly affect each other. As Deleuze writes,

> We cannot avoid the necessary conclusion – *that there must be another time in which the first synthesis of time can occur*. By insisting upon the finitude of contraction, we have shown the effect; we have by no means shown why the present passes [. . .] The first synthesis, that of habit, is truly the foundation of time; but we must distinguish the foundation from the ground. (DR 79)

Hence, we now move on to the second, disjunctive synthesis, which details how desire is the 'past' of relations in the sense of being that by which relations come to be, and that into which relations pass in a certain sense. We will also see that Deleuze's famous concept of 'becoming' is precisely meant to call attention to how relations can leave their mark on the essence of entities.

1 The Disjunctive Synthesis

Each relation concerns a comprehension of something by something else, and in this sense each relation is a present. Each present relation is an actualisation of the virtual aspect of machines (DR 83). Conversely, as they are non-relational, we can say that 'virtual objects belong essentially to the past [. . .] Virtual objects are shreds of pure past' (DR 101). This does not mean that your manifestations exist today and your real internal properties or singularities existed last year. It means that the two differ in kind, and that a power or Idea as such is never present to another machine. 'Past' thus has two senses. First, it is that which is at work in a relation without entering into it. Second, since each Idea or power must be the result of a contraction of something else, any desire at work must have been produced previously. The current *puissance* of a machine must have been fabricated earlier, but this current *puissance* is, of course, not to be found as such in that earlier moment. My capacity to speak French is not an empirically available object in Paris in 2013. Nor can it be found as an empirical object inside the machines that are regenerating or maintaining it currently. Nevertheless, my *puissance* must be at work in whatever present finds me speaking French. It is in this sense that a desire belongs to the pure past while being contemporaneous with its actualisations into a present:

> The virtual object is never past in relation to a new present, any more than it is past in relation to a present which it was. It is past as the contemporary of the present which it is, in a frozen present; as though lacking on the one hand the part which, on the other hand, it is at the same time, as though displaced while still in place [. . .] Contemporaneous with itself as present, being itself its own past, pre-existing every present which passes in the real series, the virtual object belongs to the pure past. (DR 102; cf. 81, 83; B 58–9)

The second and disjunctive synthesis concerns precisely this past which 'causes the present to pass' (DR 79), this 'pure element of the past' or '*a priori* past' (DR 81). For each machine, this past is the 'in itself of being' (B 55) as a 'substantial temporal element [. . .] playing the role of ground' (DR 82; cf. 88). Despite being functioning as ground, the difference in kind between virtual and actual always remains intact: 'you will never compose the past with presents, no matter what they may be' (B 57). As we noted earlier, even an infinity of things relating to a house cannot stand in for the house itself. Past and present always remain separated by a 'caesura which distributes a non-symmetrical before and after' (DR 89; cf. SK 210378).

Why is this synthesis disjunctive? The connective synthesis concerns the fact that each relation is a relation of a body (a point of view) with a machine (or machines) contracted into an actual, contiguous manifestation. The disjunctive aspect concerns the fact by which such a thing can happen. It concerns Ideas, as the singularities or powers of a body determine what it can do. What it can do is entertain certain relations, for which its internal reality is the reason. Disjunctive synthesis tells us that a relation is not just the contraction of other machines into actuality, but that this happens because of an activation of the powers of a machine. Here we need to remind ourselves that relations are unilateral and asymmetric, because direct Figure–Figure interaction between two bodies is impossible due to externality. I encounter the river, but the river need not encounter me. For the river and I to encounter each other requires at least two relations, with both entities registering the other on their own terms. The river, after all, does not encounter me as a raucous fluid that engulfs it. So in each relation, the disjunctive synthesis refers to the Idea of the machine that is functioning as point of view. The caesura thus marks 'the present of metamorphosis, a becoming-equal to the act' (DR 89). A relation marks the point at which the capacities of a machine become involved in something it is confronted with, in something it has to deal with. This unilateralisation is by no means an oversimplification of reality. In any specific encounter, countless machines will be at work, and the very fact that all contact is indirect will create monstrous patchworks of distributed agency everywhere. To give a very simple example, I may not have the capacity to register the existence of a certain chemical. Apples, however, may be able to respond to it, and contract the chemical in such a way that their composition alters. Suppose that this result is something I *can* register, causing me to be poisoned by apples sprayed with too many pesticides. If my severe apple poisoning motivates me to find out what is turning apples into toxic danger balls, I must design pieces of equipment that can function as intermediaries between me and the chemicals I cannot register. My instruments must contract the chemicals into something that I can contract in turn, or they must function as parts of me that generate a capacity to see the chemicals for myself. And at every step along the way, countless other machines can intervene, including farmers, insects, funding, the pesticide lobby, colleagues, textbooks on chemistry, patents, and so on.

Because of the difference in kind between virtual twofolds and actual manifestations, 'what defines desiring-machines is precisely their capacity for an unlimited number of connections, in every sense and in all directions. It is for this very reason that they are machines' (BSP 121). If desire were no 'more' than relational manifestations, entities would be reducible to their relations. Reality would be internalist rather than externalist. Being would be functional, whereas everything so far tells us the precise opposite, namely that even something as utterly utilitarian as a table is 'not intended for any specific purpose, for anything one expects of a table' (AO 17). This means that the disjunction implied in relations is not exclusive. It is not the case that a power can be actualised in only six specific ways, or even in only one way at a time. In both those cases the Idea of a machine would again be functionally defined and reduced to its (possible) local relations. Instead, 'disjunctions, by the very fact that they are disjunctions, are inclusive' (AO 56; cf. 77). The same internal reality of the table can be the ground of its encounter with me, with a small particle, with a beam of light, and with an insect. Likewise, I can use my capacities to run, to walk, to stroll, and to jump. Moreover, I can use the same powers at different moments and in different encounters. In addition, different machines can synthesise different encounters with the same machine simultaneously. The fact that I encounter the table on my own terms does not preclude that another entity encounters the table (or part of it) as yet another partial object in another relation characterised by other qualities. In all such cases, the inclusivity of disjunction points to the fact that the internal reality of entities is not reducible to their manifestation in relations. In principle, a relation never fully absorbs an entity in its being encountered, and conversely it cannot fully deploy an entity in having an encounter. Hence, as we saw earlier, the idea that each machine can in principle have an unlimited number of relations or connections.

Hence also Deleuze's tendency to refer to the second synthesis in terms of a specific understanding of the notion 'either/or' (cf. AO 86). If disjunction were exclusive, then defining a machine's being in terms of 'either/or' would indicate that a machine can only do X or Y, and only one at a time. This would violate externality, as the being of a machine would then neatly correspond with precisely two manifestations. Conversely, if disjunction is inclusive, 'either/or' refers to 'the system of possible permutations between differences that always amount to the same as they shift and slide about' (AO 24). In other words, the powers of an entity never correspond to any specific relations, but their exercise *does* result in manifestations of entities that are contiguous with the experienced world of a machine. Another way of putting this is that the number of relations that a body can enter into is infinite in principle.[1] It can do either this, or that, or that, or that, . . . and so on (which does not mean that any assemblage can do everything). This is precisely what Deleuze is after when asking readers to 'establish a logic of the AND, overthrow ontology, do away with foundations, nullify endings and beginnings' (ATP 25). Remember that in this specific passage, ontology means 'metaphysics' as we have defined it. Deleuze demands that we let go of the idea that a single relation or limited set of relations would define the being of entities (as foundations, endings, and beginnings). Instead, all connections between machines are disjunctive, which is to say local manifestations of virtual essences that remain irreducible to these essences. Deleuze is even explicit in that *'relations are exterior to their terms'* is the reason why the copula '"and" dethrones the interiority of the verb "is"' (DI 163; cf. D 55–7).

The irreducibility of a machine's distribution of singularities to its actualisations is why humans are, for example, able to waver. As Deleuze writes, 'the mouth of the anorexic wavers between several functions: its possessor is uncertain as to whether it is an eating-machine, an anal machine, a talking-machine, or a breathing-machine' (AO 11). Or elsewhere:

> An organ may have connections that associate it with several different flows; it may waver between several functions [. . .] All sorts of functional questions thus arise: What flow to break? Where to interrupt it? How and by what means? [. . .] The data, the bits of information recorded, and their transmission form a grid of disjunctions of a type that differs from the previous connections. (AO 52)

Even a lifetime of eating and speaking cannot undo the fact that a mouth can also be put to work in throwing up. As with powers, *puissance*, and potential, Deleuze's descriptions of the disjunctive nature of synthesis comes with the warning that 'the only danger in all this is that the virtual could be confused with the possible' (DR 211; cf. 212; DI 101). There are two reasons for this warning. First, 'the possible has no reality (although it may have an actuality); conversely, the virtual is not actual, but *as such possesses a reality*' (B 96). A possibility is by definition something that is not yet real. The virtual twofold, being the real internal matter or Idea of an entity, is fully real, so it is not possible. Second, a possibility is a possibility *of something*. If virtual essence were possibility, it would therefore refer to something else, which would make it relational, representational, internalist, and reducible.[2] Possibilities do, of course, exist, but they are not the being of things themselves (TRM 234). In fact, for every machine there are two interrelated types of possibilities. First, there is the infinity of possible encounters that the machine could undergo given its current capacities. Second, there are all the possible alterations that its desire could undergo as a result of these encounters.

Being at the root of each disjunction, the virtual essence of a machine is a *cause*.[3] It is the reason why a machine is able to have a specific encounter. Deleuze frequently insists on this point, for example in saying that the transcendental field has genetic power (LS 99). He writes that 'extensity as a whole comes from the depths' (DR 229), that 'a quality is always a sign or an event that rises from the depths' (DR 97), that desire is the excessive cause of processes and productions,[4] that all functioning of things is determined by power (DR 174), that corporeal causes produce sense (LS 86, 95), that with regard to singularities, '*sense* depends on the distinction and distribution of these brilliant points in the Idea' (DI 100; cf. 175), that singularities 'preside over the genesis of the solutions of the equation' (LS 54; cf. DR 75), that singularities are like 'little selves which contemplate and which render possible both the action and the active subject' (DR 75), that code 'determines the respective qualities of the flows passing through the socius' (AO 284), that a partial object is always a function of the unconscious (AO 370), that the depth of a full body has the '*power to organize surfaces and to envelop itself within surfaces*' (LS 124), that 'causes are referred in depth to a unity which is proper to them' (LS 169), that an Idea 'constitutes the sense of all that it produces' (DR 155), that desire 'is the internal causality of an image with respect to the existence of the object or the corresponding state of affairs' (LS 13), or simply that 'desire produces reality' (AO 43; cf. 151–3). This brief litany should erase any lingering doubts in readers who still resist the notion that Deleuze is a relatively classical thinker of essences that function as the ground for events.

The connective synthesis, in which a body as point of view contracts other machines into its actual experience of them, demanded further explanation: how was this possible? The disjunctive synthesis provides the answer to this question. It is the code, desire, power, Idea, or singularities of a machine, its essence or internal matter, that acts as the cause of relations. The contiguity of a world of experience is what Deleuze calls bare and material repetition: nothing will ever encounter anything but that which its point of view allows. Yet this material repetition is rooted in a 'clothed' repetition hidden beneath the envelopes of actuality, which is differenciation itself, or the jump from the virtual to the actual:

> [E]very time, material repetition results from the more profound repetition which unfolds in depth and produces it as an effect, like an external envelope or a detachable shell which loses all meaning and all capacity to reproduce itself once it is no longer animated by the other repetition which is its *cause*. In this manner, the clothed lies underneath the bare, and produces or excretes it as though it were the effect of its own secretion. The secret repetition surrounds itself with a mechanical and bare repetition [. . .] (DR 289; cf. 20)

Yet there is more to disjunctive synthesis than this. After all, if disjunctive synthesis were merely to point us to how code can function as ground, it would not be a synthesis at all. The connective synthesis would do all the synthesising by bringing irreducible rhizomes together in their being apprehended by yet another multiplicity. But the disjunctive matter of that other multiplicity would just sit there and let it all happen. So what is actually being synthesised in the second synthesis?

Recall the strange mereology of machinic being. Any relation whatsoever is a connection, contraction, or contemplation of mutually exclusive machines into a contiguous actual manifestation. To encounter is to bring others together in a relation with you, without these others having this relation to each other. We are citizens of the world, but I am not a citizen of you. Hydrogen and oxygen are components of water, but oxygen is not a component of hydrogen. I perceive a plethora of things as a landscape, but these things are not this landscape for each other. Furthermore, connective synthesis does not differentiate between what is empirically inside and outside a machine. Based on my current capacities, code, or Idea, I connect to both organs inside me and objects outside me. Ontologically, anything contracted into an encounter with me is part of me. Also recall that every machine must be produced by other machines, and that it is immediately irreducible to its component parts once this happens. When at least two other machines produce a new machine, they do not just produce a body without organs, as that would mean that every production would at first be the production of the exact same (impossible) one-fold thing, making it unintelligible why different things exist. To produce is to produce a full fourfold: a machine with a body without organs and singularities that can only be encountered in terms of partial objects and flow or qualified sense-events. As being produced by other machines means using these machines as parts, being produced implies comprehending other machines. As we have seen, comprehension is a comprehension of a qualified sense-event, as all contact must be indirect. So producing a machine must simultaneously mean being comprehended by that machine, and comprehending means to contract, to connect, to carry out the first synthesis. Hence any relation with any partial object can participate in the increase, decrease, or alteration of a machine's code, desire, or singularities. This is the full sense of 'contraction'. As we cited earlier, a plant 'contemplates water, earth, nitrogen, carbon, chlorides, and sulphates, and it contracts them in order to acquire its own concept and fill itself (enjoyment)' (WP 105). What we must here understand is that what a plant ultimately contracts from its various parts is the very code that informs its point of view.

If the initial progenitors of a machine produce an entity with an internal reality of its own, and if this production goes by way of relations that are not different in kind from subsequent relations that the machine entertains during its further existence, then all these relations have a shot at altering a machine's code.[5] The second, disjunctive synthesis points to the fact that while connectively, the powers of a machine underlie that which a machine encounters in actuality, the same actuality is having its effect on those very same singularities or desire (which can vary from being nigh irrelevant to utterly overpowering). For example, many machines are contracted in my study of French. These include textbooks, alphabets, lectures, dramatic *chansons*, elements of other languages, vague memories of Latin words, and so on. While I study French, I do so based on my powers. But the price to pay for connecting to these machines is that they become temporary parts of me, which is to say that they can alter my powers. This is of course obvious, because otherwise nobody could ever learn a new language, no castle could be modified to withstand cannon fire, and no hurricane could gain enough strength to deterritorialise cows. Deleuze indicates this with the following passage:

> Production is not recorded in the same way it is produced, however. Or rather, it is not reproduced within the apparent objective move-

ment in the same way in which it is produced within the process of constitution. In fact, we have passed imperceptibly into a domain of the production of recording, whose law is not the same as that of the production of production. The law governing the latter was connective synthesis or coupling. But when the productive *connections* pass from machines to the body without organs [. . .] it would seem that they then come under another law that expresses a *distribution* in relation to the nonproductive element as a 'natural or divine presupposition'. Machines attach themselves to the body without organs as so many points of disjunction, between which an entire network of new syntheses is now woven, marking the surface off into co-ordinates, like a grid. The 'either . . . or . . . or' of the schizophrenic takes over from the 'and then' [. . .] (AO 23)

Connections are always connections to parts. A machine's parts generate its powers, so that the flip side of connections is recording or registration, terms Deleuze uses for the second synthesis throughout *Anti-Oedipus*.[6] That which is recorded is desire or the distribution of singularities pertaining to a machine. So, while a machine undergoes a connection and contracts machines into an encounter, it also undergoes variation in the very internal matter that grounds this connection, possibly allowing new connective syntheses with these or other machines. Everything we wrote about the 'logic of the AND' and about the Deleuzian 'either . . . or' is further intensified by this insight. Most importantly, it shows how a body without organs can gain or alter its matter by appropriating entities, and that this appropriation is rather a structural feature of relations:

The body without organs now falls back on desiring-production, attracts it, and appropriates it for its own. The organ-machines now cling to the body without organs as though it were a fencer's padded jacket, or as though these organ-machines were medals pinned onto the jersey of a wrestler who makes them jingle as he starts toward his opponent. An attraction-machine now takes the place, or may take the place, of a repulsion-machine: a miraculating-machine succeeding the paranoiac machine. But what is meant here by 'succeeding'? The two coexist, rather [. . .] (AO 23)

On the one hand, a machine is a paranoiac, because the body without organs is irreducible to anything else. Like a paranoiac obsessed with eluding 'the system', the body without organs eludes all others. The body without organs keeps others at a safe distance by virtue of the difference in kind between its virtuality and their actuality. It is a point of view on others, not these others themselves. This pertains to the connective synthesis, which establishes a contiguous world of organ-entities and little else. Hence the body is 'the artist of the large molar aggregates, the statistical formations of gregariousness, the phenomena of organized crowds' (AO 320).

Yet the virtual is always a twofold, and a body's desire is far more promiscuous than the body itself. Every connection implies that something else has a shot at altering it. As behooves a promiscuous entity, the alterations, additions, or subtractions in the machine's Idea are by no means beholden to their sources, as the virtual differs in kind from the actual. Actual surfaces of entities have a shot at altering the virtual properties of others, but they cannot rely on any subsequent loyalty. No ship takes automatic care of its own wooden components. Since it concerns the creation of intensive code from extensive encounters, Deleuze also calls this aspect of the second synthesis 'miraculating', 'mystic', 'fetishistic', 'perverted', and 'bewitched' (AO 22). It is not 'paranoid' but 'schizophrenic', and concerns 'the molecular direction that on the contrary penetrates into singularities, their interactions and connections at a distance or between different orders' (AO 320). It implies a kind of circuit in which intensive matter or desire is the cause for that which is contracted, but that which is contracted is in turn that which co-generates matter or desire. In other words, 'the production of recording itself is produced by the production of production' (AO 28). Nevertheless, Deleuze warns that 'doubtless the former paranoiac machine continues to exist in the form of mocking voices that attempt to "de-miraculate" the organs' (AO 23). The irreducibility of machines and the difference in kind between actual and virtual precludes all ultimate equilibrium and integration. Nothing can undo the irreducibility of a machine: 'Although the organ-machines attach themselves to the body without organs, the latter continues nonetheless to be without organs and does not become an organism in the ordinary sense of the word. It remains fluid and slippery' (AO 27).

The production of recording in the disjunctive synthesis also tells us why machine ontology is not solipsistic. If engaging in a relation were only to encounter an actual manifestation of another multiplicity as permitted by my singularities, then the real virtuality of encountered machines would be completely irrelevant to my existence. However, the fact that machinic fourfolds are produced by machines tells us that an encountered machine definitely partakes in the generation of the encountering machine's capacities when the latter comprehends the former. At the limit, we can say that the water in which I swim has no *connective* influence on how I experience it, while at the same time it does have its *disjunctive* influence. By contracting the waves of the ocean into experience they become a part of me, and any part of me has a shot at altering my singularities. The virtual water cannot influence how I encounter it, because *my* code determines how I encounter it. It can, however, influence my code by becoming one of my generators. Through this indirect disjunctive recording, the waves thus have a say in how they are experienced by the swimming body. Take Deleuze's description of how one learns to swim:

> When a body combines some of its own distinctive points with those of a wave, it espouses the principle of a repetition which is no longer that of the Same, but involves the Other – involves difference, from one wave and one gesture to another, and carries that difference through the repetitive space thereby constituted. To learn is indeed to constitute this space of an encounter with signs, in which the distinctive points renew themselves in each other, and repetition takes shape while disguising itself. (DR 23)

He describes the process of a child learning to walk in similar terms. On the one hand, the child uses its current code to walk around a room or a garden. On the other hand, 'the child constructs for itself another object, a quite different kind of object which is a *virtual* object or center and which then governs and compensates for the progresses and failures of its real activity' (DR 99). So two things happen at the same time and 'one series would not exist without the other, yet they do not resemble one another' (DR 100). The same principle is expressed in his famous example of the encounter between a wasp and an orchid. The example presupposes that both entities encounter each other, so that they come to co-constitute each other's powers through their own respective connective and disjunctive syntheses:

> Each chain captures fragments of other chains from which it 'extracts' a surplus value, just as the orchid code 'attracts' the figure of a wasp:

both phenomena demonstrate the surplus value of a code. It is an entire system of shunting along certain tracks, and of selections by lot [. . .] The recordings and transmissions that have come from the internal codes, from the outside world, from one region to another of the organism, all intersect, following the endlessly ramified paths of the great disjunctive synthesis. (AO 53)

Both the orchid and the wasp have their respective internal chains of code. The wasp encounters the orchid, making the orchid one of the partial objects that it comprehends in being produced. Hence the actual orchid comes to co-determine the virtual content of the wasp. Simultaneously, the orchid encounters the wasp as one of its producers, so that the latter can come to co-determine the virtual content of the former. In short, all 'production is immediately consumption and a recording process (*enregistrement*), without any sort of mediation' (AO 14). The absence of mediation does not imply sudden direct Problem–Problem interaction. It merely indicates that any connective synthesis is by definition always also a disjunctive synthesis. This being established, the following long passage, which may otherwise strike us as mere poetic hyperbole, becomes deadly serious:

[B]reaks that are a detachment (*coupures-détachements*) [. . .] must not be confused with breaks that are a slicing off (*coupures-prélèvement*). The latter have to do with continuous fluxes and are related to partial objects. Schizzes have to do with heterogeneous chains, and as their basic unit use detachable segments or mobile stocks resembling building blocks or flying bricks. We must conceive of each brick as having been launched from a distance and as being composed of heterogeneous elements: containing within it not only an inscription with signs from different alphabets, but also various figures, plus one or several straws, and perhaps a corpse. Cutting into the flows (*le prélèvement du flux*) involves detachment of something from a chain; and the partial objects of production presuppose stocks of material or recording bricks within the coexistence and the interaction of all the syntheses. How could part of a flow be drawn off without a fragmentary detachment taking place within the code that comes to inform the flow? [. . .] Every composition, and also every decomposition, uses mobile bricks as the basic unit [. . .] These bricks or blocks are the essential parts of desiring-machine from the point of view of the recording process: they are at once component parts and products of the process of decomposition that are spatially localized only at certain moments [. . .] (AO 54–5)

On the one hand, there are connections (the *prélèvements*) that combine irreconcilable machines into contiguous flows. The flip sides of such relations are disjunctions (the *détachements*), which are best understood as other entities carving in, adding to, taking from, upsetting, or slightly nudging the singularities of that which they now co-produce. As all relations are on the same ontological footing, even several straws and a corpse have a shot at altering my essence, should an encounter with them happen to leave a trace. Connective synthesis 'cancels' difference by bringing entities into contiguous actuality (DR 223, 228), but disjunctive synthesis carves it into the heart of things.[7] Code, having been the cause of the actuality experienced, in a sense also causes these flows to 'pass over to the body without organs itself, thereby channeling or "codifying" the flows' (AO 373). As Deleuze writes, 'the body without organs serves for the recording of the entire process of production of desire' (AO 23; cf. 90, 144).[8] Or elsewhere: 'the event is *properly* inscribed in the flesh and in the body [. . .] only in virtue of the incorporeal part' (LS 221–2).[9]

Deleuze also has a different formulation for the same insight. Because a code, Idea, or desire differs in kind from actuality, because it is 'more' than all actuality, it would never be able to settle autonomously on precisely how to actualise a certain encounter if the machines encountered were not involved in any way. Even if I encounter another machine based on my singularities, it is nevertheless an *other* machine of which I encounter an actualisation. After all, the sense-event of a machine is an expression of its virtual essence. In fact, the point is obvious: the encountering machine must be such that it can encounter the other assemblage, but this other assemblage must be such that it can be encountered by the encountering machine. Thus, the encountered machine partakes in characterising the event. Deleuze calls this procedure 'vice-diction' (DR 189) and states that it 'has two procedures which intervene both in the determination of the conditions of the problem and in the correlative genesis of cases of solution: these are, in the first case, the *specification of adjunct fields* and, in the second, the *condensation of singularities*' (DR 190). Though in different terminology, this again expresses the notion that comprehended entities not only compose the actual manifestations (adjunct fields) encountered by a machine, but that they are in such moments also parts of the encountering machine that partake in the generation of its singularities.

This allows us to also counter a possible objection to machine ontology, namely that we are pretending that powers are internally related to their machinic bodies. After all, we have defined code or desire or an Idea as that which an entity *has*. One could accuse Deleuze of retaining transcendentally what he banishes empirically. But this is not the case, as there is no capacity without a generator. There must always be a straw, a corpse, a book, or an organ, or better yet a whole army of machines to generate my intensive matter. Hence the relation between Idea and problematic body remains indirect, as there must always be a generator to provide the latter with the former.

Fifth Intermezzo – Graham Harman and Fourfold Objects

We can now draw a comparison between Harman's object-oriented ontology and Deleuze's machine ontology, which at first sight reveals some striking similarities. Ironically, Harman is probably closer to Deleuze's machine ontology than any other object-oriented thinker, while also being the most vocal in reproaching Deleuze (*as he tends to be interpreted*) for reducing entities to a presumably more basic stratum of reality (Bryant et al. 2011: 292; Harman 2009: 6; 2011b: 63). Yet exactly like Deleuze, Harman thinks that entities such as scissors, chemicals, languages, planets, words, and circus tents are the basic constituents of reality, and that their ontological structure is a fourfold (Harman 2011a: 107).

Harman derives the basic split between an object's internal being and its manifestations to others from Heidegger's tool analysis in *Being and Time* (2010). In a nutshell, whenever a tool such as a hammer breaks, it ceases to be embedded in the context where it normally functions, for example a carpenter's workshop. Until just now, it tacitly operated within a wider system of equipment on which the carpenter could rely. She did not need to pay conscious attention to the object: she was just happily hammering away. By malfunctioning, the hammer suddenly severs its relations with that wider system *and* forges a new relation with its user in that it is now an object of conscious attention. The hammer suddenly stands out, but despite these changes in the object's relations, it is still *the same object*. For many Heideggerians this merely indicates two ways in which humans can relate to objects: practical use on the one hand and theoretical attention on the other. Yet for Harman, it tells us something important about the *object*, namely that the object itself has an extra-relational aspect (otherwise it would not be *this* hammer that used to work and now malfunctions). He also thinks that this extra-relationality is not part of *our* experience of objects, but of objects themselves. Or more precisely, other *objects* are no less unable to access the interior being of the hammer than human *subjects*. For this ontologisation of extra-relationality, he relies on the same argument as Deleuze (see section 3 of Chapter 2). If entities *are nothing but* their relations to other entities, then it is unintelligible how anything can ever change, as everything that anything could be would be exhausted in its *current* givenness (Harman 2011a: 12).

After splitting objects into a relational and non-relational aspect, Harman, too, argues that this twofold consists of two further twofolds. He agrees with Leibniz that an object *qua* object (Leibniz's monad) must consist of two aspects: one aspect to constitute its unity (accounting for why it *is* rather than *not*), and one further aspect constituting its specific character (accounting for why it is *this* rather than *that*). Whereas Deleuze calls these aspects the body and the singularities of a machine, Harman refers to them as the Real Object and Real Qualities of an object. Like Deleuze, Harman takes Husserl to have established that the relational presence of objects to others is also a twofold (2011a: 11; cf. 2005: 21–32). First, there are its qualities, which Harman calls Sensual Qualities. Yet a quality is never directly a quality of a quality (no such thing as a 'green ounce' or an 'ugly inch'). Qualities are qualities of a unified object that is *not* the real object (which remains external to relations), but a second unity of the object, wholly immanent to its givenness. Deleuze calls this a partial object, and Harman refers to it as a Sensual Object.

Harman and Deleuze would also largely agree on *how* change occurs (i.e. when an existing entity is truly altered or when a real new entity is forged). Within his object-oriented ontology, this is called 'vicarious causation', in which 'vicarious' simply means that entities can never influence each other *directly*, as externality precludes any such encounter between the private interiors of entities.[10] Harman explains the nature of vicarious causation by analogy, writing that metaphors best illustrate how it works. Take the metaphor 'the cypress is [like] a flame'.[11] To construct the metaphor, one draws upon the qualities of a flame without literally transposing them on to the cypress. The metaphor does not make for a hot, orange-red, and flickering tree. The source material of flame qualities instead becomes *other* in the metaphor, and strictly speaking the same goes for the cypress. This becoming *other* is the quintessence of vicarious causation. It is exactly why 'the cypress is a conifer' does not work as a metaphor, because in that case the source material used to generate the metaphor is overly characterised by sameness (Harman 2005: 106). In terms of Harman's fourfold, in constructing the metaphor one draws upon the *sensual* qualities of two objects in order to create a third, new object which will have *real* qualities that differ in kind from their source material (2005: 107). To coin some terrible jargon, vicarious causation consists in a *double othering*. First, the manifest qualities of an object are already *other* than the real qualities it harbours in its private interior. Second, whenever those manifest qualities come to generate another object, they always remain *other* than the real qualities of *that* object. Of course, this is not just the case for the generation of new objects, but also for alteration in existing ones. If my encounter with an object results in a change in my interior being, this is because its manifest qualities (different in kind from its real qualities) generate new or alter existing real qualities in me (different in kind from those manifest qualities).

This theory of vicarious causation is (in my view) completely commensurable with Deleuze's notion of disjunctive synthesis. If my singularities alter due to studying French textbooks or attending a festival, the result is, of course, not 'tiny textbooks' or 'mini-festivals' in my interior being. Powers generated are different in kind from whatever actualities generate them. When over the course of the centuries, a species of orchid is influenced by its exposure to wasps, the orchids obviously do not become wasps themselves. They gain the capacity to *manifest* a 'waspy' shape, but *qua* real object they never become wasps. After all, there are no reported cases of hammer orchids flying around and annoying people who are trying to have a barbecue.

Yet Harman's and Deleuze's philosophies are at odds when it comes to their respective accounts of *when* change can occur. For Harman as for Deleuze, the dyad of real qualities (Deleuze's singularities) and real object (Deleuze's body) in an entity constitutes a malleable essence. Yet for Harman, the alteration of an essence due to an entity's encounters with others is either drastic or nil:

> For me, real objects must in fact have qualities, and cannot just be virtual trajectories across many years' worth of different, shifting qualities. For this reason, I do in fact hold that we change as people either by putting

on masks and costumes that hide the fact that deep down nothing has changed, *or* by entering into combination with new things that make us something different from what we were. Or rather, both of these things happen at different times during a human life. We might go through a country music phase, or a phase in which we pretend to others and even ourselves that we are rakish womanizers when really we are nothing of the sort. But on the other hand we also go through experiences, probably rare, that turn us fundamentally into new people by making us enter into something else through an irreversible combination. If the usual alternative is that we either have no fixed identity but are in a constant flux of becoming, or that we remain as an unchanging soul from conception to death, I would suggest instead that we change on a *finite* number of occasions, so that I am no longer the same person as at age five, but may be the same person I was last year or the year before. Transformations in life would be real, but rare. (Harman 2015: 16)

This is not an off-the-cuff remark on Harman's part, as his recent book *Immaterialism* is (among other things) a sustained defence of the notion that the interior of an object can only be altered about five or six times over the course of its existence (Harman 2016: 107–18). Moreover, change is a zero sum game for Harman: one either undergoes a drastic transformation, or nothing happens at all. But what kind of game, exactly? Is change like the transformations in Ovid, so that the same entity called Actaeon used to be a human but is now a stag, and the same entity called Daphne is both a former nymph and a current laurel? If so, then for the same entity (*qua* body without organs or real object), essential qualities change either radically or not at all. Yet if we admit that real qualities can change radically, then by what argument would they not be able to change gradually as well? Why would a spell cast by Apollo change me a lot, but the acquisition of a new language not change me a little?

Or is change much more sinister? Has there been an ominous night during which events conspired to simultaneously bring about the utter annihilation of Graham Harman at age five and his instantaneous replacement by another Graham Harman, perhaps aged thirty? If that is the case, then this is not really change, but a replacement of one entity by another. The essential twofold of any single entity would then be utterly unalterable. Yet what would then be the principle or cause of change in a reality consisting only of unalterable things?

Note also that both scenarios would endow the moment of an entity's creation with a surprisingly exceptional status. Like Deleuze,

Harman holds that entities among themselves must account for the generation of new beings. Whenever a new entity is produced, everyday assemblages such as proteins, musicians, furnaces, and words must be involved in the constitution of the real qualities (the singularities) of the new thing. Producers must in a sense 'style' their product. After its moment of production, however, a Harmanian object's real qualities seem to become nigh immune to being influenced by those very same everyday things. Why? What is so different about non-initial relations? There is, of course, an abundance of existential examples to illustrate the resistance of objects to change once they have been formed, and Deleuze would completely agree that the vast majority of existing machines will not be able to affect each other in the slightest, but one cannot help but wonder about Harman's ontological argument for change as only being possible on a finite number of exceptional occasions, and then only in an extreme sense.

From the perspective of machine ontology, there is a fallacy at work in Harman's line of reasoning in the passage just cited. Harman's account of change is designed to ward off two dangers: 1) that entities are unchangeable; 2) that entities are in a constant flux of becoming. Harman is correct in refusing (1), as it would render how anything could ever happen and why anything exists at all unintelligible. Yet he refuses (2) because he thinks that if entities can in principle always be altered by their encounters, this effectively amounts to reducing all entities to their relations (hence violating the externality thesis). This is simply not the case. Recall that for Deleuze, powers or singularities are by definition different in kind from the actualities generating them. This basic fact already makes it impossible to dissolve an entity into its relations. Regardless of whether I am changed drastically, incrementally, or not at all by either a single, a hundred, or a thousand events, be they subtle or sublime, none of these relations is able to violate externality. *In principle*, any frequency and intensity of change in the interior of an entity is possible, and what actually transpires will depend on the case. Put differently, it will depend on the contingent encounters that a machine is confronted with, the manner in which its current singularities resist or resonate with these encounters, the force exercised by the powers or real qualities of surrounding entities, and so forth.

Also note that Harman should strictly speaking agree with this! In his own terms, if all change is by definition 'vicarious' or 'metaphorical', then no degree of being-constituted-by-something-else can amount to a *literal* transfer of qualities on to the object under construction (thereby equating and thus reducing the object to that which constitutes it). Hence, limiting change to a finite number of occasions at which, additionally, the alteration of an object's interior is by definition drastic requires a further argument. Harman would need to show why, for example, a slow, incremental, and somewhat continuous formation over time of an object's real qualities through a series of encounters with other objects (each exerting a minor influence) would be *different in kind* from being transformed by a single collision with a life-changing event. This seems to require a theory of two different types of relations: those that can alter the interior of objects, and those that cannot – and *in principle* at that. The least we can say here is that Deleuze's machine ontology is not where one should look for such a theory.

2 The Notion of Becoming

An essence is always undergoing a minimum of variation. This malleability of essence is why 'problematic ideas are not *simple* essences' (DR 163, emphasis added). This variation can at times be so minuscule that it can be considered zero or insignificant for all intents and purposes. The coming decade or so will see little to no change in the Idea of a gold bar locked away in Fort Knox, for example. At other times, this variation can be tremendous instead and herald the change of caterpillars into butterflies. But whatever the rate of change of desire, variation there must be. This is because each aspect of machines must be produced. Singularities are no exception, even though their production is different in kind from the generators whose comprehension grants a machine its Idea.

As Deleuze writes, all entities are endowed with a 'receptivity' (DR 98) to record or register the traces of encounters in their internal matter. The disjunctive synthesis gives us the full sense of what it truly is to contract or contemplate: 'to contemplate is to draw something from' (DR 74). The resulting variation in the essence of a rhizome is called 'becoming' or 'a change that is substance itself' (B 37).[12] Deleuze would not be Deleuze if he did not resort to misleading terminology in his explanation of this concept. Throughout *Anti-Oedipus* and *A Thousand Plateaus*, he writes about becoming in terms of an 'I feel . . .', for example in how the schizophrenic Judge Schreber would 'feel' a becoming-woman. Yet becoming is far from being that which one feels, and

Deleuze is once again asking us to abandon our normal understanding of a term. He writes that the 'I feel' of becoming has nothing to do with sensible qualities (DI 238). He is thus using 'I feel' as a 'technical, philosophical concept and not just the usual "I have the impression. . ."'[13] Becoming concerns a variation in a machine's *puissance* which, being transcendental, is not available to human feeling or any other type of direct access.[14] Instead, the 'I feel' of becoming is the indirect awareness that one's desire is changing, an always somewhat uncertain conclusion that can only be based on actual manifestations which one can try to read as signs of ongoing change.

Becoming is not exceptional. It is not a flaw or malediction (K 35). A chance encounter with something that seems unimportant now may later turn out to have radically changed the code of a machine: 'we can be thrown into a becoming by anything at all, by the most unexpected, most insignificant of things' (ATP 292). Yet by the same logic, a revolutionary event may turn out not to have changed anything at all. Whatever the nature of a sense-event, it is always a question to which extent and in what way it will be recorded: 'the eternal truth of the event is grasped only if the event is also inscribed in the flesh' (LS 161). In any case, becoming is not imaginary, but 'perfectly real' (ATP 238). It is true that Deleuze distinguishes specific cases of 'becoming-animal', or 'becoming-woman', and even 'becoming-pupil, -burgomaster, -girl, and -Mongol' (AO 109). Such anexact names are necessary to emphasise that becoming is never a becoming-in-general. Becoming is becoming with regard to specific machines (an animal, the Mongols, a woman). Becoming is always a 'block' of becoming (ATP 238) and never unlimited (N 28). Yet each such block is but a specific case of 'a more profound becoming-imperceptible' (FB 27; cf. ATP 252, 279–81; D 45). Imperceptible, because the transcendental recording resulting from an encounter is neither extensive, nor resembles the comprehended extensity that generated it. Hence Deleuze writes that becoming is the 'most imperceptible thing' (D 3) and that 'what becomes visible on the one plane is what is imperceptible on the other plane'.[15] As we have seen, Deleuze accords no special privilege to the machines that initially produce an assemblage. Each contracted machine has a shot at altering a multiplicity's code. This is why 'we oppose epidemic to filiation, contagion to heredity' (ATP 241).[16]

The machinic fourfold and the syntheses posit no particular a priori relations. This allows all existential relations of an object to have a say in what the essence of an object will become. Conversely, in a reductionist system of universal depth or height, change due to existential events is never essential, as all things remain internal to their original relation with a certain source. Yet in machine ontology everything at least has a shot:

> We [. . .] believe that everything commingles in these intense becomings, passages, and migrations – all this drift that ascends and descends the flow of time: countries, races, families, parental appellations, divine appellations, geographical and historical designations, and even miscellaneous news items [. . .] (AO 104)

Any encountered machine is a part of the machine that encounters. Everything has a shot at leaving a trace. It is in this sense that 'a tree, a column, a flower, or a cane grow inside the body; other bodies always penetrate our body' (LS 87). Yet having a shot is a tricky business, because generated code does not resemble its generator. As Deleuze often insists, becoming has nothing to do with imitation.[17] This is why we can rebel against the very institutions that have given us the capacity to do so. Becoming moves from the actual into the virtual that does not resemble it. In this sense becoming concerns 'absolute deterritorializations, at least in principle' and benefits not its source but its result: the 'unformed matter of deterritorialized flow, of nonsignifying signs' (K 14).

We saw that Deleuze refers to the connective labour of machines as 'Libido'. The disjunctive synthesis is denoted by the term 'Numen', defined as 'the energy of disjunctive inscription' (AO 24; cf. 331). Numen concerns that aspect of synthesis by which contractions result in new registrations or recordings of code, a move from actuality to virtuality that Deleuze also calls 'a transformation of energy' (AO 24). Why this name 'Numen', meaning divine presence or divine will? Precisely because in the absence of a God or sovereign subject, entities among themselves are doing the work traditionally assigned to an exceptional agent. In machine ontology, 'the sole thing that is divine is the nature of an energy of disjunctions' (AO 25).

Becoming concerns the variation in the internal matter or Idea of a machine: 'materiality, natural or artificial, and both simultaneously; it is matter in movement, in flux, in variation, matter as a conveyor of singularities and traits of expression' (ATP 409). Yet this does not mean that everything is constantly changing significantly. Everyone knows of countless machines that are extremely resistant to being altered by others, and stalwart machines number no fewer than the legions of multiplicities that can be snuffed out of existence with laughable ease. Yet whatever the strength of a machine, its unconscious is a 'factory' immersed in a process of being generated and being the ground for generations (cf. LS 90). The virtual twofold of body and desire is always an active unity of interior change.[18] This change results from a machine's encounters with other machines, but such relations always remain 'at a distance' due to the difference in kind between virtuality and actuality:

> Every force is thus essentially related to another force. The being of force is plural, it would be absolutely absurd to think about force in the singular. A force is domination, but also the object on which domination is exercised. A plurality of forces acting and being affected at distance, distance being the differential element included in each force and by which each is related to others. (NP 6)

All machines or rhizomes are irreducible entities. They are forces unleashed in the world. Nevertheless, each force must at least comprehend two other forces that are producing it. As Deleuze writes, '*you will never find a homogeneous system that is not still or already affected by a regulated, continuous, immanent process of variation*' (ATP 103). These forces act at a distance, as their actuality will be contracted into a virtuality, which differs in kind from relational manifestation. Because of this universal structure of being generated and generating, the Idea is not just a machine's matter, but a 'burning, living center of matter' and the 'beating heart of reality' (AO 32, 107).

This leads us to the distinction between what Deleuze calls 'social' and 'technical' machines. As stated in the introduction, these terms neither indicate different kinds of machines, nor a distinction in scale, as if bigger machines were social and smaller ones technical (BSP 130), nor an opposition of groups to individuals (BSP 130). Rather, each machine is both technical and social (AO 46). The technical and the social indicate a difference in 'regime', not in kind (BSP 130).[19] Now, Deleuze tells us that desiring-machines are the same entities as technical and social machines, but that desire concerns their unconscious (BSP 132).[20]

It follows that the technical and social aspect of machines concerns their actuality.[21] Desire is 'molecular' (see our earlier discussion of singularities), which Deleuze opposes to the 'molar' social and technical machines (AO 327). All machines are thus 'desiring-machines in one sense, but organic, technical or social machines in another sense: these are the same machines under determinate conditions' (AO 328; cf. 387).

A machine is social in so far as it contracts a multitude of other machines into being its generators. To be social is to take things into one's 'stock' (D 104). It is to 'intervene' or 'repress' (AO 46, 70, 166), meaning that 1) contraction brings otherwise isolated entities together, and 2) the comprehension of a machine is always based on the capacities of the machine doing the comprehending. This is why Deleuze writes that 'it is *in order to function* that a social machine must *not function well* [. . .] The dysfunctions are an essential element of its very ability to function' (AO 176–7). Remember that contraction is based on the essence of a machine, but that this essence in and of itself is not functional. This non-functionality is precisely why *new* relations can be forged with *this* machine (otherwise it would be restricted to its current actuality).

Conversely, a machine is technical in so far as it is being comprehended by other machines. To be technical is to function for something. Hence technical machines 'point to the social machines that condition and organize them, but also limit and inhibit their development' (AO 165). The table is a social machine for its parts. As long as these other machines are parts, they are made to deploy their excessive desire in actually functioning as part of the table. Technical machines 'are definable extrinsically' (ATP 458), as being-technical is being-for-others.

This simple division harbours some strange consequences. Take, for example, a phalanx of hoplites. In a very important sense, the phalanx is taking *itself* as its parts.[22] After all, it is the phalanx that, based on its code, contains other machines as members of itself. Each machine can only be generated from its own parts. Moreover, the individual hoplites relate to one another asymmetrically and unilaterally. Each experiences the actual others from his own virtual perspective. Each uses his shield to protect another hoplite to his left, but remains exterior to this other. But in the experience of the phalanx, the hoplites are encountered symmetrically and continuously, in accordance with the rule of rupture and contiguity. The virtual phalanx truly experiences the hoplites as a unity. Additionally, the same machine can, of course, simultaneously be technical and social; for example, 'the clock as a technical machine for measuring uniform time, and as social machine for reproducing canonic hours and for assuring order in the city' (AO 165). Technically, the clock functions as a thing people look at to see the time. Socially (imagine a village with only one clock), the clock does not just comprehend its physical components, but also the people abiding by it. Is this last thought a strange one? Not in machine ontology. Recall that only contraction by a third machine can bring two machines together. We can only meet somewhere because there is somewhere to meet (a bar, a university, a prison, an online forum). Is the clock not among those machines that make people converge at certain hours? There is certainly a sense in which the time has us . . .

3 Assemblages and Intensities

Because of becoming, a machine is an assemblage and not just something assembled (an *agencement* and not an *agencé*). Desire is not just assembled at the moment of inception, 'desire is always assembled' (ATP 229). As the body without organs is only ever the irreducible unity of a machine, it could never generate its desire all by itself.[23] It needs 'organ-machines'. The body is 'pure and intensive matter, or the stationary motor whose organ-machines will constitute the working parts and the appropriate powers' (TRM 21). To be an assemblage is to have one's singularities result from encounters with others. 'We will call an *assemblage* every constellation of singularities and traits deducted from the flow – selected, organized, stratified – in such a way as to converge (consistency) artificially and naturally; an assemblage, in this sense, is a veritable invention' (ATP 407). Hence 'an assemblage is precisely this increase in the dimensions of a multiplicity that necessarily changes in nature as it expands its connections' (ATP 8). 'Multiplicity' stresses the virtual twofold which is the internal reality of all entities. 'Assemblage' stresses that despite the irreducibility of their bodies and the surplus status of their code, machines must always be generated. As we have seen, every encounter has a 'shot' at partaking in the assemblage of singularities. A machine's internal chain of code can be the result of many things, though it differs in kind from all of them:

> No chain is homogeneous; all of them resemble, rather, a succession
> of characters from different alphabets in which an ideogram, a picto-
> gram, a tiny image of an elephant passing by, or a rising sun may sud-
> denly make its appearance. In a chain that mixes together phonemes,
> morphemes, etc., without combining them, papa's mustache, mama's
> upraised arm, a ribbon, a little girl, a cop, a shoe suddenly turn up.
> (AO 53)[24]

Throughout its existence, an assemblage gets locked in fierce
battles, loving embraces, secret thefts, and public declarations with
the machines that generate it (those to which it connects) and the
machines that it generates (those to which it is connected). Some
of these encounters will be chaotic struggles for power, as several
assemblages lay claim to the same entity. Others will take the form
of veritable alliances, as several assemblages become part of a
larger and more resilient multiplicity. None of this will ever form
'an integral whole as such' (DR 209), as each contracted entity
remains irreducible. An assemblage remains 'un-attributable'
(ATP 4), which is to say external to its relations. With Deleuze,
we must never stop stressing how each machinic assemblage is an
'outsider' or 'anomaly': 'Lovecraft applies the term "Outsider"
to this thing or entity, the Thing, which arrives and passes at the
edge' (ATP 245; cf. D 42).

An assemblage can nevertheless contract code and alter its Idea.
Sometimes this variation will be minimal, at other times it will
change everything. So perhaps a better translation for *agencement* would have been 'operation', as 'assemblage' suggests something with a fixed set of components. 'Operation' would perhaps
be better at capturing the idea that a machine can remain *this*
machine while at the same time its encounters and the multiplicities to which it becomes coupled (temporarily or permanently) can
change its *puissance*. The turbulent changes that can characterise
military campaigns and storms exemplify this: 'it is the military
men and the meteorologists who hold the secret of proper names,
when they give them to a strategic operation or a hurricane' (ATP
264; cf. D 120).

It is also important to understand that the existential situation
in which an assemblage finds itself limits its ontological 'freedom'.
Neither a desert storm nor Desert Storm can just do or become
anything whatsoever. As Deleuze writes, 'whenever a multiplicity
is taken up in a structure, its growth is offset by a reduction in its

laws of combination' (ATP 6). Take, for example, a relatively big and resilient multiplicity such as a nation-state: 'States are made up not only of people but also of wood, fields, gardens, animals, and commodities' (ATP 385). Or in another example, a cavalry-man is comprised of (among other things) a man, a horse, and a stirrup (D 69). In both cases, the machines taken up in a structure, whether people, animals, or stirrups, will find that the course of their existence and even their becoming can become largely determined by the social machine that uses them as a technical machine. Once entities become functionaries of another thing, this limits what they can do by locking them into certain patterns of manifestation.

Despite its bodily irreducibility and its excessive desire, no machine can just connect with any other machine, no assemblage can contract just any partial object. Everything depends on specific, contingent encounters that match the powers that be. For example, the EU can assemble and contract citizens, laws, trade agreements, and so on, but it is highly unlikely that it is capable of registering emotions. A rock can register me handling it, but it cannot respond to me singing to it. The same spark that detonates a volatile chemical solution does nothing to a steel plate. All depends on what bodies are actually capable of. A machine simply cannot assemble just anything in its future. Conversely, neither can it retain everything it assembled in its past. In fact, most of its encounters will be forgotten. The thousand adventures one has as a child will mostly have been forgotten once one reaches the venerable age of thirty. All that remains is some traces of code or some minor machines that still function, and here one never knows precisely what created what. So a complete archive would be the rarest thing in the universe, perhaps existing only as a Borges fiction. The contraction of actual presents into pure pasts different in kind from those presents guarantees that forgetfulness is a fundamental feature of reality.[25] Therefore, 'disjunctions are the form that the genealogy of desire assumes' (AO 25). Such a genealogy of the becoming of an assemblage would in a way be 'without history' (D viii).[26] The history of an entity is thoroughly relational. It is the record of how others manifested to it and how it manifested to others.

Conversely, becoming is what happens between those two things. Because becoming concerns the production of virtual code, it 'cannot be reduced to anything that has become [. . .] Becoming is not what it becomes' (WG 82–3). We can thus answer a strange question that Deleuze asks in *Kafka*, the book in which assemblages are first mentioned: 'why have we aligned *the faraway and the contiguous* [. . .] on the one hand, with the *distant and the close* [. . .] on the other?' (K 76). Actuality, being contiguous, always remains far away from a machine because no part can ever become integrated to the point where its being fully becomes a being-for-the-other. Moreover, the virtuality of a point of view can never integrate the actuality it experiences into itself as such. At the same time, a virtual twofold is always infinitely distant from its actual objects, due to their differences in kind. Yet because the actual object is nevertheless actual *to* this virtual point of view, it is in another sense extremely close to it.

The nature of assemblages explains why Deleuze's work is riddled with terms associated with transformation and metamorphosis (e.g. C1 8; B 64; LS 221; DR 154; FLB 9). They primarily refer to becoming, to the contraction of actual presentations into virtual content. Hence all becoming is transmutation (LS 8). Transmutation is key because 'the absolute condition of non-resemblance must be emphasized' (DR 279; DI 100). This is why *What is Philosophy?* is so hostile towards the notion of transparent communication (WP 6, *passim*), as for Deleuze nothing ever manifests in relations as it is in itself. This is also the sense in which to read 'everything changes in nature as it climbs to the surface' (LS 175). It is not to say that any new situation in which I end up turns me into a radically new entity (which would be relationism). Instead, the change in nature by climbing to the surface simply reiterates that in actualised virtuality or contracted actuality, the source never resembles the result.

A reality in which entities are constantly engaged in assembling and being assembled with varying degrees of intensity or even success is, as we have seen, what Deleuze calls 'schizophrenic'. He also calls it 'delirious', taking delirium to mean the crossing of the threshold between actual and virtual by which the intensive matter of a machine is altered, but also the shifts in the actual entities that are the content of relations.[27] Delirium is thus the name for 'the recording that is made of the process of production of desiring-machines' (AO 34). This is delirious because there are no a priori ontological rules for which relations do and do not change an essence. Of course, existentially there are always plenty of constants and constraints, but in principle, even a corpse and some straws have a shot. Delirium tells us why 'I is another', as Deleuze quotes Rimbaud (AO 377; cf. C2 153; DR 58, 85, 110).[28] I is another because everything I essentially am is assembled from encounters with entities that are quite unlike me. I is also another because what I essentially am is malleable. My singularities or desire can vary over time. This, incidentally, is precisely why existence is always *dangerous*: any encounter can lead to an alteration that one's code or Idea cannot accommodate, the result being death. Finally, I is another because I cannot access my virtual self. Everything I can notice about myself is an actuality, and hence a transformation that differs in kind from my essence. Moreover, as we have seen in our discussions of contiguity and flow, each image of myself will be tied up with and informed by other machines that are not me.

As indicated, there are moments when Deleuze does not use 'event' in the sense of sense-events (see section 2 of Chapter 5). The concept has a double meaning which we can now address.[29] There are 'double series of events which develop on two planes, echoing without resembling each other: real events on the level of the engendered solutions, and ideal events embedded in the conditions of the problem' (DR 189). These two events differ in nature (LS 157). So whereas sense-events concern the local 'solutions' to problems, 'pure' or 'ideal' events concern singularities themselves (LS 52–3, 100, 103, 178; DI 100; TRM 388; WP 156). The ideal event is that which happens to the virtual aspect of a machine during its encounters. It is the variation of desire, the alteration of code, the becoming of an Idea, or the redistribution of singularities. Since desire must be produced and is therefore in principle a variation, at the limit that which fills a body without organs is the ideal event itself (LS 178; FLB 15–16). We can thus speak of a pure event that is both essence (LS 100) and pure past (LS 136). It is also in this sense that we can proclaim that 'True Entities are events' or that 'ENTITY = EVENT' (D 66). This notion of 'pure' event also allows us to grasp the meaning of 'counter-actualization', a concept introduced in *The Logic of Sense* (cf. LS 152, 161). If the virtual aspect of an assemblage were never to change because of encounters, then actuality would be utterly ineffectual with regard to the virtual. This would return us to the bland monism of an unchanging ground. The virtual would be trapped in its own unchanging eternity. Instead, the disjunctive synthesis of becoming implies counter-actualisation, which is to say becoming what it was not: 'to the extent that the pure event is each time imprisoned forever in its actualization, counter-actualization liberates it' (LS 161).[30]

Yet not all events are alike. One cannot confuse the ontological structure of entities with their existential challenges. Precisely because of ontological equality, things are unequal in their existence (this is not the case in systems of false height and depth: if God existed, everything would existentially be equal under God). Ontologically, a volcano has no more reality than a spoken word, and a mild breeze is as real as a supernova. Existentially, things are different. This brings us to the notion of intensities. Remember that Deleuze rejected his early idea that a single universal depth (or force, or process, or dimension) populated by intensities would underlie or permeate all beings (TRM 65). After this rejection, 'intensities' become strictly synonymous with singularities or the *puissance* of an entity. Like singularities, Deleuze calls them 'not the sensible but the being *of* the sensible' (DR 267; cf. 231). They are what 'occupies' or 'populates' a body (ATP 153), which itself is 'zero intensity' (ATP 31). As with code, the intensities of a body result from 'the forces of attraction and repulsion' (AO 33) and are the reality of matter.[31] Like the Idea, intensity is transcendental and always already covered and enveloped by extensity (DR 144; cf. 223, 233–5, 237, 254). It is 'neither divisible, like extensive quantity, nor indivisible, like quality' (DR 237). It is not divisible, because it is not extensive. Yet it is alterable through becoming (unlike quality: I can slice an apple, but the slices will remain just as red). So why is intensity yet another synonym for the virtual aspect of machines? Because whether or not one machine manages to alter another depends on the intensity of their encounter. And the intensity of an encounter depends on the virtual twofolds of the machines involved. Hence 'it is intensity which *dramatizes*. It is intensity which is immediately expressed in the basic spatio-temporal dynamisms' (DR 245). The essences of entities determine the dynamics of spatio-temporal encounters. And precisely because different entities have different Ideas, not all machines can connect to others, not all machines survive all encounters, not all machines even register the existence of others, and so on. This is also why the body without organs is associated with *zero* intensity. The body is precisely the aspect of assemblages that repulses all contact. It follows that the degree to which a machine *does* have its indirect encounters with others can only be accounted for by that which fills its body.[32] This is why 'intensity' is an appropriate synonym for the internal matter of multiplicities.

Let us now turn to Deleuze's notions of difference in itself and repetition for itself, his machinic alternatives for maledictory concepts of difference and repetition premised on internalism, reductionism, and representationalism. If machines are to be understood, then 'the total notion is [. . .] that of: indi-different/ciation (indi-drama-different/ciation)' (DR 246). This unwieldy term can now be dissected. The 'indi-' refers, first, to the indifference of a body without organs. No matter what happens to the internal reality or the actual surfaces of an entity, the body remains irreducible to anything else. Second, 'indi-' refers to individuation, which we have seen is the moment by which the singularities or Idea of an entity contracted into an actual manifestation, which is to say a twofold object of sense and qualities (a partial object with flow). Differenciation is the actualisation of virtual content into a manifestation encountered by another entity (DR 207). It presupposes individuation: 'every differenciation presupposes a prior intense field of individuation' (DR 247). This is just to say that individuation and differenciation both concern actualisation, but the former from the point of view of the virtual Idea and the latter from the point of view of the actual sense-event. Differentiation is 'the determination of the virtual content of an Idea' (DR 207), in other words the becoming of the code of an assemblage as a result of its encounters. As Ideas can vary over time, differentiation is the difference internal to an Idea (DR 26). This essence which differs is the ground or cause for all actualisation, the latter differing in kind from the virtual object. Differentiation is thus the differenciator: 'the differenciator differenciates itself' (DR xix). Every entity remains enveloped by its own actual surfaces. In other words, it is something that distinguishes itself (becomes actual) from itself (its virtuality) without becoming really distinct from itself (becoming enveloped instead). Hence we must 'imagine something which distinguishes itself – and yet that from which it distinguishes itself does not distinguish itself from it' (DR 28; cf. 152). Everything 'bathes in *its* difference' (DR 243, emphasis added). Each entity is 1) irreducible to all other entities, 2) has a differentiating essence, which is 3) different in kind from its own actualisations. Such is 'difference in itself'.

As for repetition, this first concerns the fact that a machine can only ever (repeatedly) register other entities on its own terms, following its own capacities, even if its code changes due to inter-actions with others. One cannot undo the fact that one's body is one's point of view. Second, repetition is the fact that in any given relation, an entity can only manifest actual profiles, never singu-larities in and of themselves (this too happens 'repeatedly'). These first two repetitions comprise what Deleuze calls 'repetition of the Same' or 'physical, mechanical, or bare repetitions' (DR xx). Such repetition is grounded in 'the more profound structures of a hidden repetition' which concerns singularities (DR xx; cf. 1). This repeti-tion concerns 'something unique or singular which has no equal or equivalent. And [. . .] repetition at the level of external conduct echoes, for its own part, a more secret vibration which animates it, a more profound, internal repetition within the singular' (DR 1; cf. xix, 17). It is aimed at 'the ground which carries every object to that extreme "form" in which its representation comes undone' (DR 57). This repetition for itself concerns the internality of an entity. First, how its becoming entails that other actual entities are always generating its internal desire, the latter differing in kind from the former. Second, how all its relations will concern its actualisations. These two directions of transmutation comprise 'eternal return' according to Deleuze (cf. NP xviii, xix, 23–4, 46, 47; DR 6, 11).[33] As he writes, 'repetition in the eternal return [. . .] consists in conceiving the same on the basis of the different' (DR 41). The full 'drama' of a machine's existence plays out along the lines of this difference in itself and repetition for itself. Deleuze seeks to capture such dynamism in the following litany:

> The first repetition is repetition of the Same, explained by the iden-tity of the concept or representation; second includes difference, and includes itself in the alterity of the Idea, in the heterogeneity of an 'a-presentation'. One is negative, occurring by default in the concept; the other affirmative, occurring by excess in the Idea. One is conjec-tural, the other categorical. One is static, the other dynamic. One is repetition in the effect, the other in the cause. One is extensive, the other intensive. One is ordinary, the other distinctive and singular. One is horizontal, the other vertical. One is developed and explicated, the other enveloped and in need of interpretation. One is revolv-ing, the other evolving. One involves equality, commensurability and symmetry; the other is grounded in inequality, incommensurability and dissymmetry. One is material, the other spiritual, even in nature and in the earth. One is inanimate, the other carries the secret of our

deaths and our lives, of our enchainments and our liberations, the demonic and the divine. One is a 'bare' repetition, the other a covered repetition, which forms itself in covering itself, in masking and disguising itself. One concerns accuracy, the other has authenticity as its criterion. The two repetitions are not independent. One is the singular subject, the interiority and the heart of the other, the depths of the other. The other is only the external envelope, the abstract effect. The repetition of dissymmetry is hidden within symmetrical ensembles or effects; a repetition of distinctive points underneath that of ordinary points; and everywhere the Other in the repetition of the Same. (DR 24; cf. 84)

We have now identified the full 'tetravalence of the assemblage' (ATP 89): first, the body (Figure, problem, plane of consistency); second, desire (code, *puissance*, powers, potential, Idea, singularities, intensities); third, sense (sense-event, partial object); fourth, qualities (flow). A body and its desire form a twofold virtual essence. A sense-event and its qualities form a twofold actual manifestation. A first, connective synthesis (habit, contemplation, contraction, production) describes what a relation is. A relation, being a combination of rupture and contiguity, brings together various otherwise irreconcilable machines into the actual experience of yet another machine. A second, disjunctive synthesis (of recording, registration, or inscription) describes what a relation is rooted in. Any relation is rooted in the essence of an assemblage, which nevertheless always retains a surplus over the sum total of its relations. This essence itself is malleable, being registered or inscribed, as the internal matter of a machine, due to the contraction of other entities. What Deleuze calls 'becoming' is precisely this malleability of machinic essence, which by no means amounts to constant and hyperactive change. Instead, the variation in a machine's essence depends on the nature and intensity of the relations it finds itself engaged in.

Yet our analysis so far may have started to frustrate some readers, because Deleuze seems to be cheating. Twice, even. First, despite having dispelled the possibility of a dualism between social and technical machines, he seems to retain a dualism between machines and their relations, betraying his own insight that everything is a machine. Such a dualism also suggests that machines are irreducible whereas relations are not, which would violate the externality thesis with regard to relations: terms would be irreducible to relations, but relations would be reducible to terms. Second, Deleuze has not yet accounted for a medium for encounters between machines. It is all very well that machines contract their desire by encountering the actual manifestations of others, but we have yet to see that in which such recording and registration occurs. The usual suspects for this medium are substrates below entities, or structures, subjects, and divinities above them, but these are unavailable to machine ontology.

This would signal trouble for Deleuze's ontology, 'unless we have not yet found the last word, unless there is a third synthesis of time' (DR 84; cf. LS 168). Deleuze is aware of the two remaining questions and notes that 'the second synthesis of time points beyond itself in the direction of a third' (DR 88). As our discussion of this third synthesis in the next chapter will show, each relation between machines is a machine as well, and machines are the media in which machines generate other machines among themselves. Being machines, relations are also irreducible entities that 'repress' their virtual body and *puissance* in an envelopment by actual surfaces. As Deleuze writes:

> Our point of departure was the opposition between desiring-machines and the body without organs. The repulsion of these machines, as found in the paranoiac machine of primary repression, gave way to an attraction in the miraculating machine. But the opposition between attraction and repulsion persists. It would seem that a genuine reconciliation of the two can take place only on the level of a new machine, functioning as 'the return of the repressed'. (AO 29)

Relations are machines, which is the full sense of relations being 'veritable external bridges' (DI 163). They too are external terms. And it is because machines are themselves local media that 'mediators are fundamental. Creation's all about mediators. Without them nothing happens' (N 125). The third, conjunctive synthesis and its implications as elaborated in the next chapter will constitute the final features of Deleuze's ontology:

> The first mode has to do with the connective synthesis, and mobilizes Libido as withdrawal energy (*énergie de prélèvement*). The second has to do with the disjunctive synthesis, and mobilizes the Numen as detachment energy (*énergie de detachment*). The third has to do with the conjunctive synthesis, and mobilizes Voluptas as residual energy

(*énergie résiduelle*). It is these three aspects that make the process of desiring-production at once the production of production, the production of recording, and the production of consumption. (AO 56)

Notes

1. Deleuze credits Freud with first realising this, specifically with regard to sexuality: 'For what Freud and the first analysts discover is the domain of free syntheses where everything is possible: endless connections, nonexclusive disjunctions, nonspecific conjunctions, partial objects and flows' (AO 70; cf. SCS 180472). This refers to the first edition of Freud's three essays on sexuality, in which human sexuality is simply what it becomes due to our contingent experiences.

2. 'The idea of the possible appears when, instead of grasping each existent in its novelty, the whole of existence is related to a preformed element, from which everything is supposed to emerge by simple "realization"' (B 19–20). This is 'the most general error of thought, the error common to science and metaphysics' (B 20).

3. The equation of desire to cause originates in Deleuze's study of Kant (KCP 3).

4. 'À savoir que le désir, en tant que émission de processus, en tant que fabrication de création de processus, que le désir n'a strictement rien à voir avec rien de négatif, avec le manque, avec quoique ce soit, que le désir ne manque de rien' (SCS 270580).

5. In jargon: 'modifications of a code have an aleatory cause in the milieu of exteriority' (ATP 54).

6. Deleuze also uses 'inscription': 'A body without organs is the surface of inscription [. . .] for every desire' (SCS 260373; cf. AO 24).

7. Even words can become 'carved into the depth of bodies' (LS 84). Disjunctive synthesis is always 'an exercise in naked flesh, in the depths of the soul' (AO 147).

8. Cf. '[L]enregistrement est un dehors-dedans, une limite envelopante, "dehors" parce que faisant intervener une surface d'extériorité sur laquelle sont transcrits des resultants, "dedans" parce que faisant partie constitutivement de la machine et réglant le procès de production' (LAT 41).

9. This is why 'desiring-production has solely an actual existence' (AO 154). Virtual–virtual interaction is foreclosed, so that all production of code (the production of desire itself) must result from the contraction of the actuality of other machines.

10. See the seventh chapter of *Guerilla Metaphysics*.

11. Harman (2005: 105).
12. By 'substance' Deleuze means the unconscious or virtual aspect of an assemblage: 'the unconscious is a substance to be manufactured' (D 78). Cf. 'being is alteration, alteration is substance' (DI 25, cf. 37).
13. 'Le "je sens", je veux dire, il y a un "je sens" philosophique. Le "je sens" c'est pas seulement "J'ai l'impression"' (SCS 270580).
14. To hold otherwise would require the mistake of 'projecting consciousness on the unconscious' (SCS 150272).
15. 'ce qui devient perceptible sur ce plan, c'est ce qui est imperceptible sur l'autre plan' (SCS 150277). See also the repeated assertion that all becomings are molecular (ATP 272; cf. 275; K 37).
16. Cf. 'The difference is that contagion, epidemic, involves terms that are entirely heterogeneous: for example, a human being, an animal, and a bacterium, a virus, a molecule, a microorganism. Or in the case of the truffle, a tree, a flu, and a pig. These combinations are neither genetic nor structural; they are interkingdoms, unnatural participations' (ATP 242).
17. 'Qu'est-ce que ça veut dire: devenir animal? Ça ne veut pas dire imiter [. . .] Ce n'est pas au moment où on imite que ça marche' (SCS 150277).
18. Deleuze also discerns this in Leibniz: 'Alors je dis juste: retenons la définition: unité active du changement intérieur'; 'la forme substantielle [. . .] l'entéléchie c'est cette unité active, c'est-à-dire ce qu'on a appelé pour le moment: monade' (SL 120587).
19. Cf. 'The truth of the matter is that *social production is purely and simply desiring-production itself under determinate conditions*' (AO 42); 'there is never any difference in nature between the desiring-machines and the technical social machines. There is a certain distinction between them, but it is merely a distinction of régime' (AO 44; cf. BSP 129).
20. *A Thousand Plateaus* repeats the same distinction in different terms. It calls social and technical machines 'collective assemblages of enunciation': 'the only assemblages are machinic assemblages of desire and collective assemblages of enunciation' (ATP 22), which are again two faces of the same coin so that one is always inside the other (ATP 23).
21. Hence a machine will socially and technically be 'caught up in this or that segment, this or that office, this or that machine or state of machine [. . .] On the other hand and at the same time, it will take flight the whole time, carried away by a freed expression, carrying away deformed contents' (K 59).

22. Contra any *causa sui* interpretation, *this* is how a machinic body implies 'its own self-production [and] its own engendering of itself' (AO 26). This is simply to say that wherever a machine is being constructed, it can only comprise its parts based on its own singularities or Idea, even if those too are under construction.

23. This is why there is no deterritorialisation without reterritorialisation, as Deleuze likes to remind his readers (cf. AO 360). It is possible for a machine to alter its relations, so that it leaves the 'territory' of that which generates it or that which it generates. It is, however, impossible for a machine to have no relations with generators or generations whatsoever.

24. Hence there are always 'a thousand beings implicated in my complications' (LS 298).

25. So that *becoming is an antimemory*' (ATP 294) and reality is permeated by an 'active forgetting' (DR 55).

26. 'L'histoire de quelqu'un, ce n'est pas la même chose que le devenir' (SCS 150277; cf. *L'Abécédaire*, 'gauche').

27. 'délirer c'est précisément, et c'est mon hypothèse puis le début, franchir des seuils d'intensité, passer d'un seuil d'intensité à un autre, c'est à dire qu'avant de délirer, le délirant, c'est quelqu'un qui sent et sentir, c'est sentir des passages intensifs sur le corps sans organes' (SCS 180472).

28. Cf. 'The schizo has no principles: he is something only by being something else' (AO 107). Deleuze also quotes Vaslav Nijinsky: 'I am God I was not God I am a clown of God; I am Apis. I am an Egyptian. I am a Red Indian. I am a Negro. I am a Chinaman. I am a Japanese. I am a foreigner, a stranger. I am a sea bird. I am a land bird. I am the tree of Tolstoy. I am the roots of Tolstoy ... I am husband and wife in one. I love my wife. I love my husband' (AO 97; original in Nijinsky 1971: 20).

29. 'Aussi faut-il distinguer dans les événements [. . .] la part qui renvoie au transcendantal, et celle qui renvoie à l'effectuation' (letter to Joseph Emmanuel Voeffray, LAT 90).

30. Contra Hallward, who misunderstands the meaning of 'unilateral', it is therefore not the case that 'since [Deleuze] acknowledges only a unilateral relation between virtual and actual, there is no place in Deleuze's philosophy for any notion of change, time or history that is mediated by actuality' (2006: 161–2).

31. 'L'intensité [. . .] est le caractère de ce qui est réel dans la matière' (SL 170387). And since machinic matter is always separated by surfaces from other machinic matter, radically different intensities exist. They

can be, for example, biological, psychological, chemical, energetic, mathematical, aesthetic, linguistic, informational, semiotic, and so on (ATP 109–10).

32. 'Mais l'intensité zéro ce n'est pas le contraire des puissances intensives, elle est la matière intensive pure que les puissances intensives viennent remplir à tel ou tel degré' (SCS 150272).

33. Deleuze's reading of Nietzsche is organised on a juxtaposition of reactive, extensive, or 'mechanical' forces (NP 41) with active forces that concern what things can do (NP 61). Deleuze treats active force as a synonym to the will to power (NP 7), which he calls the 'internality' of force (NP 47, 51). More specifically, will to power is that which 'makes a force obey within a relation' (NP 51), which points to Deleuze's own notion of social and technical machines. No force ever exhausts another force, as the latter always keeps 'enjoying' its own difference (NP 8–9). All relationality is reactive: 'the fact remains that we do not feel, experience or know any becoming but becoming-reactive' (NP 64). A becoming-active is 'neither felt nor known' (NP 68), but it can be *thought* (NP 69). According to Deleuze, Nietzsche holds that 'consciousness merely expresses the relation of certain reactive forces to the active forces which dominate them' (NP 41) and 'it is inevitable that consciousness sees the organism from its own point of view and understands it in its own way; that is to say, reactively' (NP 41). It is not hard to see that the virtual/actual distinction is at work in all of this, especially when Deleuze calls Nietzsche's philosophy a 'selective ontology' intended to 'replace the old metaphysics' (NP 72, 84).

8

The Construction of Machines

The first two syntheses do not yet reveal that in which relations happen. If only two syntheses existed, we would have to
posit a universal background (if only formally) in which relations
are forged and from which new entities emerge. Badiou's book
on Deleuze exemplifies this. For Badiou, the disjunctive synthesis is the ultimate achievement of Deleuze's philosophy (Badiou
2000: 21). Badiou's fascination with disjunctions runs so deep
that his book on Deleuze does not contain a single mention of
the third, conjunctive synthesis. Instead, Badiou simply assumes
that relations belong to some kind of universal and open Whole
(2000: 122).[1] If that were the case, everything would be rein-
ternalised into a universal One, which is precisely what Badiou
tries to convince readers Deleuze is saying (2000: 11, *passim*).
This, of course, results in a quasi-Deleuze who flagrantly violates
the externality thesis. Contra Badiou, we here analyse the third
synthesis and its consequences, among which are the theses that
relations are machines as well and that mediation is local rather
than universal.

1 The Conjunctive Synthesis

The conjunctive synthesis, Deleuze writes, implies a 'universal
ungrounding' (DR 230; cf. 292), and the birth of multiplicities
(DR 90; cf. 133). What does this mean? Deleuze calls the first
synthesis of connection a 'foundation' and the second synthesis
of disjunction a 'ground' (DR 79). Recalling what we have said
on causation and vice-diction, an ungrounding synthesis must
therefore move beyond both the machine that relates and the
machines that are related to. In the third synthesis, there must be
something that takes something 'for itself' (AO 28). This implies

nothing less than that *each relation is a machine*.[2] Machines are irreducible to their relations, and reciprocally relations are irreducible to machines. To be irreducible is to be a body without organs with singularities that do not resemble their constituents. Is this not precisely what a conjunction is? A conjunction is a compound in which two things that are the case make for a *third* thing (the conjunction) that is the case as well. Take 'I have washed the car' and 'I have taken out the rubbish.' If both are the case, then a third thing, the conjunction, is the case as well: 'I have washed the car *and* taken out the rubbish.' With the very choice of the term 'conjunctive', Deleuze signals that any relation between any two machines is a machine in turn. Each relation will therefore take something 'for itself', as its terms will function as the generators of its own virtual body without organs and Idea, by which it will not be reducible to its components (even if it existentially depends on them). This is why the third synthesis is a synthesis of 'consumption' and of 'consummation' (AO 103). This cannot refer to the becoming of the machines forming the terms of the relation, as that concerns the second disjunctive synthesis of recording. Instead, it refers to the genesis of a new machine altogether, which from then on can engage in its *own* connections and becomings.

The third synthesis therefore implies the production of a 'residue' (AO 28), not in the sense of insignificance, but rather in the sense of a result or outcome, which is why Deleuze describes the moment of consumption or consummation in terms of a 'so it's . . .' (AO 29). What can 'it' then be? It can be anything. Water is a conjunction of hydrogen and oxygen, political parties are conjunctions of their members and their demands, love is a conjunction of lovers. Even my perception of a tulip is an irreducible machine in its own right. Granted, it is weak, frail, and all too dependent on others. Nevertheless, neither I, nor the tulips, nor even a thousand other entities can ever be the being of this perception. Nothing can stand in for it. Every production, even the production of a quick glance or a thin smile, implies the genesis of new machines, because to produce something is to produce something irreducible, something with a body of its own. As Deleuze writes, 'the genesis of the machine lies precisely here: in the opposition of the process of production of the desiring-machines and the nonproductive stasis of the body without organs' (AO 20). The same thought is expressed in the following:

> [M]an is a *component part* of the machine, or combines with something else to constitute a machine. The other thing can be a tool, or even an animal, or other men. We are not using a metaphor however when we speak of machines: man *constitutes a machine* as soon as this nature is communicated by recurrence to the ensemble of which he forms a part under given specific conditions. The man-horse-bow ensemble forms a nomadic war machine under the conditions of the steppe. Men form a labor machine under the bureaucratic conditions of the great empires. The Greek foot-soldier together with his arms constitute a machine under the conditions of the phalanx. The dancer combines with the floor to compose a machine under the perilous conditions of love and death. (BSP 117–18)

There is no dualism between machines and relations, because all relations are machines. As we read in Deleuze's study of Nietzsche: 'Every relationship of forces constitutes a body – whether it is chemical, biological, social, or political. Any two forces, being unequal, constitute a body as soon as they enter into a relationship' (NP 40; cf. ATP 149; SPP 19). This same idea is expressed many times throughout Deleuze's work. For example, he writes how the individuation of singularities, which is their actualisation into a relation, organises 'a new dimension in which they form a unique whole at a higher level' (DI 87). In *A Thousand Plateaus*, he writes that 'whenever someone makes love [. . .] that person constitutes a body without organs, alone and with the other person or people' (ATP 30). Whatever the type, all relations imply that something becomes detached from the immediate production of an actuality, thus giving rise to a new nomadic entity: 'the product is something removed or deducted from the process of producing: between the act of producing and the product, something becomes detached, thus giving the vagabond, nomad subject a residuum' (AO 39). As each synthesis always implies the other two syntheses as well, this means that any connection whatsoever involves the production of a non-productive, irreducible body without organs (AO 19).

Deleuze calls this residual entity a 'celibate machine' (AO 29). And since *every* assemblage has been synthesised from other multiplicities, there is no rhizome that is not a celibate machine. Each machine is paranoiac in the sense of being irreducible, miraculating in the sense of undergoing virtual becoming, and celibate in the sense of being truly new with regard to the machines that initially produced it. Each machine is celibate, 'an autonomous figure binding to itself neutrality and genetic power' (LS 123). Each machine is 'an orphan, just as it is an anarchist and an atheist' (AO 354), precisely because it is irreducible in its own right *even if* it is but the feeblest of relations flashing between two others that utterly dwarf it. Nevertheless, even from such humble beginnings, a machine may grow to become a dominant force in its own milieu (the genesis and lifespan of storms, deserts, plagues, and ideologies exemplifies this). So we went too fast when we defined the Deleuzian 'eternal return' in the previous section. Its full and final meaning is the truth of the celibate machine (AO 33): every production produces an irreducible machine. 'Eternal return' does not just mean that every machine undergoes becomings, but also that each relation by which a machine becomes is itself a machine that becomes as well. What returns eternally is the production of the new, which is to say the genuine arrival of the future:

> Eternal return [. . .] causes neither the *condition* nor the *agent* to return: on the contrary, it repudiates these and expels them with all its centrifugal force. It constitutes the autonomy of the product, the independence of the work [. . .] It is itself the new, complete novelty. It is by itself the third time in the series, the future as such. (DR 91)[3]

We thus see another striking feature of the mereology implied by machine ontology. Not only is a poem as real as a volcano and a young woman as real as a galaxy, but the *reading* of the poem by the young woman is as real as volcanoes and galaxies as well. Machine ontology is pluralism pushed to its limits, as everywhere there will be 'the unconditioned character of the product in relation to its production, and the independence of the work in relation to its author or actor' (DR 92). Note also that acknowledging the celibacy of machines is what Deleuze calls being worthy of events:

> Accept the event. What does that mean? It doesn't mean at all to resign oneself [. . .] The event, at the same time, is effected in bodies – and doesn't exist if not in bodies, but it contains in itself something incorporeal. 'My wound existed before me, I am born to embody it.' That is to say, yes, it is effected in myself, but it contains something by which it isn't anymore 'my' wound. It is 'he' wound [« *il* » *blessure*] [. . .] To be worthy of what happens, it is to draw, in the event that is effected in me or that I effect, it is to draw the part of the 'un-effect-able' [*l'ineffectuable*]. (SCS 030680)

Being worthy of events implies acknowledging that my relations and parts are not 'me', but first and foremost a 'them' from which I draw something. So as we have seen, every entity, even a wound, will have its Libido: its connections to generators and generations. Every entity will have its Numen: the becoming of its transcendental properties as a result of its encounters. We now add that every entity will have its 'Voluptas': its contributions to the inception of other assemblages. The bullet does not just hit me, it generates a wound as it hits me. The 'residual energy' of encounters therefore indicates the production of a new machine:

> Just as a part of the Libido as the energy of production was transformed into energy of recording (Numen), a part of this energy of recording is transformed into energy of consummation (Voluptas). It is this residual energy that is the motive force behind the third synthesis of the unconscious: the conjunctive synthesis 'so it's . . .', or the production of consumption. (AO 28–9)

The conjunctive synthesis shows why machine ontology is not a dualism, but instead upholds a duality between virtuality and actuality across the board. It also gives us Deleuze's answer to the problem of mediation. Instead of positing a universal background (an 'open Whole'), Deleuze holds that relations are forged within or through machines themselves. Nothing can bridge the gap between two machines except a third machine functioning as a 'veritable external bridge' (DI 163). The bird and the river that I see may have nothing to do with each other, but they nevertheless converge within my relating to them. The same goes for the components of water, love, political systems, trees, houses, festivals, storms, and galaxies. Each entity can, in principle, function as the medium or factory in which new relations are forged. But why is it the *third* synthesis that 'organizes the converging series over which it bears as it prolongs them under a condition of continuity' (LS 175; cf. 229)? Was this not already the principle of rupture and contiguity implied in the first synthesis of habit, connection, and contraction? It was not. Take again the bird and the river in my perception. It is *through* my perception, which is a machine distinct from myself, that I connect to the bird and the river as parts of the same contiguous world. The conjunctive synthesis is distinct from the connective synthesis in that the former concerns that which must be generated (a celibate machine) *during* the connection with other machines (partial objects, sense-events) in order for the encounter to last.

Someone may point out that one cannot produce a medium (the relation) without requiring another medium in which that new medium comes to be. This is completely true. Wherever a celibate machine is produced, there must already be another machine to function as the factory or territory for that production: 'the celibate machine first of all reveals the existence of a much older paranoiac machine' (AO 30). As Deleuze writes, 'a machine is constituted from the moment there is communication between two portions of the outside world that are really distinct *in a system*' (BSP 119, emphasis added). To provide an analogy, take a meeting between two strangers. They can only meet if they are already together somewhere. If they are to meet, they must meet in a bar, a street, a metro car, a chatroom, or a prison. There must always be an encounter *in* a specific space and time (AO 259). That in which two assemblages meet is the 'older' machine that Deleuze refers to. Yet *once* they meet, they become the generators of something entirely new, and from that point on they are no longer (just) together in a bar or a street, but also in the celibate machine that they generated within the older machine. They are now together in a love, a hate, or a conversation. Since this new machine is irreducible to the older machine in which they met, they can try to use the new, celibate machine to leave the older machine while nevertheless remaining together. Lovers can, after all, leave the bar in which they fall in love. This is why every new relation is 'the nuptial celebration of a new alliance' (AO 30). It is also why conjunction or 'conjugation' always 'plugs or seals the lines of flight' and 'performs a general reterritorialization' (ATP 220). Lines of flight are plugged, because excessive desire is effectively actualised within the context of a specific relation. The generators of the celibate machine are reterritorialised, because they are now the generators of a truly new medium in which they 'coexist' (LS 225) as something specific: a person in an army becomes a soldier, someone in a club becomes a dancer, and so on. It follows that our identities (philosopher, gardener, wine connoisseur, and so on) are not so much markers of who we are as they are indicators of that which we co-generate. To be a soldier is to actualise one's virtual singularities (which differ in kind from actualities and do not resemble soldiering) within an army, a battle, a videogame, or a fantasy. But as Deleuze writes, a subject is always quick to confuse herself 'with this third productive machine and with the residual reconciliation that it brings about: a conjunctive synthesis of consummation in the form of a wonderstruck "so *that's* what it was!"' (AO 29). Any conclusion that one 'truly is' a nurse, an athlete, or a criminal is wrong, precisely because virtual being does not resemble actual identities, relations, or activities. What is true, however, is that these markers of identity can signify the machines in which we tend to dwell and to which we tend to connect, so that these could be major factors in determining our becoming.

Another way of putting this is that being public precedes being private. If two machines are to forge a relation, they must first be in a far more public place in which countless other entities may swarm as well. Soldiers and bullets meet in battle, minuscule elements are forged into more complex assemblages within the heart of stars, and ideas are born in conversations and readings. It is in this sense that a local 'height' renders possible contact, or the actualisation of machines to other machines (LS 198, 247). Such height is never a universal background that functions as the general medium for interaction and genesis. Deleuze's ontology denies the existence of something like 'the social' in general. It is always specific machines that function as the locus of encounters. Multiplicities become 'bound together' only on the full body of yet another multiplicity, so that they are in a sense 'on' its body while nevertheless remaining completely distinct (BSP 133). Conjunction thus points to the pre-existence of a *milieu* which is the 'Ambiance' or 'Encompasser' (C1 141) for the production of relations and things. As Deleuze writes in his essay on Lucretius, 'a body is born not only of determined elements [. . .] it is born also into a determined setting, which is like a mother suited for its reproduction' (LS 272). There is not just one such factory, but rather 'a pantheism of mothers' (LS 272). Such a milieu is what Deleuze early on refers to as a 'dark precursor' (DI 97, 102; DR 119–20). It is 'dark' because it is in a way absent from the sense-events for which it allows and from the celibate machines that spring forth from it. After all, I encounter my future *beloved* in the bar, and not the *bar*. The bar is just the environment in which I encounter someone. If I encounter the bar, then I do so within yet another machine. Moreover, it is by no means necessary that the lover's love remains tied to the bar in which it was conceived.

What happens when, for example, someone is being cut by a knife (LS 5)? There is, of course, the cutting of the knife and the being cut of a victim. Since relations are unilateral, these are two distinct sense-events. These must happen somewhere in a bar, in a street, or on a battlefield. And we must now add that, for as long as it lasts, there is another assemblage being generated, namely the knife fight itself, which is no less real than a war, a fire, a tank, or a flame. To take a more peaceful example, consider what happens when we drink tea. As Deleuze writes, 'the true container is not the cup, but the sensuous quality, the flavor' (PS 119). A few seconds ago, the tea and I were already together in a room, though unrelated. Yet once I drink it, the tea and I are together in a new assemblage generated by me and the tea, which we can call the drinking or the tasting, signalled to me by the flavour I experience. Like my perception of the bird and the river, it is *through* the tasting that the tea, which remains a 'sealed vessel' in itself, is translated into an 'open box', thus becoming available to being encountered (PS 140).

As Deleuze writes, in each production there is always something that 'diverts' (AO 52). We must thus conclude that *'sufficient reason or the ground is strangely bent*: on the one hand, it leans towards what it grounds, towards the forms of representation; on the other hand, it turns and plunges into a groundlessness beyond the ground which resists all forms and cannot be represented' (DR 274–5; cf. 154). This is not to say that there is a universal unground lurking behind the scenes. Rather, it is to say that each encounter implies the immediate generation of a new machine that cannot be reduced to its generators. The conjunctive synthesis thus refers to a 'synthetic progression' (DR 181) or 'progressive determination' (DR 210) by which new entities emerge, each with a contingent shot at becoming weaker or more powerful, at connections, contractions, recordings, and becomings. Yet no machine is a machine in general. Each has its own specific Idea in variation. It follows that a given machine will not be able to even register the existence of the vast majority of other machines. Another way of putting this is that for Deleuze, compossibility and incompossibility are *in this world*, as opposed to Leibniz, for whom reality is entirely compossible with itself yet incompossible with realities that God did not engender. Sometimes incompossibility is 'practical', as when we are forbidden to enter a certain bar or street, or when certain words are forbidden in certain places. At other times, it will be truly 'essential', as when we simply do not have the *puissance* to be somewhere or encounter something. Dark matter is a good example of the second type: we think we know it exists, but we are unable to encounter it until we construct the proper machines to overcome our current limits.

Any celibate machine can start to function as a 'quasi-cause' (AO 180; LS 94). Recall that a celibate machine is generated by machines that function as its parts. The celibate machine contracts its desire from them through becoming. In doing so, it does not encounter its generators directly, but as sense-events or partial objects with specific actual qualities. These sense-events, having a specificity rather than a bare particularity, retain 'a relation of causality with their physical causes' (LS 169–70), which we called 'vice-diction' or the participation of machines in how they are encountered (cf. section 1 of Chapter 7). On the other hand, sense-events have a relation with their celibate machine. As they are actual *to it*, it is the celibate machine that finds them combined into its own contiguous world.[4] Hence the celibate machine comes to function as a 'quasi-cause' for sense-events (cf. LS 5, 33, 144). Or in the terminology of *A Thousand Plateaus*: 'It is in the [body without organs] that the organs enter into the relations of composition called the organism' (ATP 159). There is, after all, no preordained togetherness for the organs of animals or the inanimate parts of buildings and planets. They are only together insofar as something makes them coexist and 'cooperate'. This is why a frequently encountered term in *Anti-Oedipus* is *se rabattre sur*, translated as 'falling back on'. As Deleuze writes:

> [The body without organs] falls back on all production, constituting a surface over which the forces and agents of production are distributed, thereby appropriating for itself all surplus production and arrogating to itself both the whole and the parts of the process, which now seem to emanate from it as a quasi-cause. Forces and agents come to represent a miraculous form of its own power: they appear to be 'miraculated' by it. (AO 24)

Wherever a machine connects to its generators, its generators may also connect to it (sometimes it may force them to do so, but this is not necessary) and make it one of the parts that partakes in their becoming. Deleuze calls such a loop 'quasi-causal' because it may lead us to think that the product (the celibate machine) did not just come to co-determine its producers, but that it preceded them in the first place (AO 22, 180). 'Trickle-down economics', 'God created man', 'you owe everything to your country', 'the hand evolved so that we could grasp', and 'the royal bloodline can be traced to the gods' are only some examples that presuppose that a product fully preceded its producers.

The quasi-causal nature of celibate machines and the insight that even relations are such machines makes machines what Deleuze calls 'paradoxical entities' (LS 40–1, 97). In functioning as a local medium,[5] a machine is two-sided and in a sense 'circulates' through the 'signifying and the signified series' (LS 40). The medium, for example the knife fight, is where the cutting by the knife and the being cut by the victim take place. Being a machine, it is displaced in relation to itself, as its virtuality cannot be reduced to its actual presence and location in other machines. As we noted earlier in section 2 of Chapter 4, a machine is absolute (*ab solus*) in its irreducibility. Hence 'the paradoxical entity is never where we look for it, and conversely that we never find it where it is' (LS 41; cf. 228). Furthermore, because its essence is malleable, it fails to observe 'its own identity, resemblance, equilibrium, and origin' (LS 41). Moreover, it is 'in excess in the one series which it constitutes as signifying, and lacking in the other which it constitutes as signified' (LS 41).[6] This is because relations are unilateral. If I look at the river, my perception is a machine that mediates my encounter with the river. My perception is irreducible to and hence excessive over me. The river, however, can remain utterly unperturbed by both me and my perception. Then what about the bar in which two future lovers meet? That bar is simultaneously excessive and lacking in two different directions, which is entirely possible since nothing forbids a machine from being the medium for the forging of multiple relations.

Now that the machinic nature of relations has been established, we can address another notorious part of Deleuze's philosophy: the theory of differential relations. For Deleuze, 'differential relation' is a philosophical concept inspired by the mathematics of differential calculus, but not equivalent to it (cf. DI 102, 176–7).[7] Furthermore, the philosophical concept can easily be explained without reference to the mathematics. As Deleuze writes, there is 'nothing mathematical' in his notion of differential relations (DR 181). He instead aims to give *ontological* meaning to differential relations (DR 170). Hence 'differentials express the nature of a problematic as such' (DR 178). We therefore require an ontological and not a mathematical analysis of Deleuze's appreciation for the notion of differential relations stemming from the fact that in them, 'dx is strictly nothing in relation to x, as dy is in relation to y' (DR 171). Now, for Deleuze, 'dx is the Idea' (DR 171). It follows that x is the body whose Idea it is. That dx is nothing in relation to x first concerns the formal distinction between a Figure and its code. Within the virtual half of a machine, the body is simple and non-productive, whereas desire is multiple and productive (as cause). Furthermore, a body is in a sense indifferent to the variations and becomings of its Idea, as its generation is realised by other machines, not by its own *puissance*. Second, dx being nothing in relation to x reminds us that the actualisation of a virtual Idea into a machine's relations is never the actualisation of its body, the latter remaining withdrawn behind its actual surfaces.[8] We can now understand the following:

> The symbol dx appears as simultaneously undetermined, determinable, and determination. Three principles which together form a sufficient reason correspond to these three aspects: a principle of determinability corresponds to the undetermined as such (dx, dy); a principle of reciprocal determination corresponds to the really determinable (dy/dx); a principle of complete determination corresponds to the effectively determined (values of dy/dx). (DR 171; cf. 172)

A machine's Idea as such is undetermined yet not indeterminate. It is the virtual being of an assemblage which differs in kind from and cannot be reduced to how it was, is, or will be determined in actual relations. It is excessive in principle. Nevertheless, an Idea *can* be translated into actual manifestations, but this requires at least one other machine. Together, two machines thus guarantee that an Idea is determinable. Should they encounter one another, the result will be a 'complete' determination in the form of a concrete manifestation, or a 'depotentialization' (DR 174) in which *puissance* is brought into actuality. As we have seen, each relation between multiplicities yields another assemblage, which is a differential relation in the precise sense that it cannot be reduced to its generators. The celibate machine will connect to and contract from its generators on its own terms, so the actualities that it encounters are 'nothing' to the virtual aspect of these generating machines, which differs in kind from their manifestations.[9] Water is a differential relation with regard to its hydrogen and oxygen, nations are differential relations with regard to their laws and citizens, a love is a differential relation with regard to its lovers, and so forth.

How, then, does the notion of differential relations testify to 'the power of Ideas to give rise to Ideas of Ideas' (DR 172)?[10] Because the Idea of a machine is generated by contracting other machines that have their own Ideas in turn. My Idea or desire is 'nothing' in relation to its generators: in and of themselves the singularities of my eyes have nothing to do with my capacity to see. Since these generating machines are again differential relations with regard to their respective generators, we can say that each Idea is tied to a group of differential relations (DI 99; DR 174). And as an Idea is strictly synonymous with desire, code, power, and singularities, we can also say that 'corresponding to the determination of differential relations are singularities, distributions of singular points' (DI 176). The notion of differential relations thus, again, emphasises the irreducibility of entities and the fundamental split within each individual assemblage (cf. DR 172).

The conjunctive synthesis, the celibate status of machines, and the differential nature or relations (hence also the celibate status of relations and the differential nature of machines) emphasise how Deleuze's machine ontology allows for surprise and novelty in reality. It is in this sense that the conjunctive synthesis is the synthesis of the future (DR 115, 90): each synthesised relation heralds the arrival of a genuinely new and irreducible entity, one for which not even the sum total of other machines can stand in.[11] This excess, this 'residue' or 'consumption' implied in all events is the promise of all emancipation, but also of 'all art, all poetry, all mythic and aesthetic invention' (PS 4; cf. DR 41). The third synthesis is the final building block of an ontology that does away with all universal grounds, all false depths and heights, all reductionism and all internalism. It is also the third synthesis that 'draws together the totality of time' (DR 89). With the birth of a new celibate machine, *it* too starts to connect (first synthesis) and become (second synthesis), giving rise to further celibate machines in the process, and so forth. As Deleuze dramatically puts it, conceiving of a reality thus operating without a transcendent height or depth is 'to throw time out of joint, to make the sun explode, to throw oneself into the volcano, to kill God or the father' (DR 89; cf. C2 xi).[12] At the end of all things, true repetition thus also comes to signify the 'emission of singularities' (DR 201; cf. LS 59), which is to say, the genesis of irreducible machines.

Deleuze sometimes calls schizophrenic reality a game without rules. Any reductionist or internalist metaphysics can be understood as a game with predetermined rules and limits. Conversely, machine ontology holds that there are no a priori rules that determine which entities will exist and how they will relate. It merely outlines a formal fourfold structure for entities and a triadic synthetic model of relations. We can compare this to a throw of the dice.[13] For Deleuze, each throw of the dice, which is to say each production of a relation, 'affirms necessity' and combines 'all the parts of chance' (NP 28). The affirmation of necessity refers to the virtual twofold of whatever machines are involved in a situation. After all, it is absolutely necessary that they encounter actual manifestations based on their singularities, and that their Idea undergoes becoming based on these contractions. Not a single entity has the choice not to have the desire it has. Yet any event is also a combination of all the parts of chance, since not a single machine *had* to exist. Existence is an existential matter, not an ontological one. Moreover, each event generates a celibate machine that is irreducible to its generators, hence further emphasising the contingent nature of existing machines.[14] This is what Deleuze means when writing that each throw results in 'the unique number which cannot be another' (NP 32). Another way of putting this is to say that the encounters between entities that result in the genesis of new machines are 'aleatory' (DR 198). Actualisations are aleatory because the virtual aspect of the machines involved differs in kind from these manifestations. Virtual properties do not imply any specific actualities. A sense-event is just what a machine 'happens' to be doing, not what it was 'meant' to do. Moreover, the point of contact between entities is aleatory in so far as their relation will be another machine that cannot be reduced to its generators, hence 'ungrounding' itself from them (DR 200).[15]

Sixth Intermezzo – Tristan Garcia and Formal Things

We have seen how there is no dualism between machines and relations. Any new relation is immediately a new machine. It follows that each machine exists sandwiched between other machines. On the one hand, there are the machines that generate it, meaning machines encountered in actuality. On the other hand, there are the machines that it generates, meaning machines to which becomes actual. Due to externality, a machine always remains irreducible to either side.

Actual presence to another machine never amounts to dissolving into the very being of that machine. From the very moment of its inception, each machine is therefore 'celibate'. Such absolute irreducibility also characterises entities as featured in Garcia's ontology, though he prefers to call them 'solitary'. Comparing Garcia and Deleuze on this irreducible 'in-betweenness' will draw attention to a fundamental difference in *how* entities are said to be irreducible. As we will see, for Garcia a thing is always *less* than its parts and environments, whereas for Deleuze it is always *more*.

Garcia adheres to a two-sided ontology that captures entities in their *formal* being on the one hand and their *objective* being on the other. This is roughly comparable to the distinction we have been making between an ontological and an existential reading of machine ontology. Ontologically, each machine is absolutely equal in being a fourfold of body, Idea, partial object(s), and qualities. No machine will ever be a fivefold or threefold, and the four aspects of a machine will always be these four and no others. Existentially, the exact opposite is the case. Machines are produced via specific and varying actualisations of specific other machines, gain specific powers, and actualise in specific ways to specific other machines. Ontologically, there is no difference between a cat and a table. Existentially, they differ tremendously. Likewise, Garcia holds that all things are *formally equal* and *objectively different*.

Much like machine ontology, Garcia holds that everything equally counts as a thing. A duck, the sky, the number six, a pebble, an impossible entity, and a word are all equally things despite their many objective differences. Nevertheless, Garcia goes further than Deleuze by also assigning thinghood to qualities. For Deleuze, 'red' is an actualisation of a machine, but it is not itself a machine. For Garcia, 'red' is simply another thing with the same ontological dignity as a sports car or a camel. Garcia's ontology is therefore significantly more 'flat' than Deleuze's. We return to this point later in our discussion. For now, we will first outline some key features of Garcia's ontology in *Form and Object*.

Garcia seeks to grasp things in their irreducibility via a method of 'de-determination' (2013: 21). For example, one de-determines a tree by abstracting it from its components, its environment, its properties, its past, and its future. In terms of machine ontology, one removes all actuality pertaining to an entity, meaning everything that generates an entity and everything that an entity manifests to others. De-determination leaves only the tree as a 'solitary' thing that is 'reducible to nothing' (Garcia 2014: 8). The parallel with Deleuze's externality thesis will be obvious here. Yet *contra* Deleuze, Garcia does not think that a solitary thing is in any sense a real being in itself. Garcia rejects all varieties of substantiality or essence under the rubric of 'compactness'. He thinks that endowing an entity with any kind of positive content to constitute *its* being always ends up in entities simultaneously trying to be a whole and the component of that whole. For Garcia, such entities are somewhat like the mythical Ourobouros serpent trying to swallow its own tail. It never works, and even if it did it would fail, because success would imply the serpent vanishing into nothingness.

Much like Gabriel, Garcia therefore concludes that being or existence is only ever being or existing *in* something: 'to be in something and to be something are equivalent' (2014: 60). How can a thing be irreducible if its being is only ever being *in* and never a proper being *it*? By defining it as the difference between what is in it on the one hand, and what it is in on the other hand: 'a thing is nothing other than the *difference* between *that which is in this thing* and *that in which this thing is*' (2014: 13). 'That which is in this thing' is whatever composes something, 'that in which this thing is' is whatever a thing composes: 'a thing is precisely the connection or relation between what composes this thing and what this thing composes' (2014: 119). This difference is not positive. There is no content standing between the generators of a thing and whatever a thing generates, nothing resembling what Deleuze calls a machine's Idea or singularities. A thing has no substantial or essential being. For example, 'a star is the difference between what composes a star and what a star is [in]. Nothing more, *nothing less*' (2014: 118, emphasis added). Hence, this difference that is thinghood is negative: the simple fact that the star is neither identical to the molecules composing it, nor to the galaxy or system in which it is found, nor to the sum of both. Again: 'a thing is nothing other than the *difference* between [. . .] content and container' (2014: 61). Garcia therefore warns us *not* to think of a thing as some kind of bag that separates an inside from an outside, because the analogy implies that a thing is comprised of some positive kind of content (here, leather or plastic).

This negative difference is insurmountable and irreducible, precisely because you can never conclude what is in a thing from what a thing is in, and vice versa (2014: 125–6). The components of a rock do not tell you whether that rock is currently in Arizona or Tuscany, and the bare fact of eating a hamburger does not tell you anything about its ingredients. Another way of referring to that in which a thing is, is to say that something *comprehends the thing*. Garcia calls this its 'form' (2014: 28) or the outline of its inclusion in the world. That which comprehends the thing is where a thing 'ends', because it is precisely the point where something else takes over. Conversely, that which is in a thing is what *the thing comprehends*. We can understand 'comprehension' as the opposite sense of being, because 'being' was already defined as 'being in'. Being is therefore identical to being comprehended in something else, and comprehending something else is equal to what we could call 'being been'. A thing is the simple difference between comprehending and being, because it can never be reduced to either side: 'a thing is emptied of its content and exiled by its container' (2014: 53). Quite simply, we can neither locate a tree among its components nor among the entities in its environment.

Things become a bit more difficult as soon as we realise that 'that which is in' a thing cannot be another thing. This is because a thing was defined as a difference, and this difference refers to two things that a thing *is not* (neither its components nor that in which it features). Saying that a thing is composed of a series of differences is therefore an incoherent statement, because it would amount to saying that things are composed by something that *is not* (i.e. neither this nor that).[16] Instead, the correct formal way of defining what is in a thing is 'no-matter-what' (2014: 19). The point of doing so is that if all entities are equally things, it makes no sense to talk about specific entities that compose things. One never knows in advance. Hence 'no-matter-what' or 'anything' or 'whatever turns out to be the case' composes a thing (2014: 21). 'No-matter-what' therefore simply means 'composed of whatever turns out to be the matter of which something is composed'.

Similarly, 'that in which a thing is' can also not be another thing, because it is equally incoherent to say that something that is not is in something that it is not. Formally, we must therefore say that a thing is in something quite unlike a thing, and Garcia calls the latter 'the world' or the 'form' of a thing (2014: 142). Such a world or form has a beginning (right where the thing ends), but it has no end. Think of the following example. If you put your hand on a wall, you can start to paint everything around your hand red. In principle, you can keep painting indefinitely. The outline or form of your hand therefore has a specific beginning (your hand), but it never ends. We should therefore understand the world as that against which a thing stands out, as everything that a thing is not, and at the limit as everything that comprehends a thing.

Both 'no-matter-what' and 'world' emphasise the formal equality of things. Existentially (Garcia prefers 'objectively'), things differ in terms of what composes them and where they feature in. Yet formally, all things are equal in being composed of 'no-matter-what' and in standing out against everything that they are not (in). If we move from this formal part of Garcia's ontology to its 'objective' double, things must be regarded as objects. This is to say that concrete entities are never composed of some undefined 'whatever' and located in some undifferentiated 'world'. Objectively, something is always composed of specific objects and located in other specific objects. Fabric is in the chair, the chair is in the room, and so on. As Garcia writes: 'things that enter into another thing, which in one way or another comprehends them, we call "objects"' (2014: 100). Note the parallel with Deleuze's machine ontology. *Qua* machine, each machine is equal in being a fourfold of body, Idea, sense, and qualities. *Qua this* or *that* machine, this formal schema is cashed out with *specific* entities generating a specific machine with specific powers defining it, and actualising in specific ways during encounters with other machines.

It should be obvious that no existential condition could ever undo the fact that entities are ontologically machines. Likewise, Garcia stresses that objecthood never replaces thinghood, but is the complement to an entity's formal being. As he quips, 'by keeping a dog in my basement, I do not remove the dog from the world' (2014: 78). The fact that the dog is in the basement changes nothing about the fact that the dog stands apart from everything that it is not (and everything that is in it). It merely indicates that the dog is somewhat more involved with *one* thing that it is not (the basement) than with most of the other things that it is not. Or take Garcia's example of the primitive sponges that some primates manufacture from leaves and twigs in order to clean their food (2014: 86). Formally, sponge, leaves, and twigs are all equal. Each is a difference between that which is in it and that in which it is. Objectively, they are unequal, among other reasons because the sponge exists through leaves composing it, while leaves are in turn not composed of leaves. In conclusion, '*Objectively*, things are together and unequal. *Formally*, things are alone and equal' (2014: 102).

Several objections come to mind when one critically assesses Garcia's ontology. First, there seems to be no identity over time for entities, neither *qua* things nor *qua* objects. This is because entities are defined as the difference between what composes them and what they compose. It follows that any change in what composes an entity or in what an entity composes engenders a completely new entity, because it yields a different difference. Since Garcia's entities have no 'in itself' to define them apart from their two types of relations, there is simply nothing that an entity can inherit from its past by which it could remain the same entity. Yet here, Garcia simply chooses to bite the bullet and assert that 'the object now' is a different entity from 'the object a few seconds ago' (2014: 115). As Jon Cogburn also notes, this assertion is supported via a new theory of time proposed by Garcia (Cogburn 2017: 117). The same theory of time also addresses the related problem that there seem to be no entities *at all*, as every thing (and object!) is defined in terms of its relations to components and that in which it features. It would therefore seem that there is in fact only *one* thing that exists, namely the totality of relations. Yet here Garcia dodges the bullet by moving to the other extreme: the difference between 'that which it is in' and 'that in which it is' that entities *are* is *so* irreducible that no entity ever dissolves into anything, up to the point that no entity can ever even be eliminated. Even entities from the most distant past remain existent and irreducible. They are never destroyed, but only become 'less present' than whatever entities comprise current states of affairs (Garcia 2014: 180–3). As there is no room here to elaborate on Garcia's theory of time that supports both claims, we can simply concede the point and move on, all the more because there is a more fundamental problem in Garcia's ontology that is more relevant in the context of Deleuze's machine ontology.

From the perspective of Deleuze's machine ontology, the real problem haunting Garcia's ontology is the infinite deferral of specification that we previously addressed in the context of Gabriel's ontology. Garcia's ontology admirably accounts for why there is something rather than nothing. Any entity is not nothing because it is irreducible to what composes it and what it features in. There is simply no way to explain it away. Yet his ontology does not account for why there is *this* rather than *that*. Why is *this* a cat and *that* a table? If this is a cat and that is table, then they must have some specific *character*. We already saw that this character cannot be derived from their formal status as things entered by 'no-matter-what' and entering 'the world', because all things are formally equal. The only remaining option is therefore that cats and tables derive their character from their objective existence. Yet note that entities *qua* objects are still defined as being *nothing but* (the difference between) other objects composing them and other objects in which they feature. This is the one point on which Garcia's formal and objective ontology are strictly identical:

> *Formally*, 'that which is a thing' corresponds to its matter, and 'that which
> a thing is' to its form, that is, to the world. From the formal point of view,
> all things have the same form, since they all enter alone into the world.
> *Objectively*, 'that which is a thing' are objects – things which are in this
> thing and which compose this thing; 'that which the thing is' can be the
> big thing into which this thing enters among other objects. (2014: 113)

Objectively, the cat can *only* be characterised by the objects featuring in it and the objects in which it features. It has no characteristics
in and of itself. Hence any explanation of why the cat *is a cat* exclusively consists of a reference to other entities. Yet the same is true for
these entities. In the cat's fur and paws, we do not find any specific
properties that could serve as a ground or source from which the cat
can derive its character. We just find *further reference* to whatever
objects compose the fur, and then of course further reference to
whatever composes those objects, *ad infinitum*. It therefore seems
that when, in the second half of *Form and Object*, Garcia introduces
objects with specific features (extensity defining where and when an
object is, and intensity roughly defining what an object is like), this
introduction is wholly unwarranted by either facet of his Janus-faced
ontology. Another passage in *Form and Object* confirms this:

> But what is the thing *really*? Does the thing have any consistency, like a
> thin layer of being separating what is in this layer and what this layer is
> in? Things really manifest a solidity or a matter, since I can touch them or
> hold them in my hand. Things have a *matter*, which is everything which
> enters into these things. But things *are* not their matter, since things are not
> *in* their matter. (2014: 108)

Put differently, if nothing is truly itself in either formal or objective
ontology, then by definition nothing can ever find a component or
environment based on which it can be *this* rather than *that* object,
because the same condition (not being a matter) holds true for each
thing among those components or in that environment. Here we see
a crucial difference between Garcia and Deleuze. For Garcia, the
difference-that-a-thing-is is purely negative. A thing is simply defined
as being neither its components nor that in which it features. A thing
is therefore always *less* than its components and the wholes into
which it enters. For Deleuze, the difference-that-a-thing-is is positive.
A machine is always *more* than its generators and its generations. It
has private, interior being comprised of what he calls its powers, sin-

gularities, or Idea. This 'more' is formally equal for all machines, but it is always cashed out *differently* depending on a specific machine's existential conditions. Depending on what a machine encounters, different internal properties or powers will be inscribed in its virtual, transcendental aspect. Depending on those singularities, it will register different entities differently. And depending on its singularities and those of machines encountering it, it will also be actualised differently to different machines.

The co-translator of the English edition of *Form and Object* also spots this problem, but suggests that it merely arises from an error in translation. He regrets having chosen 'difference' as that which is between what is in a thing and what a thing is, and he writes that he should have gone for 'differentiator' (Cogburn 2017: 180). But that would solve nothing, as Garcia's entities would *still* lack any properties that would constitute a sufficient reason for why *this* entity differentiates *like this* and *that* entity differentiates *like that*. There would still be nothing positive inscribed in the heart of beings, so that any and all specification and characterisation dissolves into an indefinite chain of references to components that are in things and 'big things' in which things are, without ever stumbling upon something that actually has *features*. This is precisely why Garcia thinks that a quality like 'red' is a thing. For Deleuze, there is a difference *within* entities, between their virtual properties and their actual manifestations to others. Therefore, machines must have actualisations that are not themselves machines, but rather translations of the *being* of a machine into the experience of another machine. But if no such being exists, then no such translation exists, which is precisely what happens when Garcia defines entities as a difference *between* entities rather than within themselves. Yet this exacerbates the infinite deferral of specification, since even a simple quality turns out to be nothing but a reference to its own components and environments.

These remarks should increase our understanding of why Deleuze assigns a positive and excessive 'content' to each machine, one that is formally or ontologically equal yet existentially different for each entity. If machines exist sandwiched between other machines, then something must characterise a machine *qua* machine if we are not to drown machines in an indefinitely proliferating network of references. Yet Garcia's distinction between things and objects also points to an important feature of Deleuze's machine ontology that is still to be addressed. If all machines are ontologically equal, then we need an explanation of why *hierarchies* of entities exist existentially. This nesting of machines in machines is addressed in the next section.

2 Rhizomes and Hierarchies

A machine is an ungrounded entity. As soon as 'older' machines enter into determinate relations and generate a new entity, this entity is fully irreducible. In this sense 'to ground is to determine the indeterminate' (DR 275). As a celibate machine will have its own virtual essence generated not from the virtuality but the actuality of other machines, it is also always a case of 'constructing the essence from the inessential' (DR 263). Each new machine is a force unleashed in the world, even if it is utterly dominated by other forces. We have seen that 'multiplicity' stresses the virtual twofold being that exceeds a machine's relation, and that 'assemblage' emphasises how this private essence is open to variation. We now come to 'rhizome', which focuses on various tensions between machines. The machine considered as rhizome focuses on how wholes relate to parts, how combat is the law of the Real, and how redundancy, fragility, and resistance are key notions in machine ontology.

To once again affirm that all machines are rhizomes, note that rhizomes are the 'nature' of multiplicities (ATP 30; cf. TRM 310), multiplicities are rhizomatic (ATP 8), and 'rhizomatics' is 'the science of multiplicities' (ATP 43). Like any assemblage, a rhizome 'has no beginning or end; it is always in the middle, between things, interbeing, *intermezzo*' (ATP 24). This simply repeats the principle that the essence of an entity is neither that which generates it nor that which it generates, but rather the Idea generated in it and by which it generates. Among other things, 'rhizome' emphasizes how such an individual essence is always constructed from heterogeneous sources. There is neither anything 'waterish' about oxygen and hydrogen in and of themselves, nor is there anything 'punkish' about electric guitars and bad haircuts. The generators do not resemble the generated machine, even though the generated machine always encounters its generators on its own terms and as parts of itself (following the principle of rupture and contiguity). As each generating part of a rhizome will in turn be a rhizome that is generated from non-resembling parts, reality can be seen as a giant system of interlocking 'caverns' or 'sponges':

> Dividing endlessly, the parts of matter form little vortices in a mael-
> strom, and in these are found even more vortices, even smaller, and
> even more are spinning in the concave intervals of the whirls that
> touch one another. Matter thus offers an infinitely porous, spongy,
> or cavernous texture without emptiness, caverns endlessly contained
> in other caverns: no matter how small, each body contains a world
> pierced with irregular passages [. . .] (FLB 5)[17]

This is why 'a rhizome is made of plateaus' (ATP 21). For Deleuze, a plateau is 'any multiplicity connected to other multiplicities by superficial underground stems in such a way as to form or extend a rhizome' (ATP 22). The comparison of multiplicities to root systems is apt. Recall that the essence of a machine is open to variation caused by its encounters. This means that anything a machine can encounter can become one of its parts, so that the relation between a machine and that which it encounters can be considered a tendril or a root leading to the transcendental, intensive matter that forms its beating and becoming heart. In this way, a single assemblage can make coexist 'engineers and parts, materials and machines person-nel, executioners and victims, the powerful and the powerless, in a single, collective ensemble – oh desire, flowing out of itself and yet perfectly determined each and every time' (K 57). The code of a human being, for example, is not determined solely by a biologi-cal blueprint, human artifice, or an ideological mould. Instead, she becomes coupled to countless machines, varying from the banal and quotidian to the sublime and exceptional, each of which can come to inscribe her code or alter her desire. For example, the being of a child is not simply determined by family and social conditions in general, but rather by its encounters with 'bread, money, dwell-ing place, social promotion, bourgeois and revolutionary values, wealth and poverty, oppression and revolt, social classes, politi-cal events, metaphysical and collective problems' (AO 121). Every rhizome is determined by others that are unlike it. Based on its desire, every rhizome relates to other machines in 'like' manner, even though these other machines do not have this relation to each other. In this sense, as Braidotti writes, Deleuze's philosophy is a 'teratology' (Braidotti 2000: 165; 2002: 172–211). In the absence of metaphysical standards, everything is equally abnormal, trans-versal, and eccentric. As machine ontology allows for no natural 'amicability' (DR 45), 'unnatural participation' (ATP 258) is every-where the principle of things.

Rhizomes thus have multiple entrances, and one can enter 'by any point whatsoever, none matters more than another, and no entrance is more privileged even if it seems an impasse, a tight passage, a siphon' (K 3). This is because each relation is ontologically equal in being a 'canal' by which desire can alter (though existentially, relations differ vastly in intensity and type). When Deleuze writes that 'only the principle of multiple entrances prevents the introduction of the enemy, the Signifier and those attempts to interpret a work that is actually only open to experimentation' (K 3), the same principle is affirmed. This is *not* to say that any machine can connect to any machine whatsoever.[18] It is also *not* to say that each relation to a machine is equally useful, good, valuable, or reliable. After all, each machine has its code and its specificity. Nevertheless, a rhizome is never exclusively generated by rhizomes just like it. As Deleuze says of Lucretius: 'there is no body composed of homogeneous parts' (LS 266). Electricity is not generated from electricity, dams are not built from dams, and cultures are not made from culture. Instead, everything is constructed from a motley crew of willing, unwilling, aware, unaware, intentional, unintentional, powerful and weak builders and supporters. Consider the following exemplary passages:

> [D]esire never stops making a machine in the machine and creates a new gear alongside the preceding gear, indefinitely, even if the gears seem to be in opposition or seem to be functioning in a discordant fashion. That which makes a machine, to be precise, are connections, all the connections that operate the disassembly. (K 82)

> [A machine is social in] taking men and women into its gears, or, rather, having men and women as part of its gears along with things, structures, metals, materials [. . .] [Kafka's] genius is that he considers men and women to be part of the machine not only in their work but even more so in their adjacent activities, in their leisure, in their loves, in their protestations, in their indignations, and so on. The mechanic is part of the machine, not only as a mechanic but also when he ceases to be one. (K 81)

> There is always an uncle from America; a brother who went bad; an aunt who took off with a military man; a cousin out of work, bankrupt, or a victim of the Crash; an anarchist grandfather; a grand-

mother in the hospital, crazy or senile. The family does not engender its own ruptures. Families are filled with gaps and transected by breaks that are not familial: the Commune, the Dreyfus Affair, religion and atheism, the Spanish Civil War, the rise of fascism, Stalinism, the Vietnam War, May '68 – all these things form complexes of the unconscious [. . .] (AO 118–19)

A rhizome or root system indeed! And this can work both ways, which is what 'extending' a rhizome means. A sailor's encounters with his ship, the ocean, and merciless storms will influence his becoming such that even when on land, he will walk, talk, and stand in a certain 'oceanic' manner, thus in a sense extending the rhizome of an ocean to places where the ocean itself cannot venture.[19] Or take the poetic description of how a man becomes a smith, which Deleuze borrows from the anthropologist Marcel Griaule:

> The shock of the hammer and the anvil broke his arms and legs at the elbows and knees, which until that moment he had not possessed. In this way, he received the articulations specific to the new human form that was to spread across the earth, a form dedicated to work [. . .] His arm become folded with a view to work. (ATP 41; cited from Griaule 1975: 38–41)

Within the rhizome of his smithy, the encounters of the apprentice with hammers, anvils, pieces of metal, scalding heat, and swarms of sparks will 'break' him, which is to say, significantly contribute to his becoming. As the years pass and the former apprentice becomes a master smith, his entire being will have become 'folded with a view to work', and even on a day of leisure with friends and family, his gestures and composure will betray his 'becoming-smith'.

Rhizomes thus emphasise the open nature of the whole constituted by a machine. As Deleuze writes,

> A whole is not closed, it is open; and it has no parts except in a very special sense [. . .] The glass of water is indeed a closed set containing the parts, the water, the sugar, perhaps the spoon, but that is not the whole. The whole creates itself, and constantly creates itself in another dimension without parts. (C1 10)[20]

The parts of a machine are other machines to which it cannot be reduced. Nevertheless, a machine is a closed, irreducible vessel in its own right, contracting its desire from other machines that it only ever encounters on its own terms. In this sense it 'creates itself' while nevertheless being generated by others. The 'other dimension without parts' is, of course, the private intensive matter of a machine's desire or code, as the Idea always 'corresponds to the objectivity of a "problem"' (DR 124). Because the Idea differs in kind from its generators and that which it co-generates, 'an element cannot be part of the sub-sets which it determines, nor a part of the set whose existence it presupposes' (LS 69). Put differently, 'a content [is] incommensurable with the container' (PS 117), because of the difference in kind between the virtuality of a body (the container) and the actuality of its parts (the content). Each whole is therefore but a part alongside parts (BSP 118; AO 58). First, it can be contracted as a part of the contiguous world of other machines. Second, these other machines can be *its own parts*, as when a love comes to co-determine the becoming of the very lovers who generate it ('my marriage is killing me'). Hence 'the body without organs is in fact produced as a whole, but a whole alongside the parts – a whole that does not unify or totalize them, but that is added to them like a new, really distinct part' (AO 371).

Despite Deleuze's association of desire with joy (ATP 155), rhizomatic being is hardly a walk in the park. As we said in the first chapter, machines are everywhere engaged in ignoring, transforming, recruiting, excluding, absorbing, consuming, producing, recording, targeting, fleeing, trapping, or displacing others. Everything exists in relations of tension (NP 40). Not everything is war, but everything is definitely cruelty and combat (ECC 132–3). In machine ontology, everything becomes a matter of violence and attack, because everywhere entities are drawn from their virtuality into actualities for others (DR 152). The transcendental becoming of all machines is 'a perpetual and violent combat' (ATP 159), which is as 'invisible' as it is 'incessant' (DR 109). Another way of putting this is to say that everything is both extremely fragile and surprisingly sturdy, depending on the case.

Everything is fragile in so far as nothing has metaphysical licence to exist. Everything is a contingent production, so that machines are 'possible although less probable' (BSP 118). Even the most resilient and eternal machines are but products. As Deleuze asks, is not each force proposed as being the One determining All (biology, language, natural laws, religion, ideology) ultimately always but a 'particular perishable and corruptible object which we consider in isolation from every other object? And what forms a whole if not a particular finite combination, filled with holes, which we arbitrarily believe to join all the elements of the sum?' (LS 267). Even the most powerful machines depend on generators whose principle has nothing to do with them. In a more intuitive example, we humans are extremely vulnerable to the tiniest of events. A single blood vessel bursts, and we die. Brief love affairs haunt us for decades. A tiny bit of metal, fired at high velocity, instantly terminates even the mightiest of generals. Yet these are not just human problems. Each machine is but a 'fragile combination' (D 5) which depends on the surface actualities of others (LS 202; cf. 81, 94). Everywhere and always, things only work 'so long as the surface holds' (LS 125), and there is 'nothing more fragile than the surface' which is always at risk of being 'overturned in a terrible primary order' (LS 82; cf. 94). This is because the virtual being of a machine can never be exhaustively deployed in a single relation, so that there is room for other entities to intervene and start relating to my bodily organs, or to my beloved, or to my most cherished possessions, and bring them to sever their relations with me. Even in the most totalitarian of systems, there is always 'the danger that a single organ might flow outside the despotic body, that it might break away or escape' (AO 243).

Is the fragility of entities not also central to Deleuze's book on Francis Bacon? Bacon is presented as the golden mean between Mondrian and Pollock. Mondrian's abstractions suggest that, behind the scenes of natural perception, everything is neatly organised into distinct fields and fixed ratios. In Pollock's abstract expressionism the opposite seems to be the case, as everything is movement, mixture, and action. For Deleuze, Mondrian clings to the vain hope that reality can ultimately be grasped *in itself* on the condition that we abstract from all representation. Mondrian offers 'an asceticism, a spiritual salvation' (FB 103). Pollock, on the other hand, is overly destructive, his paintings are 'all-over' and imply 'catastrophe' (FB 102). Machine ontology 'rejects' the false height of Mondrian and the false depth of Pollock. As Deleuze writes, 'the first danger, as we have seen, is that the ground would remain indifferent and inert, with an abstract and coagulated brightness. But there is yet another danger, namely, that the broken tones of the Figure would be allowed to blend together and become scrambled' (FB 143). Bacon, however, expresses precisely the kind of fragility that Deleuze seeks to illustrate. His Figures are always at risk of losing their flesh, meat and bone. The work and effort constantly needed to prevent parts from escaping or degenerating is what Mondrian and Pollock lack: 'tension is what abstract painting lacks the most' (FB 109). In Bacon's world it is 'as if combat had now become possible', showcasing a pluralist reality characterised by a constant 'acrobatics of the flesh' needed because everything constantly threatens to 'descend' and deterritorialise (FB 62, 23).

Yet rhizomes can be as resilient as they are fragile. For example, compare Deleuze's ontology to the metaphysics recently proposed by Quentin Meillassoux. Recall that for Meillassoux, reality is *hyper*-contingent. Everything can radically change or even disappear at any moment *without any reason*. As he writes,

> Everything could actually collapse: from trees to stars, from stars to laws, from physical laws to logical laws; and this is not by virtue of some superior law whereby everything is destined to perish, but by virtue of the absence of any superior law capable of preserving anything, no matter what, from perishing. (Meillassoux 2011: 53)

Like Deleuze, Meillassoux holds that nothing has metaphysical licence to exist. For Meillassoux, the lack of such an ultimate warrant implies the chance of instantly vanishing without any reason. For him, only superior metaphysical laws could have real traction on entities, and he thinks that such laws are impossible. For Deleuze, this is not the case. Wherever something has been generated by machines, it takes *machines* to undo it. No tree disappears without a fire burning it, termites consuming it, or thunderbolts detonating it into a swarm of splinters. *Puissance* is always something that must be overcome by other machines. If the people seek to depose a tyrant, then they will have to pit their machines against his. Deleuze would most certainly accuse Meillassoux of being a thinker of 'false height'. For Meillassoux, states of affairs emerge and change because something *beyond* any or even all specific entities makes it so, and this something, this hyper-contingency, can itself never be influenced or altered in turn, making it completely impervious to the comings and goings of the world.

Second, recall that every machine has *its* desire. This simple fact significantly limits the machines that it can encounter. A machine will be utterly oblivious to and untouchable by the vast majority of other existing machines. A single glance at the pyramids, the moon, or a religion will tell you that resilience is as much a feature of reality as fragility. Third, note that a number of parts of a machine can be redundant (ATP 98). The EU can lose some of the machines that help generate it (or gain new ones) while nevertheless remaining the EU. The same is true for the parts of a person, the stones in a volcano, the bricks in a house, and so on. Precisely because the virtual essence of a multiplicity differs in kind from the actual manifestations from which it assembles its desire, there exists a degree of resilience with regard to these manifestations. Of course, this degree may be minimal in some relations: destroy the brain and the human perishes. Yet as Deleuze writes, multiplicities 'always resist' (ATP 488), and even a sense-event is resistance (C2 256) in the precise sense that it manages to *last* for a while. As with fragility, human existence testifies to this resistance. After all, any human society is built to resist storms, riots, deaths, wars, unexpected catastrophes, the zealous infatuations of the young, and the foolish conservatism of the old. Or as Deleuze puts it, 'the prime function incumbent upon the socius, has always been to codify the flows of desire, to inscribe them, to record them, to see to it that no flow exists that is not properly damned up, channeled, regulated' (AO 47).

We can also analyse machinic encounters between machines in terms of their 'gravity', as Deleuze indicates (WP 154; D 104; ATP 386, 488–9). First, any rhizome combines heterogeneous and irreducible machines into the contiguity of its parts. Sometimes this will have little to no effect on those parts: I look at the river, the actualisation of which in my perception can slightly alter my desire, but the river remains unperturbed. At other times, however, machines can be drawn into the orbit of a rhizome that lays claim to them, becoming locked into acting as a technical machine for a social machine. The very becoming of these functional machines can thereby come under the spell of that social machine, if the whole manages to fall back on to its parts and becomes a part of these parts. The entire scene is then one of 'pieces of a puzzle belonging not to any one puzzle but to many, pieces assembled by forcing them into a certain place where they may or may not belong, their unmatched edges violently bent out of shape, forcibly made to fit together, to interlock, with a number of pieces always left over' (BSP 119). Many phenomena, ranging from human bondage to the orbits of planets around stars, illustrate this.

Second, machines make others gravitate 'towards' them by making some generations more sensible or 'better' than others. For example, 'there is a full body of the steppe which engineers man-horse-bow, a full body of the Greek city-state which engineers men and weapons, a full body of the factory which engineers men and machines' (BSP 131). Fielding horse archers in the mountainous landscapes and compact cities of ancient Greece is tactically unsound. It makes more sense to field heavy infantry who can occupy and hold narrow passages. Whoever chooses the latter over the former will win the day and continue to survive. Conversely, anyone foolish enough to rely on heavy infantry on the steppe will be destroyed in a war of attrition against elusive mounted raiders (Crassus versus the Parthians). Machines themselves can thus constitute 'territories' whose features promote some machines over others, and lock machines into stable patterns of production and behaviour. As demonstrated clearly in symbiosis, machines can even come to depend on one another for their very survival, so that their relations, though not ontologically predetermined, become what DeLanda calls 'contingently obligatory' (2016: 11). Peter Sloterdijk is therefore being shallow in saying that 'if you read Deleuze, by and by you feel a little bit uneasy because the resentment against all hierarchical structures is so strong' (Sloterdijk 2014). Sloterdijk does not see that the ontological absence of hierarchy and pre-established relations is precisely the condition for the possibility of a reality existentially characterised by *nothing but* hierarchy, *nothing but* machines functioning as technical and social machines for each other, and *nothing but* becoming because of others and making others become. As Deleuze writes, 'no doubt there is still hierarchy and distribution in univocal being' (DR 36), as 'doubtless, there is no more equality or any less hierarchy' in multiplicities than there is in a world according to metaphysics (ATP 33). There are always hierarchies based on 'things and beings from the point of view of power [*puissance*]' (DR 37). The ontological univocity of being implies nothing less than the 'great politics' of existence (LS 72).[21]

Whenever rhizomes come to lock the (re-)production and functioning of other machines into stable patterns, the former become what Deleuze calls 'strata' for the latter. Strata lock singularities 'into systems of resonance and redundancy [. . .] organizing them into molar aggregates. Strata are acts of capture, they are like "black holes" or occlusions striving to seize whatever comes within their reach' (ATP 40). Strata or molar organisations deprive desire of its 'objective being' (AO 40; cf. 163), which is to say that they enforce certain actualisations while excluding others. In and of itself, molar organisation is not something we can or even should get rid of.[22] Many machines come to function as strata, and Deleuze acknowledges the 'immense diversity' of energetic, psycho-chemical, geological, and organic strata (ATP 41). Nevertheless, three major strata are distinguished: the physico-chemical, organic, and anthropomorphic strata (ATP 502). Their existence invites the creation of 'regional' ontologies which would detail specific modes of existence in these domains based on fourfold being and threefold synthesis. *A Thousand Plateaus* attempts to outline these for a number of strata. For example, in the non-organic stratum, expressions are dependent on content (ATP 59). An entity such as sedimentary rock requires that specific machines, namely flysch, are actualised as its parts. The virtual properties of flysch must be expressed into sense-events such that flysch becomes a technical machine for the social machine of sedimentary rock. Sedimentary rock cannot but await the arrival of entities that start to express their content as its parts. Yet in organic strata, such expression is far more independent from content. After all, birds mate with birds to give rise to more birds. Even though successful reproduction requires far more machines than just two parents, it is nevertheless not the case that birds must passively await feathers, beaks, and beady eyes to arrive and accrue into more birds. Birds themselves are far more actively involved in manufacturing the proper expressions of machines that constitute birds. In the anthropomorphic strata, human activity gives rise to even more independence of expression with regard to content. Whereas a bird must definitely have the components of a bird in order to be a bird, humans seem to be able to create entities that are far more oblivious to their components. Compared to other entities, we are masters of 'multiple realisation', or the generation of the same expressions from a variety of machines. Beethoven's seventh can be played by a Japanese orchestra, a CD, or a vinyl record; wide varieties of symbols can signal the same message; the same information can be stored and retrieved from a variety of media; and so on.

We postpone further analysis of such regional ontologies to future research, and now turn to what Deleuze calls the 'principles' for rhizomes, each of which has already been foreshadowed in our preceding analyses. First, the 'principle of connection' dictates that 'any point of a rhizome can be connected to anything other, and must be' (ATP 7). Everything to which a rhizome relates is equally part of its contiguous world, of the flow of qualities over its partial objects. This 'must be', because a rhizome has no choice but to experience in terms of its code. A rhizome brings together other entities in a relation that these entities do not have among themselves. If we use a book as an example, then 'a rhizome ceaselessly establishes connections between semiotic chains, organizations of power, and circumstances relative to the arts, sciences, and social struggles' (ATP 8). The second 'principle of heterogeneity' (ATP 7) states that a rhizome does not resemble the multiplicities that generate it. Wherever at least two machines generate a third machine, none of these three is reducible to the others. There are thus only 'fragments whose whole relationship is sheer difference – fragments that are related to one another only in that each of them is different' (AO 56). The third 'principle of multiplicity' repeats that multiplicities are 'substantive' (ATP 8). A machine is neither first and foremost one of several machines belonging to the same One, nor a One that organises its many components. A machine is one *and* many in its internal reality: one in being a body without organs, many in having singularities open to becoming. Since this becoming concerns its essence, the 'nature' of a multiplicity changes 'as it expands its connections' (ATP 9). Fourth is the 'principle of asignifying rupture' (ATP 10). Though a rhizome may be actualised into many relational surfaces, these actualisations are ruptures that differ in kind from its own desire, which can never come to signify or be that into which it is actualised. There will, in short, never be anything 'waterish' about hydrogen or anything 'deskish' about the Idea of a piece of wood. Fifth is the 'principle of cartography' (ATP 13). Every machine has a specific desire, so that nothing stands in the way of labouring to create accurate, truthful, reliable, and useful descriptions of it. However, these descriptions can never *be* the machine that they describe. The map is never the territory that it maps. Moreover, each description or map 'constructs the unconscious' in the sense that it, too, is an irreducible rhizome. Finally, the sixth principle is that of 'decalcomania' (ATP 13), which states that whatever the origin and status of a machine, even if it is intended as a specific map of something else, it can always *become*. That is to say: its encounters can always lead to new or altered inscriptions of desire on to its virtual body.[23]

Our explication of the conjunctive synthesis was the final major step in our explication of Deleuze's ontology. The most important lesson learned here is perhaps that the generation of each new relation implies the production of a new machine, precisely because each relation *is* a machine in and of itself. There is no dualism between relations on the one hand and machines on the other. To forge a relation is to manufacture a new entity that Deleuze calls a 'celibate machine'. As with social and technical machines, celibate machines are not a separate class of entities. Instead, each machine is the celibate machine of its own production. It is not relevant whether such an entity turns out to be short-lived and barely noticeable or a long-lived behemoth that countless others must seek to negotiate throughout the ages. Each relation has its body and its desire, and like all other machines its presence differs in kind from its private, malleable essence. Hence in each connection-registration there is also this residue in the form of a new machine. The full threefold synthesis thus comprises 1) the manifestation of a qualified sense-event to a machine, 2) the extent to which this encounter alters the *puissance* based on which the relation was forged, and 3) the genesis of a new and irreducible entity altogether. This is the threefold of what Deleuze respectively calls 'Libido', 'Numen' and finally 'Voluptas'. We also saw that Deleuze's use of the notion of 'differential relations' precisely means that each relation, being a machine, is characterised by the now familiar internal difference in kind between its virtuality and its actuality. That relations are differential simply means that a machine, even though emerging as a celibate machine at a certain place and time, is always already excessive over all its current, past, and future relations.

Notes

1. As noticed by Arnaud Villani 'Conclure sur la conjonctive, c'est entrer dans les choses mêmes. Badiou reste à mi-chemin, suspendu' (1998: 47).
2. Hence Deleuze's claim, in one of his seminars, that a 'logic of relations' has two elements (SS 170281): first, understanding relations as external to terms; second, understanding that each individual is power, with individuals *also* including relations.

3. The past is the condition and the present is the agent (DR 93). Hence, again, Deleuze emphasises how any new machine surpasses both the actuality and the virtuality of its generators: 'all that returns, the eternal return, is the *unconditioned* in the product' (DR 297).

4. The event is 'submitted to a double causality, referring to the external and internal causes whose result in depth it is, and also to a quasi-cause which "enacts" it at the surface and brings it into communication with all the other [events]' (LS 211).

5. Again, entities 'converge not in themselves (which would be impossible) but around a paradoxical element [. . .] This element or point is the quasi-cause to which the surface effects are attached, precisely insofar as they differ in nature from their corporeal causes' (LS 183).

6. We must accord a double meaning to the term 'series'. On the one hand 'series' refers to the contiguity of events that make up the world of an entity. On the other, it refers to the serial variation of a machine's essence.

7. Philosophically, 'differential calculus is irreducible to mathematical reality' (SL 220480).

8. Deleuze explicitly relates differential relations to the externality thesis in SS 100381. Also see 'if the differentials disappear in the result, this is to the extent that the problem-instance differs in kind from the solution-instance; it is in the movement by which the solutions necessarily come to conceal the problem' (DR 178).

9. As we said earlier, a machine in a sense 'constitutes' its own parts in so far as it can only relate to things on its own terms. As Smith writes, 'the differential relation is thus not only a relation that is *external* to its terms, but a relation that in a certain sense *constitutes* its terms' (2012: 53).

10. Deleuze sometimes suggests that *only* Ideas or singularities generate partial objects or extensions, and that *only* differential relations or bodies generate qualities or flow (DI 100; DR 207, 210). Yet this is not really the case. As he writes, for example, 'there is in general no quality which does not refer to a space defined by the *singularities* corresponding to the differential relations incarnated in that quality' (DR 210, emphasis added).

11. '[L]a genèse des conjonctions [. . .] cette genèse de la nouveauté qui est essentielle, genèse de la nouveauté comme telle, c'est-à-dire qui n'implique aucune réduction du nouveau à l'ancien' (SL 100387; cf. DI 113).

12. From each encounter, a new machine springs forth as a 'congelation or condensation in a sublime occasion, *Kairos*, which makes the

solution explode like something abrupt, brutal and revolutionary'
(DR 190).

13. Cf. 'ontology is the dice throw' (DR 199). This machinic 'game' has
'no precise rules, and [. . .] neither winner nor loser' (LS 58), and
neither Man nor God is in control of the game (LS 60), because that
would violate externality.

14. Cf. 'Ideas are the problematic combinations which result from
throws' (DR 198).

15. At the limit, we can thus even say that the celibate machine or paradoxical entity *is* the aleatory point, which would make *each* machine
an aleatory point. Hence Deleuze writing about 'the erection of
a paradoxical instance, an aleatory point with two uneven faces,
which traverses the divergent series as divergent and causes them to
resonate through their distance and in their distance' (LS 174).

16. This is no complete account of how Garcia defends the formal presence of 'no-matter-what' and 'world' in his ontology, but it suffices
to grasp the gist of it. For a more extensive reconstruction, see
Cogburn (2017).

17. The reference to Leibniz is obvious: 'every portion of matter can be
thought of as a garden full of plants or a pond full of fish. But every
branch of the plant, every part of the animal (every drop of its vital
fluids, even) is another such garden or pond' (Leibniz 1989: §67).

18. 'The question [. . .] is whether the pieces can fit together, and at what
price. Inevitably, there will be monstrous crossbreeds' (ATP 157).

19. Cf. K 81. Bryant also refers to these descriptions of becomings in
sailors and smiths in his own version of machine ontology (2014: 34,
127).

20. Deleuze also approvingly notes that 'Proust maintained that the
Whole itself is a product, produced as nothing more than a part
alongside other parts, which it neither unifies nor totalizes, though it
has an effect on these other parts simply because it establishes aber-
rant paths of communication between noncommunicating vessels,
transverse unities between elements that retain all their differences
within their own particular boundaries' (AO 58; cf. PS 143).

21. Cf. 'Staying stratified – organized, signified, subjected – is not the
worst that can happen; the worst that can happen is if you throw the
strata into demented or suicidal collapse, which brings them back
down on us heavier than ever' (ATP 161).

22. 'Je ne vois pas de vie possible sans ensembles molaires' (SCS 150277)

23. Decalcomania is a technique to transfer the pattern of one surface on
to another surface.

9

Machine Ontology and Thought

With the fourfold and the three syntheses characterising machinic being now before us, we can go into further detail regarding the view of reality emerging from machine ontology. We first provide a broad and somewhat tentative account of how Deleuze's machine ontology would recast several 'standard' philosophical notions, including freedom, time, space, and selfhood. Next, we answer the question why human beings do not *naturally* think of reality in machinic terms. As we will see, *Anti-Oedipus* identifies a series of paralogisms or errors of reason that lead us astray when trying to discern the nature of reality. Each paralogism is a variation on the same mistake: to confuse a machine's relation with its proper being, for example by defining it in terms of an empirical quality or in terms of its origins. Finally, we will showcase how machine ontology accords with what Deleuze calls 'transcendental empiricism', an apt name for his overall philosophy and method of thinking. Transcendental empiricism rigorously respects human finitude in upholding that what we (and other machines) encounter is only ever a sign or manifestation of other entities, never these entities in and of themselves. This is the empiricism part. Nonetheless, Deleuze equally defends that thought can move beyond this condition. Although thought can never make the transcendental aspect of a specific entity present to itself, it can nevertheless manage to think *that* there is such a virtual side to machines. We can perhaps call this a 'formal' insight into machinic entities, in so far as it tells us *which* aspects machines have and *how* they engage with each other, but never *what* any specific machine is precisely.

1 Self and World

With the system of fourfold machines and threefold syntheses in place, and with the notion of rhizomes having served to illustrate a schizophrenic reality shaped by extreme fragility as well as stubborn resistance, and machinic behemoths as well as insignificant assemblages, we can now attend to several key philosophical notions from the perspective of machine ontology, though only in a very general way. These are selfhood, subjectivity, freedom, consciousness, space, time, otherness, and world. A short excursion into these notions may be useful in further coming to terms with machine ontology, but also in positioning Deleuze with regard to other philosophies we are familiar with.

To start, machine ontology holds that every entity is a self. It is so by virtue of the irreducible (non)-being or ?-being of its body without organs (cf. DR 64). Since every machine is a machine generated by machines, all of reality is riddled with what Deleuze refers to as 'passive' selves (DR 118). Although each self is a force unleashed in the world, these forces are passive in two senses. First and most obviously, the vast majority of these selves are incapable of intentional acts. Second, all selves, even those that take an active interest in their becomings, undergo passive syntheses in all their relations. Each such self *has* a subject, so that there is a 'larval subject' (DR 118) for each passive self. The subject of a self is its Idea: 'the only subject is desire itself on the body without organs' (AO 90). Like 'self', 'larval' has several senses. First, the subject is larval in that it is real but not actual. It is not an object of anyone's or anything's experience. Second, each Idea is larval in that its future encounters will further develop it by partaking in its becoming, even though we must once again stress that it is *not* the case that each relation will *significantly* change the Idea of a machine. Third, each Idea is larval in the sense that it may be actualised into a technical machine for a 'larger' social machine. In this sense the subject-desire of my bodily organs is larval with regard to my own subject-desire: it has become folded into functioning as a generator for me. This is what Deleuze tries to convey with his dramatic remark that 'the [body without organs] howls: "They've made me an organism! They've wrongfully folded me! They've stolen my body!"' (ATP 159). Everything Deleuze writes about folding, especially in his work on Leibniz, comes back to this same point: everywhere in reality are larval subjects made into the generators of 'larger' larval subjects, which are subjected to other social machines in turn. Plus, wherever the third synthesis takes place, a new self with such a larval subject is produced (AO 29). Each subject's openness to becoming is why the subject has 'no fixed identity, [and is] forever decentered, *defined* by the states through which it passes' (AO 32–3). As stated in our analysis of the conjunctive synthesis and Voluptas, this subject is 'defined by the share of the product it takes for itself, garnering here, there, and everywhere a reward in the form of a becoming [. . .] being born of the states that it consumes and being reborn with each new state' (AO 28).[1]

As the unconscious of a machine is the 'real subject', that with which we tend to identify ourselves is but an 'apparent residual subject' (AO 376). As we have shown, identity markers such as 'parent', 'lover', 'judge', 'Dutch', 'Hindu', and 'cheap wine aficionado' refer to that into which we tend to translate our desire, which first and foremost concerns machines generated in our relations with other entities. When it comes to our 'real' subjectivity, like all other selves, human beings are simultaneously absolutely solitary and utterly social beings. Recall what we cited earlier: 'any agent is all the more collective because an individual is locked into it in his or her solitude' (K 18). We are solitary in so far as our body without organs and our malleable singularities are irreducible to any other entity that ever was, is, or will be. Nothing can replace any of us, and not even our images of ourselves can stand in for our singularities. Like all machines, we are so solitary that we cannot even reach our own desire. Yet simultaneously, since nothing exists by itself, we are produced, kept intact, and essentially altered by relations with other machines. We also cannot even lift a finger without mobilising a veritable infinity of smaller and larger entities. We are all utterly alone, but simultaneously we are 'like a conspiracy of criminals' (D 9), engaged in unnatural participations to bring about unforeseen events:

> When you work, you are necessarily in absolute solitude. You cannot have disciples, or be part of a school. The only work is moonlighting and is clandestine. But it is an extremely populous solitude. Populated not with dreams, phantasms or plans, but with encounters. An encounter is perhaps the same thing as a becoming, or nuptials. It is from the depth of this solitude that you can make any encounter whatsoever. (D 6)

Nothing in this is exclusively human. Human existence does not imply an ontological rupture with the formal structure of fourfold beings and threefold synthesis. The progression from inanimate assemblages to living beings, to sentient beings, and then to reasonable beings can only be an increasing intensification of the irreducibility of entities to their generators and generations. So as with any entity, human beings enjoy a fundamental double freedom (LS 6). First, we can never be reduced to or integrated in what produces us. Second, we can never be reduced to or integrated in what we (co-)produce. This is a tragedy when it comes to good things as much as it is a blessing regarding evil things. Yet the irreducibility we share with all existing multiplicities is neither good nor bad in and of itself (cf. DR 19).

Yet surely human beings are at least conscious whereas other entities are not? And does not consciousness warrant that we are caring, fearing, doubting, wondering, active, moral, memorising, sympathising, artistic beings, vastly different from almost everything else? This is certainly the case, but such matters are existential and not ontological. Not even consciousness violates machine ontology. Here is Deleuze:

> What appeared finally to be a dead end was the confrontation of materialism and idealism [. . .] It was necessary, at any cost, to overcome this duality of image and movement, of consciousness and thing. Two very different authors were to undertake this task at about the same time: Bergson and Husserl. Each had his own war cry: all consciousness is consciousness *of* something (Husserl), or more strongly: all consciousness *is* something (Bergson). (C1 56)

Machine ontology follows what Deleuze here ascribes to Bergson. Because of the externality of relations to terms, to be conscious of something implies that there is a third thing in addition to whoever is conscious and what she is conscious of. Of course, a relation (of perception, attention, feeling, or thought) with something requires an 'old' machine in which the relation is forged. Yet more importantly, the *being conscious* itself is a relation, and therefore it is an utterly irreducible machine. Seeing, feeling, perceiving, engaging, attending, and all other varieties of being conscious of something imply the first, second, *and third* synthesis. Each relation is a new, celibate machine. If I perceive a blackbird, then my perception in itself is as impenetrable to all relations and as withdrawn from all presence as the blackbird itself.

Next, if that in which entities encounter one another is always another rhizome, then space and time are not universal and homogeneous containers that serve as media for entities and events. If everything were internal to space and (or) time, the externality thesis and the machine thesis would both be violated. Instead, spaces and times must be local phenomena rooted in machines themselves (cf. DR 51). According to Deleuze, space primarily relates to the singularities of machines (DI 111). As the fourteenth chapter of *A Thousand Plateaus* ceaselessly affirms, we must distinguish between two kinds of space (cf. ATP 474): first, the transcendental 'smooth space' of machinic singularities, and second the actual 'striated' space of actual manifestations. Any machine is confronted with the contiguity of actual sense-events that constitute its striated world, but these striations do not correspond neatly to the smooth spaces underlying them. This implies, first, that not all machines are part of all spaces. The windows in my living room co-constitute space for me, but not for the minuscule particles that pass through it unobstructed. Additionally, things are never located in space in general, but always in other machines. Two lovers are in a love, in a bar, in a street, in a city. Planets are in solar systems, in galaxies, in the universe. Everything is alone in itself and irreducible in its own virtual space. Yet simultaneously, machines are together in other machines, and never somewhere in general.

Time, too, must be separated into two halves (LS 5: cf. 21; DI 180). Deleuze calls the one 'Chronos' and the other 'Aion', with 'reciprocal exclusion' existing between them (LS 61). We can distinguish the two by looking at the characteristics that Deleuze ascribes to them. Chronos is 'the present which alone exists' (LS 77), concerns 'the action of bodies and the creation of corporeal qualities' (LS 165), and is 'the limit or the measure of the action of bodies' (LS 163). It is 'the present of the pure operation, not of the incorporation' (LS 168) and this operation '"regularizes" in an individual system each singular point which it takes in' (LS 77). Chronos, so Deleuze writes, 'is an encasement [and] the time of mixing and blending' (LS 162). Finally, it is 'limited but infinite time; infinite because cyclical, animating a physical return as the return of the Same' (LS 61). In other words, Chronos concerns the contiguous flow of actual encounters that a machine undergoes.

It is the passage of actual events for machines, or the changes that they experience. Chronos concerns how machines exist for (stand out to) other assemblages in being translated into actuality. It 'limits' the actions of bodies, because it concerns the contractions of their excessive virtual desire into actual manifestations. It 'regularizes' singular points because it concerns the relation of a machine to other machines that do not have this relation with each other. Chronos thus concerns the mixing and blending of machines, irreducible in themselves, into the contiguous world of yet another machine. This is a return of 'the Same', as no machine can ever go beyond registering other entities on its own terms.

Conversely, Aion concerns the 'unlimited past and future' (LS 61), 'attributes which are distinct from qualities' (LS 165), the 'already passed and eternally yet to come' (LS 165). It concerns that which becomes 'autonomous in the act of disinvesting itself from its matter and flees in both directions at once, toward the future and toward the past' (LS 62; cf. 5). It is the time of that in which singularities subsist and insist (LS 53), that which puts 'time inside the Figure' (FB 48). Aion 'can only be thought' (LS 74) as it divides what transpires into 'an already-there that is at the same time not-yet-there, a simultaneous too-late and too-early' (ATP 262), whereas Chronos is 'the time of measure that situates things and persons' (ATP 262). Aion is the time of becoming or counter-actualisation. It is the variation of essence inscribed on or incorporated into the virtual surface of rhizomes. As it concerns virtuality, it is distinct from actual qualities. Given the surplus nature of transcendental desire, it escapes each present, which is to say each relation. It is thus already passed and eternally yet to come. Taken together, Chronos and Aion account for time among machines: the alterations in transcendental singularities interwoven with the changes in actual and individually contiguous worlds.

But what is this world, and what are the others who populate it in addition to myself? Starting with the latter, an 'other' is, of course, just a machine that is not me. It is another distribution of singularities on another body enveloped by its actual surfaces (DR 260). As we have seen, what we usually take ourselves to be (mother, hoplite, horse archer, bureaucrat, and so on) is in fact always such an other: a machine that I generate and that in turn comes to generate me. Hence, we can say that 'I is another' (DR 261) in yet another sense than those already described in section 3 of Chapter 7. I am another in that I identify myself with some of the machines I generate. Yet Deleuze also mentions an Other, which is not the machine I encounter, but yet another machine that is announced yet not present in my encounter. This Other is 'neither an object in the field of my perception nor a subject who perceives me' (LS 307; cf. 309). It is something wholly other than the quotidian other (LS 317).[2] Deleuze defines this Other as *the expression of a possible world*' (DR 261; cf. LS 309). Consider the example of seeing a terrified face, 'under conditions such that I do not see and do not experience the cause of this terror' (DR 260). Such a face is 'the expression of a frightening possible world, or of something frightening in the world – something I do not yet see' (LS 307). The Other is thus a sign of a machine according to which another machine is found to function. It is a possible world to the extent that I can also become grasped by the machine that the sign announces. The terrified face makes me glance at the horizon, I see the approaching monster, and now I find myself in terror as well. Hence the Other announces a 'transition in the world' (LS 305). Deleuze calls this Other an always pre-existing 'structure' (LS 307), because machines are always located in other machines. The structure-Other fills the world with 'possibilities, backgrounds, fringes, and transitions' (LS 310). These Others certainly exist, as everywhere machines are functional machines to yet other machines, but it takes a being that is at least alive to discern them.[3] In its relation to me handling it, a book cannot discern the signs of contempt that announce that I am about to commit it to the flames. As Deleuze describes in his essay on Michel Tournier's Robinsonade, to lose the practical ability to discern the Other in others is to lose oneself in a world of immediacy: 'in the Other's absence, consciousness and its object are one' (LS 311).

But again, what is this world Deleuze speaks of? A world cannot be *the* world for the same reasons that space and time are not universal and homogeneous media. If *the* world existed, there would be something non-machinic containing all machines. Instead, 'an individual is [. . .] always in *a* world as a circle of convergence' (LS 110, emphasis added). A world is the contiguity of actual and qualified partial objects that a machine encounters. So first, a machine's world can vary as its desire, or that of the machines it encounters, changes. Second, each world is 'infinite in an order of convergence' (LS 110), as there is no predetermined quantity of machines that a machine can encounter. Third, each world has 'a finite energy' (LS 110) since each machine has its specific code and thus cannot discern just anything. Recall the example of the tick from section 1 of Chapter 6. Its world is everything it encounters based on its three powers (registering light, sweat, and blood). Our tick's world does not contain haikus, nuclear weapons, the German language, sharks, dinosaur fossils, and many other entities besides. It follows that there are always more entities than one finds in a world. It also follows that the same entity can be part of multiple worlds, as its vague essence can be actualised in multiple ways to multiple beings (LS 114).

The world does not exist, but we must nevertheless affirm that there is *one* reality.[4] There is one reality in the precise sense that there is not more than one. There is not the world of Matter and then the world of Spirit, with different principles for both. There may exist a theory, book, story, or anecdote about two distinct worlds of Matter and Spirit, but such an entity will just be a fourfold machine generated from other machines via three-fold syntheses. There are not, as for example Karl Popper would have it, metaphysically distinct realms for physical objects, mental states, and abstract entities such as numbers.[5] Machine ontology posits one reality in the precise sense that all machines and all their singularities are generated from *local* outsides, which is to say other machines with their own irreducible and withdrawn virtual aspect, but never from a *total* outside, which is to say something transcending machinic being.

Yet if there is one reality, then we must ask if there is a machine of all machines, despite the non-existence of the world? As Deleuze writes, 'the problem [. . .] becomes: *is there a totality of all [bodies without organs]?*' (ATP 154; cf. 165). Is there 'a Universe which is taken to be the system of all systems' (LS 77)? Deleuze's own answers to this question are contradictory. Sometimes he suggests that there exists a single 'abstract machine' that sweeps everything along (ATP 4) or that constitutes an 'unlimited social field' (K 87). At other times, he writes about a plurality of existing abstract machines and equates the notion to the singularities of a machine or the 'diagram' of an assemblage (ATP 91, 511). He posits a 'mechanosphere' which would be the 'set of all abstract machines and machinic assemblages' (ATP 71), but at the same time he tells his students that he does not believe there is a final region for all regions.[6] So which is it? We can take our clue from the following: 'there is no abstract machine, or machines, in the sense of a Platonic Idea, transcendent, universal, eternal. Abstract machines operate within concrete assemblages' (ATP 510). Even a machine for all machines will not be a Platonic entity with which other entities entertain internal relations. So even if all machines somehow co-produce a single 'huge' machine called 'the abstract machine' or the 'mechanosphere', then this 'ultimate' machine will still not violate externality. The existential possibility that this machine may exist is irrelevant to machine ontology. A shoe, a horse, and a person would be as irreducible to this ultimate machine as they are to a shoebox, a meadow, and a classroom. Like any other machine, the mechanosphere would simply be a part among parts, an entity produced by others and undergoing becoming, and something never integrated in anything. So there is one reality, but this reality is a 'chaosmos and no longer a world' (LS 176; cf. DR 199). Being is not a cosmos, which is to say a well-ordered set of domains. Reality is schizophrenic instead, meaning that it is nothing beyond machines and what happens among them.

Seventh Intermezzo – Bruno Latour and Irreducible Actants

Our reflections in the previous section bring us to this brief comparison between Deleuze's machine ontology and Bruno Latour's philosophy. Like Deleuze, Latour approaches reality as comprised of irreducible entities and their mutual associations, meaning as lacking a final layer or primordial source to which concrete existents can be reduced. Indeed, the parallel between Deleuze and Latour is so strong that the latter suggested at one point that his famous actor-network theory really ought to be called 'actant-rhizome ontology' (Latour 1999a). After outlining some key features of Latour's thought, we will see that his philosophy proposes a (re)definition of both 'self' and 'world' similar to Deleuze's recasting of those concepts. Our comparison also allows us to start zooming in on the relation between object-oriented ontology and empiricism. An ontology that treats all entities as being equally real can easily be accused of disregarding the many differences that exist between beings, not to mention of always already knowing 'what' everything is. This seems to devalue empirical work (not just in the sciences, but also in arts and politics), as one could think that the actual *study* of things and events can yield nothing but accidental (and therefore unimportant) properties if their ontological structure is already known. We will see how, for Latour as well as for Deleuze, such accusations ultimately rely on erroneous reasoning.

Latour's philosophy spans roughly two dozen books and dozens of articles, and its full scope cannot be addressed in this brief intermezzo. Our interest in the basic features of entities, however, provides for some focus. This is because, wide variations in subject matter notwithstanding, Latour's analyses are always grounded in a single and ultimately quite concise theory about how entities (which he calls 'actants', 'actors', 'existents', or 'hybrids') work. The most systematic and complete presentation of this theory is arguably still 1984's *Irreductions*, the programmatic complement to Latour's study of Pasteur in *The Pasteurization of France.*[7] Some of Latour's disciples will immediately take issue with this, for reasons we will address shortly. First, let's take a look at the theory of actants as presented in *Irreductions*.

Like Deleuze, Latour flat-out denies that beings or 'actants' can ever be fully reduced to or fully explained in terms of something else. Reality contains neither a mysterious depth from which all things emerge, nor a lofty height from which everything emanates. The multitudes of entities comprising reality are neither the mere reflections of macro-entities like Capitalism or Evolution, nor mere aggregates of micro-entities like subatomic particles or strings. Instead, everything that populates reality is a real being in its own right, an 'actant' that leaves its own mark on other actants. Actants can, of course, be stabilised into playing a certain role or fulfilling a certain function, but such identities can never be naturalised, meaning that circumstances can always conspire to make an actant start doing something else. Latour calls this the 'principle of irreducibility': 'nothing is, by itself, either reducible or irreducible to anything' (1998: 158). In short, any temporary 'reduction' of an entity to a certain role (say, being a component of a smartphone or a piece of pipe in a sewer) is always the result of contingent labour by other actants, and can in principle be undone by other actants still. This principle of irreducibility animates Latour's actor-network theory to this day (Latour 2013: 33). Much like Deleuze's machines and rhizomes, actants can combine into networks, but the latter are not ontologically different from the former. Instead, each network simply comprises another actant, and each actant within the network can always be revealed as another network, which is to say, as constructed and given potency by still other actants. For example, Deleuze's machine ontology would define a city as both a machine and a rhizome: a machine because of its irreducibility and a rhizome because it is generated by countless other machines. For the same reason, a city for Latour is both an actant and a network of actants.

The parallels with Deleuze's externality thesis will be clear, and there is similar proximity with regard to the machine thesis. Latour upholds no a priori divisions of reality into different domains or levels. Reality has no separate 'real', 'imaginary', 'figurative', and 'symbolic' zones (Latour 1998: 159, 181, 188). There is no ontological separation between 'natural' entities on the one hand and 'cultural' entities on the other (1998: 167). Finally, Latour explicitly denies that his theory of actants is just an economic, legal, technological, linguistic, scientific, social, human-centred, or naturalising discourse (1998: 203–6). Instead, actants are simply what entities *are* (or rather: how they work). As with the machine thesis, Latour's theory of actants places all entities on the same footing, allowing for no pre-established and metaphysically ordained hierarchies in the world.

Whatever happens, then, results from interactions between actants. Or as Latour puts it, actants must be taken as speaking for themselves (1998: 299). If we want to explain what happens, we must trace the actions of actants with regard to each other, because nothing leads back to a final substance or principle that explains everything. Or as Latour puts it with a tip of the hat to Leibniz: 'no matter how far we go, there are always forms; within each fish there are ponds full of fish' (1998: 161). States of affairs are therefore not determined by some transcendent order, but 'locally', 'on the field of battle' (1998: 164). Any investigation into what exists or happens will therefore only ever reveal more actants. Any hope of stumbling upon some final X by which to simplify, hierarchise, totalise, and reduce everything 'once and for all' is simply in vain (1998: 169). The only difference in actants is whether they – depending on the situation – are dominating something else or being dominated by something else, which is no different from Deleuze's distinction between 'social' and 'technical' machines (Latour 1998: 168).

Actants are thus never merely 'intermediaries' that simply reflect the nature or passively execute the commands of some other entity or structure. They are 'mediators' that add their own difference to what transpires, much like that primary school whispering game in which each child slightly distorts the message in the act of passing it on. Just as Deleuze's machines interpret their encounters on their own terms, each actant 'translates all the other forces on its own behalf' (Latour 1998: 166–7). Moreover, the weight that an actant gets to throw around in the world is never simply 'its', but always and everywhere bestowed upon it through 'associations' or 'alliances' with other actants (1998: 180, 160, 195).

In short, Latour sees reality as comprised of nothing but actants and their associations. Actants never derive their strengths and weaknesses from some transcendent beyond, but always from their engagements with further actants. He therefore also refers to them as 'hybrids', 'quasi-objects' and 'quasi-subjects' (Latour 1991: 51). Hybrids, because reality is not neatly cut up into distinct zones where only like engages with like. Anything ranging from cities to scientific theories only exists because of the conjunction of countless actants of various types and from different domains. Quasi-objects, because every entity truly counts as a real *thing* (hence 'object'), yet never as a passive object that simply represents a set of mechanistic laws (hence 'quasi'). Quasi-subjects, because every entity *acts* (hence 'subject'), yet never as some kind of Kantian subject that also accounts for the action of *every-thing else* (hence 'quasi'). The parallels with Deleuze are again undeni-able, as Latour's quasi-object or quasi-subject is no different from what the former calls 'larval subjects'. Unsurprisingly, then, the two thinkers are also in agreement on their notion of the 'world'. Latour would also deny that a 'world' exists, if by that we mean an always already exist-ing totality that pre-unifies everything in a single overarching order. As actants always encounter other entities on their own terms and resist being assimilated into something else, anything we could call a 'world' must always result from what Latour calls 'progressive composition' (2004: 18, 47). And of course, whatever is composed can always be altered or undone whenever new actants make themselves felt.

This brief outline of Latour's metaphysics allows us to pose two ques-tions. The first is whether it is coherent, and the second is whether it even makes sense to call his position a 'metaphysics' in the first place. The first point has been discussed at some length in Harman's recon-struction of Latour's metaphysics (Harman 2009). Harman points to something of a paradox central to Latour's position. On the one hand, Latour insists that actants are irreducible, that they make their own difference in the world, and so on. Yet on the other hand, actants are defined in terms of their actions. As Latour writes in *Pandora's Hope*:

> [T]here is no other way to define an actor but through its action, and there is no other way to define an action but by asking what other actors are modified, transformed, perturbed, or created by the character that is the focus of attention. (Latour 1999b: 122)

For Harman, this suggests that Latour's philosophy is a relationism in which actants are ultimately reduced to their relations with (i.e.

their effects on) other entities (Harman 2009: 81). If this is indeed the case, then Latour's position falls prey to all the problems haunting internalism and relationism that we have already discussed extensively: the impossibility of accounting for change, the infinite deferral of specification, and so on. Latour seems to be aware of this difficulty. There are moments in his writings when in addition to actants, he also posits the existence of a 'plasma', a decidedly non-ontic reservoir of unformatted energy or potential that would somehow infuse actants with an excess over and above their current engagements (Latour 2007: 244).

Yet note that the passage just cited from Latour is about the *definition* of entities, which is not necessarily the same thing as their *being*. If entities are truly irreducible, then there is no unmediated and transparent way of presenting their interior being to humans, because such presentation is by definition relational. In the absence of that possibility, the *only* way to define an entity is to observe *what it does*, meaning to register it in the act of translation. The cited passage therefore leaves some room for doubt as to Latour's real position. Is there *true* irreducibility for actants, such that they would be *more* than their deployment in relations? In a recently published discussion between Harman and Latour called *The Prince and the Wolf* (2011), Latour seems to affirm this. He denies that he adheres to a relationism and insists that actants are irreducible singularities (Latour et al. 2011: 41, 43). He also adds that the fact that things are never their relations is the very reason that they must always be 'translated' by other entities instead of simply being given to them, without such translations 'ever emptying their kernel' (Latour et al. 2011: 49). Finally, he notes that things are not their relations, but what relations with other actors bestow upon them (Latour et al. 2011: 122), a remark that suggests even more overlap with Deleuze's machine ontology (specifically concerning virtual singularities). Nevertheless, Harman could easily counter that despite Latour's assertions, the latter's writings are somewhat saturated with remarks that suggests that things really *are* nothing but the marks they leave on others. As the final verdict in this matter is, of course, up to Latour himself, we move on to the second point.

To which 'genre' does Latour's theory of hybrid actants belong? His *We Have Never Been Modern* repeatedly calls it an ontology (Latour 1991: 51, 77, 86, 123). Then again, *Irreductions* denies that his position amounts to anything resembling a system (Latour 1998: 198, 206). During a discussion recorded in *The Prince and the*

Wolf, Latour first doubts and then simply denies having a metaphysical system (Latour et al. 2011: 41, 46). Following that, however, he immediately adds that he *does* have an 'experimental metaphysics'. That last distinction between 'metaphysics' and 'experimental metaphysics' is also stressed by authors critiquing Harman's reading of Latour as one of the more refreshing metaphysicians of the twentieth century (Hämäläinen and Lehtonen 2016). How to make sense of this?

As with Deleuze, the solution is to distinguish between metaphysics and ontology. For Latour and some of his readers, the problem with the term 'metaphysics' is that it suggests having a theory that can map reality without having to do any experimental or empirical work to find out which entities exist and what they are doing (Hämäläinen and Lehtonen 2016: 20). This concern is also raised by Noortje Marres in *The Prince and the Wolf*: any claim to having a metaphysics is at risk of neglecting the fact that what exists is fundamentally and drastically variable (Latour et al. 2011: 97–8). A classical metaphysician would always already know what exists and what things are, so that any empirical work could only ever yield ultimately accidental (in the Aristotelian sense) features of objects. It should be obvious that neither Latour nor Deleuze has a metaphysics *in this sense*, because such a metaphysics is the quintessential example of the very type of reductionism that both philosophers spend much of their writings arguing against.

Yet like Deleuze, Latour most definitely has an *ontology*, which is to say a basic theory of *how beings work*. This is evident, for example, in how Hämäläinen and Lehtonen argue *against* the idea that Latour would have a metaphysics. Their basic argument is that a metaphysics would *not* allow for the notions that actors make sense of their own activities, that reality unfolds among things themselves, that entities have their own mediations, and that there exists a democracy of objects rather than a transcendent order that forces entities into submission (Hämäläinen and Lehtonen 2016: 25). These features of existents, they argue, are 'distorted' in metaphysical systems (2016: 27–8). Point granted. But to what else do these very features of entities and their associations amount than an ontology? If the features of actants that Latour outlines in *Irreductions* and elsewhere are not ontological statements, then surely no statement was ever ontological! To clear up the discussions concerning the status of Latour's position, all that is needed is to distinguish between metaphysics on the one hand and ontology on the other. And even though he is not a metaphysician, it is quite clear that Latour is definitely an ontologist. Here is the simple proof. Neither Latour nor any Latourian would *ever* expect to find entities that do *not* conform to his theory of actants, just as no Deleuzian would ever find anything in reality but multiplicities. A Latourian investigation will never stumble upon a Platonic form, nor will it find that some subatomic particle is the ultimate root of reality, nor will it ever conclude that a signifier like 'Capitalism' or 'Evolution' unexpectedly *does* explain everything that happens. And the reason for this is that Latour holds that *such things do not exist*. All that exists is actants and their associations, and the continuous affirmation of that basic thesis proves that his philosophy is premised on a single account of what it means to be a real entity. Nothing more is needed for a philosophy to be ontological.

This leads to our final point of comparison between Latour and Deleuze, which is the importance of empiricism. As noted, a metaphysician might be somewhat committed to holding that she always already knows the essential features of the furniture of the world. By contrast, *an ontologist knows nothing*. This is precisely why Latour stresses the importance of empirical investigations in his work (Latour et al. 2011: 44), and why Deleuze calls for a 'transcendental empiricism' (on which we elaborate later in this chapter). By placing all entities on equal ontological footing, an ontologist has no a priori clue whatsoever as to how *specific* machines or actants ever go about their business. *That* actants exist and *that* they are produced in mutual associations is an ontological thesis, but *which* actants and *which* associations exist in any given case can only be established empirically. Likewise, *that* machines exist and *that* they are fourfolds engaged in various syntheses is an ontological thesis, but *which* machines exist, *which* powers they have, and *which* ties they have to each other can only be established empirically. Latour is quite clear about this in his recent *An Inquiry into Modes of Existence*. Actor-network theory *as such* can only ever tell you the same exact thing about everything whatsoever: that it is 'composed in a heterogeneous fashion of unexpected elements revealed by the investigation' (Latour 2013: 35). Deleuze would say the exact same thing about machine ontology *as such*. This is precisely why Latour's *Modes* project tries to identify similarities between various 'types' of actants and associations, so that we can start making useful distinctions and differentiations in the ontologically flat plane of actants. After all, that actants are irreducible does not mean that all actants are absolutely incomparable. On the contrary, the world is 'stable' or 'regular' enough to warrant an investigation into the modes, fields, domains, or zones into which entities can be grouped.

Note that Deleuze tried to do the exact same thing in *A Thousand Plateaus*. He explicitly states that *A Thousand Plateaus* remains premised on a general logic of assemblages (TRM 177), but that it tries to invent or identify fields that we can use to classify different types of assemblages (TRM 179). Such fields or 'plateaus' are characterised by 'intensive continuity' (TRM 179), which is to say that they contain machines whose singularities are sufficiently alike to be meaningfully classified as belonging to the same domain. Much like Latour, such a domain, plateau, or 'mode of life' (!) must in each case be identified through 'experimental practical reason' (TRM 179). Much as Latour cuts up the world of actants in *Modes*, Deleuze divides the world of machines into separate investigative domains, including language, music, politics, history, and so on. This is also why he classifies machines into different 'strata', most notably a physico-chemical, an organic, and an anthropomorphic one (ATP 502). Each stratum contains a diversity of machines, but also has a certain 'unity of composition in spite of the diversity in its organization and development' (ATP 502).

Both *An Inquiry into Modes of Existence* and *A Thousand Plateaus* respond to the basic fact that an ontology (as opposed to metaphysics) never 'already knows' what exists and how it exists. Hence, both Latour and Deleuze have a healthy respect for empirical investigations, and both thinkers see the necessity of using the results of such investigations in attempts to discern specific fault lines and domains within a reality in which everything is equally real, but existentially different. This opposes Latour as well as Deleuze to a host of other types of philosophies. Think, for example, of the scientistic realist who always already knows that everything is subatomic particles. Or take the stereotypical Marxist who always already knows that whatever has occurred is just one more ideological mystification to add to the ever-growing pile. Or imagine the equally stereotypical Freudian who always already knows that anything you do is the expression of some repressed sexual trauma involving your parents. Unlike any metaphysical or critical philosopher, Latour and Deleuze *never* know in advance what exists, what produced something, what something produces, and so forth, *precisely* because the only thing they know in advance is equally true for all possible entities.

This should suffice to identify some basic yet key parallels between Latour and Deleuze. To further stress the importance of empiricism to machine ontology, this chapter will end with a section that further elaborates on Deleuze's notion of 'transcendental empiricism'. First, however, we will pay some attention to Deleuze's view on why human beings do not 'naturally' register reality in machinic terms. This, incidentally, makes for a slight difference between Latour and Deleuze. For Latour, our tendency to reduce things to transcendent or otherwise overarching structures is largely the result of the historical and contingent emergence of a 'modern' way of thinking. For Latour, modernity establishes the belief that reality can be divided into two domains: a 'natural' one in which all entities can be reduced to passive executors of mechanistic natural laws, and a 'cultural' one in which everything is reduced to sovereign human freedom (Latour 1991). Yet for Deleuze, reductionism is not rooted in a historical event, but rather in *paralogisms*, which is to say in errors of thought engendered by the very way in which machines appear to each other (and hence also to human beings). We now turn to these paralogisms.

2 Platonism and Paralogisms

By systematically outlining a theory of entities among themselves, machine ontology hopes to achieve what Deleuze, following Nietzsche, sees as philosophy's mission: 'to overturn Platonism' (DR 59; cf. LS 253). To overturn Platonism is to remove all traces of full presence, reductionism, and relationism. It is to remove simple, stable, eternal, general essences and replace them with individual distributions of malleable singularities (cf. LS 53). As Deleuze writes, machine ontology aims to replace 'the Idea as the goal of reminiscence [and] the stable Essence' by Ideas conceived as subject to 'qualitative transition' and 'mutual fusion' (PS 109).

For the sake of argument, let us call 'Platonism' any philosophy defending the thesis that the being of some or all entities is secondary (LS 255). Secondary, because their principle, truth, or essence is found in something else that possesses (or simply is) this principle, truth, or essence primarily and fundamentally. For example, the Platonist holds that those who are just participate in justness, but only the Eternal Form of justness has or is justness in a primary way. In other words, Platonism is internalism: 'Platonism thus founds the entire domain that philosophy will later recognize as its own: the domain of representation filled by copies-icons, and defined not by an extrinsic relation to an object, but by an intrinsic relation to the model or foundation' (LS 259).[8] Deleuze's machine ontology inverts this idea:

> If bodies with their states, qualities, and quantities, assume all the characteristics of substance and cause, conversely, the characteristics of the Idea are relegated to the other side, that is to this impassive extra-Being which is sterile, inefficacious, and on the surface of things: *the ideational or the incorporeal can no longer be anything other than an 'effect'*. (LS 7)

In machine ontology, bodies and their virtual content become the cause of what transpires. Actual qualities such as being just are no longer references to eternal forms, but hallmarks of the sterile surfaces of neutral sense-events. In Platonism, things are 'copies' or representatives of something that determines their being (LS 256). In Deleuzism, things are 'simulacra' that always retain a difference in kind between what they are in their virtual becoming and what they manifest to others. The Platonic copy is an image with a resemblance, the Deleuzian machine produces images without resemblance (LS 257). This is not to say that resemblances do not exist, but that resemblances are productions between machines rather than predetermined identities (LS 258, 262). Hence Platonism and Deleuzism find themselves at odds: 'one invites us to think difference from the standpoint of a previous similitude or identity, whereas the other invites us to think similitude and even identity as the product of a deep disparity' (LS 261).[9]

Our reason for returning to this opposition is that 'the simulacrum implies huge dimensions, depths, and distances that the observer cannot master. It is precisely because he cannot master them that he experiences an impression of resemblance' (LS 258). According to Deleuze, all Platonism or internalism results from the fact that precisely because the private depth of machines is irreducible to and different in kind from their actualisations, we constantly make the error of thinking that the contiguity, identity, and resemblance that characterises actuality also characterises things in themselves. In *Anti-Oedipus* Deleuze details this error of thought by outlining five 'paralogisms of psychoanalysis', which are misinterpretations of the nature of the unconscious. As Deleuze considers any entity whatsoever to have a virtual twofold 'unconscious', these errors of thought do not just concern human beings, but also machines as such. They are metaphysical as much as they are psychoanalytic.[10] A paralogism can be unmasked but never eliminated by thought, precisely because it results from experience and thought itself. It presents something thought must perpetually strive to overcome in itself. For Deleuze, all paralogisms 'revolve around the same error' (AO 132), which is thinking the virtual in terms of the actual, the ontological in terms of the existential, and the transcendental in terms of the empirical.

Deleuze first describes the 'paralogism of extrapolation' (AO 132), which concerns the opposition between 'two uses of the connective syntheses: a global and specific use, and a partial and non-specific use' (AO 88). It corresponds to what we called objectivism in the introduction, and is caused by the experienced similarity between entities as a result of the principle of rupture and contiguity. In machine ontology, any relation is a connection with a partial object, that is to say an actual sense-event that differs in kind from the virtual being of the machine of which it is a manifestation. It is not just partial, but also non-specific: the concept, quality, or membership assigned to an assemblage points to that in which it is (placed), to its desire translated into a technical machine for a larger social machine, but not to its Idea itself. In a paralogism of extrapolation, however, we *do* take an assigned quality, concept, or membership to accurately express the being of another machine. As Deleuze writes in another context: 'what is apprehended when we touch the surface of the object is perceived as residing in its innermost depth' (LS 274). This is 'global' because it equates the being of an entity to its belonging to a category (of dogs, of red things, of Italian people). In principle each such category can contain an infinity of entities, each made identical through their membership. It is 'specific' in that it narrowly identifies the being of an entity with a single relation. In short, we 'extrapolate' an actual manifestation into the being of a multiplicity. It follows that each entity receives a 'global object' to which it can never conform (AO 88). No specific dog can be the dog that all dogs are, nothing can be the red of all reds, and nobody is the quintessential Italian. The paralogism of extrapolation gives rise to impossible standards, as the extrapolated X is simultaneously posited as the being of an individual and that which an individual always lacks (AO 90). The quality, concept, or membership then becomes a 'despotic signifier' (AO 91, 132–3). The paralogism of extrapolation is the erroneous thought that 'real desiring-production is answerable to higher formations that integrate it, subject it to transcendent laws, and make it serve a higher social and cultural production' (AO 92).

The second 'paralogism of the double-bind' concerns the disjunctive synthesis of recording (AO 133), and takes the first paralogism a step further. After the equation of an entity's being to a privileged relation, it starts to make sense to interpret all of its other relations and actions as expressions of one particular quality. Disjunction then becomes exclusive (AO 94). Everything something or someone does (this, or that, or that . . .) is then seen as a mere variation on one specific trait which remains identical. Deleuze gives the example of the Oedipus complex. As soon as one decides that our unconscious is defined by the Oedipus complex, then *all* our actions, even mutually contradictory ones, are mere expressions of that complex. We are then 'in good health because of Oedipus, sick from Oedipus, and suffering from various illnesses under the influence of Oedipus' (AO 100). Stereotyping is also based on this logic, whereby mutually unrelated or even opposing behaviours are seen as 'typical' expressions of one's membership of a certain group.

Next, the third 'paralogism of application' is a misinterpretation of the conjunctive synthesis (AO 133). The previous paralogisms equate the being and behaviour of an entity with a single quality (or a limited set of qualities) that it nevertheless lacks. The next logical step is to deny a subject all agency and to appoint a 'symbolic organizer' as the determinant and cause of all its actions (AO 111). The being of the subject, which cannot but lack what it must nevertheless be, undergoes 'an explicit reduction to an *empty form*, from which desire itself is absent and expelled' (AO 216). The subject comes to be seen as a mere representation, mirror, moment, or position of something with which it is presumed to have an internal relation. Or as Deleuze writes, the 'polyvocity' implied in the third synthesis is reduced to a 'biunivocity' (AO 127).[11] Instead of new relations implying new and irreducible entities, all novelty is reduced to a mere variation on the same *Spiel*. The 'nomadism' implied in the logic of the celibate machine and differential relations is then replaced by 'segregation'. If everything is essentially assigned to an inescapable organiser, then nothing can ever escape anything. This is not just a psychoanalytic mistake, but the very core of all relationism and reductionism (cf. AO 125). Everything that transpires is 'applied' to privileged organisers, with the manifold of irreducible fourfolds and their becomings reduced to a simple view in which the three elements of an event (two terms and a relation) are always rigidly overdetermined by and mere representations of a third entity or structure. It is 'as if a tablecloth were being folded, as if its 4 (=n) corners were reduced to 3 (+1, to designate the transcendent factor performing the operation)' (AO 123; cf. 68, 91, 117).[12]

The fourth 'paralogism of displacement' (AO 138) is a variation on the combined effect of the first three paralogisms. It exists by virtue of our ability to realise that keeping an entity in a certain relation is a matter of exerting force. In machine ontology, this simply results from the thesis that virtual code differs in kind from actual manifestations. Hence, something must always be *happening* wherever a certain relation is to be forged, maintained, or broken. Yet in the fourth paralogism, we once again think empirically where we should think transcendentally. Instead of opposing the exertion of a force to the excessive and surplus nature of desire, we conclude that a relation includes force because that which is related to 'strives' to be in relations that are the exact opposite to this relation of force. One example Deleuze gives is the idea that incest is forbidden *because* we want to commit it. We would 'naturally' tend towards incestuous relations, which would explain why the prohibition of incest takes the form of laws that are pedagogically, religiously, and legally enforced. Because of the paralogism of displacement, laws and proscriptions come to point, via the now naturalised tendency they presumably negate, to the 'animal in us' (AO 201). Another example would be the Aristotelian idea that heavy objects 'strive' to be at the centre of the universe, which is then used as an explanation for why it takes effort to lift them. As Deleuze describes it, this logic of displacement involves a 'repressed representative', a 'repressing representation', and a 'displaced represented' (AO 138). The repressed representative is desire, singularities, or code outside of its relational coding. The repressing representation is the law of relation that exerts force on the entity. Finally, the displaced represented is the negation of this exertion of force, or the 'natural' tendency that holding the entity in a specific relation is meant to ward off.

The fifth and final error of thought is the 'paralogism of the afterward' (AO 154). It is a perversion of the idea that desiring-production (i.e. connecting, becoming, and generating according to the three syntheses) must always involve an actuality. As we have seen, each entity only ever relates to the actual manifestations of other entities. It can only register that which it takes as its parts in so far as it is actual. So, there is a sense in which the being and becoming of entities comes 'after' the constitution of something actual: something must actually happen if an entity is to be generated. The paralogism consists in thinking that this actuality itself does not refer to a virtuality of its own. Deleuze gives the example of someone who thinks that the Oedipus complex is the actual generator for certain thoughts, behaviours, and events, without being generated in turn. The Oedipus complex would then be an actuality without any virtuality generated from other entities involved in its becoming. It would be self-identical and unengendered. Of course, in reality, the Oedipus complex is just another machine with its own generators and its private virtuality (AO 154). It is only through the paralogism that we come to misinterpret it 'in isolation, abstractly, independently' (AO 154). This paralogism of the afterward also lurks behind all forms of bland materialism. Such philosophies of false depth think that all entities take something quite unlike themselves for their matter, without this matter taking something quite unlike itself for *its* matter. The result is the positing of an ultimate and final layer of reality constituting a homogeneous and universal ground for everything, a gesture that must always be refused on the grounds presented in previous chapters.

These paralogisms demonstrate how the nature of direct experience and the fact that the transcendental being of beings can only be *thought* always tempts us to return to variations on Platonism, which is to say to reductionism and relationism. We never cease projecting actuality on to virtuality. Moreover, that entities are existentially locked into hierarchies, regularities, patterns, and relations further increases the risk that we keep thinking reality metaphysically rather than ontologically. Deleuze's proposed alternative is precisely a mode of thinking that constantly emphasises the transcendental, malleable essence of individual entities.

3 A Transcendental Empiricism

We thus arrive at what Deleuze calls a 'transcendental empiricism' (B 30; DR 57, 240; LS 20; LAT 89; TRM 384). If machinism is Deleuze's ontology, then transcendental empiricism is an apt name for his overall philosophy and the method of thinking implied by this ontology. As he writes, 'pluralism (otherwise known as empiricism) is almost indistinguishable from philosophy itself. Pluralism is the properly philosophical way of thinking, the one invented by philosophy; the only guarantor of freedom in the concrete spirit, the only principle of a violent atheism' (NP 4; cf. PS 4). Deleuze opposes this pluralist transcendental empiricism to Kantian transcendental philosophy, which for him is 'too general or too large for the real' (DR 68). By its very nature, Kantian transcendental subjectivity foregoes the possibility of conceiving of different relations and interactions between entities themselves, committed as it is to reducing all such activity to apparitions to a subject. In this sense, it is internalist through and through. Conversely, transcendental empiricism is rooted in a theory of a schizophrenic reality in which entity is a machine with its own malleable and transcendental essence, an internal 'matter' based on which it encounters its world.

Deleuze nonetheless remains wholly Kantian on two points, namely human finitude and the power of thought. Because of the externality of relations and terms, we are necessarily finite beings. We can only learn about the interior of others by taking their extensive and actual manifestations as signs of their virtuality, hence the name transcendental *empiricism*. Thought can think how entities work and it can realise that entities have an individual transcendental reality, but it cannot make this transcendental reality present to us. It cannot give us what this reality is in a specific case, even though science demonstrates how we can arrive at incredibly accurate accounts of how machines manifest under determinate circumstances. Nevertheless, not even the most accurate and reliable descriptions or experiences of an entity can stand in for its being. Atoms as classically conceived, or any of their contemporary equivalents, which each seem to be identical to each other, are only ever identical in their actuality. They may differ only minimally in their virtuality, but that is enough to guarantee their irreducibility: '*however small* the internal difference between two series, the one story does not reproduce the other, one does not serve as model for the other: rather, resemblance and identity are only functional effects of that difference which alone is originary within the system' (DR 126). Moreover, in many cases we cannot even determine which or even how many machines are involved in a given experience. Who will say, for example, how many entities are folded into a pointillist painting, a rock concert, or a forest?

Yet despite our finitude, which we share with all machines, Deleuze nevertheless accords a certain privilege to thought.[13] Thought can think that which can never be present, namely the irreducibility and transcendental nature of entities. Thought can move beyond the sensible and consider 'the being *of* the sensible' (AO 237).[14] Even though Deleuze is often presented as privileging feeling over thinking, the opposite is in fact the case. As he writes, that which is excessive or measureless (desire) 'can only be conceived by a thinking soul' (C1 47), the body or 'atom' is addressed only to thought (LS 268), essence can only be grasped by pure thought (DR 140, 143), so that pure thought is the faculty of essences (PS 86), thought can thereby surpass the mere appearance of things in consciousness (SPP 18), which is why as far as philosophy is concerned, 'only intelligence extracts the truth' (PS 23).

Yet in thinking machines, thought also encounters its own limits. It realises, quite simply, that the empirical is never the transcendental. No specific Idea is ever directly available as 'the goal of reminiscence' and as a 'stable Essence' (PS 109). Each Idea is instead withdrawn in its virtuality where it undergoes its own 'qualitative transitions' (PS 109). So as Deleuze notes,

> thought is also forced to think its central collapse, its fracture, its own natural 'powerlessness', which is indistinguishable from the greatest power [. . .] Difficulty as such, along with its cortège of problems and questions, is not a *de facto* state of affairs but a *de jure* structure of thought [. . .] (DR 146)

This difficulty is the fact that we can realise that the fourfold machinic model and the threefold theory of synthesis applies to a rock striking the surface of Mars, but everything about the rock, the striking, Mars, and its surface is only ever available to us based on our own *puissance* as generated by the machines coupled to us. Every possible description of the event thus moves away from machine ontology: 'the moment that one describes [. . .] the material process of production, the specificity of the product tends to evaporate' (AO 37). Or in different terms, language 'incessantly slide[s] over its referent, without ever stopping' (LS 2). Moreover, if everything is a machine, then so is each formula or description or perception that ties us to the event of the rock striking Mars. Like all relations, concepts and symbols are machines in and of themselves (cf. AO 36; DR xx–xxi; LS 60, 87; SL 150480).[15] In short, we can theorise the being of beings generally, but the price to pay is that we cannot think the being of a being accurately. Machine ontology formally describes that which does not allow for substantial definitions.

As a consequence, we must reaffirm the old wisdom that philosophy is not knowledge: 'the philosopher, as philosopher, *is not a sage*' (NP 92). From the point of view of transcendental empiricism, 'nothing can be said in advance, one cannot prejudge the outcome of research' (DR 143). The great question of 'what can a body do?' (cf. D 60; NP 41; SCS 150277; SPP 17) cannot be answered by a philosopher *qua* philosopher. To even begin answering the question for any given body or bodies always involves non-philosophy, and even then we are only ever categorising and examining signs of machines in order to construct maps of their being. This would be the process of determining '*who? how? how much? where and when? in which case?*' (DI 96; DR 188). Since we cannot know essences, such indirect approximations are our only means of coming to terms with the being of machines. As Deleuze writes, the inner being of things can only be understood 'from the outside and through successive experiments' (FLB 55). The virtual–actual distinction must everywhere be upheld, and the philosopher must refuse 'to be drawn out of the cave, finding instead another cave beyond, always another in which to hide' (DR 67). Even an infinitely more reliable and useful description of a thing than its givenness to direct perception is still relational, and should not be believed when it claims no longer to be a curtain or mask hiding the entity.

Hence Deleuze writes that 'the masks do not hide anything except other masks' (DR 17).[16] What we call knowledge usually concerns 1) the actual components generating an entity or 2) the actual part an entity plays in the generation of something else. Neither of those yields the virtual being of a machine itself. They are functional masks of that which generates it or that which it generates. Not that there would be nothing behind the curtain, but that that which is behind the curtain cannot be revealed: 'There is nothing behind the curtain except unnamable mixtures' (LS 133). Consider:

> Given a certain effect, what machine is capable of producing it? And given a certain machine, what can it be used for? Can we possibly guess, for instance, what a knife rest is used for if all we are given is a geometrical description of it? (AO 13)

The point is that *no* description, experience, or other type of relation can give us the knife rest in and of itself. Ontology must remain silent on which machines exist and what their internal being is. As Deleuze notes with regards to machine ontology: 'we shall not inquire how all this fits together so that the machine will run: the question itself is the result of a process of abstraction' (AO 19). This is to say that how specific machines work and how specific relations form between them is not for ontology to say. It can only say that every entity is equally real in being a fourfold machine engaged in threefold syntheses. Ontology can draw no lines in the sand of Being, because even impossible objects, as soon as they are generated as thoughts or riddles, are no less real than concepts, slogans, laws, languages, mathematical formulas, pies, crumbs, and particles:

> At the very moment you say 'this machine is impossible', you fail to see that you are making it possible, by being yourself one of its parts, the very part that you seemed to be missing in order for it to be already working [. . .] You argue about the possibility or the usefulness, but you are already inside the machine, you are a part of it, you have put a finger inside, or an eye, your anus, or your liver [. . .] (BSP 129)

In fact, Deleuze thinks impossible objects even *confirm* the split nature of machines, as an impossible entity can never manifest *as such*. There can be no accurate representation of a square circle or a mountain without a valley. Nevertheless, they are distinct, irreducible, and have their own virtual aspects:

> [Contradictory objects] are without signification, that is, they are absurd. Nevertheless, they have a sense, and the two notions of absurdity and nonsense must not be confused. Impossible objects – square circles, matter without extension, *perpetuum mobile*, mountain without valley, etc. – are objects 'without a home', outside of being, but they have a precise and distinct position within this outside: they are of 'extra being' – pure, ideational events, unable to be realized in a state of affairs. (LS 35)

Yet if even impossible entities are machines, then how are finite creatures such as ourselves ever able to determine *when* there is a machine, *how many* machines are at stake, *which* machines we are dealing with, and so on? Our preceding analyses give us several characteristics that can put us on the scent of machines. First, there is emergence. With machines being irreducible to their generators, we can set out to discover what their 'proper' manifestations are (water at a hundred degrees being wet and boiling, which are not features of hydrogen and oxygen). Second, there is redundancy. Due to the difference between the virtual and the actual, it will often be the case that not all relations with its generators are necessary for a machine. We can always experiment with selectively adding and removing generators and generations and seeing what 'stays' proper to a machine (a practice we try to perfect in scientific experiment). Third, there is the 'falling back' on generators that is often a feature of bodies without organs. Machines can loop back into becoming generators for their own components, changing them in the process by influencing their becoming (human membership of religious groups, for example). This effect on their parts can be used as yet another method to detect them and to gain knowledge about their mode of existence. Fourth, there is, of course, resistance. As each machine is a force in and of itself, it will always require force to 'move' it. So, wherever force is exerted, a machine is resisting. Fifth and finally, there is the generation of specific parts. Nothing appears out of nowhere, so wherever something is generated, a machine must be at work.

These are but very general pointers, but nevertheless it is safe to say that human beings (along with many other sentient creatures) are surprisingly skilled at distinguishing things from one another and at noting regularities, patterns, locations, and interactions concerning the assemblages that interest them. To engage with machines is to undergo an apprenticeship in signs, as each actual surface is a sign of one or more virtual objects being translated into extensity. What we wrote earlier about schizoanalysis and ethology comes back to this point.[17] To become more familiar with a machine is to know more and more of its signs, as when one comes to 'know' a beloved by seeing her or him go through a lifetime of different situations and actions, or a material by spending decades on manipulating it with tools and one's bare hands. Only through such an apprenticeship can we get any idea of how another machine experiences its world. As Deleuze writes, defining a multiplicity is best done by such 'accumulations' of signs:

> To learn is first of all to consider a substance, an object, a being as if it emitted signs to be deciphered, interpreted. There is no apprentice who

is not 'the Egyptologist' of something. One becomes a carpenter only by becoming sensitive to the signs of wood, a physician by becoming sensitive to the signs of disease [. . .] Everything that teaches us something emits signs; every act of learning is an interpretation of signs or hieroglyphs. (PS 4; cf. ATP 486)

In his book on Proust, Deleuze argues that such apprenticeships should not just teach us about the entities that make up our world, ourselves, and each other. It should also, philosophically, teach us what signs are *themselves*.[18] To go through the apprenticeship of signs is to slowly come to terms with the schizophrenia of reality, the problematic nature of entities, and with the finitude of both humans and other machines.

A first way to think about our experience is in terms of 'worldly signs' (P 6). Signs are worldly to the extent that we treat the entities as if they *are* their actual qualities. It is to define things in terms of their colours, actions, components, locations, origins, and so on: 'the worldly sign does not refer to something, it "stands for" it, claims to be equivalent to its meaning' (PS 6). Practical life is full of worldly signs, to the extent that we say and think that trees *are* green, some of us *are* Dutch, the couch *is* heavy, war criminals *are* evil, the coffee *is* horrible, water *is* H_2O, parmesan cheese *is* Italian, all of us *are* other people's children, and so forth. There is absolutely nothing wrong with such identifications, except that they are philosophically misleading and contribute to a host of political problems.

It is fairly easy to move beyond the naïve relationism, reductionism, and objectivism of worldly signs. Life, after all, contains many moments in which we realise that things are more than meets the eye, and that they instead have hidden realities that one can set out to explore. To love someone is the example Deleuze gives, though many more of course exist: 'love does not concern only [. . .] loved beings, but the multiplicity of souls or worlds in each of them' (PS 9). What he calls 'signs of love' are the same signs as before, but apprehended differently. A sign of love is taken as but an initial experience of something deeper: 'to love is to try to *explicate*, to *develop* these unknown worlds that remain enveloped within the beloved' (PS 6). To see the world in terms of signs of love is to realise that 'names, persons, and things are crammed with a content that fills them to bursting' (PS 122).

In a third moment, our hypothetical apprentice of signs realises that signs do not communicate with that which they envelop. Deleuze constantly uses the example of a jealous lover, who despite all kinds of subtle or even brutal manipulations never gains full control over the beloved. The jealous lover is precisely *jealous* on account of being constantly aware of the fact that the real interiority of the beloved remains forever out of reach. As Deleuze writes, 'the truth of love is first of all the isolation of the sexes' (PS 80), as love 'makes it a principle to renounce all communication' (PS 42). At this point we realise, as Deleuze writes elsewhere, that 'animal and reasonable, green and color are two equally immediate predicates which translate a mixture in the body of the individual subject, without one predicate being attributed to it any less immediately than the other' (LS 112). In this third stage, one must abandon the hope of bringing the inner reality of another machine as such to the surface. Signs of love turn out *not* to reach the depth, and are inseparable from actuality, from 'the weight of a face, from the texture of a skin, from the width and color of a cheek' (PS 85). Not even love is powerful enough to overcome ontology. Signs then appear as what Deleuze calls 'sensuous impressions or qualities' (PS 9). As he writes, 'the quality no longer appears as a property of the object that now possesses it, but as the sign of an *altogether different* object' (PS 11). That is, the lover can at least take the sign for a sign of being *in* something with the beloved. The jealous lover is, after all, *in* love. This can be done because every connection demands a medium. Deleuze notes that the three preceding signs are 'too material' (PS 58). 'Material' does not mean 'made of tangible stuff', nor does it mean 'matter' as we have defined it in previous chapters. 'Material' means 'in something else': 'all the signs we meet in life are still material signs, and their meaning, because it is always *in something else*, is not altogether spiritual' (PS 41). This is to say that all the signs we meet are *relational*: 'what we call an "object" is only the effect an object has on our body' (EPS 146).

In a fourth and final stage of what is ultimately the process of coming to terms with Deleuze's own philosophy, we understand that 'material meaning is nothing without an ideal essence that it incarnates' (PS 13). This is the stage of what Deleuze calls 'signs of art': 'the world of art is the ultimate world of signs, and these signs, as though dematerialized, find their meaning in an ideal essence' (EPS 13). It is at this point that we realise that individual entities have virtual essences that withdraw from all relations. We accept that signs are in an ontological sense signs of the imperceptible (DR 140). We never have the truth of an other's being, but only ever 'machinic indices'.[19] Only through such signs can we achieve notions of what bodies can do:

> We know nothing about a body until we know what it can do, in other words, what its affects are, how they can or cannot enter into composition with other affects, with the affects of another body, either to destroy that body or to be destroyed by it, either to exchange actions and passions with it or to join with it in composing a more powerful body. (ATP 257)

To get to know something implies becoming its 'Egyptologist'. Only signs give us a sense of that which we will never truly know. Only through signs can we come, as Pierre Klossowski puts it, to 'teach the unteachable' (2005: 44). Put differently, becoming familiar with machines implies working through a 'symptomatology' of signs in order to find out which signs belong to which machines:

> Precisely, symptomatology is located almost outside medicine, at a neutral point, a zero point, where artists and philosophers and doctors and patients can come together. (DI 134, translation modified; cf. 140)

If Deleuze identifies seeing the world in such terms with art, it is because art is precisely the domain in which we constantly realise that all reduction fails. It simply never 'works' to reduce a work of art to that which was used to generate it, to how we experience it, to its previous or current social and political context, and so on. With art, we always notice that such clarifications somehow distance us from the work itself, that is to say, from a piece of art being a Figure with its own Idea. Hence 'it is only on the level of art that the essences are revealed' (PS 38). This is again not true merely for a select number of cases. Instead, we should learn from works of art that all actualisations or signs are at the end of the day always already signs of art, which is to say manifestations of transcendental Ideas: '*once* they are manifested in the work of art [. . .] we learn that they *already* incarnated, that they were already there in all these kinds of signs' (PS 38).

Notes

1. The subject 'can situate itself only in terms of the disjunctions of a recording surface, in what is left after each division' (AO 28).

2. '*Non pas un autrui, mais un tout-autre qu'autrui.*'

3. Of course, being able to 'handle' the Other structure does not make living beings infallible. Success and failure in negotiating the Other structure contingently depends on powers and circumstance. Hence life has many moments in which we notice that the Other structure is by no means attuned to us: '[T]he absence of the Other is felt when we bang against things and when the stupefying swiftness of our actions is revealed to us' (LS 306).

4. *This* is what Deleuze means with the 'One-All' in *What is Philosophy?* (WP 35). Badiou may suggest that Deleuze holds there to be 'a single clamor of Being for all beings', but Badiou forgets the second part of the statement, which clarifies what this clamour implies: 'a single clamor of Being for all beings: on condition that each being, each drop and each voice has reached the state of excess' (DR 304). Badiou wants Deleuze to say that the Whole or the One is always more than the All of existing entities, but Deleuze is saying the exact opposite: every single thing is always 'more' than everything else, so that there is no possibility whatsoever of a single world containing everything else.

5. The 1978 'Tanner Lecture on Human Values' in which Popper defends this can easily be found online.

6. 'je crois plutôt qu'il y a – qu'il y a pas une grille, qu'il y a pas, finalement, une région de sens de toutes les regions. C'est pas possible' (SC 141282).

7. With the still recent publication of *An Inquiry into Modes of Existence*, Latour's philosophy has perhaps entered a truly new phase. Though we do address this work later in this section, we still mostly focus on what would now be 'early Latour', not in the least because the *Inquiry* is still too fresh to understand its full scope and consequences.

8. Cf. how in Platonism entities 'are endowed with resemblance. But resemblance *should not be understood as an external relation*. It goes less from one thing to another than from one thing to an Idea, since it is the Idea which comprehends the relations and proportions constitutive of the internal essence. Being both internal and spiritual, resemblance is the measure of any pretension' (LS 257).

9. Cf. 'What are these systems constituted by the eternal return?

Consider two propositions: only that which is alike differs; and only differences are alike. The first formula posits resemblance as the condition of difference [. . .] According to the other formula, by contrast, resemblance, identity, analogy and opposition can no longer be considered anything but effects, the products of a primary difference or a primary system of differences' (DR 116–17).

10. The term 'paralogism' invokes Kant, and indeed, as with Kant, Deleuze's paralogisms are cases in which we think empirically when we should instead think transcendentally.

11. 'Biunivocity' is a precise correspondence between two systems of magnitudes, for example 'three chairs for three guests'. The term thus suggests a situation in which elements rigidly belong to one another.

12. This transcendent factor can be conceived as a single thing or as an entire 'presupposed aggregate of departure' (AO 133).

13. As Knox Peden also notes (2014: 241).

14. As Rancière calls it, a metaphysics of 'insensible sensation [*sensation insensible*]' (2004: 150).

15. Hence Deleuze defines a concept in machinic terms, as having its own virtual being: 'what is distinctive about the concept is that it renders components inseparable *within itself*. Components, or what defines the *consistency* of the concept, its endoconsistency, are distinct, heterogeneous, and yet not separable' (WP 19). See also, throughout *What is Philosophy?*, Deleuze's statements about concepts being multiplicities, having an incorporeal side, relating to sense-events, simultaneously being absolute and relative, and so on. Like any rhizome endowed with virtuality, a concept, too, 'is real without being actual, ideal without being abstract' (WP 22).

16. 'The mask is the true subject of repetition. Because repetition differs in kind from representation, the repeated cannot be represented: rather, it must always be signified, masked by what signifies it, itself masking what it signifies' (DR 18; cf. 42, 84, 106).

17. It is obvious that, for Deleuze, schizoanalysis and ethology indicate the study of any entity whatsoever. Much as 'differential relations' have little to do with mathematics within machine ontology, 'ethology' has little to do with biology. We therefore cannot agree with Howard Caygill when he writes that 'Deleuze's ethology in the final analysis employs a biological rhetoric to evoke an anti-human, anti-ethical, anti-political, anti-philosophical pathos which sentimentally avoids the implications of biological selection' (Caygill 2002: 160). Caygill forgets that any rigorous ontology cannot be 'anti' humans,

ethics, and politics, but rather *must* rigorously purge itself of all human, ethical, and political concerns if it is to avoid the twin traps of subjectivism and historicism.

18. The full sense of 'learning' is therefore not just to learn about this or that entity, but also about the *being* of entities in general. '[An] apprentice is someone who constitutes and occupies practical or speculative problems as such. Learning is the appropriate name for the subjective acts carried out when one is confronted with the objecticity [*l'objectité*] of a problem (Idea), whereas knowledge designates only the generality of concepts or the calm possession of a rule enabling solutions' (LS 164).

19. 'Atteindre aux machines désirantes de quelqu'un et on ne peut jamais les saisir directement, on n'a que des indices machiniques, autant être le plus obscur que possible, c'est chouette, c'est forcé, il n'y a que des indices' (SCS 180172; cf. K 47); 'It seems that schizoanalysis can make use only of indices – the machinic indices – in order to discern [...] the libidinal investments of the social field' (AO 398).

Conclusion:
Ontology and Discontinuity

This study has aimed to reconstruct Deleuze's hitherto overlooked machine ontology and to critically compare it to a number of contemporary object-oriented philosophies. As for the reconstruction, what have we learned? Machines are the 'minimum real unit' (D 51). Each machine has four aspects. Two of these comprise its virtual and non-relational aspect, two others comprise its actual manifestations in relations. A machine's body comprises its virtual unity, so that it exists rather than not. A machine's Idea (its singularities or powers) comprises its virtual specificity, so that it is this rather than that machine. Body and Idea comprise a machine's virtual being. Its other two aspects comprise its actually being experienced by other machines. A sense-event or partial object is the bare fact of a machine being encountered by another machine, rather than not. Finally, flows and qualities are the content and specificity of such an encounter as this rather than that experience.

Externality dictates that the virtual aspects of machines never meet directly. A machine can only encounter the actual manifestations (sense-events and flows) of other machines. Such manifestations are translations based on the virtual aspects of whatever machines may be involved, but never direct presentations of those aspects. How a machine registers the manifestations of others depends on the capacities or powers that it has. We saw how this accounts for interaction in the minimal sense of simple contact.

A machine's body and Idea comprise its essence. Each such essence is malleable. A machine's own manifestations in terms of sense-events obscure its virtuality from other machines, but in so far as a machine experiences the qualified sense-events of other machines, its virtual aspect is open to those manifestations. After all, the aspect of a machine that encounters the manifestations of others are its body and Idea, not its sense-events and qualities (because that would lead to the absurdity that when I see my friend Simon, that which is doing the seeing is me being seen by my friend Stefan). Therefore, there is nothing that *de jure* precludes that which a machine encounters from altering its Idea. Whether and to what extent this *de facto* occurs depends on the machines involved in a given encounter. We have seen how this accounts for interaction in the wider sense of engendering change.

Any relation between machines immediately engenders a new machine. Whether such a machine will be short-lived and largely at the mercy of others, or a durable entity that can bend others to its will depends on the circumstances. It does not matter whether I am among the machines generating a tune in my head, a philosophy book, a perception of a river, a house, a nation-state, or a thought about jazz music: each of those would be a new machine that is irreducible to its generators. We saw how this accounts for novelty.

Reality, then, is first and foremost characterised by discontinuity. Machines are the minimum real unit, and there is no direct contact between the interior and real being of machines. No machine is ever reducible to any other machine that ranks among its components or its environment, because a machine's actual manifestations to other entities differ in kind from its virtual aspect, which constitutes its non-relational excess over and above all relations. Conversely, continuity is only ever a contingent, temporary, and local effect engendered by whatever force machines manage to exert on others. Such continuity depends on the Idea, powers, or singularities of the machine in question. I may perceive the Waal river and the Waal bridge as parts of a single landscape, but this depends on my capacities to do so. In no way does it mean that the river and bridge are somehow ontologically one. Moreover, even this simple example emphasises discontinuity in that the perception is immediately a new machine that cannot be reduced to its generators.

We can now resume the discussion (from section 2 of Chapter 1) about the proponents of the 'virtual realm' interpretation, who claim that the opposite is the case. For them, the actual reality of what humans and others experience is characterised by discontinuity in the sense that things manifest separately in space and time. Conversely, the virtual realm 'behind' or 'under' (neither term is really satisfactory) such actualities would be characterised by continuity, which is to say direct contact between the intensities or processes that comprise it. Is there any way to reconcile machine ontology with virtual realm ontology? There is not.

First, machine ontology cannot be integrated into virtual realm ontology. This is because the basic premise of machine ontology is that the virtual aspect of whatever entity is *never* in direct contact with the virtual aspect of whatever other entity. In a virtual realm ontology, however, the virtual aspect of actualities *is* continuous with the virtual aspect of everything else that exists (strictly speaking, we should say that the virtual realm as such is the virtual aspect of everything that exists, and that actualities merely differ because they express it to different degrees). Such continuity is impossible in machine ontology, because there is always a sense-event that precludes the virtual aspects of any two machines from coming into direct contact. Second, virtual realm ontology cannot be integrated into machine ontology. The basic premise of virtual realm ontology is that anything virtual exists in continuity (and therefore possible direct engagement) with all else that is virtual. As discussed, there is no way in which machine ontology can accommodate that (due to the externality thesis, the unilaterality of relations, and so on).

If reconciliation is impossible, we will simply have to choose. Two arguments speak in favour of machine ontology. First, machine ontology has its own account of interaction, change, and novelty, which means that positing a virtual realm is neither warranted nor necessary. Of course, proponents of virtual realm ontology can try to make the same claim: the virtual realm accounts for interaction, change, and novelty, so that there is no need for ontologically real machines. The only problem (and this is the second argument), is that virtual realm ontology is inconsistent. Note that the virtual realm cannot be homogeneous, as that would make it impossible to explain why it generates qualitatively different actualities. It must therefore be diverse, hence the diversity of events, intensities, and processes that would comprise it. The continuity ascribed to the virtual realm demands that any such process can directly relate to at least some other process. The question is then whether or not such a process is *more* than its relations with other processes. If this is *not* the case, then change and novelty are impossible. If processes *merely are* their current engagement with other processes, then no process has a surplus or reserve from which new relations could be forged (Chapter 2 discussed this theme at length). If processes are *more* than that, then they have an interior that is external to their current relations. Not only would that violate continuity, it would also be inconsistent with the sole reason to posit the virtual realm in the first place. The whole point of the virtual realm is to account for change, interaction, and novelty *for the part of reality where externality holds sway*. So, if there is externality between processes, proponents of a virtual realm would need to posit a second virtual realm to animate the first, then a third to animate the second, *ad infinitum*. For these reasons, virtual realm ontology must be abandoned in favour of machine ontology.

The previous chapters have tried to show that this is precisely Deleuze's project after *Difference and Repetition*. What then about the mature Deleuze's mentions of continuity and univocity, of a 'plane of immanence' or 'plane of consistency' that would underlie all things? These have been read in the wrong key by those who have overlooked Deleuze's shift to machine ontology. Take continuity. In *The Logic of Sense*, continuity is no longer a given feature of a virtual realm, but pertains rather to sense-events, which is to say to actuality. Moreover, Deleuze is clear that continuity is contingent in that it needs to be established and in that it can collapse (LS 125). Continuity now pertains to actual surfaces that are apprehended by some entity (LS 236), which is exactly how we described it earlier in this section. In short, continuity is but a local and temporal achievement in actuality, one that is 'conditioned' by the ontological break or externality between machines (AO 38). Something similar is true for univocity. Recall from section 2 of Chapter 1 that the Deleuze of *Difference and Repetition* associates univocity with the ontological dissolution of all things. In *The Logic of Sense*, however, univocity 'does not mean that there is one and the same Being; on the contrary, beings are multiple and different [. . .] That of which it is said is not at all the same, but Being is the same for everything about which it is said' (LS 179). Machines are univocal in the sense that each has the same fourfold ontological structure, and each of them is different in that no two machines cash this out in exactly the same way. As for the plane of immanence and the plane of consistency, these do not refer to a separate realm or thing that would exist in addition to assemblages. They are simply synonyms for the virtual aspect of machines (section 1 of Chapter 9 covered why the same is true for 'abstract animal' and 'abstract machine'). As Deleuze writes, 'in effect, the body without organs is itself the plane of consistency' (ATP 40; cf. 43). The body is simply a plane of immanence or consistency in the sense that it is the interior where the desire or Idea of a machine coagulates: '[the body without organs] is the plane of consistency or the field of desire' (ATP 165; cf. 270). No wonder that 'we can and must presuppose a multiplicity of planes' (WP 50) and that 'there are varied and distinct planes of immanence' (WP 39). Whenever Deleuze writes about all assemblages 'opening up' to a plane of immanence or consistency, he is most certainly not alluding to some *thing* that would exist in addition to all machines, let alone some thing that would perform causal work *instead* of the machines, thereby degrading the latter to mere representations. There is only 'the' plane of immanence in the minimal sense that the machines *themselves* comprise, alter, and renew reality, given that there is no transcendent entity or structure to do that work *for* them. The only consistent or even meaningful way to refer to 'the' plane is therefore as a synonym for 'all machines'.

What about Deleuze and object-oriented philosophy? Deleuze's machine ontology is both a speculative realism and an object-oriented philosophy. That much should be absolutely clear by now. If we consider how machine ontology compares to other positions associated with speculative realism, we can note how this genre of new metaphysics consists of both *internalist* and *externalist* philosophies. There are three ways of being an internalist within this context. First, one can hold that all seemingly discrete entities are in fact internal to a larger and continuous domain (which can be matter, 'the virtual', pure productive force, chaos itself, or anything else). We saw how this seems to be the position of Bryant and DeLanda.[1] Second, one can hold that reality exists independently from human experience and thought, but that it can be grasped *as such* by application of a privileged procedure, for example mathematics or the natural sciences.[2] Third, one can hold that individual entities are the fundamental texture of reality, while defining these entities as *being* their relations to their components and environment. This characterises both Gabriel's and Garcia's position, and possibly that of Latour. What all internalisms have in common is a denial of a truly *private* and *non-relational* aspect to beings. In the third chapter and throughout the seven intermezzos, we have seen how (from the perspective of Deleuze's machine ontology) such a denial creates serious problems and inconsistencies in internalist ontologies – the infinite deferral of specification being the most significant among them. By contrast, Deleuze adheres to a staunchly externalist ontology in which every machine has an interior that can never be reduced or even presented to other beings. Every entity is an irreducible singularity that can only ever be translated into relations, and 'translation' should here be understood in the strongest possible sense of there being a *difference in kind* between what entities are in themselves and what entities manifest in their relations. In addition to Deleuze's ontology, the only other speculative realist philosophy premised on this *absolute* externality is Harman's, though we saw how Latour might still turn out to be part of the externalist rather than the internalist camp. The major difference between Harman's ontology and Deleuze's machine ontology is that, from the perspective of the latter, there is no good (or even valid) reason to restrict the number of occasions on which the interior of an entity can change.

Hopefully, these initial comparisons will serve as productive points of departure between contemporary speculative realists and Deleuze. In any case, what we have tried to demonstrate is that when it comes to speculative realism, Deleuze falls squarely in the camp of object-oriented ontology. Object-oriented thinkers should therefore think twice before dismissing Deleuze as yet another reductionist, just as their opponents should not be so certain that Deleuze is on their side.

Notes

1. It also seems to be the position of Bennett, Barad, Grant, and Grosz.
2. As proposed by Meillassoux and Brassier, respectively.

Bibliography

Primary Sources: Published

L'Abécédaire de Gilles Deleuze – avec Claire Parnet (1996). DVD. Directed by P. A. Boutang. Paris: Editions Montparnasse.

Bene, C., and Deleuze, G. (1979). *Superpositions. Richard III suivi par 'Un manifeste de moins.'* Paris: Les Éditions de Minuit.

Deleuze, G. (1984). *Kant's Critical Philosophy – The Doctrine of the Faculties*. Trans. H. Tomlinson and B. Habberjam. London: The Athlone Press.

Deleuze, G. (1986). *Cinema 1 – The Movement Image*. Trans. H. Tomlinson and B. Habberjam. London: The Athlone Press.

Deleuze, G. (1988). *Spinoza – Practical Philosophy*. Trans. R. Hurley. San Francisco: City Lights Books.

Deleuze, G. (1989). *Cinema 2 – The Time Image*. Trans. H. Tomlinson and R. Galeta. Minneapolis: University of Minnesota Press.

Deleuze, G. (1990). *Expressionism in Philosophy – Spinoza*. Trans. M. Joughin. New York: Zone Books.

Deleuze, G. (1990). *The Logic of Sense*. Trans. M. Lester. New York: Columbia University Press.

Deleuze, G. (1991). *Bergsonism*. Trans. H. Tomlinson and B. Habberjam. New York: Zone Books.

Deleuze, G. (1991). *Empiricism and Subjectivity*. Trans. C. Boundas. New York: Columbia University Press.

Deleuze, G. (1993). *The Fold – Leibniz and the Baroque*. Trans. T. Conley. London: Continuum.

Deleuze, G. (1994). *Difference and Repetition*. Trans. P. Patton. New York: Columbia University Press.

Deleuze, G. (1995). *Negotiations*. Trans. M. Joughin. New York: Columbia University Press.

Deleuze, G. (1997). *Essays – Critical and Clinical*. Trans.

D. W. Smith and M. A. Greco. Minneapolis: University of Minnesota Press.

Deleuze, G. (2000). *Proust and Signs*. Trans. R. Howard. Minneapolis: University of Minnesota Press.

Deleuze, G. (2002). 'Description of a Woman – For a Philosophy of the Sexed Other'. *Angelaki*, 7(3), pp. 17–24.

Deleuze, G. (2004). *Desert Islands and Other Texts – 1953–1974*. Trans. M. Taormina. New York: Semiotext(e).

Deleuze, G. (2004). *Francis Bacon – The Logic of Sensation*. Trans. D. W. Smith. London: Continuum.

Deleuze, G. (2006). *Two Regimes of Madness – Texts and Interviews 1975–1995*. Trans. A. Hodges and M. Taormina. New York: Semiotext(e).

Deleuze, G. (2006). *Nietzsche and Philosophy*. Trans. H. Tomlinson. New York: Columbia University Press.

Deleuze, G. (2007). 'Responses to a Series of Questions'. *Collapse*, III, pp. 39–43.

Deleuze, G. (2010). *Foucault*. Trans. S. Hand. London: Continuum.

Deleuze, G. (2015). *Lettres et autres textes*. Paris: Les Éditions de Minuit.

Deleuze, G. (2015). *What is Grounding?*. Trans. A. Kleinherenbrink. Grand Rapids: &&& Publishing.

Deleuze, G., and Guattari, F. (1977). 'Balance Sheet Program for Desiring-machines'. *Semiotexte*, 2(3), pp. 117–35.

Deleuze, G., and Guattari, F. (1986). *Kafka – Toward a Minor Literature*. Trans. D. Polan. Minneapolis: University of Minnesota Press.

Deleuze, G., and Guattari, F. (1994). *What is Philosophy?*. New York: Columbia University Press.

Deleuze, G., and Guattari, F. (2005). *A Thousand Plateaus*. Trans. B. Massumi. Minneapolis: University of Minnesota Press.

Deleuze, G., and Guattari, F. (2013). *Anti-Oedipus*. Trans. R. Hurley, M. Seem, and H. R. Lane. London: Bloomsbury.

Deleuze, G., and Parnet, C. (1987). *Dialogues*. Trans. H. Tomlinson and B. Habberjam. New York: Columbia University Press.

Primary Sources: Unpublished

Deleuze, G. (1971–80). Seminars on *Capitalism and Schizophrenia*. http://www.webdeleuze.com/ and http://www2.univ-paris8.fr/deleuze/article.php3?id_article=215 (accessed 27 May 2015).

Deleuze, G. (1978). Seminars on Kant. http://www.webdeleuze.com/ (accessed 27 May 2015).

Deleuze, G. (1978–81). Seminars on Spinoza. http://www.webdeleuze. com/ and http://www2.univ-paris8.fr/deleuze/rubrique.php3?id_rubrique=6 (accessed 27 May 2015).

Deleuze, G. (1980–87). Seminars on Leibniz. http://www.webdeleuze. com/ (accessed 27 May 2015).

Deleuze, G. (1982–83). Seminars on Cinema ('classification des signes et du temps'). http://www2.univ-paris8.fr/deleuze/rubrique.php3?id_rubrique=10 (accessed 8 December 2015).

Secondary Sources

Agamben, G. (1998). 'L'immanence absolue'. In E. Alliez (ed.), *Gilles Deleuze, une vie philosophique*. Le Plessis-Robinson: Institut Synthélabo, pp. 165–88.

Althusser, L. (2006). *Philosophy of the Encounter – Later Writings, 1978–87*. Trans. G. M. Goshgarian. Ed. F. Matheron and O. Corpet. New York: Verso.

Aristotle (1991a). *Categories*. In *The Complete Works of Aristotle – Volume I*. Trans. and ed. J. Barnes. Princeton: Princeton University Press.

Aristotle (1991b). *Metaphysics*. In *The Complete Works of Aristotle – Volume II*. Trans. and ed. J. Barnes. Princeton: Princeton University Press.

Badiou, A. (2000). *Deleuze – The Clamor of Being*. Trans. L. Burchill. Minneapolis: University of Minnesota Press.

Baugh, B. (2006). 'Real Essences without Essentialism'. In C. Boundas (ed.), *Deleuze and Philosophy*. Edinburgh: Edinburgh University Press, pp. 31–42.

Beaulieu, A., Kazarian, E., and Sushytska, J. (eds) (2014). *Gilles Deleuze and Metaphysics*. London: Lexington Books.

Beistegui, M. de (2010). *Immanence – Deleuze and Philosophy*. Edinburgh: Edinburgh University Press.

Bennett, J. (2010). *Vibrant Matter – A Political Ecology of Things*. Durham, NC: Duke University Press.

Bergen, V. (2001). *L'ontologie de Gilles Deleuze*. Paris: L'Harmattan.

Bergen, V. (2006). 'Deleuze et la question de l'ontologie'. *Symposium – the Canadian journal for continental philosophy*, 10(1), pp. 7–24.

Bergson, H. (1914). *Laughter: An Essay on the Meaning of the Comic*. Trans. C. Brereton and F. Rothwell. New York: Macmillan.

Bergson, H. (1999). *An Introduction to Metaphysics*. Trans. T. E. Hulme. Cambridge, MA: Hackett.

Bouaniche, A. (2007). *Gilles Deleuze, une introduction*. Paris: Pocket.

Braidotti, R. (2000). 'Teratologies'. In I. Buchanan and C. Colebrook (eds), *Deleuze and Feminist Theory*. Edinburgh: Edinburgh University Press, pp. 156–72.

Braidotti, R. (2002). *Metamorphoses*. Cambridge: Blackwell.

Brassier, R. (2007). *Nihil Unbound – Enlightenment and Extinction*. New York: Palgrave Macmillan.

Bryant, L. R. (2008). *Difference and Givenness – Deleuze's Transcendental Empiricism and the Ontology of Immanence*. Evanston: Northwestern University Press.

Bryant, L. R. (2011). *The Democracy of Objects*. Ann Arbor: Open Humanities Press.

Bryant, L. R. (2014). *Onto-Cartography – An Ontology of Machines and Media*. Edinburgh: Edinburgh University Press.

Bryant, L., Srnicek, N., and Harman, G. (eds) (2011). *The Speculative Turn – Continental Materialism and Realism*. Melbourne: re.press

Buchanan, I. (2008). *Deleuze and Guattari's Anti-Oedipus – A Reader's Guide*. London: Continuum.

Caputo, J. (1987). *Radical Hermeneutics: Repetition, Deconstruction, and the Hermeneutic Project*. Bloomington: Indiana University Press.

Carrouges, M. (1976). *Les machines célibataires*. Paris: Arcanes (Collection Chiffres).

Caygill, H. (2002). 'The Topology of Selection – The Limits of Deleuze's Biophilosophy'. In K. A. Pearson (ed.), *Deleuze and Philosophy – The Difference Engineer*. London: Routledge, pp. 149–62.

Clancy, R. (2015). *Towards a Political Anthropology in the Work of Gilles Deleuze – Psychoanalysis and Anglo-American Literature*. Leuven: Leuven University Press.

Cogburn, J. (2017). *Garcian Meditations – The Dialectics of Persistence in Form and Object*. Edinburgh: Edinburgh University Press.

Colebrook, C. (2002). *Understanding Deleuze*. Sydney: Allen and Unwin.

David-Ménard, M. (2005). *Deleuze et la psychanalyse*. Paris: Presses Universitaires de France.

DeLanda, M. (2002). *Intensive Science and Virtual Philosophy*. London: Continuum.

DeLanda, M. (2011). *Philosophy and Simulation*. London: Continuum.

DeLanda, M. (2013). *A New Philosophy of Society – Assemblage Theory and Social Complexity*. London: Bloomsbury

DeLanda, M. (2016). *Assemblage Theory*. Edinburgh: Edinburgh University Press.

DeLanda, M., and Harman, G. (2017). *The Rise of Realism*. Cambridge: Polity.

De Sanctis, S. (2015). Interview with Maurizio Ferraris. In S. de Sanctis and A. Longo (eds), *Breaking the Spell – Contemporary Realism under Discussion*. Padua: Mimesis, pp. 221–7.

Descartes, R. (1994). *Discourse on the Method*. In *The Philosophical Writings of Descartes, Vol. I*. Trans. J. Cottingham, R. Stoothoff, and D. Murdoch. New York: Cambridge University Press.

Empedocles (2001). *The Poem of Empedocles*. Trans. B. Inwood. Toronto: University of Toronto Press.

Ferraris, M. (2013). *Goodbye, Kant! – What Still Stands of the Critique of Pure Reason*. Trans. R. Davies. Albany: State University of New York Press.

Ferraris, M. (2014a). *Manifesto of New Realism*. Trans. S. de Sanctis. Albany: State University of New York Press.

Ferraris, M. (2014b). *Where are You – An Ontology of the Cell Phone*. Trans. S. de Sanctis. New York: Fordham University Press.

Ferraris, M. (2015). *Introduction to New Realism*. Trans. S. de Sanctis. London: Bloomsbury.

Foucault, M. (1970). 'Theatricum philosophicum'. In *Dits et écrits II*. Paris: Gallimard, pp. 75–99.

Foucault, M. (2013). 'Preface'. In G. Deleuze and F. Guattari, *Anti-Oedipus*. Trans. R. Hurley, M. Seem, and H. R. Lane. London: Bloomsbury, pp. xi–xiv.

Freud, S. (1961). 'Neue Folge der Vorlesungen zur Einführung in die Psychoanalyse'. In *Gesammelte Werke XV*. Berlin: S. Fischer Verlag.

Gabriel, M. (2013). 'The Meaning of "Existence" and the Contingency of Sense'. *Speculations*, 4, pp. 74–83.

Gabriel, M. (2015). *Fields of Sense*. Edinburgh: Edinburgh University Press.

Gandillac, M. de (2005). 'Vers une schizo-analyse'. In *L'Arc: Gilles Deleuze*. Paris: Inculte, pp. 145–58.

Garcia, T. (2013). 'Crossing Ways of Thinking – On Graham Harman's System and My Own'. Trans. M. A. Ohm. *Parrhesia*, 16, pp. 14–25.

Garcia, T. (2014). *Form and Object – A Treatise on Things*. Trans. M. A. Ohm and J. Cogburn. Edinburgh: Edinburgh University Press.

Grant, Iain Hamilton (2006). *Philosophies of Nature after Schelling*. London: Continuum.

Gratton, P. (2014). *Speculative Realism – Problems and Prospects*. New York: Bloomsbury.

Griaule, M. (1975). *Dieu d'eau*. Paris: Fayard.

Grosz, E. (1994). *Volatile Bodies: Toward a Corporeal Feminism*. Bloomington: Indiana University Press.

Guattari, F. (2006). *The Anti-Oedipus Papers*. Trans. K. Gotman. New York: Semiotext(e).

Hallward, P. (2006). *Out of this World: Deleuze and the Philosophy of Creation*. London: Verso.

Hämäläinen, N., and Lehtonen, T.-K. (2016). 'Latour's Empirical Metaphysics'. *Distinktion: Journal of Social Theory*, 17(1), pp. 20–37.

Harman, G. (2002). *Tool-Being – Heidegger and the Metaphysics of Objects*. Chicago: Open Court.

Harman, G. (2005). *Guerilla Metaphysics – Phenomenology and the Carpentry of Things*. Chicago: Open Court.

Harman, G. (2009). *Prince of Networks – Bruno Latour and Metaphysics*. Melbourne: re.press.

Harman, G. (2011a). *The Quadruple Object*. Winchester: Zero Books.

Harman, G. (2011b). 'Realism without Materialism'. *SubStance*, 40(2), pp. 52–72.

Harman, G. (2015). 'Strange Realism: On Behalf of Objects'. *The Humanities Review*, 12(1), pp. 3–18.

Harman, G. (2016). *Immaterialism – Objects and Social Theory*. Cambridge: Polity.

Heidegger, M. (1976). *An Introduction to Metaphysics*. Trans. R. Manheim. New Haven, CT: Yale University Press.

Heidegger, M. (2010). *Being and Time*. Trans. J. Stambaugh. Albany: State University of New York Press.

Hegel, G. W. F. (2010). *The Science of Logic*. Trans. and ed. G. di Giovanni. Cambridge: Cambridge University Press.

Holland, E. W. (2001). *Deleuze and Guattari's Anti-Oedipus – Introduction to Schizoanalysis*. London: Routledge.

Hughes, J. (2008). *Deleuze and the Genesis of Representation*. London: Continuum.

Hughes, J. (2011). *Deleuze's Difference and Repetition*. London: Continuum.

Husserl, E. (1982). *Ideas Pertaining to a Pure Phenomenology and to a Phenomenological Philosophy – First Book*. Trans. F. Kersten. The Hague: Martinus Nijhoff.

Jameson, F. (1997). 'Marxism and Dualism in Deleuze'. *The South Atlantic Quarterly*, 96(3), pp. 393–414.

Jameson, F. (1998). 'Les dualismes aujourd'hui'. In E. Alliez (ed.), *Gilles Deleuze, une vie philosophique*. Le Plessis-Robinson: Institut Synthélabo, pp. 377–90.

Kant I. (1991). 'On the First Ground of the Distinction of Regions in Space'. In J. Van Cleve and R. E. Frederick (eds), *The Philosophy of Right and Left*. Dordrecht: Springer.

Kant, I. (1996). *Critique of Pure Reason*. Trans. W. S. Pluhar. Cambridge, MA: Hackett.

Kant, I. (2007). *Critique of Judgment*. Trans. J. C. Meredith. Oxford: Oxford University Press.

Klossowski, P. (2005). 'Digression à partir d'un portrait apocryphe'. In *L'Arc: Gilles Deleuze*. Paris: Inculte, pp. 51–68.

Lacan, J. (1972). 'Seminar on *The Purloined Letter*'. *Yale French Studies*, 1(48), pp. 39–72.

Latour, B. (1991). *We Have Never Been Modern*. Trans. C. Porter. Cambridge, MA: Harvard University Press.

Latour, B. (1998). *The Pasteurization of France*. Trans. A. Sheridan and J. Law. Cambridge, MA: Harvard University Press.

Latour, B. (1999a). 'On Recalling ANT'. In J. Law and J. Hassard (eds), *Actor Network Theory and After*. Oxford: Blackwell, pp. 15–26.

Latour, B. (1999b). *Pandora's Hope – Essays on the Reality of Science Studies*. Cambridge, MA: Harvard University Press.

Latour, B. (2004). *Politics of Nature – How to Bring the Sciences into Democracy*. Trans. C. Porter. Cambridge, MA: Harvard University Press.

Latour, B. (2007). *Reassembling the Social. An Introduction to Actor-Network-Theory*. Oxford: Oxford University Press.

Latour, B. (2013). *An Inquiry into Modes of Existence – An Anthropology of the Moderns*. Trans. C. Porter. Cambridge, MA: Harvard University Press.

Latour, B., Harman, G., and Erdélyi, P. (2011). *The Prince and the Wolf – Latour and Harman at the LSE*. Winchester: Zero Books.

Lecercle, J.-J. (2002). *Deleuze and Language*. New York: Palgrave Macmillan.

Leclaire, S. (1996). 'La réalité du désir'. In *Écrits pour la psychanalyse, tome 1: demeures de l'ailleurs 1954–1993*. Paris: Seuil.

Leibniz, G. W. (1989). 'The Principles of Philosophy, or, The Monadology'. In *Philosophical Essays*. Trans. and ed. R. Ariew and D. Garber. Cambridge, MA: Hackett.

Lyotard, J. F. (1997). *Heidegger and 'The Jews'*. Trans. A. Michel and M. Roberts. Minneapolis: University of Minnesota Press.

Maimon, S. (2010). *Essay on Transcendental Philosophy*. Trans. N. Midgley et al. London: Continuum.

Massumi, B. (1992). *A User's Guide to Capitalism and Schizophrenia.*

Deviations from Deleuze and Guattari. Cambridge, MA: MIT Press.

Meillassoux, Q. (2011). *After Finitude – An Essay on the Necessity of Contingency*. Trans. R. Brassier. London: Continuum.

Merleau-Ponty, M. (2005). *Phenomenology of Perception*. Trans. C. Smith. London: Routledge.

Michaux, H. (1974). *The Major Ordeals of the Mind*. Trans. R. Howard. New York: Harcourt Brace Jovanovich.

Moore, A. W. (2012). *The Evolution of Modern Metaphysics – Making Sense of Things*. Cambridge: Cambridge University Press.

Nancy, J.-L. (1998). 'Pli deleuzien de la pensée'. In E. Alliez (ed.), *Gilles Deleuze, une vie philosophique*. Le Plessis-Robinson: Institut Synthélabo, pp. 115–24.

Negri, A. (1995). 'On Gilles Deleuze & Félix Guattari, *A Thousand Plateaus*'. *Graduate Faculty Philosophy Journal*, 18(1), pp. 93–109.

Nijinsky, V. (1971). *The Diary of Vaslav Nijinsky*. Trans. R. Nijinsky. Berkeley: University of California Press.

North, M. (2009). *Machine-Age Comedy*. Oxford: Oxford University Press.

Patton, P. (2007). 'Utopian Political Philosophy: Deleuze and Rawls'. *Deleuze Studies*, 1(1), pp. 41–59.

Peden, K. (2014). *Spinoza Contra Phenomenology*. Stanford: Stanford University Press.

Plato (1997). *Parmenides*. Trans. M. L. Gill and P. Ryan. In *Plato – Complete Works*. Ed. J. M. Cooper. Cambridge, MA: Hackett, pp. 359–97.

Rancière, J. (1998). 'Existe-t-il une esthétique deleuzienne?' In E. Alliez (ed.), *Gilles Deleuze, une vie philosophique*. Le Plessis-Robinson: Institut Synthélabo, pp. 525–36.

Rancière, J. (2004). 'Deleuze, Bartleby, and the Literary Formula'. In *The Flesh of Words*. Trans. C. Mandell. Stanford: Stanford University Press, pp. 146–64.

Rancière, J. (2006). *Film Fables*. Trans. E. Battista. New York: Berg.

Roderick, N. (2016). *The Being of Analogy*. London: Open Humanities Press.

Rosset, C. (1971). *Logique du pire – éléments pour une philosophie tragique*. Paris: Presses Universitaires de France.

Sartre, J. P. (1960). *The Transcendence of the Ego*. Trans. F. Williams and R. Kirkpatrick. New York: Hill and Wang.

Sartre, J. P. (1993). *Being and Nothingness – An Essay on*

Phenomenological Ontology. Trans. H. E. Barnes. Beijing: China Social Science Publishing House.

Sellars, W. (1962). 'Philosophy and the Scientific Image of Man'. *Frontiers of Science and Philosophy*, 1, pp. 35–78.

Sellars, W. (1991). *Science, Perception and Reality*. Atascadero, CA: Ridgeview.

Shaviro, S. (2014). *The Universe of Things – On Speculative Realism*. Minneapolis: University of Minnesota Press.

Sibertin-Blanc, G. (2010). *Deleuze et l'Anti-Oedipe: la production du désir*. Paris: Presses Universitaires de France.

Sloterdijk, P. (2014). 'Satan at the Center and Double Rhizomes'. http://lareviewofbooks.org/interview/satan-center-double-rhizomes-discussing-spheres-beyond-peter-sloterdijk (accessed 15 May 2015).

Smith, D. W. (2012). *Essays on Deleuze*. Edinburgh: Edinburgh University Press.

Somers-Hall, H. (2012). 'Deleuze's Philosophical Heritage: Unity, Difference, and Onto-Theology'. In D. W. Smith and H. Somers-Hall (eds), *The Cambridge Companion to Deleuze*. Cambridge: Cambridge University Press, pp. 337–56.

Stengers, I. (n.d.), 'Gilles Deleuze's Last Message'. http://www.recalcitrance.com/deleuzelast.htm (accessed 4 December 2015).

Sutton, D., and Martin-Jones, D. (2008). *Deleuze Reframed – A Guide for the Arts Student*. London: I.B. Tauris.

Świątkowski, P. (2015). *Deleuze and Desire – Analysis of The Logic of Sense*. Leuven: Leuven University Press.

Tarde, G. (2012). *Monadology and Sociology*. Trans. T. Lorenc. Melbourne: re.press.

Villani, A. (1998). 'Deleuze et l'anomalie métaphysique'. In E. Alliez (ed.), *Gilles Deleuze, une vie philosophique*. Le Plessis-Robinson: Institut Synthélabo, pp. 43–55.

Villani, A. (2006). 'Why am I Deleuzian?'. In C. Boundas (ed.), *Deleuze and Philosophy*. Edinburgh: Edinburgh University Press, pp. 227–49.

Widder, N. (2012). *Political Theory after Deleuze*. London: Continuum.

Williams, J. (2003). *Gilles Deleuze's Difference and Repetition: A Critical Introduction and Guide*. Edinburgh: Edinburgh University Press.

Williams, J. (2008). *Gilles Deleuze's Logic of Sense: A Critical Introduction and Guide*. Edinburgh: Edinburgh University Press.

Zepke, S. (2008). 'The Readymade: Art as the Refrain of Life'. In S. Zepke and S. O'Sullivan (eds), *Deleuze, Guattari and the Production of the New*. London: Continuum, pp. 33–45.

Žižek, S. (2004). *Organs without Bodies – Deleuze and Consequences.* London: Routledge.
Žižek, S. (2006). *The Parallax View.* Cambridge, MA: MIT Press.
Zourabichvili, F. (2012). *Deleuze: A Philosophy of the Event, Together with The Vocabulary of Deleuze.* Trans. K. Aarons. Edinburgh: Edinburgh University Press.

Names Index

General Index

EU Authorised Representative:

Easy Access System Europe Mustamäe tee 50, 10621 Tallinn, Estonia

gpsr.requests@easproject.com

Printed and bound by CPI Group (UK) Ltd, Croydon, CR0 4YY

07/05/2026

02104613-0011